ALCOHOLISM

Eva Maria Blum &
Richard H. Blum

FOREWORD BY MORRIS E. CHAFETZ

ALCOHOLISM

MODERN PSYCHOLOGICAL
APPROACHES TO TREATMENT

Jossey-Bass Publishers
San Francisco · Washington · London · 1976

ALCOHOLISM
Modern Psychological Approaches to Treatment
by Eva Maria Blum and Richard H. Blum

Copyright © 1967 and 1972 by: Jossey-Bass, Inc., Publishers
615 Montgomery Street
San Francisco, California 94111
&
Jossey-Bass Limited
44 Hatton Garden
London EC1N 8ER

Library of Congress Catalogue Card Number LC 67-13278

International Standard Book Number ISBN 0-87589-005-9

Manufactured in the United States of America

JACKET DESIGN BY MEL BYARS

FIRST EDITION
 First printing: *May 1967*
 Second printing: *September 1967*
 Third printing: *May 1969*
 Fourth printing: *November 1972*
 Fifth printing: *February 1974*
 Sixth printing: *June 1976*

Code 6745

THE JOSSEY-BASS BEHAVIORAL SCIENCE SERIES

To the memory of

E. M. JELLINEK

Foreword

As I sat at my desk to read this interesting new book on alcoholism, the quick climatic changes common to New England weather manifested themselves in the warmth of the traditional January thaw. A January thaw in alcoholism is similarly evident: from the ice-age days of moralism, punitive measures, and dogmatic assertions concerning alcoholic persons, we are entering a period where scientific rationalism, liberal legal decisions, and national concern are melting the glacial front. Instead of Alcoholics Anonymous self-help groups alone protesting our lack of interest in this enormous group of people in trouble, instead of disdain by most caretaking professionals, and instead of fanciful pronouncements about the cause and course of alcoholism, we see eminent institutions and their clinicians, researchers, and teachers working in the field; we see landmark decisions by district courts of the United States, the *Driver* and *Easter* cases stating that an alcoholic person can no longer be arrested for public drunkenness; and we see the creation of the National Center for Prevention and Control of Alcoholism by the National Institute of Mental Health.

These are heady times for those of us in academic life who by accident or choice find ourselves enwrapped in the delights or frustrations of dealing with the complexities of alcoholic casualties. We are no longer alone.

If a new moment of scientific and humane concern has replaced the subjective times of yesterday, then it behooves us to re-

examine with care baselines of clinical and therapeutic endeavor. Too
often we assume much when we know little. For example, few would
consider and far less state that all treatment may not be for good.
Since we know next to nothing about the natural history of alcoholism,
spontaneous recovery, success rates of treatment, and so forth, we do
not know who should be treated, who little treated, and who is better
left without formal treatment. (I am, of course, not referring to the
punitive neglect of treatment of vast majorities of alcoholic persons
through disinterest and moralism but to the carefully studied decision
that a patient would be the worse for being treated.) Not all treatment—our caretaking egos aside—is beneficial!

When we question the basics of what we bring to people in
trouble, our knowledge grows and our patients receive better care.
We understand our limitations, and what we do apply is more appropriate to the given case, is surer, and ultimately more ameliorative.

For these and other reasons the Blums' book is timely. The
rapidly burgeoning interest in alcoholism requires the broad, yet detailed examination of alcoholism treatment these authors have lent
themselves to. On the one hand, avenues of psychological factors
underlying treatment modalities are explored; on the other, the by-
ways wherein may be found the details and concrete applications of
treatment are thoroughly searched and presented for the reader's consideration. The questions the Blums ask demand to be asked, even
though not all answers can be supplied now.

Solutions to important psychosocial problems such as alcoholism do not come easy; they may never come at all. This does not
mean that we must sit idly by as casualties continue to accumulate.
Any questionings that open new possibilities for greater insight and
action than we had before are all to the good. We workers in the field
of alcoholism herald the dawn of a day of fruitful questioning: the
Blums' book is a ray from the rising sun.

Baltimore, Maryland

Morris E. Chafetz
Principal Research Scientist, Fac-
ulty of Arts and Sciences, Center
for Planning and Research, The
Johns Hopkins University, and
President,   Health   Education
Foundation, Inc., Washington,
D.C.

Preface

Alcoholism: Modern Psychological Approaches to Treatment presents
information on current methods for the psychological and social treatment of alcoholism. We seek to provide a perspective on treatment
that takes into account cultural values, social goals, and individual
needs, and to evaluate prevailing therapies. This book is for professionals in the healing arts, in pastoral and welfare counseling, and for
others whose work is with alcoholics and their families. This book is
also for civic leaders and concerned citizens whose responsibilities,
social endeavours, or personal interests will benefit from an overview
of what can be done for alcoholics.

   The reader will find it valuable to know what alternatives are
at hand as he considers how alcoholism as an individual, group, or
community problem can be treated. He will also find it worthwhile to
keep in mind some of the moral and social issues that are encountered
as he selects one or another method for handling alcoholics.

   This is not a treatment manual—for it makes no effort to give
detailed instructions on how to become adept at the therapies described—nor is it a guide to the medical handling of physical disorders
associated with alcoholism. It *is* a treatment aid—for it offers guidance to those who work with alcoholics. The book is an invitation to
consider what alcoholism treatment has to offer, how treatment can
be improved, and what the implications are for the evolving trends in
the handling of alcoholic disorders.

Alcohol studies are plagued by particularly awkward vocabulary problems. Many of the words commonly used to refer to alcohol problems or alcohol-use habits are charged with emotion. When employed in clinical or research writing these words bring with them contaminating prejudices or misconceptions. Consequently, alcohol studies—and students—make an effort to use words that are less biased and do not perpetuate inaccurate conceptions. A specialized vocabulary has inevitably emerged. We employ it as well as the technical vocabularies of psychoanalysis, learning theory, and community psychiatry.

The term, "change–agent," which we employ frequently, requires explanation. Relieving the distress of the patient and those with whom he lives is the basic concern of treatment. Since the treatment of the alcoholic usually requires intervention from another person or persons, one necessarily focuses on the people who intervene. In traditional clinical work these persons are psychotherapists, physicians, social workers, and pastoral counselors. In other aspects of work with alcoholics, those who intervene may be vocational rehabilitation workers, probation officers, police officers, educators, and nurses. We need a term that includes all who work to change the actions or feelings of an alcoholic; we use "change–agent."

Various phrases are used to refer to the alcoholic. In order to avoid misconceptions, prejudice, and emotionalism, many writers on alcohol avoid popular terminology. They speak of "persons with alcohol-related problems," "problem drinkers," or "excessive drinkers." We find these phrases awkward and say instead, "alcoholic." Many people—from all walks of life, with an immense range of signs, symptoms, and degrees of impairment—have one problem in common: their difficulties are associated with alcohol use. "Alcoholic" refers to the common denominator; it implies no causative role for alcohol as the source of all difficulty, nor does it presume any typology or common characteristics among persons tagged with that label.

We are indebted to the Cooperative Commission on the Study of Alcoholism and in particular to Commission members Nevitt Sanford, Erich Lindemann, Benson Snyder, Ruth Fox, Mark Keller, and Ernest Shepherd for their comments on drafts of the manuscript. We are grateful for the helpful and detailed criticism offered by Morris Chafetz, David Myerson, Keith Ditman, Alfred Bochner, Joseph Rosenfeld, and William Henry. A special note of thanks is due to Robert Wallerstein for his many excellent suggestions which we have tried, as best we can, to utilize. Those who assisted us are in no way responsible for the views we set forth. Finally, and more generally, we acknowledge the great contributions, scientific and humane, of the many dedicated professionals and laymen whose clinical, social, and research efforts comprise the field of alcoholism treatment.

Stanford, California   *Eva Maria Blum*
April, 1967   *Richard H. Blum*

Contents

ALCOHOLISM

PART ONE

WHAT IS TREATMENT?

Chapter I

~~~~~~

A Perspective on Treatment

In this chapter we shall attempt to put modern approaches to the alcoholic in perspective. To do this we shall draw on historical and cultural illustrations. In pursuit of that perspective we state our first thesis, namely that the greater the perceived threat of deviant behavior to established values and life styles the more stringent and intense are the protective measures of a community. Thus the response to alcoholism depends upon the kind of behavior valued by the community, upon the kind of behavior that drinkers in that community display, upon the disparity of the two, and, inevitably, upon the available methods for modifying behavior known to a community at any given time.

When there are both drinking and disapproval of drinking (or its consequences) and when the methods for modification or control of drinking are either ineffective or so extreme that they arouse disapproval on the part of respected citizens, there will be not only "alcohol problems" but also disputes over "treatment" as well. Let us offer an ancient example.

When Dionysus, the god of wine, first came to Thebes, he was imprisoned by King Pentheus; and the worshipers of the god, those perpetrators of obscene disorder, were hunted down, as Pentheus put it, "like the animals they are." But Dionysus soon invoked his powers, and before long his followers were in the ascendancy. Pentheus' own mother, Agave, was a Dionysian; and she, along with other orgiasts, killed Pentheus, tearing him from limb to limb. Euripides, in writing his tragedy about this legend, *The Bacchae,* suggested that the conflict between the power of the state, standing as it did for order, and the power of wine, whether serving divinity, lust, or chaos, was not satisfactorily resolved either by imprisoning the intoxicated women or by dismembering the authority who opposed them. Euripides was a very wise man.

With the demise of Pentheus, the Dionysian cult became institutionalized. Rituals, a priesthood, and early bureaucratization occurred as the cult itself was absorbed into the general context of Greek religion. Dionysus, by becoming an acceptable god, also became innocuous. By that time the maenads (bacchantes) were no longer a menace or the vanguard of frightening change; the community itself could be at ease with the wine god's followers. But this comfortable familiarity did not mean that drinking itself no longer caused trouble, for there were other more individual matters of conduct and respect to be considered.

In ancient Greece (and in modern Greece as well), a man's pride did not allow him to lose such control that he was unable to compete with other men in athletics, in dancing, in singing, and in drinking itself. Plato tells us (*Symposium,* 223) that a man who drank so much that he lost his capacity to best another man in argument was shamed indeed. And shame in Greece is real, for a shamed man is ridiculed cruelly. For this reason, and in order to protect himself from the physical consequences of overindulgence, a man must be ever alert to the consequences of his drinking.

Perhaps energy can be devoted to the hygiene of individual drinking—that is, to protecting a man from the social (*e.g.,* ridicule), psychological (*e.g.,* loss of self-esteem), and physical ill effects of alcohol—only when the community itself is convinced that a menace to the society does not exist. At that time, the communiy can devise individual remedies and protections which become part of acceptable drinking behavior. Thus, as one would expect, the ancient Greek society developed many remedies in the form of herbs and chiropractic and magical manipulations to combat whatever pain and disability an individual might suffer from drinking.

What we would suggest from these illustrations is that if new forms of drinking behavior emerge, whether in association with major social change or with the availability of new forms of alcohol (or, of course, if alcohol itself becomes available for the first time), there is likely to be a sense of community danger or disintegration. When that occurs, the major focus of the community will be not on the prevention of individual distress after indulgence but rather on the restraint of the new drinking behavior. At this stage community power will be exercised to control or coerce. On the other hand, once drinking is accepted there can be a more rational and less punitive effort to influence drinking behavior. Some of these will be through the provision of controls in drinking situations; others will teach persons how to drink without harming themselves and others; still others—therapeutic or correctional in intent—will be directed to those who do suffer or cause harm. Few modern societies are simple. The chances are that both the menace-suppression emphasis and the gentler harm-preventing, hurt-healing orientations exist within a given culture. We believe that is the case in the United States today.

It seems likely that a community applies the strongest measures to prevent or control drinking behavior when drinkers are considered to be both unusual and dangerous. When such efforts are not successful and, further, when there are value conflicts within the community that arise out of or focus on one versus another control method, there will be unresolvable disputes among the contending factions that will curtail further attempts at treatment. It is our belief, in consequence, that *treatment* as such—that is, a humane effort that concerns itself with the drinking individual's own situation and feelings—will more often occur when the community does not consider drinking behavior to be dangerous. Having presumed this much, we think it well to comment further on deviation and treatment.

When coercive measures are applied to drinkers to make them alter their drinking behavior, we think it is likely that the drinking involved will be "deviant" in two different ways. One is that the subject's drinking activities will be considered by the community to be morally inferior or delinquent. The other is that his disapproved drinking habits will be shared by only a minority of others in that community. The implication is that not only must the drinker be denigrated but he must be politically weak before coercive measures are commonly applied. For treatment to be given, deviancy is also implied, but it is of quite a different order. The deviancy is defined by a subject-oriented standard of ideal drinking, the notion that the person himself is experiencing a state that is not desirable.* The occurrence of treatment also presumes an optimism about the capacity of healers to return the drinker to a more desirable condition. One would assume that such optimism would be based on past experience, although such empiricism is, of course, not necessarily operative. It is only necessary that the optimism—or faith, if it be that—exist either in the healer or in the one being healed. There can be optimism about treatment, even when there is no empirical basis, so long as there exists some other basis—for example, a psychological one derived from hope for the concurrent gratifications of either party (healer or patient) in the treatment process. An example of this kind of gratification can be found in Christian tradition (Weber, 1963), where the act of benevolence increases the comforter's chance to achieve "grace" regardless of whether the sufferer or sinner is eased.

If the presence of humane endeavors to return an individual to a state of greater comfort, or to prevent his discomfort from drinking without preventing drinking itself, does depend on a kind of optimistic, individual-centered, distress-oriented idealism but does not depend on "statistical" definitions of deviancy, it follows that the presence of treatment in a given group or society is independent of the frequency of drinking in that society. Thus, a community can have a very considerable amount of drinking in terms of either per capita amounts consumed or of frequency of drunkenness, without developing the idea that to drink or to be intoxicated is deviant and a menace—or that it requires treatment. A number of recent splendid cross-cultural studies make that point. Child, Bacon, and Barry (1965), for example, conclude that "A high rate of consumption does not necessarily mean that alcohol is disruptive of social life" and further that a culture with socially integrated drinking does not necessarily have any less drunkenness than a culture where drinking is not integrated.** Similarly, a comparison of French with Italian and North American drinking (Sadoun, Lolli, and Silverman, 1965) discusses

---

* Cultures vary in their drinking patterns and their standards of drinking behavior. For example, in Chichicastenango, studied by Bunzel (1940) and where we made observations as well, acute intoxication is "integrated" into the culture; it is part of religious ritual and is therefore deemed necessary. The intoxication is incidental and no effort is made to forestall its aftereffects.

** See Chapter 4 for a discussion of culturally integrated drinking.

the fact that a high rate of alcoholism exists in France and a low rate in Italy, even though per capita alcohol consumption is much higher in Italy. (See also Efron and Keller, 1963). Finally, results of a recent national survey in the U.S. (Cisin and Cahalan, 1966) make it clear that heavy drinking occurs in socioeconomic groups which generally suffer few adverse effects from alcohol, whereas problem drinking occurs in groups where drinking itself is much less frequent.

To have suggested that coercion is sustained by moral intolerance of certain kinds of drinking behavior, whereas treatment requires an ideal for drinking as such, does not logically require that treatment is unrelated to morality. Nor, in fact, is it.

Moral judgments are linked with experiences of pleasure and pain, with gratifying or distasteful interpersonal events, and with the control of impulses. Even in a society where drinking is itself approved, if there exists an ideal about human conduct and human feeling that recognizes undesirable aspects of drinking and that seeks to prevent or treat these, we think it unlikely that views of drinking will be unrelated to morality.

How does it matter? It matters only if moral judgments, even if they are made without disparagement of the excessive drinker, intrude upon the choice of treatment methods, treatment subjects, or treatment occasions, so that relatively straightforward ideals about the relief of pain or disability are complicated by less straightforward attitudes toward the business at hand. By "less straightforward" we mean that the healer's approach to the problem drinker, and the latter's approach to the healer, necessarily become part of a larger and more complex fabric of ideologies and feelings in which it is difficult to separate empirical evidence from convictions or to separate the facts of the treatment situation from the feelings and fantasies of the participants. We do not pose these eventualities in any critical sense. We merely propose that under these circumstances any treatment effort—necessarily humane by definition—is complicated by emotion and belief. At least for the present we believe this is the state of affairs for almost everyone involved in the treatment of alcoholics. Since that is the case, it is well to admit it and, if possible, to make the most of it.

Interestingly enough, the nineteenth-century pioneers in the treatment of mental illness profited considerably by not only recognizing but also emphasizing the moral component in therapy. These pioneers employed a method called "moral therapy," which was ac-

tually initiated at the end of the eighteenth century under the leadership of Pinel, Tuke, and others. This method stressed friendly associations with the patient, a discussion of his difficulties, programs of
constructive daily activity, and, of course, a rather clear statement of
socially approved ends. In modern terms, it was planned psychological
retraining within a positive sympathetic social milieu, where structure
was clear and groups were cohesive. Cope and Packard (1841) observed that by means of moral treatment "90 per cent of the recent
cases can be restored so as to be able to maintain themselves and
family."

Despite this evidence of effectiveness, moral therapy was quietly
abandoned in American and British mental institutions after 1860 and
later was almost completely forgotten. Adams (1964) states that data
from the Worcester State Hospital show that recovery rates declined
over 90 per cent after 1860 and reached their lowest point between
1923 and 1950. He agrees that one may raise questions about old
statistics and the validity of conclusions drawn from them but adds
that, nevertheless, every recent study on the subject of moral therapy
agrees that the results of that method have not been surpassed during
the contemporary period despite all the advances made by physical
medicine since 1860.

One may conclude with Rees (1957) that "the great irony is
that after a hundred years the laboratory-centered, physically oriented
research efforts have failed to produce techniques for the 'treatment'
and 'cure' of functional personality disorders significantly more effective than the best techniques of the 1840's." Actually the most progressive, contemporary, mental hospital programs are those that have
revived practices much like those generally prevalent during the moral
therapy era, as we shall see later on.

Why did moral therapy disappear to be replaced by less effective methods? Adams proposes that the development of physical medicine during the late nineteenth century showed such promise that
clinicians and researchers believed it a model for the proper approach
to mental disorders, which included addictions and, of course, alcoholism. Moral therapy was regarded as "unscientific" in an era that in
its beginnings, at least, held that science must be impersonal and concerned with material things. Social and psychopathological phenomena would be reduced, it was anticipated, to molecular causes.
(Barzun [1958] describes how these expectations remain powerfully
with us.) Objective, "toughminded," but otherwise amoral approaches

began to characterize hospital procedures and the "ideal" behavior of modern clinicians. Adams believes that as recovery rates fell, one could chart the rise in detachment and objectivity in treatment styles. Increasing efforts were made to identify physical-disease entities associated with addiction; most of these early efforts understandably assumed that mechanistic and simple deterministic processes underlay alcoholism, as well as other behavior disorders.

Perhaps the culmination of this trend was reached in the 1950's when eminent investigators hoped to find that a disturbed neuro-chemistry was responsible for the disturbed interpersonal relations of the patient. Certainly we share the physicalistic optimism that hopes to identify neuro-physiological correlates of behavior disturbance. However, the point is that, even in a scientific era, treatment methods express the hope and biases of the times fully as much as they represent, at least to date and with reference to behavior disorders, a body of scientific evidence—including careful programs of treatment evaluation.

If we examine what is happening to alcoholics in the United States today, we can easily see how methods of approach reflect the special situations, backgrounds, and interests of those in contact with the alcoholic. As Myerson (1957) has pointed out, alcoholism reaches deeply into many aspects of community life; legal, religious, social institutions are inevitably touched by alcoholics and in turn attempt to influence them. Because of the antisocial behavior associated with excessive drinking, law-enforcement agencies necessarily handle alcoholics. Their methods range from kindness and exhortation through incarceration and, for the homicidal drinker, the death penalty. The methods of the churches also vary: some preach abstinence, the worldly as well as other-worldly condemnation of drinkers, and the public-be-damned enactment of Prohibition. Others, more sophisticated, seek self-control. They may also operate rehabilitative groups utilizing morality, zeal, and cohesive group interaction. In addition, many pastors provide counseling that seeks psychological as well as spiritual insights. The medical profession, because excessive drinking leads to physical illness, because alcoholism is currently described through the disease model, and because society puts "doctors" in charge of such conditions, applies to alcoholism whatever methods of hospitalization, drug treatment, or psychiatric care are available or seem promising at any given time.

In each of the above instances, the institution applies—with

whatever modifications it can—its own current methods and philosophies to the handling of problem drinkers whose deviant conduct
brings them to the attention of the institution. We would restate this
observation in terms of a principle that appears to describe all forms
of therapeutic intervention: any treatment of alcoholics will be understood, carried out, and rationalized in terms of the prevailing beliefs
and orientations and the available facilities and methods of a culture,
of an institution, of a group, or of individuals for whom the deviant
behavior is a problem. This is simply to say that the treatment of
alcoholism is compatible with whatever else a person or group thinks
and does. Therapy depends upon the climate of thought. Alcohol treatment methods are specific only insofar as deviant drinking behavior
provides special problems that are not amenable to prevention or
correction using the ordinary facilities and procedures of the person
or institution. Even with these special problems, specific alcohol treatments will not vary dramatically from the conventional ways in which
persons or groups handle other deviants, problems, patients, clients
(or whatever else they are called) with whom they come in contact.

    One must conclude that the kinds of intervention, the goals of
intervention, and the choice of those who will be subjected to intervention are all consonant with cultural values and styles. If a society
insists that treatment be scientific and not magical, then nobody will
be treated with magic (at least not called by that name). If a society
abhors drunkenness more than it abhors cruelty, then it will allow
cruelty to be employed to deter drunkenness. If a society believes that
physicians are exceptionally capable in restoring desirable states of
body and mind, then alcoholism will be perceived as a disease and
doctors will be asked to study and treat it. And if a society cares how
individuals feel and if it believes in brotherly love, then that society
will devote immense efforts to alleviating pain so that in their caring
the less fortunate brother is not forgotten.

Chapter II

~~~~~~

Unexamined Factors in Treatment

It may be that much of what people do takes place for reasons that are not too clear or, if clear, not too rational. How a man acts does not always square with how he says he wants to act or even with how he says he is acting. Possibly some of his vagaries are due to a certain functional randomness, for randomness can be quite useful for anyone who lives in a world that is without certainties—such behavior allows exploration and discovery and even change. Some human inconsistencies are probably due to hidden constants rather than demonstrable randomness. These constants are determinants even if they are unutterable or unacknowledged, whether one calls them motives, unconscious defenses, habits, or biochemical processes. And, finally, some human irrationalities result from a clinging to beliefs or ideologies even when the truth or the appropriateness of these systems is in doubt.

A man must have a chart to go by, for he seems an order-loving creature who enjoys justifications and purposes. Rock-solid knowledge is not so abundant and enlightening as to allow any man to guide a whole course by the landmarks of irrefutable evidence and sweet reason alone. What is a man to do? A course he must have; neither friends, wives, nor a hungry stomach tolerate too much drifting. And so he prefers a map, even if the islands are mythical and some ports an Ithaca that may never be reached.

We propose that therapists and change-agents are people, and that they will neither always be rational nor should they want to be. We further propose that, as far as their treatment activities are concerned, much of what can be termed irrational is at least understandable if considered as magic. And, as a final proposition, we shall say that magic is not necessarily a bad thing.

THE ROLE OF MAGIC

It is understandable in this era that a healer eschews the irrational—especially if the irrational, in the form of magic, is believed to be as ineffective as it is unfashionable. After all, ours purports to be an eminently practical age. If one defines magic as the practice of thoughts and actions that aim to control events, but that evidence no relationship between the wish or ritual and the outcome, then clearly much of what people do is magical. When magic occurs as part of medical or psychological treatment, its components include a consensus of faith among the participants and the use of mechanics, or rituals, which have a compelling nature; that is, they draw upon "powers" in the patient, in the healer, and perhaps in the evironment (worldly or supernatural) which induce a particular outcome. Accordingly, at least something of what happens in many forms of treatment is magic. Paradoxically, these magical treatments seem to work. Clinicians wisely speak of the efficacy of "faith" on the part of the patient and of the importance of the patient's "motivation" and "will power." Researchers as well as clinicians document such phenomena as "suggestion," "experimenter effect," autohypnosis, "the placebo effect," etc. Although no one is yet quite sure what the ingredients of these curative influences are, there seems little doubt that people respond to as yet poorly identified components of treatment. Jerome Frank (1961) has done scholarly work in analyzing these elements in *Persuasion and Healing*, Kiev and his colleagues (1964) have considered them in folk psychiatry, and we (1965) have observed them in folk medical practices in Greece.

Perhaps a special reason why magic plays a role in alcoholism treatment is that alcohol itself has long been a magical drink; it has unseen powers, divine potentials, or can be, in William James' (1954) words, a source of "anesthetic revelations." Given the magical qualities of alcohol, it is no wonder that in the past the cures applied to alcoholism have been magical in themselves.

Hsu, quoted by Paul (1955), notes that the common man of this modern age will accept magic only if it is disguised as science. There may be good psychological reasons for singling out the alcoholic for need-fulfilling ritualistic care. "Treatment is to be carried out with pomp, emphasis, and regularity. Faith in treatment is to be encouraged, and suggestion is to be used (deliberately)" recommends an associate of the British Society of Addiction (1947). And why not? For as Sillman (1948), Silber (1959), and Weijl (1944) all observed, the alcoholic himself is very likely to have magical beliefs that the treatment process may not only accommodate but also put to use.

As every magician knows, magic itself is merely power. It is, magicians say, amoral, but can be used for either good or bad. In more modern terms, it appears that therapists who manipulate the magical components of patient thinking may do so artfully, knowingly, and with success, or blindly, or compulsively, and therefore with danger. For example, the psychoanalyst Balint (1957) speaks of the "doctor's apostolic function." Balint means by that the mission that the doctor feels to convert his patients to his own conceptions of how a patient ought to behave when ill. Analyzing physicians' attitudes, he concludes that "it was almost as if every doctor had revealed knowledge of what was right and what was wrong for patients to expect and to endure, and further, as if he had a sacred duty to convert to his faith all the ignorant and unbelieving among his patients" (Balint, p. 216). Balint points out that it is difficult for the physician to avoid showing his hand—to avoid disclosing what, in his opinion, is right and proper for a patient to do in a given situation. The result is that the patient has either to accept the doctor's "faith and commandments" and be converted, at the least, superficially; or to reject the "rules" and settle down to chronic haggling. Of course, as a last resort, the patient may change to another doctor whose "faith and commandments" are more congenial.

The difficulty of magical thinking in both therapist and patient are illustrated by Erikson (1956), another psychoanalyst. He tells of patients in whom one may sometimes observe a sudden, intense impulse to destroy the therapist. Their underlying wish is a cannibalistic one—to devour his essence and his identity. At the same time, or in alternation, there may occur a fear and wish to be devoured, to gain identity by being absorbed in the therapist's essence. If the therapist were to share the patient's magical thinking, he would feel extremely threatened by these fantasies. If he can understand them for what they are, then he will be able to prove to the patient "through many severe crises, that he can maintain understanding and affection for the patient without either devouring him (himself) or offering himself for a totem meal" (Erikson, p. 91). Not all physicians can be so sanguine about their own role.

Roth (1958) studying hygienic rituals in hospitals finds that activities which are magical can also be functional. The less certainty there is about regularities in nature, the more likely it is that a man, upon whom there are demands to act, will develop rules that are ritualistic and supportive of necessarily irrational beliefs. Treatment is conducted in the face of uncertain etiology (except for the certainty that it is complex!); knowledge of the relative merits of one or another form of therapeutic intervention is limited; and information on the concurrent aggravating or ameliorating factors in the outcome of treatment is nonexistent.

Ambiguity in important matters leads to anxiety. One way to handle anxiety is to engage in activity that aims to reduce ambiguity. When that activity is a clinical art—one including both the theory and practice of treatment—uncertainty can be eliminated by fiat rather than fact. One becomes "convinced" and dedicated to particular methods. Insofar as anxiety is thereby reduced, the activity is its own reward, but it contains many other rewards as well. The humane wish to help, the pleasure of interpersonal relations, the gratifications of action and achieving: all these and more can operate to cement therapies into unchallenged belief systems. That this happens is no surprise; what is surprising is that it occurs infrequently, for many therapists avoid the plunge into total conviction, instead abiding ambiguity and suffering the attendant anxiety.

In spite of these uncertainties, a healer may wish to convey confidence to his patients lest they become despairing. Since the primary purpose of treatment is to allay distress, how painful it is when a healer, conveying his own doubts or inadequacies, fails to comfort or to reassure. It is no surprise that many healers respond to the demands upon them by becoming what their comfort-needing patients would have them be—that is, confident and action-oriented men. (In other places, writers such as Balint or ourselves [R. Blum, 1964, 1960], have discussed the dangers of reassurance and apparent omnipotence.) The healer's confidence or sense of personal invulnerability have important historical roots; for in times past the healer has been priest, magician, and physician all in one.

Fejos (1959) has described the dangers of not fully crediting the role of magic in modern medicine. Fejos writes of having attended a discussion in which physicians tried to determine which drug in the pharmacopeia is the most important and the most needed. His colleagues considered morphine and its derivatives as the most important—the drug that enables the physician to allay speedily the anxiety component in pain.

Fejos suggested that magic should also be cited, "for without it, without the mana of the qualified physician, there would be no faith in the quality of the physician to heal, and only a physician could tell you how difficult, how almost impossible, it is to effect therapy in such a case . . ." (Fejos, pp. 29–30). In a similar vein, the English psychopharmacologist Richard Joyce once said to us how remarkable it was that a physician using placebo attributed so much to the pill or injection itself and failed to note that it was himself, the physician, who could be the source of the placebo effect. Why, Joyce wondered, would a man credit a sugar pill but doubt or disown the effectiveness of his own interpersonal impact?

The compelling use of oneself in the treatment situation—the willingness to share feelings or to be inventive; the active, perhaps "existential" intervention that acknowledges that what goes on in the treatment process is as yet not completely known—this is what many modern clinicians refer to when they speak of utilizing magic or faith in their practice. To admit to the "art" of treatment is not to be anti-rational nor anti-intellectual; nor is it an invitation to mysticism or autistic thinking. We would argue that to be really alive one must be more than a rational animal and that when one undertakes treatment it is the vital healer who, taking the patient for what he is and from where he is, stands a good chance for success. The work of Whitehorn and Betz (1960, 1957) lends support to the notion that it is the active rather than the objective therapist who succeeds.

That man cannot live by reason alone nor the physician practice by science alone has been emphasized in the profound writing by Dubos (1959). He proposes that to fulfill its potentialities, scientific medicine may once more need the help of bold amateurs willing to use empirical methods based on "philosophical, humanitarian, and esthetic beliefs. Medical statesmanship cannot thrive only as scientific knowledge, because exact science cannot encompass all the human factors involved in health and in disease. Knowledge and power may arise from dreams, as well as from facts and logic" (Dubos, p. 183).*

A number of investigators subscribe to the same fundamental principle. In a brilliant analysis of the concept of mental health, Hartmann (1964) states "the rational must incorporate the irrational as an element in its designs" (Hartmann, p. 10). He believes that the denial of irrational elements in human nature is not the most promising method to achieve adaptation to reality. He points out that insight into the interrelationship of rational and irrational behavior is incomplete, and many times what one considers rational behavior is merely *rationalized* behavior stemming from the reservoir of irrational drives and emotions. This is not to say that the author condemns the irrational; quite the contrary. He decries "totally rational" action as a caricature of human endeavor. He points to the psychoanalytic process itself as a model of the successful use of irrational elements of behavior for purposive rational actions. "Here, obviously, in the plan of a rational technique, devised to alter the patient's behavior, the fact of irrationality is included. Rational means are used even in order to mobilize irrational forces which, as we know from experience, will finally become integrated into a new state of balance" (Hartmann, p. 67).

We have mentioned the excellent discussion of the resemblances between the conditions for magical cures and successful psychotherapy that is found in Frank's *Persuasion and Healing* (1961). The patient must be emotionally aroused in the healing situation; he must expect healing efforts to be beneficial, or relevant; the healer's prestige or social role must be such as to inspire expectations of health; finally, the patient and healer must reach a consensus about what each expects of the outcome. According to Frank, psychotherapists and magicians achieve beneficial results insofar as they are able to reinterpret the patient's unpleasantly ambiguous and frightening inner state in the light of shared belief systems. Formerly anxiety-arousing signals can thereby become innocuous or even pleasurable anticipations. Indeed, according to Cofer and Appley (1964), to change anticipations and the stimuli that arouse them is to alter "motivation."

Medical intervention by means of drugs may be viewed in the same benevolent, structure-giving light. Lindemann and Clarke (1952)

* See also Ackerknecht (1942) and Kiev (1964, 1962).

in a very important paper* suggest that the beneficial effect of psychotropic drugs, given concurrently with psychotherapy, occurs because
the therapist interprets the confusing and frightening array of drug-
induced sensations and thoughts in a manner that gives the patient a
new structure and orientation that are cohesive and meaningful. The
use of pharmacologically active substances, including active placebos
as agents, produces disorganization, ambiguity, anxiety, and—as is
typical in organic states—dependency and perplexity. If a therapist
gives personal and situational support during this critical period of
dependency and felt inadequacy, he can at the same time provide a
new order, which—tailored to the therapist's best estimates of the
patient's life situation and personality dispositions—can become salient
in the life of the patient.

NEITHER MAGIC NOR FACTS

Not all of the unrecognized components in treatment are
directly related to those wishes, rituals, shared beliefs, or actively imposed orientations that we include under "magic." Some aspects of
treatment seem simply to be bits and pieces of tradition, comforting
biases, or incorrect understandings of matters of fact. Their presence
can inhibit treatment.

Take the selection of patients as an example. Many clinicians,
whatever their speciality or the settings for their practice, believe that
certain patients will benefit from treatment and that others will not—
or that there are the "good" patients and the "bad." If these expectations are not based on careful follow-up studies of all kinds of
patients on whom treatment has been attempted, the prejudice can
never be challenged. Yet such unfounded beliefs operate as gates to
shut out many people from the touch of the healing hand. Now, if it
happens that the belief has a latent function—in the sense that the
clinician or agency is incapable of treating any more patients or clients
than it already has—it may not matter so much that the excuse used
to keep the flow of admissions geared to treatment capabilities is itself
probably nonsense. The trouble is that there may be better ways for
selecting patients than the application of inappropriate criteria, even
in overworked facilities.

* See also Lindemann and von Felsinger (1961).

As another illustration, one finds psychotherapists—or physicians—requiring that a patient be "motivated" for treatment. Certain alcoholics are typically "unmotivated," in the traditional definition, and are thus rejected on these grounds. And much of the "evidence" for the "wisdom" of these rejections comes from self-fulfilling prophecies or contaminated judgments. There is, in fact, reason to believe that so-called "unmotivated" patients can respond to at least some forms of psychotherapy as well as motivated patients. Furthermore, the new concepts of motivation offered by Cofer and Appley (1964)— who posit anticipation and invigoration rather than permanently delineated "drives"—suggest that motivation, in the sense of arousal or interest, can be produced by presenting stimuli appropriate to the person. Motivation may be interpreted in terms of expectations. Thus, if one can alter by experience what a person anticipates, then one can alter his later expectations, his motivation, and his behavior as well. Using this approach, therapists who are not so demanding of immediate acceptance by their patients could consider the change of treatment motivation as a task similar to the change of any other set of expectations or consistent behaviors on the part of the patient. This discussion is not the place to discuss the difficult business of changing levels of arousal or learned anticipations; but it *is* the place to point out that unexamined beliefs, of which the notion of the need for patient "motivation" may be one, are widespread in treatment and can interfere with both the acceptance and cure of alcoholics.

Another inhibiting factor in treatment is the folk notions of beneficial or desirable diseases (R. and E. Blum, 1965), which are probably related to some professionals' beliefs about alcoholism; for example, that alcoholism is preferable to its presumed alternatives. There is a good deal of evidence (Selye, 1956, 1955) that illness symptoms are the manifestations of natural defenses against trauma, pathogens, or, in the psychological realm, threats to ego, esteem, adaptation, and so forth. With reference to psychopathological states, it is commonly held that symptoms should not be removed until the underlying problem has been resolved—that is, until the stressors have been eliminated, modified, contained, or compensated for; so that the disabling symptoms need no longer occur as part of defense and adaptation. Those who consider alcoholism to be a symptom of a hidden psychological difficulty are reluctant to interfere with drinking behavior for fear that something worse will occur, such as depression, suicide, psychosis, or criminality.

Psychoanalysts have long debated this point, and there are competent change-agents on both sides of the fence. Recently the advocates of hypnotic-aversion treatment for alcoholism have faced the same issue, and they are now in general agreement that there is no great danger in interfering with the drinking, that is, in removing the symptom (Abrams, 1964). Other clinicians point out that because alcoholism generates so many other difficulties, somatic and social, it is the least preferable of conditions, even if it is likely that interference with drinking would bring on such acute disorders as psychosis or delirium tremens. They note that these conditions are themselves amenable to control and cure. Antagonists disagree, pointing out that untreated withdrawal symptoms (the DT's) lead to death just as psychosis may lead to suicide. Death, they say, or even permanent psychosis is less preferable than alcoholism, especially if the excessive drinking is treatable. In this debate there may be many hidden issues; the only ones we would decry are folk assumptions to the effect that alcoholism as such is beneficial* or that one dare not try to suppress it for fear of inevitable alternatives that are worse.

Another of the false assumptions that hinder the progress of extending care to those who need it is the widespread public belief that none of the presently existing treatment methods for alcoholics are effective. This belief is groundless, as anyone who is acquainted with studies evaluating treatment could testify. Nevertheless, the prejudice against alcoholism treatment, expressed in this defeatist attitude, cannot help but discourage many potential patients and their families, as well as persons who would otherwise refer an alcoholic.

Human endeavours will, it seems, inevitably be characterized by inconsistency, conflict, inefficiency, and the like. To us it appears that the best the therapist or change-agent can do is to be as explicit as he can about what he wants to achieve, to be as well informed as he can about how to achieve it, to be as objective as he can about what he is actually doing and achieving, to be as curious and flexible as he can about trying new methods, and to be as brave as he can when results fall short of his hopes. With these challenges in mind, we shall now turn to a direct consideration of treatment methods themselves.

* One finds among artists and literati the romantic notion that drug use or drug dependency is necessary for virility, spontaneity, or artistic creativity. Some say it is not to be interfered with lest artistry suffer. (See Roe's [1946] findings about beliefs related to alcoholism among painters.)

Chapter III

~~~~~~

Treatment Defined and Goals Considered

There are some very broadminded views of what constitutes "treatment" for the alcoholic. There have been recent arguments to the effect that any effort at change—either in personality or behavior and whether by environmental control, physical intervention, or symbolic interchange—is a form of treatment. The change-agent may be an expert or an ordinary citizen; the alcoholic may consider himself sick or well, a patient or a problem drinker or neither. Still, it is "treatment" as long as someone undertakes to alter another's drinking for the benefit of the community and the patient. Ideally, "treatment" *is* for the benefit of both alcoholic and the community, but it is well to keep in mind that what is of benefit to the one may not be of benefit to the other.

As for our own definition, we shall not be quite so broadminded. However, we shall not distinguish, as some do, between care, treatment, rehabilitation, and reeducation; for each of these words implies humane attention to the alcoholic that attempts to alleviate distress, to heal, and to encourage steps toward a better life. We naturally include the many varieties of group and individual care—for example, crisis intervention (Lindemann, 1944; Caplan, 1961)—and

20

the many programs of community psychiatry (Caplan, 1961; Bellak, 1964); so that "treatment" necessarily applies to acute and chronic care and to social, psychological, or medical interventions.

Conflicts arise over the definition of "treatment" when the intervention brings distress to the patient. For example, the traumatic procedures of aversive conditioning (disulfiram, succinylcholine, emetine, electric shock) sometimes make patients deathly ill and dreadfully frightened. The cure is often so hard on the patient—and the outcome so uncertain that some observers are hard put to call these "therapies." On the other hand, although it is easily agreed that a typical jail is an atrocious place, some modern jail programs, while perhaps claiming only to offer humane imprisonment and to prevent inmate degradation, do offer deputy-level counseling, a supporting milieu, and in certain facilities, much more. Are these facilities "treatment" centers, even if they make no claim to heal or rehabilitate their inmates?

The answer, and the whole definition problem, rests upon the weight given to three components in treatment: one is the intent of the change-agent, whether humane or punitive; the second is the style of actual intervention, whether pain relieving or otherwise; and the third is the actual outcome in two theaters—one, the patient's own health and satisfactions; the other, the welfare and sensibilities of other citizens in the community. We would suggest that disputes over the definition of treatment can be clarified by deciding which component is under discussion. For ourselves, we shall require that in a process called "treatment" the overt and covert intent of the change-agent is to produce a beneficial change in the alcoholic.

A definition such as this, based on expectations and goals, has its drawbacks; it is in fact quite permissive. But every definition will have its own disadvantages, and each person in the field must define the term in a way that will cover the situation he is concerned with. In this book, where a great variety of interventions are described— those engaged in by individuals or groups from many specialities and walks of life, those with outcomes unknown or with varying degrees of success—it is evident that we need to encompass a multitude of procedures that seem held together only by a common thread: that the change-agents *do* wish to help both patient and community.

Some who are professionally parochial prefer to define treatment in terms of who gives it and what steps a change-agent takes rather than to rely on concepts as soft-headed as expectations and intentions. These authorities would limit "treatment" to actions taken by professional healers. Using this definition, a kindly jail administrator could never give treatment, nor could a nurse unless her actions were part of a program laid down by a senior healer. This definition implicitly emphasizes the importance of training, professional responsibility, and rational programs of care. No one would doubt that these are valuable ingredients, but to rest solely upon them is to be too exclusive—at least for us and this book.*

It has been demonstrated in offender rehabilitation, in therapeutic communities (Jones, 1953), in Alcoholics Anonymous (A.A.) fellowships,** and in the Synanon program*** that meaningful communication can be promoted between client and change-agent if both do come from the same background and can share each other's point of view. One of the arguments for the treatment of alcoholics by recovered alcoholics rests on these grounds. We propose that there is likely to be gain by admitting to treatment teams persons from all walks of life—persons with a variety of experiences and with all sorts of personality structures including defects as well as assets—in short,

* There are a number of controversies that swirl around treatment definitions. Who evaluates the patient? Who decides on programs and referrals for the patient? Who does the better job after all? One can follow an interesting exchange of ideas by referring to the debate between Krystal and Moore (1963). Krystal defends the view that only professionals are qualified to treat alcoholics; Moore takes the position that non-psychotherapists do very well in producing behavior change. Other participants in this controversy include Agrin (1964), Bortz (1964), McGoldrick (1964), Hiltner (1964), Chafetz (1964), E. Blum (1964), Lemere (1964), Roger J. Williams (1964), and Mowrer (1964). Quite recently a similar debate, one which bears on the same problems, has emerged in regard to the treatment of schizophrenics. Poser (1966) found undergraduates achieved better results in group therapy than did psychiatrists and social workers. Margaret Rioch (1966) suggests that professionals are slow to adopt new methods, and Rosenbaum (1966) points to basic problems in the definition of "helping."

The reader will recognize that the debate about who should provide treatment goes considerably beyond matters of demonstrable fact and strikes deeply into matters of social status, political power, and economic advantage for the professions involved. Diverse viewpoints also arise because of differing role responsibilities, theoretical backgrounds, and personal values among alcohol workers. One hopes that the debate, rather than being resolved by fiat, would continue and lead to further research on the treatment process.

** See Chapter 12.

*** See Chapter 11.

anyone who is likely to have a constructive impact on patients and whose presence allows for experimentation in treatment. One task of treatment programs is not to exclude potential change-agents but to discover who can be of greatest value to which type of patient at what point in his therapy career. As Chafetz (1964) has stated, "We cannot close a door that is yet to be opened."

Fundamental to any definition of treatment is the expectation that intervention can produce change. Treatment is a future-oriented, optimistic business. All treatment methods for drug-dependent people are based on a theory of change. The methods differ in what they require to induce the change. The professional approach usually implies that a considerable effort—a treatment program—is required. On the other hand, there have been cases in which apparently minor events have led to considerable change. The broader definition of treatment that we propose is more likely to allow for the good results of nonprofessional change-agents. It suggests that the search for means of bringing about change in human beings need not be limited to the fruitful but traditional methods of licensed or certified clinicians, but rather that the searcher may curiously consider all manner of events and stimuli as possible forces that can alter drinking behavior. We do not mean to contend that professionals do not recognize such possibilities; we wish only to emphasize that many people can be change-agents and that elaborate programs of hospital care or psychotherapy need not be the only ways of helping alcoholics.

Take, for example, one of our cases. An alcoholic and his wife were both members of a therapy group composed of alcoholics and their mates. The woman was very protective of the group leader, taking her side whenever a group member was critical. This behavior was typical of a life-long style: she had always been overprotective of those who were supposed to support her, beginning with her mother— a selfish, childish woman who threatened to abandon her unless she was thus catered to—and ending with her husband, with whom she once again played the role of protector to a spoilt, childish, and frightened adult. She recognized that her nurturant behavior was called out whenever she thought she might lose the person on whom she depended—the triggering occasion during treatment was the leader's announcement that a new therapist was to take over the group. She quickly understood that her fear of abandonment was expressed in this devious way, and she ceased giving support to her husband's drinking. As soon as she found a more direct form of behavior, which dealt in a straightforward way with the perceived threat of her husband's drinking, the husband was much relieved of guilt and less often seduced into a passive, self-indulgent role. He in turn became more capable of adult behavior. His own more masculine and assertive demeanor made it easier for his wife to abandon vestiges of excessive overprotectiveness, and, as a result, they were both considerably less hostile toward each other. He did not give up his drinking, but there were now several sectors in his life that afforded him new gratification. It seems that a change in behavior originating in one marriage partner effected a change in personality in the other. This example shows that one should not minimize the therapeutic potentials of apparently minor and peripheral intervention in the "life space" (the internal and external environment) of a patient with alcohol problems.

It is our first assumption in treatment that something favorable can be done for the alcoholic in relatively simple and seemingly unsophisticated ways: by helping him with economic problems; by untangling recurrent job difficulties; by offering him a sympathetic ear, and not necessarily a professional one; and by maintaining contact with him while he waits to be admitted to some other form of treatment. No specialists are needed for these tasks. What is needed is *supervision* and *training* for lay persons, who can then reach out to a troubled person and tide him over a crisis until self-healing processes have had a chance to take over.

Our second assumption is that in a person there exist self-healing processes that require a favorable external environment before they can be set in motion. This idea is well known in medicine, where the practice is not to disturb these self-healing processes with well-meant but ill-advised procedures. One must provide a sterile (aseptic, not antiseptic) environment for the wound so it may heal; one must provide a rigid frame in which a bone may knit; similarly, in the treatment of the mentally upset person, one must provide ego support so the patient may gather his inner strength and begin to mend. In periods of relative psychological unbalance (such as adolescence, combat fatigue, and the psychotic breakdown of the personality), one may witness similar phenomena of seemingly spontaneous reintegration of the personality when a supportive environment is provided.

Third, we assume in treatment that when we learn more about what actually does induce personality change—either for the better or for the worse—we can apply the principles discovered by psychological research to the deliberate constitution of home and institutional environments that will promote healing and personality growth most effectively. Further, we believe that these principles governing psychotherapeutic changes will be of assistance to those who are charged with organizing a *safe* pattern for dealing with alcoholics in settings where the major task of treatment has to rest in the hands of the average, well-intentioned, interested change-agents (lay or professional), and not in the hands of the rare, outstanding, and highly specialized therapist with unusual understanding and great gifts. Finally, we contend that such principles of treatment as are relevant to promoting the alcoholic's well-being *without* risk to him can indeed be taught to change-agents, whatever their calling.

In summary, we propose a relatively broadminded definition of what constitutes treatment. We assume, optimistically, that important changes for the better can occur with seemingly minor therapeutic interventions. We also assume that, given an appropriate environment, self-healing processes can be initiated in the patient and that, knowing the principles governing changes that occur during intensive psychotherapy or personality growth, change-agents from many walks of life can accordingly create such self-healing environments. Thus a far larger reserve of helping hands can be provided than is usually conceived.

TOTAL ABSTINENCE

Probably most of the people who come in contact with alcoholics would say, if asked what the goals of treatment ought to be, that the alcoholic should give up drinking entirely. A few who are less categorical in their thinking would say that alcoholics should be made into normal people, who can drink socially like everyone else. Professionals as well as lay people subscribe to both of these goals. As one talks to change-agents, one learns that many are discouraged with their efforts; some feel defeated, others bored, some have become angry at alcoholics in general. One finds competent and dedicated people giving up the treatment of alcoholics after many years of hard work. Why? Because too often the goals to which they and their patients subscribe are not achieved.

We think there would be more joy in their work and less personnel turnover in the field if it were recognized that total abstinence permanently maintained is improbable. Even more improbable is a return to normal social drinking without further periods of drug-dependent disability. Addictions are hard to cure. Given that fact, and given the limitation of present methods, it is unrealistic to demand a complete resolution of an alcoholic's problems. There can be other goals for treatment.

A heartening trend is the growing recognition that it is not necessary for the therapist to share the patient's unrealistic ideas as to what is required for a satisfactory transaction between patient and therapist. Generally speaking, a satisfactory transaction is one in which some profit accrues—be it that the patient has learned a little; or that he has experienced a positive relationship; or, best of all, that he has developed greater strength, warmth, and confidence in himself and the world. In the case of alcoholism treatment, the change-agent should be gratified if there is some progress, some relief of pain, or if the groundwork has been laid for later growth and enrichment.

Such a reasonable approach has been proposed by Lolli (1955). He suggests that the therapist abandon the goal of "success" and substitute for it the aim of beneficial interactions between therapist and patient. Lolli believes that the results of a therapeutic effort can be evaluated only within the frame of the concluded life history of the alcoholic. The existential philosophy of Sartre is evident in Lolli's position. Lolli warns the therapist not to fall into the trap of sharing the alcoholic's delusions of grandeur; for the alcoholic considers an endeavor a success *only* if it is immediate and complete, and treatment successful only if it brings him relief as tangible and concrete as abstinence. Perhaps people are attracted to the treatment of alcoholics, suggests Lolli, because they too hold unconsciously the same absolute definition of therapeutic success. He recommends that the ability to delay full gratification and to have modest goals should characterize the therapist. "More than the alcoholic who, inherently unstable and intolerant of stress, is 'impatient' by definition, the word 'patient' should qualify the good therapist who is most successful when he least strives for success" (*ibid.*, p. 62).

It is not only the patient who has a distorted view of the goal of therapy; it is also the general public. Perhaps the mental-health movement has had its share of the responsibility for fostering the misconception that total cure is possible—at least some persons in that movement believe that to be the case. The very notion that there is such a thing as a mental health comparable to physical health, with its relatively clear-cut criteria; or that mental illness exists in the sense of physical illness (specifically, that alcoholism *is* a disease like a physical disease for which specific cures exist) has created unreasonable hopes. Further, the mental-illness concept of alcoholism has resulted in largely futile controversies among the public.

If the view of alcoholism as a "curable disease" is to be modified—for instance, in the direction of likening it to other chronic conditions amenable to partial or temporary control and to symptom relief—then we must consider as worthy a large number of modest goals to which treatment can address itself with some hope of success. For ourselves, we are content to believe that important contributions can be made to the patient's well-being, even if they are only to interest him in acquiring a few more successful techniques in the art of living.

REALISTIC AIMS TAILORED FOR INDIVIDUAL PATIENTS

If one agrees to be satisfied—at least until better methods are found—with modest goals for treatment, one is faced with choosing which goal of many is to have priority in treatment. Certainly it is clear than any treatment that does not expect a complete cure must be prepared to cope with a variety of continuing problems—acute life crises, chronic irritations, possible deterioration, and the like. Some of these difficulties will be experienced more by the persons around the alcoholic, some will be his own felt distress; in either event, the alleviation of one may exacerbate the distress of the other. Furthermore, there may well be conflicting demands from the environment or conflicting needs within the alcoholic. As a result, one finds that change-agents, whether or not they make formal diagnoses and plans, usually must look at the total life situation of their patient. Necessity requires that treatment efforts change their focus in response to new difficulties and emergencies, so that while the prevention and anticipation of problems is an ideal goal, just coping with them and reducing their destructive impact is a critical task.

It is not trite to set forth, at this time, the cardinal treatment rule that the treatment aims for alcoholics must be tailored to the alcoholic's person and to his social situation. When considering aims, it is useful to be able to group patients or clients by some category that enables one to say that there are common aims for patients who show some features in common. Building typologies or diagnostic categories—in work with alcoholics as with any other problem group— is always a troublesome as well as a useful business. For our purposes here, it is useful to group alcoholics rather crudely in terms of their apparent aims in drinking, either as reported directly by the patients or as inferred from their life style. This assessment of the stated or inferred function of drinking can be put either in terms that stress the alcoholic's position vis-a-vis certain social conventions or cultural values, or in terms that individually and psychodynamically infer certain levels and structures in personality or neuropsychopharmaco-logical processes. Proceeding from categories based essentially on social conduct, and relating these groups to kinds of treatment aims, we find the groups and the aims falling rather easily into place by virtue of the strong value components underlying both. The two groups of drinkers to be considered at this point are the "convinced" drinkers and the "non-conformist" drinkers. These two categories need not be mutually exclusive, for a convinced drinker who also is socially non-conforming will fall into both. Attention here to these two groups should not lead us to ignore a third large group of drinkers whose social backgrounds, personality, and psychophysiological response to their drug-dependency are such that they still subscribe to conventional goals held both by society and the change-agent.

THE CONVINCED DRINKER

This group comprises alcoholics who conduct themselves so as to maintain their addiction to alcohol. Like persons dependent on other drugs, these patients appear for treatment, or succumb to its im-position, in order to obtain symptom relief from bothersome side effects and disorders and to dry out or "lay up" for only a short time. The aim most of these patients express, when they are frank about it, is to reduce their tolerance level so that they can resume drug use at lower cost, with greater initial drug reactivity, and without the con-current discomfort of whatever related ailments they have had. Al-though few change-agents can disagree with a patient's desire for im-proved physical health and even temporary reduction in drug use, the short-range "unregenerate" nature of the patient's aim leaves some-thing to be desired—that "something" usually being the change-agent's notion that the patient himself should want to abandon rather than continue his drug dependency.

However, regardless of what the change-agent thinks the patient ought to want, society will require or, to say it more exactly, will set forth some probabilistic conditions upon which any further drinking is contingent. If the "convinced alcoholic" fails to meet these conditions, he is likely to cease to be an object of treatment and to become instead subject to punishment or control. Thus, these societal requirements become realistic aims or subgoals for treatment—although it must be made clear that they are society's goals (and the change-agent's because he represents the community) more often than they are the aims of the convinced alcoholic. Society requires simply that the conduct of the continuing drinker become more conventional, regardless of what happens to his drug habit. That is, he may continue to drink if (1) he does not cost anybody any money; that is, neither he nor his family live on welfare; (2) he does not display his deviancy in unacceptable ways such as loitering, vagrancy, being a public nuisance, being an unwashed and badly dressed "bum," and so on; and (3) he does not harm anyone else physically or socially, as for example by endangering lives on the highway, being violent, robbing to sustain his "habit," being socially boorish, bringing disrepute on his family or friends, and so on. A fourth point seems less certain; whether society demands that the alcoholic not harm himself. Certainly no flagrant suicide attempts are tolerated, and obviously self-destructive drinking bouts are responded to with care; but whether there is any strong public feeling to the effect that a man cannot destroy himself quietly, discreetly, without making a nuisance, we can't be sure. The patient himself may not be sure either; some alcoholics are not pursuing a destructive course by accident. The change-agent can, however, be certain that, at least for him, an additional treatment goal will be to prevent slow and quiet suicide as well as the more dramatic form.

NONCONFORMING DRINKERS

A second large group of alcoholics, defined again by social standards, complicate their alcoholism by being unwilling to subscribe to even moderate conformity in return for being allowed to continue their drug use. Society appears to be willing to grant considerable private freedom, even for drug dependency, provided that the conditions of not being burdensome, shocking, or dangerous are met. Among the alcoholics who are unwilling to adopt discretion, whatever the etiology and psychodynamics, the community is highly sensitive to those who reject the work ethic; that is, those who do not work and do not even lie about not wanting to work to support themselves and their family. The community is also sensitive to those whose alcohol use seems to be associated with a desire to stand out as deviants, either as a symbolic expression (one is reminded of how marijuana plays this role for some rebellious young people) or as an anxiety-reducing or inhibition-reducing agent that allows the gratification of exhibitionist, asocial, or otherwise offensive behavior. Finally, the community is necessarily intolerant of those drinkers who pose genuine dangers to others. These are the alcoholics who are either aggressive or criminal, or who continue while intoxicated to engage in tasks—such as driving, flying, running dangerous equipment—which result in harm to others.

For these particular problem drinkers, the goals of the change-agent and society are incompatible either with the functions alcohol has for the drinker or with the satisfactions and activities correlated with being an alcoholic. As a result, there can be no aims that, as in the earlier cases, are a compromise between social demands and individual predilections—as, for example, increasing discretion and conformity in return for not being forced to abandon drinking entirely. In the case of the alcoholic who repeatedly challenges conventions or public safety, the change-agent will be unable to please or protect society without displeasing the patient himself. It is under these circumstances that the problems of goal setting and type of intervention become most acute; for as the demands for safety or propriety increase, the community becomes more strongly opposed to the patient's drinking behavior. It is at the very point when the patient is least amenable to treatment that society insists he must change or be changed. The likely consequence of the patient's deviant behavior is community control or coercion, without regard to its impact upon the alcoholic. Under those circumstances the means employed are no longer treatment as we have defined it, for the intentions of the change-agent are no longer benevolent; they exclude a primary interest in the satisfactions or special welfare of the defiant. When the change-agent must be simultaneously concerned both with the alcoholic's and the community's welfare, the problem of reconciling these two incompatible viewpoints becomes a primary treatment consideration and goal.

Whose side is the change-agent on? Our discussion so far has assumed that the change-agent will be on the side of society—that he will act to oppose, control, or otherwise change the unacceptably deviant acts of the alcoholic. There are at least three good reasons for that assumption; one is that most change-agents (physicians, judges, jailers, nurses, ministers, teachers) are respectable citizens who share the convictions of the community about what behavior is right and what is wrong. As community members they sense a threat to their own and others' welfare (and here we do not imply they are necessarily in error). If they were to take any different stand—one, for example, that upholds the right to drive while "under the influence" or advocates the use of marijuana as a substitute for alcohol—they would mark themselves as deviants, and they would be subject to pressures to conform. It is also usually the case in the treatment of alcoholics that change-agents are in the direct employ of the community and are assigned the task of using their skills to serve the interests of the larger community.

A private practitioner, on the other hand, has more freedom from explicit community demands since the alcoholic client, not the public, is the contracting agent. Furthermore, the client who comes to private psychotherapy is an "easier" case in terms of the aforementioned social goals; for by virtue of having the funds and the desire to seek such care, the client also demonstrates that he is already well socialized and, as a correlate, less likely to be a gross deviant. Nevertheless, for change-agents in either private practice or public agencies there arise conflicts over their professional identity and responsibilities, their notions of what is best for the patient, and their feelings of obligation to the community itself or to agencies for which they work. Many of these conflicts are expressed in debates about what must be and what should not be confidential about the information a client or patient communicates. These conflicts are also expressed in debates about problems of "over-identification" or "counter-transference" in cases where the change-agent "takes the side" of the patient; versus charges of "manipulation," "brain washing," "violation of trust," or "conformity pressures" (when the change-agent works to bring the alcoholic around to a conforming position). It becomes evident that confidentiality, professional identity, the incompatible loyalties to the many groups and their values which the change-agent shares, are all part of the problem of setting realistic social goals for the treatment of the alcoholic patient. The continuing pressures of employing agencies or public voices (the press, laws, citizen groups, informal conversations and so forth) also enter into consideration.

Since it is axiomatic that treatment goals must also be based on the patient's situation and needs, it follows that the position of the change-agent cannot be totally dictated by society, employment, or professional rigidity. There must be some freedom for the change-agent as well as the patient to act, some chance for the community to develop toward deviancy a tolerance that is essential for the treatment of the alcoholic. We do *not* argue for permissiveness in the face of an actual threat to anyone's safety; but we do argue that mistaken community notions of menace or horror attributed to drug-use (see R. Blum and Associates, 1964) are inappropriate to anyone's best interests—patient or citizen. Inevitably a change-agent, whatever the treatment setting, will have to work with his own group or institution in order to set goals for its alcoholic clients that are not only in keeping with its public mandate but also permit adequate tolerance limits for actual treatment to proceed. The responsibilities of change-agents are to help create structures or climates in which treatment is possible. Insofar as they are able to meet this responsibility, it is probably because they have called attention to the problem of alcoholism, have engendered in policy makers optimism about success in treatment, have educated policy makers and their constituents to discriminate between real dangers and imagined ones, and have thereby both extended the targets for service to encompass other than acceptable alcoholics and reduced the shock, fear, loathing, and anger which are directed toward those alcoholics who are distressingly deviant without actually being dangerous.

Now to summarize the foregoing: Treatment goals depend on what the patient is doing and seeking. They also depend upon the role of the change-agent and the setting for his interaction with the alcoholic. For example, the goals may be medical and aimed at physical health or psychiatric improvement; they may be psychotherapeutic and aimed at changes in personality structure, conduct and feelings; or they may be educative or spiritual and aimed at awareness, at non-alcoholic ways of having religious experiences, or at the development of a community-based morality. Treatment is an attempt to channel as well as facilitate change. Consequently treatment goals must differ from step to step, or problem to problem, as it may be. We shall attend more to the treatment process in a later chapter. Finally, these goals will reflect the situation of the change-agent himself, since they are determined not only by the nature of the community and the particular change-agencies, but also by the personal and idiosyncratic nature of the change-agent as an individual.

Chapter IV

~~~~~~

Whom Are We Treating?

If change-agents must set their treatment goals and tailor their programs to the life situation and personal characteristics of the patient, as Chapter Three declared, it is appropriate to ask, what *are* the characteristics of alcoholics? Do they all have features in common? If not, do their subgroups share common features and syndromes about which general statements relevant to treatment may be made? This chapter addresses itself to these questions.

Several points must be emphasized at the outset. First, any effort to set up a typology or diagnostic category into which people are fitted can be a source of trouble as well as convenience. Diagnoses of psychopathology are notoriously unreliable, especially for subgroups within a major classification of disorder (Ash, 1959). Disagreement rather than agreement is to be expected when clinicians try to assign alcoholics to one or another subclassification. Secondly, although individual evaluation is critical for most treatment endeavours, it may not be either necessary or possible to achieve a complete description of a patient and his situation at the beginning of contact. Understanding a patient is a continuing task, one leading to revisions in appraisals throughout the relationship—not only as the therapist gains more knowledge of the patient, but as the patient himself, and perhaps also the therapist, changes over time. Only a few treatment endeavours depend upon detailed personality descriptions; most endeavours assess major features but do not require knowledge of intricate psycho-dynamics. Probably psychoanalytically oriented therapists are the change-agents most attentive to planning treatment in terms of detailed patient studies; in contrast, many change-agents will be operating in settings where no psychological diagnosis is attempted. They will rely on common-sense evaluations based on easily observed features of the case. A third point to be made is that many different schemes for the classification of people with alcohol-related problems have been developed. Although these are often of considerable interest from a theoretical standpoint or in terms of planning personality research, the exposition of these systems derived from various schools of personality, sociological, or psychiatric theory is beyond the scope of this book. Here we limit ourselves to descriptive classifications which we believe are most relevant to treatment as we view it.

THE BACKGROUND CHARACTERISTICS
OF ALCOHOLICS

Of primary importance (but easily overlooked by clinicians pre-occupied with the pathologic aspects of patients seen in one office or institution) are the general social characteristics of alcoholics. These characteristics are, of course, not enlightening unless we are able to compare alcoholics with the non-alcoholic members of the popula-tion. Much recent work in sociology, anthropology, and psychiatric epidemiology focuses on those groups whose members are more than ordinarily prone to become alcoholics. People in these groups will be most likely to be in need of care. Whether or not they will receive that care is another matter, for if there are selection factors at work which restrict their access to caring agencies, they may not be seen in treat-ment regardless of their alcohol disorders.

To identify the social characteristics of problem drinkers one must know about normal drinking. We therefore present data about drinking behavior in the United States. Many of these data are directly quoted from a review prepared for the President's Commission on Law Enforcement and the Administration of Justice (R. Blum, 1966).

On the basis of the work of Cisin and Cahalan, who have done a national study (1966), it can be said that 68 per cent of all American adults have had at least one drink within the past year. Twenty-two per cent of the population report they have never tried an alcoholic beverage.

In regard to estimates of drinking prevalence among children there are no national studies. A number of excellent local surveys have been done. Maddox (in Pittman and Snyder, 1962) reviews those describing high school age drinking and finds that estimates of high school use—at any frequency—range from three in ten students (Utah, Michigan) to eight in ten (New York). Low alcohol content beverages such as beer and wine are most typically consumed and frequent use is rare. Maddox suggests that the range of teenagers having one drink or more a day is between two and six per cent. Straus and Bacon review college-age drinking findings. Patterns vary by college but combining data from a number of colleges (Straus and Bacon, 1953) one arrives at an estimate of less than half of the students drinking more than once a month, fewer than one-fifth of the men and one-tenth of the women drinking more than once a week. Alcoholism as such does not ordinarily occur among youth.

It must be kept in mind that the extent of use varies considerably over time. For example, it is estimated (Jellinek, 1947) that a century ago most Americans were either heavy drinkers or abstainers; the drink of choice being distilled spirits. Present drinking is more extensive but also more moderate; beer and wine now account for more than half of the per capita consumption (Leake and Silverman, 1966).

Differential drinking patterns occur among various groups. On the basis of the national Cisin and Cahalan study it is found that the largest proportions of drinkers are among males, younger persons in their twenties and thirties, and among people of higher socio-economic status. Among young well-off males 88 per cent drank. In contrast among poor, old women only 34 per cent have had a drink during the year prior to interview. Religious differences also obtained: Jews, Episcopalians, Catholics and Lutherans drank more than Baptist and other anti-alcohol religious groups.

Cisin and Cahalan show a marked difference between the characteristics of drinking groups as such and the groups composed of persons who are heavy drinkers and also the groups that are "problem" drinkers. Using a complex drinking measurement method which included frequency of drinking, amount drunk per occasion, and the variability in drinking, they found that "heavy"* drinking takes place among persons of low socio-economic status, especially older men and in particular ones of Puerto Rican or Latin extraction, Negroes, and Protestants not affiliated with churches, and among service workers. Heavy drinking occurs most often among big city dwellers and in more urbanized regions of the country. The investigators call attention to the fact that the heavy drinkers are found among groups with over-all low rates of drinking (e.g., Fundamentalists) meaning that moderation is not the drinking style, but rather either high or low extreme drinking patterns prevail. That is the same pattern of "extremism" that characterized last century's U.S. drinking and which allowed temperance workers to describe a high rate of alcoholism for those who did drink. It is noteworthy that the contemporary high risk groups are not socially integrated into the American "moderation" mainstream which has developed during this century, especially after Prohibition. As these groups are successfully integrated into American life—which is the historical pattern for urban immigrants—their second and third generation offspring should show moderate drinking and reduced alcoholism risk. Such "integration" aims not only at reducing the strains associated with vulnerability to drug abuse, but at learning cultural techniques of moderation in alcohol use per se, this necessarily resting upon a more cohesive family life in which drinking as well as other conventional behavior can be transmitted.

Among the twelve per cent of the total population classified as heavy drinkers, six per cent were found to be escape-oriented heavy drinkers or "problem" drinkers. Not all of these are alcoholics as such. These escapist drinkers were older, of lower socio-economic status and included more than an expected number of Negroes. They were people not well integrated in society. They were also people who worried about their drinking, who said they had more than their share of problems, who had unhappy childhoods, who claimed poor health, and who were dissatisfied with their achievements in life.

Cisin and Cahalan asked people what they did to relieve tension and anxiety. They found first, on a scale measuring tension, worry, depression and the like, that women reported being more "upset" than men and that persons in lower socio-economic situations had more tension than upper level people. When men are upset they say

* "Heavy" drinking is defined by the investigators as three or more drinks of alcohol consumed on three or more occasions per week—or more drinks consumed on fewer occasions.

they drink; women use tranquilizers or other pills more often. Generally, low status persons use more drugs and smoking—as well as eating—to relieve tension. In discussing their findings the authors observe that (social) drinking is an approved behavior among groups high in the power structure but that escape drinking is permitted, at least in the sense that others are indifferent to it, in low power groups.

The Cisin and Cahalan work is the basic national study. From other local inquiries one affirms that there are clear drinking pattern differences between ethnic groups (Knupfer and Room, 1966), for example between Irish Catholics (high), Protestants (middle), and Jews (low drinking rate) (Skolnick, 1954), that women drink less than men (Knupfer, Fink, Clark and Goffman, 1963), that younger people drink more than older but that heavy* drinkers are older (Knupfer *et al.,* 1963), that frequency of drinking increases with family income, and that variability in drinking behavior is greater within the lower income groups than within higher income groups (Knupfer *et al.,* 1963). It has also been found that expressed attitudes toward drinking are associated with actual drinking patterns (Knupfer *et al.*), that drinking to escape or relieve tension is associated with heavy drinking, that alcohol dependence is highly correlated with heavy drinking, and that emotional distress is related to heavy drinking *only* when the motivation of "escape" is offered by the drinker; that is, escape heavy drinkers do report other emotional distress, non-escape drinkers do not. So it is that "problem" drinking must be linked to escape motivation as well as to amount of alcohol used. Heavy drinking by itself does not mean that any psychological or social problems are present; it is often just part of a middle and upper class male way of life. The authors (Knupfer *et al.,* 1963) wisely note that "behavior is influenced, not determined, by social pressures."

Clark (1966) has examined "alcoholism" in a study of a Western city. He suggests that alcoholism definitions share four elements: excessive intake, a mental disturbance due to drinking, disturbed social and economic behavior, and loss of control over drinking. Constructing a measure which includes all these items, he found among a representative adult city dweller sample that alcoholism prevalence varies depending on the kind of index constructed but that by any measure men are more alcoholic than women. Women and

---

* See the definition of "heavy" drinker by Cisin and Cahalan, footnote page 36.

men were more nearly equal in the matter of using alcohol to excess in coping with tensions, but men much more than women were likely to get into trouble with other people and with public agencies, for example the police. Plaut (1967) has set forth an alternative complex definition for alcoholism; his key point is social behavior, how a person conducts himself, not drug ingestion per se, as the criteria for the judgment of alcoholism (or drug abuse as such). Plaut describes the steps to the development of drinking behavior as these can be derived from epidemiological and clinical studies; the period from beginning drinking to identification as an alcoholic takes from nine to fifteen years, with alcoholism usually emerging between the years of 35 and 55.

How children are introduced to drinking depends upon the ethnic group of which they are members, and on the correlated fact of the cohesiveness of families and the extent to which families "teach" drinking behavior. Most studies are in agreement (Plaut, 1967; Knupfer *et al.*, 1963) that within the United States Italian, Greek and Jewish families introduce their children to wine—and other mild beverages—early in life and as part of family dining or in religious rituals and festivals (what is called "integrated" drinking). Irish and Yankee offspring begin their drinking later in adolescence, more often use hard liquor, more often do their drinking outside of the home, and learn to attach different significance to drinking as such. When these findings for groups within the United States are combined with a number of cross-cultural studies (Child, Bacon and Barry, 1965; R. Blum and E. Blum, 1963; Sadoun, Lolli and Silverman, 1965; Jellinek, 1960; Leake and Silverman, 1966) a very consistent picture is presented. When drinking is part of an institutionalized set of behaviors which include important other people in roles of authority and when drinking is part of ritualized or ceremonial activities (*e.g.* family meals, festivals, religious occasions, etc.) as opposed to leisure time or private use, it is *not* likely to be associated with high individual variability (unpredictability, loss of control) in conduct nor with the growth of drug dependency nor with the judgment by observers of "abuse" or "alcoholism." Further, when parents themselves reflect safe or model drinking behavior (*i.e.* are not problem drinkers), when drinking occurs shortly before or with food-taking, and when the drinks used are wine or beer, the risks of either long-term or short-term adverse effects are slim.

Plaut, in a careful review of epidemiological work (1967, unpublished), examines various estimates of alcoholism prevalence in the United States. The best known method is based on the Jellinek formula (Jellinek, 1947) which in turn rests on cirrhosis liver deaths per annum. That formula, although subject to later criticism by Jellinek himself (see also Leake and Silverman, 1966), remains an estimation device which is still of considerable usefulness according to Keller (Keller in Pittman and Snyder, 1965). The Jellinek formula, as applied recently by Keller in 1960, gives an estimated four and one-half million alcoholics in the United States. Most criticisms of the Jellinek formula contend that it under-reports alcoholism. Plaut reviews the local and regional studies which compare other case-finding methods with the Jellinek estimation and finds that these either support the Jellinek estimate or, as critics anticipated, yield higher rates. Some of the higher regional rates show nearly twice as many alcoholics as would the Jellinek formula, for example rates of 43/1,000 as opposed to about 25/1,000. Bailey, Haberman and Sheinberg (1966) in a New York City study obtained an initial rate of alcoholism of 19/1,000 for adults, but found that the survey method led to under-reporting. Changes over time in individual reporting also ocurred, but these tended to cancel each other out so there was no major rate change. The highest rates for alcoholism were among men as opposed to women, among divorced or separated males (68/1,000), among Negro Fundamentalists (40/1,000), and among poorly educated persons (33/1,000). Alcoholics were found to be more emotionally upset, to be poorer, to have greater occupational and residence mobility, and to have more illnesses. The Cisin and Cahalan national study did not identify "alcoholics" but did seek "escapist heavy drinkers." Their findings yield an estimate of 6,800,000 Americans with alcohol problems. Reviewing these estimates of alcoholism prevalence, it is clear that the figures arrived at depend upon the methods of case finding and case definition employed. By any estimation method alcoholism is an extensive disorder.

CHARACTERISTICS OF ALCOHOLICS: PERSONALITY

Studies of personality in relation to alcohol use have mostly been confined to the clinical cases which come to the attention of psychiatrists and psychologists in treatment or incarceration situations. Such studies do not usually have the chance to compare these "identified" cases with heavy drinkers as such; the kind of comparisons which are built into the survey studies of Cisin and Cahalan, or of Knupfer and her colleagues. Clinical population studies also suffer from the fact that alcoholics who come to the attention of clinical professionals have usually been drinking for years, many of them being chronic cases. Their common experiences in drinking—and the common long-term effects of that drug—lead to similarities in behavior which may not be due to any pre-alcoholic personality traits. The study of such persons is difficult because chronic alcohol use "masks" what may be underlying traits. An additional problem is that findings are often predicated on theoretical expectations, for example that alcohol abuse is associated with "dependency" so that "dependent" personalities are then identified. Other methodological deficiencies that have plagued clinical studies of *all* types of drug-dependent persons include small sample studies without statistical tests of the data, failure to control experimenter bias, and lack of reliability shown for diagnoses employed.

It can also be awkward trying to divorce the personality traits of individuals from the social environments in which these personalities have emerged. We may infer from the survey studies of Cisin and Cahalan, from the work of Knupfer and her colleagues, and from the other studies cited, that "involved" or "escapist" heavy drinking, or alcoholism otherwise defined, is most frequent among poor and disadvantaged city dwellers who see themselves as failures—which is as others see them too. These suffering souls report themselves, in contrast to non-problem drinkers, as more unhappy and as having more personal problems. The feelings of misery so common in that group of socially maladjusted persons are very likely to be reflected on diagnostic measures as one or another kind of psychopathology. Review of clinical reports finds that to be the case (M. C. Jones, unpublished 1962). This is not to say that chronic drinkers are not psychopathological; to the contrary their backgrounds and presenting symptomatology (alcoholism) almost demand such a diagnosis. M. C. Jones (1962), in her review of prior work, summarizes as "well worn" the following descriptions of alcoholics: restless, angry, insecure, depressed, conflicted, anxious, deeply guilt ridden, lacking in self-esteem and self-assertion, emotionally unstable, with low frustration tolerance, and high but unfulfilled aspirations. One cannot know, on the basis of most of the present work, whether the same descriptions would have been offered had well-designed observations been made during the early years before these patients or inmates—and their cohort controls—either began to drink, or after they began drinking, before they became identified as alcoholics.

Two longitudinal studies throw a little light on the childhood characteristics of persons who later develop alcoholism compared to their peers who do not. The McCords (1962) did an after-the-fact study using records of children described as part of the Cambridge-Sommerville youth study. A search found 29 boys who had become alcoholics to compare with 158 from the same neighborhood who had become neither alcoholic nor criminal. Compared to these the alcoholics had been described when they were children as more "self contained," outwardly more self-confident, indifferent toward their siblings, disapproving of their mothers, more unrestrained in their aggression, and more anxious about sex. These findings, although limited by the nature of the original records, do suggest that psychological differences exist to predispose one but not another person to later alcoholism. A more extensive study by M. C. Jones (1967, 1965) followed up normal public school children over a thirty plus year period. In their forties their drinking behavior was observed. Done in a metropolitan area, nearly half of the men and more than one third of the women were heavy drinkers (every day). Less than ten per cent did not drink. As adults the problem drinkers were aggressive, attention-seeking, acting out, socially extroverted, lacking impulse control, resentful of authority, and lacking feelings for others; power-seeking and self-destructive impulses were also noted. At the other extreme, abstainers were lacking in social poise, the males were more feminine, and they were rigid and self-righteous. When they were children the persons now defined as problem drinkers had mothers who were indifferent or rejecting and lived in families that lacked warmth and understanding. From early life they had more tensions, less satisfactions, and fewer ways of handling life difficulties. Moderate drinkers, compared either to problem drinkers or to abstainers, were better adjusted children, adolescents, and adults. The Jones study has the advantage of comparing non-clinic cases of adults showing a range of drinking behavior. It shows that persons who become problem drinkers could be distinguished from others on psychological traits and family circumstances as children. It also calls attention to the other extreme of drug behavior, alcohol abstinence, finding that abstainers also have—in a metropolitan "drinking culture"—more maladaptive personality features than do moderate drinkers. These studies, when combined with the more usual clinical observations, reinforce the notion that personality problems precede problem drinking for at least some portion of the alcoholic population. Using this finding as a hypothesis for experimental studies, some exciting recent research by Karp, Witkin, and Goodenough (1965) shows that personality factors related to ways of perceiving the world ("field dependent" versus "field independent") are stably related to differences between alcoholics and others. It is unlikely that any one personal characteristic or psychodynamic constellation is *the* predisposing one for alcoholism (Syme, 1957). It *is* likely that among various subgroups (age, sex, ethnic, socio-economic class, etc.) with equivalent life experiences and exposure to alcohol use that those who become drug dependent will more often than their better adjusted peers show preexisting as well as alcohol-caused personality defects. One cannot conclude that personality disorders must exist in order for alcoholism to occur; one can propose that among populations subject to high risk of alcoholism many disordered personalities will be found and that the specific expression of their disorder (crime, psychosis, drug dependency, etc.) will be associated with psychodynamic factors.

CHARACTERISTICS OF ALCOHOLICS: THE DISEASE CONCEPT OF ALCOHOLISM

Jellinek, the acknowledged dean of alcohologists, has proposed that alcoholism is best understood as a disease, one in which various body systems are progressively involved, and one in which the etiology varies depending upon the alcohol-use syndrome presented by the alcoholic. These syndromes (a group of signs and symptoms appearing together and associated with etiology and prognosis as well as being prime diagnoses) are referred to by Jellinek (1960) as "species." The Jellinek classification is one of drinking patterns, progression, and effects; one assuming a disease process, but not assuming a common psychological substrate. Only one of the Jellinek syndromes—the Alpha species—attributes alcoholism to purely psychological dependency including the relief of emotional (or physical) pain. Jellinek held that all psychological formulations attributing alcoholism to underlying personality pathology are limited to the Alpha species.

His contention is that these formulations do not recognize that psychological vulnerability can be minor but that cultural or socio-economic factors lead to drinking and the alcohol itself leads to the observed effects. It is a point well made, for with large and frequent alcohol intake, for whatever reasons, exposure to the risk of dependency (or "addiction") becomes great. As alcohol use continues it can produce liver damage and reduced adrenocortico (stress) responsiveness.

Chronic use is strongly associated with nutritional deficiencies—since alcohol supplies calories but not nutritional needs—and these deficiencies lead to diverse organic pathology (Leake and Silverman, 1966). Much cirrhosis, for example, may be attributable to nutritional deficiency in combination with alcohol toxicity. In any event the direct toxic effects of alcohol plus the associated consequences of an alcohol-centered life style (insufficient food, exposure to trauma, etc.) are productive of further disorder; Jellinek suggests that this vicious circle leads to further (defective) alterations in central nervous system functioning. There is also further reduction in the capactiy of the liver to detoxify alcohol and, Jellinek hypothesizes, additional susceptibility to neural tissue degeneration and to uptake of alcohol as part of cell metabolism, a process biochemically intrinsic to physical dependency and demonstrated, in vitro, for morphine.

If genetic or pre-existing illness factors account for initial organ or metabolic deficit, then stress due to alcohol can be less well handled and a quicker addictive process, *i.e.* a faster disease progression, is to be expected. Similarly, on the basis of a growing literature showing how stress responses are interrelated, it can be expected that chronic environmental stress (as in crowding, continual threat, heavy noise levels, hostile interpersonal relations) may predispose an organism to reduced capabilities (defined physiologically and endocrinologically as well as in terms of performance) under a new stressor. If one conceives of the life of the metropolitan poor as heavily loaded with such environmental stress (a reasonable hypothesis which also relates to population rates for many other diseases), and if one conceives of continued alcohol ingestion (regardless of the circumstances or motives associated with initial or developing use) as a "stress," then the risk of alcohol addiction for such exposed populations is better understood.

ALCOHOLIC CHARACTERISTICS: GENERAL SUMMARY

In the United States, since the majority of persons drink alcoholic beverages, use itself is normal and persons with widely differing personal and social characteristics employ—and enjoy—the drug (wine lovers naturally prefer for wine to be called a food; others prefer it to be called only a beverage). Heavier alcohol use without frequent problem drinking is concentrated in well-off younger males; heavy use itself does not imply an alcohol problem. Alcoholism as such is concentrated among the poor and disadvantaged older males in metropolitan areas, most often persons with histories of work and family troubles and with personality defects. After alcohol use has begun, especially among persons who have not learned to use it in family settings and where use is unusual among the person's social peers, a chain of events leading to dependency or sporadic problem drinking can be set in motion. These events include the discovery by the drinker that he can relieve his emotional tensions and "escape" through alcohol, or he may find that physical pain relief or simply the prevention of withdrawal symptoms (the "abstinence syndrome" of opiate users) can be prevented through further alcohol use. Alcohol itself, perhaps in combination with pre-existing or associated physiological disorders, plays a role as a disease or toxic agent, being capable of producing further metabolic and tissue pathology as well as disordering personality and social relations. The social background, residential, and psychological characteristics of persons with alcohol problems are very similar to the features of persons who suffer high probabilities of other forms of medical or mental health disturbance, and who, as groups "at risk," challenge the nation with high rates of crime, welfare needs, unemployment, and the abuse of mind-altering drugs other than alcohol as well.

Emphasis on the association between alcoholism and general misery should not let us overlook that alcoholism can also occur among the better-off citizenry and that it is not just a disease of the poor. Illustrating the dangers of that misconception Blane, Overton, and Chafetz (1963) in a Boston study found that physicians were likely to diagnose alcoholism (*i.e.* identify it) when the patient was a Skid-Row derelict or obvious social misfit but were more likely to miss the diagnosis when the patient was well-groomed, lived with his spouse, and had no police record. Thus there is a danger of "false negatives" in identification which arises from the association between alcoholism and social misery. A "false positive" danger also exists, for not all Skid-Row types are alcoholics; for example, Straus and McCarthy (1951) showed that only 43 per cent of New York's Bowery homeless men were alcoholics.

Emphasis on the multifactorial approach, one which points out that a variety of forces contribute to the development of alcoholism, should not lead to the conclusion that for any one alcoholic all determinants have equal weight. To the contrary, examination of individuals will reveal that particular events and processes have played paramount roles in the development of drug dependency. Jellinek's (1960) description of the various syndromes or "species" of alcoholic disease represent an effort to distinguish essential case characteristics. Clinicians will necessarily be attentive to the relative importance in each patient of family experience, personality, socio-economic-ethnic circumstances, and the chain of physiological events associated with alcohol use and associated life style.

ALCOHOLIC CHARACTERISTICS: IMPLICATIONS FOR TREATMENT PROGRAMS

We need not belabor the point that there is no alcoholic personality as such nor that alcoholism may occur for a variety of reasons among persons in all walks of life. Communalities do exist—these most generally in relationship to being a member of deprived or out-of-the-mainstream urban groups—in developing addiction in response to continued exposure to heavy alcohol use and in suffering personality defects or distress of the sort that links alcohol to neurotic symptoms or reactions, to psychotic compensations, or to acting-out or escape from anxiety in character disorders. Even these generalizations are inadequate: the point is that treatment facilities must be prepared to cope with a variety of patients' personalities and problems.

On the other hand, the concentration of alcoholism among certain urban groups—Negroes, Puerto Ricans, Irish Catholics, males, the poor, and the like—points up the need for treatment agencies to emphasize methods for patient "recruiting" which will insure not only that these persons are brought into treatment but that they remain there. A critical feature is that this majority of cases who are underprivileged are the ones least likely to seek care and least likely to speak the same language or have the same values as the middle class professional who traditionally has supervised treatment programs. At every point one expects incompatibility rather than compatibility between the views of these alcoholic patients and the most prevalent healers. What the healer sees as disorder or disease the outcast alcoholic might view as the will of God, his last revolt, or perhaps the best alternative available to utter despair.

A common point of dispute occurs when the psychologically oriented healer focuses on the individual alcoholic and demands that the alcoholic recognize his own role in his "responsibility" for his troubles. Even if the alcoholic admits to troubles, he is very likely to be "irresponsible," attributing their source to the cruel world rather than himself. He may well be correct in his assessment, given the likelihood that he has been reared in misery and deprivation. Thus, the so-called "rationalizations" and "projections" of the alcoholic must be taken seriously, for they will be part of the etiology, even if not the whole story.

Throughout treatment there is likely to be continuing failure of communication between patient and healer on matters of fundamental belief and experience. The typical lower class alcoholic will be likely to have different standards from the typical middle class healer in evaluating his own bodily functions, different definitions of what constitutes illness and what should be done about it, different expectations in regard to interpersonal aggression or cooperativeness, a different "conscience" about being dependent on or exploitative of others, and certainly a different philosophy in regard to a man's chances in life for being happy, becoming a success, staying well, or being able to cope with others.

As one reviews the characteristics of the "typical" alcoholic and finds the profound relationship between alcoholism and the other social and physical disorders that affect city people in disadvantaged groups, one concludes that alcoholism is indeed but a symptom—not only of individual psychological distress or an addictive disease process but of disordered social backgrounds and painful interpersonal experiences as well. One also sees not only that the groups from whom the typical alcoholic comes share a wide number of distressing characteristics— disease, unemployment, unhappiness, powerlessness, drug addiction, criminality—in proportion far beyond their due, but also that the individual patient is likely to demonstrate these same correlative disorders in his life. Whether considered as a disease, a reaction, an acting-out, or a learned addiction, alcoholism in each patient will be a multidimensional problem which can be defined in a variety of ways, that is, economically, criminologically, educationally, socially, or in terms of public health or psychiatric disease. A successful treatment program can not be simple when the patient is complex, nor can it be narrow in scope when the patient's problems encompass a broad range of activities and community effects.

PART TWO

THE TREATMENT
PROCESS:
STAGES AND HURDLES

Chapter V

The Treatment Process: Beginning

In this and the following chapter we describe some of the stages and hurdles in treatment. The reader may ask, what kind of treatment? The answer is, all kinds; for we wish to present those elements that are essential and therefore common to treatment in general, whether it takes place in a private office or in an institution, whether it is group work, psychoanalytic therapy, or behavior therapy. Since treatment is a process, whether contact is continuous or intermittent, its division into stages is a convenience useful for identifying particular problems and procedures. The therapeutic hurdles which the patient faces differ depending upon his stage of progress, and so we shall discuss the characteristic obstacles the patient must overcome and tasks he must master before he can advance to the next step.

There is, of course, nothing inevitable about the sequence. A patient may bypass a given stage, several stages can occur simultaneously, the cycle of stages may be repeated several times during an alcoholic career, or progress can be made without evidence of passage through the particular steps set forth here. Nevertheless we believe that enough patients will progress a common path to make it worthwhile to consider how the sequences in the treatment career are best handled.

Our discussion follows Levinson (1962) in speaking of the preparatory stage, which is preliminary to formal treatment; the initial-treat-
ment stage, which includes candidacy, intake, and agreement on a
therapeutic "contact" defining patient-therapist roles and relationship;
the problem-solving stage, during which much of the "working
through" of personal difficulties occurs; the pre-termination stage;
and finally the post-treatment and follow-up stages.

One recognizes that there are a number of ways to look at
treatment; the overall process and stage analysis here presented are
but one of these ways. In later chapters we shall examine treatment
from other standpoints—for example, in terms of kinds of treatment
and noteworthy problems. Necessarily there will be some hearkening
back in those discussions to the hurdles and sequences under consideration here.

PREPARATORY STAGE

Before official treatment can begin, the alcoholic himself must
become concerned about his problem. Usually he will become concerned only after persuasive efforts are made by a person who is close
to him. Therefore, such a person must be able to recognize symptoms
of impending or present drug dependency—an ability that cannot be
assumed to exist without instruction. An educated and involved public
is *essential* in providing the necessary first aid and in laying the groundwork for treatment. Therefore, *we recommend that a wider and
broader community-teaching program be undertaken, one aspect of
which would be to give instruction on how to recognize the potential
or actual alcoholic.*

Those persons who are close to the prospective patient, the
alcoholic, need the advice of professionals to help them free themselves from inner hesitations (imposed by misunderstanding, false
psychological principles, false hopes, and false "kindness") that hamper
their efforts to steer the patient toward treatment. *We recommend
that, as part of the public education on alcoholism, professional time
be made available for the express purpose of counseling people how to
use their personal ties to the threatened drinker most effectively for
his benefit.* First-aid courses for wives, friends, interested bystanders,
and employers can be organized as group discussions or lectures. Advice about the possible contents and procedures of such courses can

be obtained from community mental health consultation services * or from the National Council on Alcoholism.** Such discussion should include emotional support for the participants. They should also include information about available community resources, instruction in referral procedures, descriptions of the nature of treatment offered, the kind of improvement that can be expected, and the support that will be necessary for optimal results during, between, and after treatments. Inevitably, such orientation will point to deficiencies in the community-care facilities. In the long run, this kind of education of the public by concerned professionals and laymen will make the public more aware of the needs of the community and of the alcoholic. Insofar as we are a democratic society, a broad base of public support is essential for the maintenance of existing treatment facilities and the creation of needed new ones.

CASE FINDING AND RECRUITING

Many alcoholics will not come of their own accord to the change-agency. Recall from Chapter Four that the typical alcoholic is poor, uneducated, a minority-group member, a person not likely either to know about or to feel comfortable with the various facilities run by the "establishment." These are the people who need a variety of health and social services but who are themselves not likely to know what they need nor where nor how to get it. It is ironic that these people who most need care are the ones least likely to receive it (Morris, 1957). In addition to these large numbers of potentially visible alcoholics not seeking care and not identifying themselves as needing it, there are an unknown number of hidden alcoholics whose very existence as "cases" will be unknown. Consider, for example, that Clark (1966) found that men but not women alcoholics were likely to be identified as alcoholics by public agencies, for it was the men who got into trouble. We must presume that women constitute a reservoir of hidden alcoholic disorders. Remember too the complete findings of Blane *et al.* (1963) to the effect that physicians diagnosed

* See Haylett and Rapoport, 1964.
** N.C.A., located at 2 East 103 Street, New York, New York 10029, is a voluntary agency which is a major resource for individuals, groups, and organizations seeking information, advice, or assistance in dealing with a particular alcoholic patient or with the planning of a program for alcoholism.

alcoholism among Skid Row patients but missed the diagnosis among well-dressed and respectable people. Some of these undiscovered alcoholics will be unknown to public agencies and to healers but not to their families and employers. However much these concerned relatives and associates may urge it, some number of alcoholics will be unwilling to make any move toward identifying themselves as having a problem, seeking aid, or accepting the "patient" or "alcoholic" role necessary to initiate them into most treatment programs.

What this means is that many, if not most alcoholics, will never receive treatment if treatment personnel sit in their offices waiting for the clients to come in. The police, of course, are case-finders par excellence in the community; but subsequent to police identification of alcoholics through arrest, there is in most communities no automatic provision for treatment. The A.A. fellowships have set a fine example in seeking out alcoholics. Salvation Army Social Service Centers provide splendid on-the-spot services. A few progressive community mental-health agencies have combined epidemiological research with consultation services and on-the-street or poverty-neighborhood health centers in an aggressive effort to find and recruit persons in need of care. On the whole, however, change-agents have been passive rather than active so that one must assume that most alcoholics have yet to experience treatment as we define it. *We recommend that the change-agents adopt an aggressive policy of community case finding and client recruiting.* It is the healer who is strong and resourceful and the alcoholic who is weak. Upon the strong must fall the burden of seeking out the weak to provide them with care. Since the task is immense, it must be done in cooperation with other community agencies and as part of broad programs which seek to provide opportunities, development, and community services to those who do not now share in our national health, wealth, and power.

REFERRAL

In conventional treatment services, part of the pretreatment stage is referral. By referral is meant some contact which introduces the patient to the change-agent prior to actual appearance of the patient on the premises. The aim of referral is to get the patient started in the appropriate change-agency. If indoctrination during the preparatory stage has been successful, the patient will be a willing one, however tentative his first steps may be.

Some agencies require that the prospective patient take the first step himself—*i.e.*, that he phone for an appointment or present himself in person.* This requirement assures a modicum of motivation in the patient and saves the therapist from wasting his time on a broken appointment. Even compulsory patients (under court order) have been required to make their own appointments.

The telephone self-referral must be handled carefully. In some clinics the initial telephone conversation becomes a hurdle, for it is used by receptionists or nurses to discourage presumably undesirable patients. The impatient or haughty telephone girl, or simply the one who naively allows herself to be trapped by the patient into acting in a rejecting fashion, can herself be the first and last treatment experience for the prospective patient. In consequence *we recommend that it be mandatory that persons who handle patient telephone calls be taught the skills required for that work.* They must be taught how to recognize the rejection-demanding patient—a delicate task. They must be taught how to use the telephone conversation as a positive referral channel should it be learned during that talk that the patient is ineligible for the particular agency which he has called. That means the receptionist must be well informed about all appropriate community resources and about patient eligibility for each.

One important feature is the provision of actual service; the telephone girls, social workers, or other persons handling calls can secure the caller's name, number, and address and can make an appointment at the appropriate agency, then call back to tell the prospective patient what has been accomplished. A further call-back is in order as a follow-up to make sure that the patient has taken advantage of the referral, has been accepted, and is satisfied with arrangements. In some communities it will be useful to create central facilities for receiving all telephone applications and for referring them to appropriate agencies directly rather than by inter-agency referral.

When the referral is not a self-referral; that is, when someone else calls to arrange an appointment for a person with an alcohol problem, the requirements for sensitivity in the receptionist are the same. When the caller is not a change-agent already acquainted with office or agency procedures, it is well to arrange for the caller himself to come into the agency either prior to or with the patient. The pur-

---

* Of course, in an emergency the patient will have to be brought to the hospital or the emergency ward; the treatment of the acutely ill person is beyond the scope of this volume.

poses are several: one is to enlist the caller—whether it be wife or employer, neighbor or pastor—in the evaluation and treatment program.
The first act of this new ally will be, of course, to get the patient to
come to the appointment—or to receive the home visitors—as has
been arranged. By working together at the outset, the referral source
can be made a treatment partner. What he learns at the agency or
office will be translated into greater influence at home to get and keep
the patient in treatment. It may also be the case, depending upon the
approach of the change-agent and the nature of the patient's circumstances, that the referral source will be directly involved as a treatment
object as well as a treatment resource. A number of agencies simultaneously smooth the referral path and develop a treatment program
by setting up get-acquainted sessions in which the patient and the
referral source meet together with the responsible change-agent.

The important therapeutic principle to which we adhere is
that no matter how many different treatment agents deal with the
patient, he must always be in contact—*constant contact*—with one
person whom he depends upon and trusts. (For a more detailed discussion of this management role, see R. Blum, 1964b, 1960.) He must
never be passed from one person to the next, becoming a cog in the
inexorable wheel of a treatment bureaucracy. This can be avoided by
consistent attention and sensitivity to the patient's relationships with
change-agents. Like the nursery-school child, he is not to be abandoned
to a new group or a new person until the new relationship has been
securely established. A concerned family member should also be in
some way part of the treatment beginnings until the relationship between patient and change-agent has become sufficiently strong to
continue on its own.

In some change-agencies, provisions for continued contact, even
before the official program begins, are made automatically (Trice,
1957). For instance, some A.A. fellowships send one of their group
to the prospective member to get acquainted with him for a period
of time before taking him to the group and introducing him to the
rest. Similarly, a sensitive and skilled therapist, Lincoln Williams, recognized in his alcoholic patients the feeling of "ships that pass in the
night" (1948) and instituted periodic dinners for them. He made sure
that all new members were introduced to older members, who took
them under their wing. Williams states that "this procedure helps that
lost capacity for relationships with others so characteristic of the
alcoholic."

This principle of continuing contact has been made maximum use of in some of the modern community mental health programs. In one case, the Northern San Mateo Mental Health Services, self-referrals are not accepted; instead, it is insisted upon that a person be recommended or referred by another agency, be it a social welfare agency, the A.A., a minister, a private physician, or other agent. In this fashion responsibility for the patient remains partly with the referral agent, who serves as a permanent treatment resource when difficulties arise: missed appointments, illness in the family, reintegration into the community. This system assures that the patient has at least one concerned person besides the therapist to rely upon. Finally, this referral method assures a close liaison between the public and the change-agency. Since the most common referral sources (aside from self, family, and friends) are clergymen, police or courts, A.A., physicians, mental hygiene clinics, social agencies, and personnel departments in industry, it is evident that the change-agent should establish a durable liaison with these referral sources as an important step in alcoholism treatment. These sources can provide political support for treatment programs, and the interchange affords educational and preventive advantages.

INTAKE STAGE—CANDIDACY

When the alcoholic has been successfully referred and has arrived—preferably, accompanied—at the change-agency, a new hurdle appears: the intake procedure. If intake is therapeutically planned, it may become a constructive experience in the patient's life. Too often, however, intake and termination become one and the same thing.

Once at the change-agency, the first person a patient encounters is frequently not the one to whom he has come for help; rather, it may be a receptionist, a clerk, a nurse, or sometimes the cashier. These seemingly auxiliary staff members are often closer to the patient in background and outlook than the therapist. If properly used, they can be exceedingly helpful—an important part of the treatment team. They should therefore be selected carefully for capacity to make the patient feel welcome and respected; they should be given necessary training and instruction in their roles; and they should be treated with the same interest and with the same consideration by other staff members as one hopes they will in turn accord to the patient.

How the patient is received the first time, as well as subsequently, is of fundamental importance in his treatment career. Complaints are legend about alcoholics discontinuing treatment after only one or two appointments. Chafetz *et al.* (1962) consider five return appointments a victory; and indeed he and his co-workers make every effort to assure this victory.

What can be done to improve the office conditions surrounding treatment? We review briefly some of the typical fears and complaints of patients about change-agencies. In the first place, patients are depressed by the very act of going to a physician's office or to a hospital, not only because of the cost but also because of its associations with pain and with death. Therefore, anything that takes the patient's mind off these thoughts is of help: furniture that looks bright and new, green plants, even an aquarium or an aviary—anything that gives a general impression of health and life. To be avoided, if possible, are sights, sounds, and especially smells that remind one of operations, emergencies, and tragedies. The laboratory coat and the important-looking stethoscope should be kept out of sight. But far more important are the human qualities that pervade the change-agency. Under no circumstances should it have the feel of an assembly line where the patient is made to wait, where he is summoned over a public-address system or, if his name be forgotten, is called by some generic name such as "boy," "grand-dad," or "dear." These practices are not only unnecessary and undignified but intolerable. Simple means to avoid dehumanizing clinic procedures can be effective, as the experience at the Alcohol and Drug Addiction Research Foundation* ilustrates. There the sensitivities and unspoken needs of the alcoholic are considered with care. Immediately on arrival the new patient is offered a cup of coffee by the receptionist; next, the physician meets him in the waiting room where he introduces himself and shakes hands before they walk together to the treatment room.

In some of the modern multiprofessional state clinics the intake procedure itself can intimidate the prospective patient, especially where his first task is to fill out a number of forms required for statistical reports. It cannot be argued that these forms are for the patient's im-

* Gooderham, M. E. W., *Manual of the East Toronto Branch, Alcohol and Drug Addiction Research Foundation,* 1966 (mimeograph).

mediate benefit, nor can he be expected to view them in this fashion. If he is more or less illiterate, or very nervous and apprehensive, the filling out of forms will do nothing for his self-esteem or for his peace of mind. As a next step he may have to be interviewed about his capacity to pay, at which time it will be determined how much each appointment will cost him. He will have to answer questions that are designed to test his motivation for treatment, his reasons for seeking it, his sincerity in doing so; and he will have to give details about his present and past life—details that may very well seem irrelevant to him. Unless this step is therapeutically handled, the patient may rightly feel that he has been doing all the giving and has received nothing in return except a bill. He may also have been given a series of appointments with different people for evaluations: medical, social, psychological, and psychiatric. After all of these, the chances that the patient feels he has obtained any help will depend pretty much on his capacity for hope and for imagination. The chances are great that he will have to repeat his story several times to these different examiners upon subsequent visits, and he is likely to resent it. The chances that he will remain firmly resolved to cooperate will approach zero if he learns that, for one reason or other, a decision has been made to defer treatment and to place him on a waiting list (see J. Sapir, 1953).

Two points need to be made here. One is that the waiting list is sometimes used by clinicians as a means of warding off patients, the less attractive patients being rejected by this round-about device. Being "less attractive" as a patient is likely to be associated with class origins lower than those of the clinician and with having characteristics judged "undesirable" in patients like being non-verbal or old. One suspects that the better-looking, more charming patient will be last to go on a waiting list. (For a further discussion of class variables affecting treatment assignment, see Hollingshead and Redlich, 1958). The second point is that being on a waiting list has a differential impact depending upon the patient's personality and social class. Rogers (1951), for example, has shown that students respond well to being placed on a waiting list; essentially a student views this deferral as proof of the mildness of his disorder and, as a future-sighted fellow, he looks forward to later contact. Lower-class patients, on the other hand, are seeking immediate relief and expect something to be done for them. Furthermore, they must be educated to the entire concept of psychotherapy. A waiting list is likely to be, for such a patient, a proof of a "runaround," another rejection which he is impotent to counteract. One must not expect to see again the lower-class patient placed on a waiting list. Since the majority of alcohol-problem patients are from the lower class, the waiting list can be designated as a major subversion of a proper treatment program.

It is clear that the intake procedures prevalent in some agencies are destructive of treatment goals whenever the patient perceives them as a hindrance, a personal slight, or a painful demonstration of the higher power and status of agency personnel vis-à-vis the lower applicant.

Those who plan for the patient's welfare must tailor all procedures to suit not only their own needs but also—and most important —the needs of the patient. The program initiated by the Alcohol Clinic at the Massachusetts General Hospital is an outstanding example of effective planning (see Chafetz, Blane et al., 1962). In 1957 a survey of alcoholics admitted to the emergency ward of the Massachusetts General Hospital revealed that the annual admission rate for alcoholics was over 1,200; however, less than one per cent of these subsequently sought treatment at the hospital's outpatient alcohol clinic. In an effort to counteract this lack of follow-through, members of the hospital staff decided to examine emergency-ward procedures and those at the alcohol clinic for possible causes of the low rate of follow-through on treatment recommendations. Upon learning just how complex the intake procedures were—as many as fourteen different professionals before a permanent therapist was assigned (and that after four to six weeks)—the staff actively started to develop an approach designed to avoid these difficulties that keep alcoholics out of treatment. As a starting point, they assumed (1) that the individual's initial contact with a medical institution reflects a physical, psychological and/or social crisis; and (2) that motivation for treatment is higher at times of crisis than at times of non-crisis, not only for the immediate disorder but also for alcoholism itself (Lindemann, 1957, 1956). From this, they concluded that the mere fact of admission to the emergency ward furnishes the opportunity to effect a rehabilitative relation with the alcoholic with a more than usual chance of success.

Using these guidelines, the staff set up suitable treatment conditions at the emergency clinic and proceeded to treat 100 alcoholics (the experimental group) by providing comprehensive medical, psychological and social care based on understanding of the dynamics of the individual patient from the time of initial contact. Another 100 alcoholics treated routinely comprised a control group. Results of the experiment show that 65 per cent of the experimental cases made initial visits to the alcoholic clinic, in contrast to five per cent of the control cases; 52 per cent of the experimental cases made five or more visits, in contrast to one per cent of control cases. It appears, then, that alcoholics do form therapeutic attachments if at the initial contact emphasis is placed on "action rather than words, on gratifications rather than frustrations, and on placing the responsibility for achieving a therapeutic alliance on the care-taker rather than the patient." Chafetz, Blane, *et al.* (1962, p. 407).

Blane and Meyers (1964, 1963) emphasize that by varying the approach to the individual patients to take into consideration their counter-dependent needs, greater cooperation can be obtained from the patient. (Counter-dependent alcoholics were those who became very anxious when the initial approach to them was very nurturant.)

As an illustration, rather than asking the patient what the clinician can do they asked the alcoholic how he could help the healers: "What is it like to have a drinking problem, or how may we best help alcoholics?" If he denies a drinking problem, Blane and Meyers asked the patient if he could tell them how he has been able to avoid it. We venture to guess that the success of such imaginative methods depends in part upon the sincerity of the questioner, for used merely as a clever device such questions would undoubtedly backfire. Beyond the difficulty of initiating a therapeutic alliance with a counter-dependent alcoholic is the problem of continuing it. Entirely new methods, which allow self-direction and autonomy, may have to be devised for counter-dependent alcoholics. Slack's (1960) success in engaging (presumably counter-dependent) juvenile delinquents in relationships suggests that methods can indeed be developed.

Frank *et al.* (1957) have discussed the initial contact between patient and therapist from the patient's point of view. They believe that the patient's perception of the treatment situation as useful or useless depends in part on its place in his current life situation. Aside from this, the personal qualities of the therapist and the nature of the specific treatment situation influence the patient's judgment as to whether he will find the help he expects, and so determine whether or not he remains in treatment. "The patient's experience in the initial interview, however, may be sufficient to counteract his initial unfavorable or defensive attitude toward therapy" (*ibid.,* p. 298). Once again we see the necessity of paying special attention to minute details in intake procedures so that the new patient will be agreeably surprised instead of having his own worst fears and suspicions confirmed.

Chafetz (1963) and Chafetz *et al.* (1962) recommend that *reasonable* requests be granted in order to cement the initial therapeutic relationship: the patient should be given cigarettes; concrete advice on personal, financial, and job difficulties; help with lodging if he is homeless. Getting a patient a shave or a meal are some of the measures employed at Massachusetts General Hospital. Another legitimate means for showing the patient that someone is interested in him is to provide immediate medical treatment when symptoms associated with alcoholism appear. In some cases, it is advisable to minimize anxiety or depression, or to fortify the alcoholic—if such is *his* express wish—against his need for further drinking. These are problems of medical management and are not the subject of this book; however, we do wish to point out the importance of having medical facilities available from the very moment the alcoholic enters the change-agency. *We recommend that all those who have dealings with alcoholics establish a close liaison with members of the medical profession who have experience in treating the medical complications that are associated with alcoholism.*

Initially, treatment should be geared precisely to the emotional level of the patient at the moment of first contact: he should be helped, insofar as possible, with the specific problem he seeks help for and in such a way that he understands what is being done for him and why. He should be given another specific appointment time; and, since any delay is extremely destructive to the tenuous tie between patient and treatment-agent, means of cementing, supporting, and implementing this tie during times between appointments must be found. Simple devices can be effective, like writing in the therapist's *own* handwriting—not the secretary's—the name of the therapist and the date of the next appointment with a reminder not to lose the paper.*

Aside from giving the patient help that he can understand, that makes sense to him, and that is useful, one may tide him over the be-

---

* Many excellent, sensitive, and tender means are to be found in Sechehaye (1951), who presents an extraordinary and original approach to the problem of dealing with individuals who cannot wait. See also Bettelheim (1950), Redl (1963), and Redl and Wineman (1952).

tween-appointment periods by *assigning an expert lay person to him.*
Such a person would maintain daily contact, provide a channel
through which emergency appointments may be reliably obtained, and
help with day-to-day problems in living. He must, of course, be given
adequate instruction and supervision so that he does not overstep his
limits and so that he will not be an obstacle to the therapeutic process
by permitting himself to be played against the therapist. The experience with therapeutic communities for delinquents has taught that the
most crucial variable in the management and eventual rehabilitation
of the delinquents is the close cooperation—indeed, daily exchange
of information—between all members of the staff who have been seeing
the offender in one capacity or another.* The same is necessary with
many alcoholic patients who—in their "acting-out behavior" and their
exploitations, manipulations, and other trouble-making activities—resemble delinquents.

It is probably evident from the above that *we propose to abolish
the intake phase in the patient's career.* Instead, we wish to promote
the notion (not a new one, to be sure) that treatment begins as soon
as the patient has decided he wants something done; and at the moment *something that is intelligible to him* must be done for him. It
follows from this that *all* personnel whom the patient sees in the treatment context have an impact upon him—whether for good or bad
depends upon the skill, intuition, and *training* of the gate-keepers and
the auxiliary and professional staff. It also follows, as we have said,
that the gate-keepers must know about the resources of their community and about their own function in the treatment of the alcoholic
as gate-keepers—opening the gates—rather than as watchdogs who
chase away the undesirables.

In some progressive organizations, research has been done to
study the intake procedures; to observe what happens to the patient
from the minute he gets in touch with the treatment facility to the
time he sees the change-agent proper; and to note the patient's reaction and understanding of the whole procedure. If one wishes to
reorganize a facility according to psychiatrically sound principles, such
systems analysis can be invaluable to pinpoint areas that need to be

---

* The reader is referred to the pioneering work initiated by Professor
P. A. Baan at the Vanderhoeven Clinic in Holland, and presently directed
by Dr. Roosenberg.

remedied and to specify what training the auxiliary personnel (including the reception clerk) need in order to create an overall therapeutic atmosphere.*

We recommend that the established principles for care which guide the modern mental health center be followed with alcoholics, whether or not they are being seen in mental health facilities. These principles include immediacy of care and continuity of care (as well as diversity of care, adequacy of records, and built-in evaluation). It is the task of the administrator and the clinician to ensure that these are practiced.

* Among the writers who have investigated the effects of the total treatment atmosphere and who have made cogent recommendations are: MacGregor (1960), Belknap (1956), Stanton and Schwartz (1954), Simmons and Wolff (1954), Saunders (1954), Titmuss (1959).

Chapter VI

The Treatment Process: Later Stages

INITIATORY STAGE

Unofficial treatment begins when pressures arise to change the patient's behavior and, perhaps, his personality. The processes set in motion at this time continue into the period when patient and change-agent meet for the first few times, that being the time when they must agree on the treatment contract. During these early meetings not only will the practical matter of appointment times, fees, provisions for emergencies, and instruction in agency procedures be handled, but teaching begins as to the nature of the treatment process itself. That teaching, which is rarely recognized as such, is also the beginning of the effort to trade points of view, to evaluate one another, and to build a relationship of trust. During this initiatory stage the patient tries to explain his problem, and he may also express his hopes about what the agency can do for him. He is likely also to talk about the people around him, especially those who have been instrumental in bringing him into contact with the change-agent. The change-agent uses what he sees and hears to assess the patient's needs, his strengths and weaknesses, and the assets and liabilities present in the patient's life situation—his family, job, neighborhood, leisure-time acquaintances, and the like. These others in the patient's life who appear to be potential help are noted, and plans are tentatively laid for bringing them into the treatment program. The treatment plan should be both broad and flexible, but it necessarily contains key propositions. One of these will be the estimate of the patient's view of the change-agent and the treatment situation. The proposition's complement will be the change-agent's own views of these same factors and an evaluation of the gulf between the two. The successful management of the beginning phase of treatment depends upon the adequacy of the change-agent's estimates of those matters of fact, morals, motives and need-determined perceptions that constitute the patient's position. Successful management also depends upon the change-agent's abilities to mold the patient's position into one which is compatible with his continuing in treatment. Molding does not mean that the patient is either persuaded, manipulated, or coerced into accepting the healer's view of things;* it does mean that in the treatment positive aspects of the patient's personality, situation, and philosophy are accentuated so that a relationship between patient and therapist emerges. Full agreement between them is not necessary, nor could it exist. One might look at the initiatory phase as a problem in small group dynamics. The goal of the change-agent is to create at least a two-person group, perhaps a larger one. For a group to be viable it must have agreement on its composition, task, and on minimal working rules. The group will dissolve if there is disagreement on critical issues of purpose or method; it may also dissolve if disagreements in other areas are allowed to intrude. The change-agent has both an overt and covert task in the group. His overt task is to work on the problem at hand; his covert task is a diplomatic one which aims to emphasize points of agreement, to maximize group cohesion, and to exclude temporarily irrelevant issues which might threaten the life of the new endeavour.

The initiatory stage of treatment cannot be considered successfully completed unless the change-agent has tested to what extent the patient actually shares his ideas about the treatment that is to follow.

---

* According to Frank (1961) the patient may be considered "cured" only after the therapist has persuaded him of the correctness of his (the therapist's) interpretation of his illness and personality structure.

The patient may have been well prepared in these initial proceedings so that he understands the kind of treatment he is about to receive and his and the change-agent's roles and responsibilities; however, only in the actual situation does he learn what treatment is really like, what his reaction to it will be, and—most important—what sort of person he is in relation to the new people that he must learn to deal with.

At the end of the discussion of treatment, the therapist should ascertain from the patient what he thought went on during the session and request him to repeat the instructions, if any were given. Similarly, the patient should tell the therapist what difficulty he anticipates the instructions or procedures will create for him, and how he thinks he might meet them. Since patients tend to feel extremely guilty if they fail to follow instructions, and as a result often cannot face the therapist, and since alcoholics are particularly prone to be uncooperative and remiss in keeping their appointments, the therapist may well anticipate such reactions; he may, for instance, indicate his awareness that the patient may not always be able to adhere to the treatment program, and point out that disobedience* is not an insurmountable obstacle. He may remind the patient that therapists must establish certain limits, in the form of rules and prescriptions; and that the patient may feel compelled to test these limits. His purpose is to attempt to alleviate the patient's guilt over infractions. With certain kinds of intellectual patients, he may even explain that in general an overly guilty conscience indicates that a person does not wish to abandon the behavior he feels badly about; for as soon as he starts making an effort to relinquish it, he need no longer feel guilty about it.** With patients who are afraid of their own destructiveness and violence, he may point out that people and facilities are available to protect the patient and the environment. Since by and large alcoholic patients are impulsive, hard to contain, and indifferent to the rules of society when they are intoxicated, therapists who deal with them should work closely with those agencies (*e.g.*, the courts, law-enforcement personnel, and hospitals) who can exert controls that may not be directly available to the therapist himself.

* If the patient is in psychoanalytically-oriented psychotherapy, he learns that disobedience will also come under his and his therapist's scrutiny.
** The reader is referred to an excellent discussion of guilt in C. Russell and W. Russell (1961).

PROBLEM SOLVING OR WORKING-THROUGH STAGE

Depending upon the goals for treatment, the middle stage can be a period of "working-through" of emotional conflicts; a period whereby insight is gained into the sources of problems; or it can be a period in which old behavior patterns are unlearned and new ones are acquired. Depending on the kind of treatment, the emphasis varies from activities *initiated by the change-agent* (administering protective or mood-altering drugs or conditioning alcohol-aversive responses) to different degrees of *patient-initiated* activities (acquiring insight, working in A.A. fellowships, joining resocialization and remedial education activities, and engaging in other self-improvement efforts such as vocational rehabilitation).

We call attention to the dimension of patient versus therapist-initiated activity because we believe it to be an important yet neglected one in studies of the relative effectiveness of treatment. That it is important has been demonstrated by studies on the prepotence of active versus passive learning (Cofer and Appley, 1964), on action as a primary means for changing attitudes (Lane and Sears, 1964), on "functional" autonomy (Cofer and Appley, 1964), and on imprinting (Hess, 1959a, 1959b; Moltz, 1960; Kovach and Hess, 1963; Rosenblum, 1959).

Some puzzling experiences in reducing anxiety too quickly in alcoholic patients may be related to general principles underlying learning. It has been found that certain patients do not return to treatment if their initial anxiety is allayed by the therapist too effectively and too soon (regardless of whether this is done by means of emotional support or by anxiety-reducing drugs). Perhaps we have here an analog to imprinting, for not only does the strength of the imprinted response depend upon the respondent's being sufficiently alert (ducks who have *not* received a tranquilizer, or a patient *not* sedated by an anxiety-producing drug) to make the necessary following movements, but apparently the object which is imprinted (by being followed) must in some way be associated with a fear-reducing situation. Therefore, unless fear is present, it cannot be reduced; this was true of drugged ducks whose "following" response was weakened; it may also be true of tranquilized alcoholics who fail to return for further treatment. Our case here is not to set up imprinting as *the* learning model but to contend that activity—and anxiety—are critical elements in the acquisition of new behavior (see also Cofer and Appley, 1964). On the other hand, until we have better evidence than analogs and theoretical deductions, we are not in a position to specify *what* activity on the part of the patient is to be fostered during the problem-solving stage. A guiding principle of treatment is that it should be started at a level neither too low nor too high but at the level where the patient *is* at the moment. The principle is easy to state but difficult to practice even, for example, in deciding upon the correct dosage of a mood-altering drug, and it is harder yet to decide upon the dosage of support needed by the patient and the amount of responsibility he can take and in what areas. Nor can a decision, once made, remain constant during the process of treatment. When to withdraw supportive drug treatment, when to push the patient to take greater initiative, when to confront him with a description of what he is doing: all these decisions requiring great sensitivity, experience, and courage. We make no specific recommendation other than to urge therapists to consult freely with others as a matter of routine *before* difficulties arise. *We believe that supervision of therapists with an aim to broaden their experience and to enhance their self-confidence as well as to maintain "quality control" should become far more widespread practice than it is presently.*

We should also like to suggest experimenting with giving certain patients a relatively free hand in choosing their own form of treatment. We believe that self-selected treatment will increase the patient's active participation and his sense of responsibility for treatment outcome. It is to be noted that some of the success of the "therapeutic community" (M. Jones, 1953) may be attributed to the patients' being given as much (and sometimes more) authority and responsibility for their welfare as is commensurate with their ability: they are expected to be maximally active on their own behalf.

This is by no means a new concept, certainly not in medicine, although it is often overlooked in the welter of magic bullets which science has showered upon us. The traditional role of the physician has been to set the stage so that the natural forces of the healing process have a fighting chance. We emphasize this point, for it is easily forgotten; especially since it is more flattering to think of the helper as doing rather than as merely assisting. Modesty on the part of the helper ensures that the patient's contributions will not only be appreciated but also that they will be sought out by every means.

It is indeed crucial in treating the alcoholic that the therapist succeed in teaching him during the problem-solving phase whose the problem is and whose salvation is at stake. The patient must learn that the business of getting well is his own, that recovery does not demonstrate the therapist's competence any more than failure to recover demonstrates his impotence. Certain patients would infinitely prefer to kill two birds with one stone: retain their bottle and thereby prove what a failure their therapist has been. The battle for supremacy by sabotaging treatment is especially acute in patients who perceive the change-agent as having a more powerful, respected, or superior position. The sick, miserable, jobless, humiliated alcoholic who meets an obviously well-to-do, successful, educated professional cannot but make the unfavorable comparison and hate both himself and his "helper." If he can't compete successfully—and indeed, he cannot—the patient can at least defeat the therapist by not getting well. This issue occurs even in the psychoanalytic situation where the patient and therapist are often matched for education and for wealth (and sometimes perhaps even in terms of "mental health"), how much more so in the medical clinic setting, where the combatants are patently unequal? In psychodynamically oriented therapy the patient's reaction of hate and envy engendered by his own self-deprecatory feelings are brought to light and dealt with for what they are, a pervasive interpersonal problem that vitiates not only the treatment relationship, but others as well. The cure? Less time spent on vain comparisons and more effort toward honest achievement, which results in justifiable pride and for which social approval is the reward. Increase in self-respect and decrease in envy follow; hence the beneficial effects of encouraging the patient in self-initiated activities that lead to greater mastery and more skill. This is the principle inherent in all programs designed to foster personality growth and inner strength by making success experiences possible and helping the patient to take note of them—the latter also a necessary task, for often his emotional difficulties prevent him from believing himself capable of achievement or even worthy of improvement. Traditionally the educator's and the minister's contributions have been especially valuable in reorganizing the alcoholic's self-perception, whereas in a strictly medical program there is less opportunity for the patient to learn to know himself as a worthwhile person. In this situation it becomes the more important to manage the patient's self-hatred and resulting resentment and to counteract the self-defeating and treatment-defeating attitudes that often result from his sense of inferiority.

How is this to be done? We can learn a great deal from studying the successful operations of organizations such as the A.A. fellowships or Synanon.* In these patient-created facilities self-respect is not only protected by various devices but is nurtured and made to blossom. As one Synanon member said: "We have over 500 patients, that means we have over 500 therapists!" Each member is made responsible not only for himself but also for the rest, who are seen as similar to oneself. If one asks them how it is that members are similar and why it is that they "understand" more than the outsider (the "square"), the answer often given is that only the alcoholic or drug addict has had the experience, empathy, and so on, to be really helpful and able to deal with others of the same type as himself without being fooled ("conned"). This may well be the case, but there is more to the matter. The doctrine that only an addict can help another illustrates the desperate need to belong to a group that does not despise one, and where the therapist need never be regarded as a person better than oneself.

Synanon's founder, Dederich (1958), believes that strengthening "the emotional muscles" by inducing activity in the members is one of the important steps in rehabilitation. Members of Synanon must therefore perform tasks for the group—helping in the preparation of meals, housecleaning, and so forth—regardless of their rebellion at being "told what to do." This activity stimulates emotions of giving or creating which have lain dormant, says Dederich, thereby dissipating resistance to cooperation. Permissiveness is in the area of *verbal* resistance or rebellion to authority which is encouraged rather than discouraged. *The insistence is on performance.* For example, if one of the members is asked to help in the kitchen, he is free to gripe as loudly as he wishes; but he is required to comply in the area of action. "It has been observed that the verbal rebellion towards authority seems to relieve inner tension, and that compliance in the action area seems to exercise the 'muscle of giving.' " In effect, such organizations create a new way of life, one in which the contribution of each person is essential and in which the place and role and value of each member are clear.

We recommend that a hard, cold look be taken at professional facilities and that remedial steps be considered. Further, we recom-

* A number of alcoholics take part in the Synanon programs although the general public conception is that their treatment facilities are for drug addicts only.

mend that organizations created by alcoholics or addicts themselves, such as Synanon and A.A. fellowships, be observed in person by professionals, so that "experts" gain a better understanding of the factors in their success and of what alcoholics think should and can be done. Finally, we recommend that one employ as a general guideline the principles that underlie A.A. fellowships and Synanon; namely, that patients are indeed capable and inventive, that they should by all means be consulted about how they can best utilize each other and their own therapeutic potential in a given treatment situation. (Madsen's [in press] and Yablonsky's [1964] studies of A.A. and Synanon, [see also Cherkas, 1964] respectively, are illustrative works.)

We also recommend that professionals treating persons with alcohol-related problems establish liaison with patient-run organizations. In the case of A.A. relatively good working relationships exist with jail and prison programs in many communities, as well as with state alcohol rehabilitation programs and mental-health facilities. There is every reason to experiment with the use of Synanon members as resource persons and counselors and as expert volunteer participants in all stages of the treatment process at a treatment facility.

We would point out in particular one principle employed at Synanon that is relevant to other treatment situations as well—with the necessary modifications, of course. The principle is to acknowledge negative feelings aroused in patients. A physician has every reason to help patients vent their anger or disappointment during the course of medical treatment of their alcoholism as long as it is clearly understood that they have to comply with the treatment regimen nevertheless. There is also every reason to give the patient alternatives in treatment processes.

PRE-TERMINATION STAGE

Patients frequently have only a vague notion how long the treatment process—whatever its nature—will last. It is therefore important to explore with them their expectations and uncertainties and, when possible, to come to a consensus about the anticipated duration. In some treatment methods the pre-termination phase actually begins in the initiatory stage, during the orientation with the therapist. In a sense, the "working-through" stage is also a preparation for the time when the patient is ready to leave since it readies him for a more independent life. But the pre-termination stage has its own special task, which is to let the patient gradually disengage himself from his relationship to the therapist and to the change-agency. The emphasis is on *gradual,* for the alcoholics are "all-or-none" people who give up treatment suddenly on an impulse—witness the high dropout rates in treatment. As a transition from reliance on therapists to reliance on persons outside the change-agency and eventually to self-reliance, the therapist may refocus the treatment from actual problem solving to a review of what has been accomplished and what remains to be achieved. If *expert lay personnel* are available (or those persons who have referred the patient to the treatment agency and have maintained contact with him throughout the treatment), they may be deliberately brought into the treatment situation to aid in this transition. *Patient groups* may be utilized for the express purpose of (a) discussing the problems of leaving; (b) becoming a core around which new attachments can be formed to make up for what the patient loses by graduating from treatment; and (c) serving as a potential nucleus for self-maintaining groups which augment the patient's social resources, permit follow-up contacts, and serve as a preventive measure.*

Another means of refocusing treatment of the alcoholic during the pre-termination stage is to encourage him to test out his new skills and *independence.* Trial visits or visits into town if he is hospitalized or lives at a facility; shifts to day-only or night-only treatment centers; experimentation with more widely spaced interviews; reduction of the medication; and similar measures are recommended. At this stage, the therapist must be prepared for considerable increase in symptoms, even though the patient previously has made very good progress. Backsliding is especially frequent during this difficult transition period, when many problems emerge as a result of fears of being abandoned and of having to be "grown up" and stand on one's own feet. A rigid insistence by the therapist on orderly and predictable progress will necessarily lead to disappointment. Like the adolescent, the *pre-termination alcoholic and even the alcoholic who has completed his course of treatment should be encouraged to try his wings with the secure*

---

* Physicians have found patient groups a useful and even a time-saving tool in handling patients with chronic illnesses; for instructional purposes, for mutual emotional support and reinforcement, especially when the treatment regimen poses difficulties (diet, sexual abstinence, exercises, and the like; see R. Blum, 1960). In various progressive prison systems patient group discussion is utilized to get inmates ready to face once again the world of employers, friends, and family.

knowledge that the doors remain open for his return when he needs to do so.

Certain schools of psychotherapy, especially the Rankian, consider transition periods to pose the utmost difficulty for the patient. Therapists so oriented bend every effort from the inception of treatment to uncover and deal with all problems which termination presents for the patient. Rank believed that the trauma of birth is the prototype of all later separation anxieties; it stands to reason that whether or not there is actual as well as symbolic truth in his theoretical contention, managing the separation anxiety constructively must be made a central task of treatment. Those concerned with patients who have a low anxiety threshold—the alcoholic patient *par excellence*—should be prepared to handle this pre-termination period with as much thought, planning, and ingenuity as it deserves. Most important, this is not only true for psychotherapeutic treatment of the alcoholic but for the physical treatment of patients with alcohol-related problems. The physician must realize that the patient does indeed depend upon him personally, that he does have a relationship with him from the minute he calls for an appointment—even if the treatment consists, from the physician's point of view, simply of dispensing medication. The patient sees the situation otherwise. To him the significance of the treatment is not just in the medicine he had been ordered to take, but in the "being given" the order and the drug. Therefore, what is being said about managing the pre-termination stage applies even in those cases where the change-agent regards his own activity as merely routine and impersonal. *Sufficient time should be allotted for the pre-termination stage,* so that all the anxieties and problems that come to the fore during this period can be dealt with therapeutically. *It also follows that similar time and care must be used in response to treatment interruptions cause by the therapist—including the change of treatment personnel.*

Ideally, the patient should be able to count on one and the same change-agent during his entire treatment course. In practice this is unfortunately rarely the case. But when changes in personnel are made, when the therapist is *unavoidably* absent, provisions should be made to prepare the patient for this beforehand and to give him an opportunity to form a relationship with the new person *before* the trusted one has left.

At present the most forward-looking concept in treatment of chronic illness—including alcoholism—is the one of "progressive care" according to which the patient is moved from one type of treatment program to another depending upon how fast he is recovering (or deteriorating). While this concept has great merit—and we shall discuss how it functions in a later chapter—one of its drawbacks can be, but need not be, that the patient is not given sufficient chance to establish a significant relationship before he has to abandon it for a new one. However, provisions can be made to obviate this disadvantage if attention is paid to the pre-termination stage each time the patient must make a shift to a new program, or if he is allowed to maintain his relationship to one primary change-agent throughout his progress through the various treatment programs.

We do not hold any brief for the view that the patient makes his relationship mainly with the change-agency and not with a particular person there. This theory has been advanced for the purpose of excusing the shifting around of patients that occurs in large treatment facilities that subscribe to the "progressive care" point of view and where the patient is funneled as quickly as possible from one quasi-independent program to the next. In highly diversified modern "progressive care" facilities the primary remedy is an organizational one: an organized unity must be built into the overall program; a unity that is created from assuming responsibility for treating the whole human being, instead of a single symptom by a specific method. For this purpose the various departments treating special aspects of the problem must keep their channels of communication open with each other as well as with the alcoholic, regardless of which department has the main responsibility for him at a given moment during his treatment career.

TERMINATION AND FOLLOW-UP STAGES

If the pre-termination period has been properly managed, it fades imperceptibly into the last stage, that of actual termination. During that last phase of treatment, all the necessary arrangements must be completed for the patient's resuming independent functioning: job placement, foster-home placement,* reunion with the family, and so forth. But that is not all. At the present stage of knowledge, the alcoholic has to be regarded as a chronic patient. For this and other

---

* For adults in transition from institutions to the community, especially for those for whom return to the family will accelerate difficulties.

reasons, post-treatment follow-up is essential in maintaining his recovery. Reunions of alcoholics who have stopped official treatment
have been found a practical means of keeping up the contact with
ex-patients. If a given patient is maintained on medication, it is useful
to have him come in at regular intervals for the purpose of checking
on the effect of the drug. Refilling of prescriptions is one means of
ensuring regular contact; the most useful part of this type of control
is not the medication itself but the opportunity it affords the doctor
to maintain a personal tie with the patient while he is adjusting to the
world outside.

Another means of keeping contact with ex-patients without
interfering in their growth toward independence is to make them
collaborators in the treatment program. Ex-patients, for example, may
be asked to take over some of the treatment functions; they may become co-leaders of treatment groups; they may become case finders
and sponsors of new or potential patients; or they may organize programs for which they feel a need exists but which are not yet available
at the treatment facility or in the community. It is, of course, essential
that sufficient prestige and social approval be attached to the role and
function of the ex-alcoholic in these positions. *We recommend that,
following the example of A.A. and Synanon, a hierarchial reward
system be provided by the organizational structure.* The aim is not
only to keep the ex-alcoholic an "ex," but to utilize him to ensure that
other alcoholics may emulate his successful treatment career.

PART THREE

KINDS OF TREATMENT

Chapter VII

~~~~~~

Psychoanalytic Treatment

We turn now to the currently employed treatment methods. Of these, many have been evolved from empirical observations in clinical practice, others are based on psychological principles, and most of them employ the knowledge gained from the work of both clinician and theoretician. To guide the reader through the maze of sometimes closely allied and sometimes diametrically opposed approaches to the alcoholic patient, we present two psychological theories that set the major divergent paths of treatment. One is the psychoanalytic theory of personality and psychotherapeutic change; the other is the body of learning and conditioning theories. The great variety of philosophies and practices in the psychological management of the alcoholic can be traced to one or the other of these theories, or to their modifications, adaptations, and intermixtures. We begin with a necessarily condensed and oversimplified exposition of psychoanalytic theory.

PRINCIPLES

The cornerstone of "classic" psychoanalytic treatment is the assumption that unconscious conflicts that cannot find an expression in socially approved activities cause mental illness (the individual

suffers) or delinquent behavior (the environment suffers.*) The
patient is unaware of unconscious conflicts that determine his conduct, influence his moods, and frequently prevent him from achieving
his conscious aims. When he is under the sway of an inner need that
is unconscious because it cannot be accepted, he must act in accordance with it even if it will not give him the greatest satisfaction *in the
long run.* Ignoring the true nature of an inner need, he will have to
invent a rationalization of his actions and his feelings—thus becoming
even more of a stranger to himself.

　　One aim of psychoanalytic treatment is "to make the unconscious conscious"—that is, to enable the patient to take stock of his
motivations, to liberate himself from blind obedience to forces within,
and to return to himself the capacity of deliberate choice. Self-knowl-

---

　　* For first-hand information on various aspects of psychoanalytic
thought and its changes from its inception until 1939, the reader is referred
to A. Freud (1953–1964). In Fenichel (1945), the reader will find an
authoritative and comprehensive statement of classical theory and principles.
A less technical presentation is that of Kubie (1936). A brief and excellent
overview of the history of psychoanalytic discoveries, the evolution of psychoanalytic concepts and hypotheses, and their subsequent refinements—
including recent and current studies to verify them—is to be found in Ross
and Abrams, "Fundamentals of Psychoanalytic Theory" in Wolman, ed.,
Handbook of Clinical Psychology (1965), pp. 303–340. The same volume
(pp. 1168–1199) also contains a useful summary of "The Psychoanalytic
Technique" by Bernstein. Here the reader will find a concise discussion of
the characteristics and the rationale of psychoanalytic treatment procedures
and "rules," as well as their modification and development by Freud's followers, and their adaptation to the treatment of children and psychotics. Indications and contraindications in the use of psychoanalysis and the proper
screening of patients are presented by Greenson, "The Classic Psychoanalytic
Approach" in Arieti, ed., *The American Handbook of Psychiatry* (1959),
Vol. II, pp. 1399–1416. The reader who wishes to become rapidly con-
versant with technical aspects of psychoanalytic treatment is referred to
Greenson's chapter.

　　Remaining within the main body of psychoanalytic teachings, but adding departures in technique are the writings of Alexander (1956), *Psychoanalysis and Psychotherapy: Developments in Theory, Technique, and Training* being the most recent. Others who have discussed variations of classic
procedure are Fromm-Reichmann, "Recent Advances in Psychoanalytic
Therapy" in Mullahy, ed., *A Study of Interpersonal Relations* (1949); and
Thompson (1950).

　　A review by E. Blum (1966) provides an extensive bibliography of
psychoanalytically oriented literature on alcoholism, its genesis, treatment,
and research.

edge is the prerequisite of choice, and choice implies inner freedom: freedom from having to repeat habitual and unsuccessful or painful behavior patterns; freedom to direct his life insofar as this is ever possible, and freedom to exert mastery over his own actions. Choice implies foresight and strength enough to wait it out until alternatives have been weighed, consequences assessed, and plans made according to his ability to endure the risks and results, including the effect on others. Psychoanalytic treatment attempts to bring about the growth necessary for facing reality within and without and for clearing away the obsolete, the forgotten, and the repressed by the scrutiny of old problems and the discovery of new solutions.

The most general and abstract description of unconscious conflict shows two diametrically opposite forces in a dynamic equilibrium. One of these strives permanently for discharge (expression), the other for repression. The patient is aware of neither, only of their resultant, the overt symptom from which he suffers. Oversimplifying for brevity's sake, one may visualize the needs that seek fulfillment as those that are expressed in interpersonal relations and the needs that oppose fulfillment as those that are expressed as prohibitions and feelings of guilt and shame, which deny pleasure for the sake of prudence, decorum, and morality. In childhood such conflicts occur typically at certain developmental periods when mastery over an impulse has to be achieved —that is, at those times when impulse and impulse control are bound to clash, as in learning to wait for food without temper tantrums, learning to give up the bottle or the breast and accept a cup, learning sphincter control, and learning to share the love of parents with others. Maturity is built of self-control, of denial and inevitable conflict. Neurosis or character disorder results when the balance of power between expression and repression has inclined in the direction of excessive and unnecessary repression in the first case, or in the direction of unmodulated and unrestrained expression in the second. Psychoanalytic procedure is designed to reactivate pathogenic childhood conflicts—to bring them out in the open once again, to relive them, and to bring the opposing forces into a better balance.

The objective of bringing unconscious conflict into the open can be realized because the patient acts according to the dictates of his unconscious no matter where he is—in treatment, or among friends and family. During treatment, his relationship to the psychoanalyst is indicative of the current state of equilibrium between the warring factions in his unconscious. His positive and negative feelings towards the psychoanalyst are the tell-tale signs of impulses that strive for fulfillment and also of impulses that oppose such discharge. These positive or negative feelings constitute the "transference reactions"; so called because they do not correspond to current reality, but to a childhood reality—or fantasy—transferred from past to present. Inasmuch as forces are at work to keep unconscious strivings repressed, the goals of therapy are circumvented. Hence the term "resistance" (to treatment, to change) is applied to that side of the unconscious conflict that maintains the pathological *status quo.*

It is to be noted that this formulation is merely a schematic diagram of the pathogenic conflict as it is manifested in the treatment situation. It is similar to what occurs also on the outside, but there the psychoanalyst speaks of symptoms instead of transference reactions. Like a transference reaction, the symptom consists of behavior that embodies simultaneously both the impulse and the defense against it and is the result of a compromise between the two.

Impulse and defense against it, force and counterforce, must be disentangled; their origins must be discovered. This process, the gaining of insight, is made possible by the very phenomenon that causes distress to the patient: the dynamic quality of the unconscious strivings, which are continuously seeking discharge in feelings (the transference repetitions) towards the psychoanalyst. To facilitate their development in a pure culture, so to speak, the psychoanalyst offers himself as an objective, neutral, nonpunitive recipient for the patient's unconscious strivings. It is in analyzing transference repetitions, in learning about their childhood origin, that the patient begins to understand that he reacts to others (psychoanalyst as well as family and associates) in very much the same way as he did earlier towards his parents and siblings. He learns that long ago his behavior was useful, even necessary, to get along or to get attention and satisfaction; but that today the same behavior is ineffective, or self-defeating and painful.

One way of helping the patient to recognize that he is reacting in terms of the past is to direct his attention to the inappropriateness of the transference responses to present-day circumstances that only *seem* to have precipitated them. Another way of assisting the patient is to eliminate as much as is humanly possible all intrusions that the psychoanalyst's personality, views, values, and feelings might contribute to the patient's ultimate responses. Neutrality of the psychoanalyst serves to protect the patient's responses from extraneous contamination and is an essential feature of classical psychoanalytic procedure. It includes the attempt to remain as unknown to the patient as possible, to avoid revealing personal reactions to what the patient says, and to give no clues about his expectations of the patient other than those made explicit in the treatment contract. The purpose of a psychoanalyst's neutrality is to provide the patient with a blank screen on which he can project the fantasies and memories that he builds into an image believed to portray the therapist. Of course this image, in reality, corresponds to the image of his parents or of other significant persons. Since the therapist has deliberately kept his own personality out of the picture, the patient has had in fact nothing to go on but his own imagination; and it is the product of his imagination that he is invited to study. For instance, when the patient shows up late for an appointment and mentions apologetically, "I know you are mad at me, Doctor, for being late," he is making an inference based on past experience with authority figures. The therapist is probably not angry at all; on the contrary, he may have used the extra time quite happily to look after some matters of his own. Rather than accepting the apology of the patient, he will delve into the patient's reason for assuming that lateness made the therapist angry. He and the patient will learn what it means to the patient nowadays to get an important person angry, and also what it has meant to him as a child.

The feelings that the patient develops towards the therapist and, more important, the feelings that he fails to develop because he cannot allow himself to experience them, provide a clue for understanding his habitual reactions to intimacy, to disappointment, to giving and receiving, to waiting, to being dependent, and to difficulty. But that is not all, for an analysis of transference reactions is complicated by resistance.

Resistance prevents the full development of transference repetitions even when the psychoanalyst has succeeded in his efforts to inject nothing of his own self that would account for the patient's feeling toward him. In spite of the psychoanalyst's neutrality, the patient will sometimes not be able to fall as desperately in love with him as once he did, for example, with his mother; nor will he be able to show as bitter a hate towards him as he felt towards his father at a time when he competed unsuccessfully for his mother's affection. Instead the patient may experience an opposite emotion, behind which hides the transferred ones, too dangerous and frightening to unleash. Or he may focus on nothing but these emotions refusing to analyze their illusory character. Or he may repress them altogether, complain of the boredom of the treatment, and break it off to flee possible self-revelation. All of these alternative reactions are termed resistances when they occur in treatment, since they not only interfere with the full flowering of the transference reactions and their resolution but also cause the forgetting of significant events, the lapses of memory, and the self-critical attitudes that prevent the patient from revealing all he does know about himself to his therapist.

Properly understood as the manifestations of repressive forces, the resistances can become an effective tool in treatment. In dealing at the same time with the resistances and the strivings that are defeated thereby, the psychoanalyst brings about in the treatment situation a reenactment of the original pathogenic conflict when wish and prohibition met in irreconcilable opposition. As the patient experiences this once again, he has an opportunity to become acquainted not only with his needs but also with the ways in which he has habitually frustrated these needs. As a result, he can modify either or both sufficiently to circumvent the previous stalemate. To this end he is invited to examine his rationalizations—to take note of his self-critical attitudes and of the various ways in which he shows his unwillingness or inability to cooperate with the treatment requirements (violations of the rules, silences, tardiness, broken appointments, falling asleep during sessions, misunderstanding or not hearing what the psychoanalyst says, failing to pay his fees and so on).

Resistance can be recognized as well in more subtle behavior of the patient: talking incessantly so that what is really meaningful remains unsaid; advance preparation of what will be mentioned instead of spontaneous discovery of important causal relationships; discussion of problems with persons other than the psychoanalyst to remove the emotional charge before it can be utilized in treatment; dwelling on the same subject to avoid more difficult ones; rigid overcompliance, which looks like active participation but is really a shifting of the responsibility onto the psychoanalyst; and many other defensive maneuvers designed to prevent insight and a change in the alignment of the conflicting forces, which would allow progress.

Analysis of the resistances results in the patient's becoming aware of his fetters and blindfolds; he is helped to do this by constant attention to them whenever they become apparent. It is not exaggerated to say that focusing on resistances, working with them, and analyzing their role and their roots is the first task for the analyst—one that takes precedence over analyzing the unconscious strivings they are designed to keep at bay.

The method of *free association* is designed to assist unconscious strivings (or at least their derivatives) in becoming conscious. The patient learns to relax his guard, to suspend judgment, and to allow anything to come to mind—be it seemingly irrelevant, insignificant, ridiculous, shameful, or shocking. To foster relaxation and spontaneity, the patient is invited to lie on a couch; and the psychoanalyst sits out of sight in order to avoid influencing the patient through accidental gesture or expression. The patient's restricted motility creates a condition analogous to that which results in dream production, and, presumably, associations will be allowed to flow more easily.

In spite of these procedures and instructions, it is quite difficult for most patients to learn to relax and to permit themselves free reign over the relatively harmless activity of speech and imagination. Resistances in the form of blocking, forgetting, falsifying, and suppressing are not easily overcome. Nevertheless, free association has proved an invaluable tool in recapturing repressed and forgotten childhood memories and in establishing links between apparently unconnected experiences, which become meaningful when they are brought into relationship once again. Viewed by the more mature eyes of the adult, many of the traumatic events of childhood fall into proper perspective: fears and worries that a child was not able to deal with but that the adult can take in stride; dissatisfactions and frustrated longings that the dependent and immature child was in no position to gratify but that the more capable and resourceful grown-up can give up as irrelevant to his present state, satisfy directly, or find substitute satisfactions for; hatred and envy that no longer have any object or reason; misconceptions and misunderstandings that could have long since been clarified had they come to light instead of lingering as unexamined nightmares, phobias, and compulsions.

Dream analysis is another means by which access is gained to previously hidden motives in the patient, since wishes and fears are often more clearly expressed in dreams—albeit in their symbolic form—than during waking hours when rational thought processes and practical considerations impose controls and distortions. As in the other analytical procedures, the patient is expected to introduce the material for analysis himself (this time in the form of dreams) and to engage actively in the attempt to interpret it. And just as in the analysis of transference repetitions and free associations, resistances make their presence felt in dream analysis and must be dealt with.

One of the striking features of the "classical" psychoanalytic method, which differentiates it from other psychoanalytic methods, is *restraint*. Relatively strict rules govern the conduct and the relationship of patient and therapist in order to ensure optimal opportunities for the emergence and analysis of unconscious materials. The psychoanalyst protects the "purity" and usefulness of the patient's transference repetitions by avoiding any judgmental or emotional contributions of his own. He also restricts professional contact with the patient to the psychoanalytic hour, refers the patient for medical examination to another practitioner, and abstains from social contacts. The psychoanalyst is enjoined to analyze his own counter-transference responses (inappropriate feelings elicited not by the patient but by the psychoanalyst's own unconscious) in order to resolve them or, at least, to keep them under control.

Another restraint is the therapeutic silence, designed to allow maximal spontaneity to the flow of free associations. The psychoanalyst must refrain from answering questions, giving directions, and offering reassurances or solutions until such time as he and the patient have thoroughly explored the hidden reasons for the patient's questions or requests. Included in the injunction of noninterference with the patient's responses are the technical problems of how and when to give interpretations of feelings and of behavior. Only when the patient himself is on the verge of grasping connections may the psychoanalyst offer—not impose—an explanation or provide a missing link. When the patient is at a total loss—overcome by resistance or completely blocked by such defense mechanisms as the phobias—interpretations are given to allow him to proceed with treatment. The matters of timing, dosage, and depth of interpretations are meticulously observed by the analyst; when in doubt, the maxim to abstain from interpretations applies.

However, the discipline that the analyst imposes upon himself is felt by the patient as frustration, for the patient would prefer to have immediate help and answers rather than to undergo the rigors of examining his actions and feelings. He would like it if the psychoanalyst would return his feelings of affection or respond to his manipulations instead of insisting on the analysis of this behavior. There are further frustrations: while the psychoanalyst must abstain from injecting himself into the situation, the patient must abstain from conventional concealments and agree to hide none of his thoughts and feelings (insofar as he can). He must go regularly for many months, even years, to the psychoanalyst; and during the course of treatment, he must avoid major commitments, changes, and decisions at least until they are fully analyzed. He must not discuss his treatment with others. In some cases he must try to abstain from certain pleasures and activities (drinking, for example), that in the past have afforded a tolerable solution for conflicts and anxieties. Many psychoanalysts who have treated alcoholics consider it important that drinking activities be either given up completely or controlled during psychoanalysis in order to bring out for analysis the difficulties that the drinking was designed to eliminate from the conscious mind.

The demands made on psychoanalyst and patient by classical psychoanalytic procedure are great; consequently, only relatively few can use it, either to treat or to be treated. It is no wonder that modifications have been proposed and developments have taken place that, although based on psychoanalytic principles, do not adhere strictly to all of the rules that have been outlined above. These changes enable children, delinquents, addicts, and psychotics, as well as persons with physical handicaps and other chronic difficulties, to benefit from treatment. Variations in technique to suit the special needs of many different types of persons are constantly being introduced into the body of psychoanalytically oriented therapies.

APPLICATION TO ALCOHOLISM

Neurotic patients are *relatively* easy to treat by the "classic" psychoanalytic method because their symptoms cause them suffering and they seek relief. "Symptomatic" alcoholics and "reactive" alcoholics, as Knight (1938, 1937a) defines them, belong in this category of neurotic patients. The "symptomatic" alcoholic drinks only incidentally—the drinking is not his major difficulty; the "reactive" alcoholic's drinking is triggered off by a traumatic event. In both of these classes of patients, alcohol-related problems are symptoms of underlying neurotic conflicts, reactions to an experience that could not be integrated and was repressed, or responses to seemingly intolerable or insoluble life situations.

But there is another group of patients whose illness is not necessarily caused by unconscious conflict alone; it stems instead from a maldevelopment of their personality and from an arrested emotional growth at an early maturational level. Among such cases are those said to be psychotic and also the group said to suffer from a character disorder. (Occasionally, one still hears the latter designated as psychopaths, although the use of this term has come into disrepute.)

Character disorders present particular difficulties because, usually, the environment is made to suffer more from their problems than are the patients themselves. In contrast, it is generally the neurotics themselves who suffer the most from their own problems. The asocial acts of people with character disorders are directed first to the outside rather than towards themselves. It is only later, through the consequences of their acting out, that these patients eventually succeed in inviting retribution and pain.*

According to Knight's (1938, 1937a) scheme, a third category of alcoholics—"essential alcoholics"—belongs with the character-disorder grouping. Acting out is a particularly common behavior pattern for essential alcoholics, and lack of motivation for change is a particularly common attitude. Aside from the difficulty of inducing a wish for change in this type of alcoholic and in reducing the incidence of their "acting out" episodes, of which delinquent behavior under the influence of alcohol is an example, another obstacle to treatment is the damage done to personality by a very early arrest in emotional development. At present, very little is known about the methods for stimulating necessary growth processes in an adult.

While Knight's classification into essential (primary) alcoholics and symptomatic or reactive (secondary, neurotic) alcoholics has proved useful and is frequently employed by other investigators, we must mention that it contains ill-defined areas and boundaries at which the groups overlap—as is the case with most theoretical schemes. For instance, many clinicians would agree that the majority of alcoholics do suffer from neurotic conflicts; yet they would also stipulate that at the same time these patients also "act out" both conflicts and impulses, as is shown by their drinking behavior.

In spite of this shortcoming, Knight's distinction between neu-

---

* "Acting out" is the technical term that describes the manner in which persons with character disorders translate impulse into immediate action or use the world they live in as a stage upon which conflict between impulse and its control is dramatically acted out by agonist—the patient—and protagonist—the law. As long as the protagonist is lax, the agonist can enjoy real benefits from his deeds and therefore reinforce his reluctance to wish for change.

rotic disorders and character disorders is an important one. The psychoanalyst keeps it in mind in setting treatment goals for, and in adjusting his methods to, a given patient. With the neurotic patient (reactive or symptomatic drinker), the psychoanalyst's aim is to remove the blocks to full emotional capacity by giving the patient insight. In the case of the character disorders (essential alcoholics), the goal is to initiate maturational processes by providing external structure and direction so that (hopefully) the patient will internalize both the structure and direction and will achieve thereby the inner strength necessary for his resocialization and self-control. The latter two aims are also appropriate for psychotic patients, with an additional effort directed at improving their reality contact and their ability to distinguish between what is going on in the outside world and what is going on within themselves. To implement such a program modifications in the classical procedures are necessary, including abandonment of the psychoanalytic detachment and neutrality. The psychoanalyst must play a much more active part in the treatment of essential alcoholics; in many cases, he must resort to institutionalization of the more disturbed and disturbing individuals.

We would emphasize that, almost from its beginning, the psychoanalytic treatment of persons with drinking problems has had to be varied depending on whether the patient was neurotic or had a character-disorder, and on which facet of his problem was most salient at a given moment in treatment. With most cases, one must expect a chaotic course in which there is an alternation and intermingling of internalized and of "acted out" conflicts. One must be prepared for intense and difficult transference reactions, since alcoholics tend to be particularly immature emotionally. An alcoholic has seldom developed the capacity to withstand frustration, nor can he wait for gratification that might be forthcoming in the future. It is evident that classical psychoanalytic treatment—based as it must be on learning to wait and learning to delay impulse-gratification until it is safe and appropriate —is an extreme if not impossible undertaking for most alcoholic patients. The history of psychoanalysis reveals the many changes which have occurred to provide alternative methods of dealing with alcoholics and persons suffering from other than neurotic problems. Let us review the course of events.

In the early days of psychoanalytic treatment it was believed that alcoholics could be cured within a period of months (Coriat, 1917,1912). As experience accumulated and theory was expanded, early optimism gave way to experimentation. With the exception of "symptomatic" alcoholism and "reactive" alcoholism (drinking to solve primarily neurotic conflicts [Knight, 1938, 1937a, 1937b]), alcoholism was regarded as akin to the character disorders and acting-out disorders (delinquency) and to disorders of the earliest ego-stages— that is, the narcissistic disorders and ambulatory schizophrenia. Consequently, techniques that had been developed for use with children (A. Freud), with delinquents (Aichhorn, 1936), and with the severely disturbed were adapted for alcoholics.

One of the pioneering experiments was that of Simmel (1929), who attempted to treat alcoholics as in-patients at the Tegel Clinic near Berlin. In addition to regular psychoanalytic interviews, he provided an institutional setting intended to substitute for the maternal care and discipline presumed to have been lacking during the infancy of his patients. Medical personnel and auxiliary staff were taught to give symbolic and direct gratifications with suitable amounts of frustration. This method fostered emotional growth, redirection of asocial impulses into socially accepted channels, and self-control. The psychoanalytic sanatorium at Tegel was to replace the patients' own "bad" mother with a new and better one who could succeed where the first one had failed in furthering personality development. A similar philosophy has guided the efforts at the Menninger Foundation (Knight, 1938; Menninger, 1938). The treatment procedures in both the Tegel sanatorium and Menninger's are described below in some detail since these were the first attempts to use psychoanalytic methods with alcoholics as in-patients.

The very fact that patients are treated in a hospital setting represents a departure from the strict psychoanalytic method, which traditionally consists of daily 50-minute interviews during which the therapist remains as anonymous as possible. In the hospital setting, the basic assumption cannot be made that the real personality of the therapist remains unknown to the patient since there are daily encounters, informal and unplanned, which help the patient form a pretty good idea of what the therapist is really like. To counteract this eventuality, the Menninger Clinic made special efforts to minimize the number of *unplanned* patient-therapist encounters by assigning to the patient a special hospital physician separate from the psychotherapist. Still, *planned* informal and recreational contacts do take place; for instance, Knight (1937a) tells of playing tennis with some of his patients. Certainly he did not remain unknown and enigmatic to his partner as "classical" procedure would have required.

At the Tegel sanatorium it was felt that there is no special value in allowing patients to struggle alone for a long time in their efforts to abstain from alcohol. Simmel states that in this very struggle lurks an element of pleasure—the pleasure of repeating the battle which took place when the patient was trying to give up his infantile masturbation. The patient may defer drinking in order to enjoy the *craving* or the masochistic torment of abstinence. Dread of loss is characteristic for the alcoholic patient. The process of "weaning" himself from drugs represents a mixture of giving up masturbation, of learning habits of cleanliness (it is interesting in this context to note that addicts refer to some ingested substances as "pot" and "shit," and to abstinence or kicking the habit as "staying clean"),* and of weaning from the breast. Treatment is fraught with great danger to a patient whose drinking behavior is intended as self-punishment, self-destruction, and as sadistic gratification of a murderous impulse that was originally directed against a frustrating mother. At the Tegel sanatorium the patients are protected by the therapeutic management of the transference situation. The patient's destructive aims *intended* against the mother and *neurotically directed* against himself are *redirected* against the therapist and translated into a symbolic reality. Simmel permits the patient to act out the killing, devouring, or castrating fantasies on acceptable substitutes. Treble amounts of food, gardening tasks that involve the cutting off of branches, smashing coffee services, and similar acts are permitted. Later, self-understanding must replace "acting out"; the destructive relationship must be resolved by means of analysis. Thus, the patient learns that his behavior represents a dramatic but nevertheless only symbolic representation of the unconscious conflict between his irrational and rational self; he learns that he has projected this conflict onto the therapist. At that point, the patient is ordered to bed for a while with special nursing care. The exultation, anxiety, or depression that results from his abstinence is analyzed. At the same time, the patient's unconscious need receives the utmost fulfillment possible: he is allowed to be a little child again—in bed—and to have

* The reader is referred to the discussion of the scatological implications of addictive substances in R. Blum (1964).

a kind mother tending and feeding him. This situation in turn is utilized during the psychoanalytic sessions by exploring the meaning it holds for the patient.

From the psychoanalytic point of view, the sanatorium plays an important role as a symbol of the mother's womb. This conceptualization has served as a model for a number of psychoanalytically oriented treatment methods based upon the principle of allowing the patient to regress to an early stage of emotional development, providing him at that point with the gratification he originally missed at this stage, and then encouraging him to progress to a more mature level of development. For instance, Azima *et al.* (1960), using prolonged drug-induced sleep as a treatment method, have produced even more drastic regression and need gratification. Other investigators have employed the various methods that have a disorganizing effect upon cognitive function—such as the hallucinogens, hypnosis, and sleep treatment—to produce a return to earlier stages of mental functioning in order to resolve the problems that occurred at those stages. It is assumed that after resolution has taken place, the patient may once more retrace his developmental steps forward without being encumbered any longer by past traumata and vulnerabilities, and without the burden of longing for missed indulgences. In psychoanalytically oriented regression treatment, nursing care is of utmost importance, symbolizing as it does the right kind of maternal nurturance and *rebirth* (from a "good mother" instead of a "bad" and depriving one).

The correspondences among "rebirth," initiation rites (especially in totemistic societies), and drinking customs (including the symbolic significance of intoxication) has been described by Weijl (1944, 1928, 1927), who sees a link between these phenomena and those that occur in the manic-depressive psychoses. Weijl uses the term "social-ritualistic" neurosis to characterize alcoholism, for he believes that drinking facilitates socializing and group-formation on the one hand; while, on the other, he views the compulsive drinking of the alcoholic as closely similar to those obsessional acts which, he claims, are part of ceremonial and ritual customs. He suggests that the "death-instinct" (self-destructive strivings) and repetition compulsion play important roles in alcoholism since one result of drinking is somnolence (a representation of death), while repeated awakening serves to circumvent the alcoholic's fear of death—the root of his compulsion to drink to stupefaction. Weijl points out that many puberty rites are connected with drinking customs and that there are many indications in customs and manners supporting the hypothesis that alcohol is the symbolic representation of the totem animal that is devoured at certain feast days. In some of these interpretations he follows the psychoanalyst-anthropologist Reik (1915), who has described revival rebirth as principal motives of puberty rites. The adolescent is "killed" in a symbolic way, after which he revives as an adult and is admitted to manhood. Crawley (1931), a folklorist-anthropologist, cites many examples of the belief in rebirth and in immortality achieved by ingesting magic substances.

It is interesting to observe the extent to which speculations about the symbolism of drinking and of intoxication have had an influence on the treatment of alcoholics. Particularly interesting is the extent to which successful treatment has, in some cases, quite unwittingly followed the magical ideas that underlie puberty rites, like the utilization of rebirth fantasies and fantasies of initiation into manhood by relinquishing the former "unworthy" or "childish" alcoholic self as one becomes a member of a new group. Dederich, an Alcoholics Anonymous graduate, and not a psychoanalyst, modeled self-help communities (Synanon) for alcoholics and other drug addicts to take full advantage of the member's covert hopes for rebirth as more capable individuals. Dederich (1958) states that Synanon deliberately fosters a group climate resembling that of a family in a primitive tribal structure. He believes that Synanon members can thereby be affected at an unconscious level. The purpose, as in other regression techniques, is to allow the addict a fresh start; in this case, by simulating the conditions necessary for his rebirth as a person who can learn to abandon drug-dependency, and by initiating him into a family-type organization that requires from him increased responsibility and independence.

It cannot be determined at this time what it is in the Synanon methods—stimulation of symbolic rebirth fantasies, "tribal" group-life, or continuous re-education (some of it using psychodynamic techniques)—that is most helpful to its members. Many psychoanalysts, among them Knight (1938), agree that re-education in a controlled environment is extremely effective—especially with alcoholics who really wish to be helped and, more particularly, when the change-agency is organized on psychoanalytic principles and offers psychoanalytic treatment. Such an environment provides outlets for aggressive drives and at the same time alleviates anxiety and gives praise and affection when appropriate. Knight advocates that an especially affectionate bond (good and enduring rapport) be encouraged between alcoholic and therapist; he points out that alcoholic patients cannot endure a passive, withdrawn attitude. Consequently "unorthodox" techniques must be employed. He recommends specifically that patients be allowed to sit up instead of lying on the couch; that there be no condemnation of the patient's excessive drinking; that the analyst may call patients by pet names and even engage in sports and recreation with them; and that a patient's great need for affection must be met directly, rather than only analyzed and interpreted. It is the emotional relationship with the therapist that acts as a partial substitute for drinking. The psychoanalyst should make no initial demands upon patients, nor should he mention the underlying dynamics of the drinking, such as homosexuality, too early. Rather than strictly forbidding alcohol intake from the outset, he should suggest substitutes for alcohol. It is of special interest to note that, contrary to the classical requirement of unflagging motivation for therapy, Knight has treated involuntary patients who had been committed to the Menninger clinic.

It has often been stated that psychoanalysis is not a treatment of choice for patients with addictive personalities. Nevertheless, and in spite of the strict criteria for improvement and the high goals set by this method, the success reported by Knight (1938) of between 60 per cent and 70 per cent improvement compares favorably with any other technique employed in the treatment of alcoholics.

Menninger (1938) also recommends a controlled environment, psychoanalysis, and increasing the patient's capacity to redirect aggressions as the best program for alcohol addiction. He concedes that this is not always successful, but a few individuals have been cured by these means and have stayed cured, not only of drinking but of the infantilism that accompanies it and the character deformities that produce it. He states that "this cannot be said, so far as I know, of any other treatment of alcohol addiction at the present time." He advocates that treatment focus on the "gradual elimination of the tendency of over-reaction to frustration, and the progressive relief of those deep, inner feelings of anxiety, insecurity, and of child-like expectation and resentment which so regularly determines [alcoholism]."

These examples illustrate a few of the modifications in technique and the theory developments that psychoanalysts have introduced in the past. They are by no means exhaustive. More recently B. Lewin points out that it is impossible for the psychoanalyst to keep to the usual analytic procedure whenever an unusual situation occurs during the course of analysis.* He noted, as an example, that the analyst, when faced with the suicide attempt of a patient, will drop quickly what he considers appropriate neutrality and will concentrate instead on saving the patient's life. Anna Freud (1954) suggests that although a therapist learns in classical technique that there is little chance for the successful therapy of any disturbance that approximates an addiction as long as the addiction has free scope, psychoanalysts do not usually *interfere* with their patient's behavior by using prohibitions. Instead, patients are asked to *postpone* the pathological form of satisfaction for periods of increasing lengths while tolerating as much as possible of the ensuing anxiety, which is used to intensify the wish for and the depth of treatment. In the case of a homosexual patient, however, whose difficulty was complicated by severe alcoholism, A. Freud *did* apply the analytical rule of prohibiting the activity and found that eventually he became heterosexual and free of his alcoholism. "There was no doubt that in his case cutting down on his perverse practices had played a most beneficial part in the technique" (*ibid.*, p. 51). She summarizes the treatment of her alcoholic patient by saying that his addiction to alcohol decreased because he transferred it to a new addiction: the analyst. "He gave me the role of protecting him against his dangerous, masculine, destructive impulses, in short, of 'holding him down.' While I filled the role in his imagination, he could do without alcohol or male partner. This implied, of course, that I had to be at his disposal without fail, and that interruption of analysis could not be tolerated. He would find me at the other end of the telephone even in the middle of the night, which is, of course, the usual striking deviation from the orthodox technique whenever it is applied to an addiction . . . When the relationship to the analyst takes the place of the satisfaction or reassurance gained from the symptom, the analysis turns into a battle between the two addictions, the addiction to the analyst holding the fort temporarily until the unconscious material appears and is analyzed" (*ibid.*, p. 51).

The question of modifying classical techniques has also come up in the dispute among psychoanalysts whether alcoholic patients can drink again. Knight believes that an alcoholic never can resume normal drinking. Shea (1954) reports on a case who seemed to be an exception to the rule that no alcoholic can ever become a moderate

---

* Lewin's remarks were made during the symposium held at the New York Society on "The Widening Scope of Psychoanalysis."

social drinker. His patient was a middle-class, college-trained man who had been married four times and had been drinking to violent excess constantly for more than 20 years. Following his psychoanalysis, he maintained an unbroken abstinence for five years and since then, for five years continuing, has been a controlled drinker. Shea felt impelled to modify some of the classical procedures of psychoanalysis by offering support and guidance during the course of treatment. Aside from this remarkable cure, Shea is not confident that the same can be accomplished in other patients: "The healthy mature elements of the personality can prevail and rule under certain circumstances, but theirs is an insecure majority indeed. The opposition—the unhealthy and primitive elements—lurk in great numbers, ready to seize power given any chance. The first drink of alcohol constitutes such a chance, paralyzing as it were, the will and tenacity of the healthy elements" (*ibid.*, p. 602). He recommends abstinence for alcoholics of this sort, in order to protect the healthy elements of their personality. He hopes to bring them to a state where they are obsessed with the idea of being sober, just as obsessed with this as they formerly were with the notion of being drunk. "These limited goals," says Shea, "should not be despised." A number of psychoanalysts have pointed out that the A.A. fellowships can be understood as just such a substitute obsession, albeit a more benign one than the obsession to drink.

EMERGING TRENDS

The pioneering days are not over. Recently, psychoanalytically oriented treatment methods have been employed with alcoholic patients to suit their particular needs and circumstances as much as possible. Of great interest is Silber's treatment approach (1963, 1959). He bases his therapy on the assumptions that arrest at an early developmental stage is one of the etiological factors in alcoholism, and that alcoholics can be manipulated through their childish desire for a powerful protector, all-giving and all-understanding. Silber recommends that the patient's attachment to the therapist be strengthened by means similar to those employed in treating children, which include openly expressed signs of shared and personal interests, the giving of gifts, visiting home and school, and even physical contact. Silber would have therapists focus on relieving guilt and on strengthening the patient's ability to discriminate between fantasy and reality by stressing the difference between wish and deed. At the State University

Alcohol Clinic, Brooklyn, New York, alcoholics are treated by residents under Silber's supervision. The cases are selected by staff psychiatrists on the basis of acuteness of need. Silber warns that most of the alcoholic patients start treatment with marked anxiety, which the residents are taught to consider as a signal indicating a great deal of suppressed rage that must be squarely faced. One way of doing so is to help the patient understand that he is *entitled to the feelings* but that the *action* which would follow *is to be inhibited*. Another source of the patient's anxiety is often a feeling of helplessness, not necessarily corresponding to a real inability to cope. Silber's experience in helping the patient view in a more realistic light his unrealistic feelings of inadequacy has convinced him that anxiety can be greatly diminished. The reduction in anxiety itself helps to strengthen the positive relationships between patient and therapist, deemed a prime requisite for psychotherapy of alcoholics. Silber, like many other psychoanalysts, believes that one must give the alcoholic patient something initially, since he has great difficulty in waiting and in sustaining tension (these are signs of an early oral fixation and of tremendous acting-out potentials).* According to Silber the alcoholic looks to his therapist to satisfy essentially insatiable demands. It is inevitable, therefore, that the therapist will eventually frustrate the patient; and the patient often responds to this frustration as he did in childhood with an unconscious (repressed) rage. In place of a conscious fury, the patient experiences a feeling that somehow he himself is no good—he doesn't deserve anything and he should be punished. He is not aware that it is the unconscious rage that produces these guilt feelings. At this point provocative behavior designed to get the therapist angry—to make him punish the patient in order to assuage his guilty conscience—often occurs. That is the very point where many treatment failures take place. To avoid them, the therapist must first of all realize that alcoholics develop a strong wish to be punished and are very skillful in provoking the therapist's retribution. Second, the therapist, instead of obliging the alcoholic, should instead remain consistent and fair, pointing out to the patient that he seems to want to be punished, and why,

---

* See also Chafetz's handling of the initial contact with alcoholic patients, which is based on the same psychodynamic principles of encouraging a positive relationship and demonstrating affection and helpfulness by acceding to patient demands, within reasonable limits. For an explicit description of how these and other psychoanalytically based techniques can be successfully applied to alcoholic offenders, see Margolis, Krystal and Siegel (1964).

explaining how he seems to equate thought and wish with actual deed and crime, thus being needlessly overwhelmed with remorse for actions committed only in fantasy. The purpose of this kind of interpretation is to decrease guilt feelings and subsequent need for inviting punishment, and to cut down on the patient's tendency to translate his feelings into action instead of talking about them. Silber recommends as a third step that the therapist attempt to play the role of the consistent parent, sharply differentiating himself from the inconsistent one whom the patient has regarded as so frustrating during his childhood. In a fourth step, the therapist should demonstrate that the patient has endowed the therapist with imaginary qualities which the therapist in fact does not possess, but which are related instead to the patient's past expectations of his parents.

After the patient understands that his hopes and fears of the therapist as all-powerful and punitive are only fantasies, standard psychotherapeutic treatment can be initiated. Emphasis should be placed on current difficulties and on exposing some of the patient's defensive maneuvers. It is especially important to help the patient become aware of negative feelings toward the therapist as soon as they arise; later on in treatment, close and constant attention should be paid to the patient's current relationships other than the one he has to his therapist. As treatment nears the end, the relationship to the therapist should move into the background, even though it supplies the motive force for the therapeutic process. Silber believes his method to be very promising: approximately 60 per cent of the patients who were referred have remained in this kind of therapy and seemingly have derived benefits from it.

Among other therapists who have recently made extensive use of psychoanalytic principles in the treatment of alcoholism should be mentioned Bochner (1962), Chafetz (1963, 1959), Chafetz et al. (1962) and Margolis, Krystal and Siegel (1964), among others.* Common to most of those who use modifications of the psychoanalytic method is (1) the care with which they treat the alcoholic's tenuous self-respect; (2) the importance they attach to establishing and maintaining a continuous, positive relationship with him by reducing anxiety and guilt through teaching the difference between aggressive fantasies and hostile deeds; and (3) their effort to promote greater

---

* For a comprehensive review of psychoanalytic writings on alcoholism the reader is referred to E. Blum (1966).

emotional maturity in the patient. This maturity is generally fostered by providing the patient initially with whatever emotional crutches he may need and leading him gradually from dependence and pleasure within the treatment situation to a greater reliance on finding the same satisfactions in his environment by acquiring more appropriate and rewarding social techniques than the ones that brought him to treatment in the first place.

Modified psychoanalytic procedures have also been adopted in a number of different approaches to alcoholism: in hypnotherapy, group psychotherapy, milieu therapy and even in drug therapy (notably using LSD-25 and others based on regression methods). Any of these approaches, which we shall discuss in later chapters, may qualify as "psychoanalytic" treatment whenever *transference* and *resistance* are presumed to be the two major processes operating in the patient and are therefore utilized for treatment purposes. Paraphrasing her father's dictum, A. Freud (1954) declared therapeutic procedure to be psychoanalytic that recognizes and works with transference and resistance to resolve unconscious conflicts.

With the present much broader applications of psychoanalytic principles to the treatment of alcoholics, the question what kind of patients can be treated has become academic. The more important question is how psychodynamic principles can be made useful to a given patient. Nowadays, it is only the rare "symptomatic" or the "reactive" alcoholic who is treated by classic psychoanalytic procedures. The most effective practice is to adapt principles from psychoanalytic theory and practice to the treatment of many kinds of alcoholics in a variety of different settings and conditions. The trend of fitting treatment to the patient, instead of rejecting patients who do not fit past notions of suitability, is a most promising one.

Chapter VIII

~~~~~~

Conditioning and Learning

We should like to give the reader an orderly picture of the contrast between psychoanalytic theory and learning theory in their attempts to explain why a human being acts as he does. A very neat distinction could be drawn if the theory of association—upon which conditioned aversion to alcohol is based—were the only learning theory extant. That is not the case, for there are a number of different schools of thought regarding the circumstances under which persons behave in a certain way, learn new behavior, and unlearn the old.*

According to some learning theories, a response that occurs in *association* with a particular stimulus occurs again when the stimulus is repeated. Such a stimulus may be one that existed in the external

---

* Readers who wish to become more fully acquainted with learning theories are referred to the following classics: Tolman (1932), Guthrie (1935), Skinner (1938), Hull (1943), Miller (1951), Spence (1951). Lucidly presented summaries of various learning theories are found in Hilgard's (1956) textbook. For a thoughtful discussion of the concept of reinforcement in the light of recent theoretical developments and experimental findings in animal learning psychophysiology and neurophysiology, the reader is referred to Pribram (1963). Sophisticated expositions of the subtleties of various theories are available in Estes *et al.* (1954) and in Koch (1959), Vol. II. An excellent work is that of Cofer and Appley (1964).

environment, or it may be one that was internally produced by the responding organism itself. Learning theories of this kind are based upon the idea that two events—stimulus and response—that are contiguous in time and space will be associated.

Other learning theories are based on *reinforcement*. These theories state that responses are learned when they are followed either by reward or punishment. Dollard and Miller (1950) hold that an individual will learn only when he *wants* something, *notices* something, *does* something, and *gets* something. Reinforcement theories of learning introduce the concept of motivation (drives and strivings), as does psychoanalytic theory. In contrast, the association theories of learning make no assumption about what the individual wants to achieve or to avoid, nor do they assume that the organism is consciously aware of the stimulus that triggers the response (as in autonomic conditioning).

The difference between associative learning and reinforcement learning is essentially one of levels of discourse. Associative learning theories describe in *what* manner and *how* learning takes place. Reinforcement theories of learning go one step beyond in inferring *why* learning takes place.*

In the last ten or fifteen years learning theories have become more sophisticated in defining what a reinforcer is. Reinforcement used to be thought of as either reward or punishment, depending upon whether the behavior was repeated or whether it was extinguished** (did not occur again). Rewards were considered to be those environmental changes that were accompanied by drive-reduction (*e.g.,* a person drinks when he is thirsty to reduce his thirst). Alcoholism can very simply be explained as a method of *drive-reduction*: anxiety or any other unpleasant feeling is reduced by means of alcohol ingestion; therefore, by definition, the drinking will be repeated. This would have been the earlier, simple formulation; currently, however, learning is viewed as a more subtle and complex process. Drive-reduction or tension-reduction can no longer be considered as its basic motivational principle. Animal psychologists have noticed that rats are curious, exploratory, and intent on a variety of experiences. Objective studies

* If one wishes to translate psychoanalytic theory into learning theory, one has to use some form of the reinforcement theory, rather than a pure form of association theory.
** Extinguished means that a sequence of behavior that has been learned will be forgotten or at any rate not repeated again.

of children show that they not only act to appease hunger, thirst, and discomfort but also to pursue change and thrills; they engage in playful activity and in inventiveness for its own sake. Consequently, learning theories have had to concern themselves with the *tension-increasing* aspect of behavior. By the same token, one can no longer view alcoholism solely as a tension-reducing device if one wishes to apply learning theory to study its genesis and function.

The second assumption of reinforcement theory, as applied to alcoholism—namely, that punishment leads to avoidance of the punished response—must also be revised in the light of new knowledge. Animal experiments have shown that what has been considered as punishment, electric shock for instance, does not necessarily lead to disruption of the punished behavior; rather, it may serve as a signal or as the conditioned stimulus for the repetition of the behavior the experimenter was hoping to extinguish. Extinguishing a behavior sequence by means of aversive conditioning has been a time-honored method of teaching the alcoholic to unlearn drinking. We present therefore a brief exposition of the concepts underlying this type of conditioning. The basic assumption is that if a rewarding stimulus like alcohol is presented simultaneously with another stimulus that has been punishing drinking, like nauseating drugs or electric shock, in time the two stimuli will become associated so that the one comes to herald the effects of the other: alcohol will mean discomfort instead of comfort. The result is an aversion response to alcohol instead of the previous drinking response. Common sense confirms this: if a certain activity is sufficiently punished, it will not be repeated.

But what is punishment? Common sense and subjective experience tell us that pain, displeasure, and fear serve as punishment even if no one but the culprit feels them. But learning theorists require more. For example, one would consider imprisonment as punishment, whether the offender changes his delinquent behavior or not; but learning theorists would not be content with this. Instead of defining punishment by its subjective effect, they define it by its results. They insist that a scientific statement be objective, not subjective; that it include only observable data (and that means, in the case of punishment, some sort of measurable behavior change).

Solomon (1964) offers the following operational definition: Punishment must be (among other things) "a noxious stimulus, one which will support, by its termination or omission, the growth of new

escape or avoidance responses.* It is one which the subject will reject, if given a choice between the punishment and no stimulus at all."
One of the advantages of this definition over the common-sense notions
of punishment is that it makes it immediately clear that one and the
same stimulus (however noxious) need not always be a punishment. It
is quite conceivable that it will pass unnoticed—for example, when
the subject is unconscious; or that it will become a signal for the re-
newal of the same activity; or even that it will become rewarding in
itself. All these possibilities have been observed in the alcoholic who
returns to his drinking regardless of, or perhaps just because of, the
painful experiences associated with it. Under suitable conditions in the
laboratory it is possible to bring about the aforementioned effects of
noxious stimuli such as becoming a signal for stopping or for resuming
an activity. That such findings have important implications for the
treatment of alcoholics is evident, and we shall presently discuss them
more fully.

Formulating treatment in terms of learning theory provides
the possibility of discovering refinements that had heretofore escaped
attention. As a case in point we mention the distinction made by
Solomon (1964) between two kinds of aversive conditioning: one
teaches *what to do;* the other teaches *what not to do.* In animal experiments, for example, the animal may be put into a situation
whereby he learns to avoid punishment (electric shock) by pressing a
bar. In other experiments, he learns to avoid punishment by *not* pressing a bar. One procedure is called *active avoidance training;* the other
is called *passive avoidance training.* In most aversive conditioning
treatments of alcoholics, it is the second procedure that is used. The
alcoholic patient undergoes passive avoidance training in all those
situations where he is given a noxious stimulus (drugs, electric shock,
hypnotically induced suggestions that he will feel nauseated at the sight
of alcohol, and so on) in order to teach him what *not* to do. It should
also be noted that most of the literature on the aversive controls of
behavior have, at least in the past, emphasized passive avoidance
learning and ignored active avoidance learning in the treatment of
alcoholics.

Let us examine some of the experimentally established facts
about the nature and effects of punishment and *passive avoidance*

---

* Hence the term aversive or avoidance conditioning.

learning that are relevant to the learning and unlearning of alcohol-ism. Solomon distinguishes among the effects of punishment on the following types of behavior: (a) behavior previously established by *rewards* (or positive reinforcement); (b) *consummatory responses;* (c) complex sequential patterns of *innate responses;* (d) *discrete re-flexes;* (e) responses previously established by punishment, or *active escape* and *avoidance responses.* It is not easy to decide whether in a given person alcoholism was established by the *rewards* drinking brought (either temporary relief from anxiety, guilt, tension; or feel-ings of warmth, excitement, assertiveness, and sociabiilty), or whether, on the contrary, alcoholism became established as a result of *punish-ment* consequent to drinking: by shame and guilt, social ridicule, and other painful experiences that occurred along with the drinking. A third possibility is to consider alcoholism as a *consummatory response.* In patients where this is the case, the effects of punishment will be different altogether from those in alcoholics for whom drinking has become, by association, in itself a punishment, instead of a consum-matory response.

Punishment procedures may either suppress behavior, facilitate the extinction of existing response patterns, serve as a signal, or as a reward in itself. Let us consider the variables that determine the effects of a noxious stimulus. Many experiments have shown that the in-tensity of a stimulus is related to its effectiveness. The following dif-ferent results can be obtained depending on variations in intensity: (a) *detection and arousal,* wherein punishment becomes a signal or a cue (discriminated stimulus), a response intensifier, or even a sec-ondary reward (secondary reinforcer), (b) *temporary suppression,* wherein punishment results in suppression of the punished response, followed by complete recovery of the response, such that the subject later appears unaltered from his pre-punished state. Alcohol may act as a mild punisher inasmuch as it becomes a cue for more drinking; as a response intensifier and secondary reinforcer, especially in patients who have lost control over their drinking; or as a temporary suppres-sor, where drinking leads immediately afterwards to temporary ces-sation of drinking, as in the case of the binge-drinker, (c) *partial suppression,* wherein the subject always displays some lasting suppres-sion of the punished response, without total recovery, (d) *complete suppression* with no observable recovery of the response. Any of these outcomes can be produced merely by varying the intensity of the noxious stimulus when responses previously established by reward or positive reinforcement are being punished (Azrin and Holz, 1961).

Another variable that determines the results of punishment is its *duration*. A third and very important variable is the *proximity* in time of the punishment to the punished response (gradient of temporal delay of punishment). An essential feature in conditioning is to present the unconditioned stimulus (nausea, apnea, EST) *after* the conditioned stimulus (alcohol). As Eysenck (1960, p. 12) points out: "It is quite elementary knowledge that the conditioned stimulus must precede the unconditioned stimulus if conditioning is to take place; backward conditioning, if it occurs at all, is at best very weak. Yet some workers in the field of alcoholism have used a method in which the unconditioned stimulus regularly preceded the conditioned stimulus; under these conditions learning theory would in fact predict the complete failure of the experiment actually reported." We may add that the precise timing has frequently been overlooked as well, and although many have insisted on the need for rigorous procedures, few have heeded this counsel.

A fourth variable is the *strength* of the punished response. The more a response has been learned, or overlearned, the less likely is it to be forgotten. This is an important factor to remember in the treatment of alcoholism, regardless of the method employed. It means that prognosis, other factors being equal, will depend on the *length* of the drinking habit. A fifth variable is the *adaptation* to punishment. New, intense punishment are better than old, intense punishments (Miller, 1960). The adaptation factor is crucial for any aversion treatment of alcoholics as has been noted, for instance, by Voegtlin (1955) at Shadel Sanatorium (Seattle). He reports that patients treated by aversive conditioning who had relapsed after a period of abstinence subsequently had shorter and shorter periods of abstinence with each successive reconditioning treatment, until finally no practical benefits were obtained from retreatment. Pareja (1947), as well as many others, has also observed adaptation to aversive conditioning.

Solomon (1964, p. 241) notes that, in general, resistance to extinction is decreased whenever a previously reinforced response is punished. However, if the subject is habituated to receiving punishment together with a reward (*positive reinforcement* during reward training), the relationship can be reversed and punishment during extinction can actually increase resistance to extinction. It is very likely that in many cases of alcoholism this is precisely the situation. Drinking, even though it is initially pleasurable and rewarding, has many disagreeable punishing consequences built in, at least in our society. The alcoholic learns at a very early stage in his drinking career to associate both reward and punishment with drinking. Consequently, additional punishment for his drinking may not deter him at all; on the contrary, it can come to serve as a *signal* for renewed drinking. Evidently, punishment so employed will functionally operate as the *secondary reinforcer,* or as a cue for reward, or as an arouser!

Under what conditions can punishment become a reliable suppressor of a response? The experimental psychologists tell us that if a *rewarded alternative* is provided which is under discriminative control (one that the subject will notice and distinguish from other alternatives), passive avoidance training can become an effective means of influence. Punishment is extremely useful when the response suppression period is used to *teach a new response that is incompatible with the punished one.* Under those circumstances, punishment of even very low intensity can have very long-lasting suppression effects.*

Self-evident as this learning principle may be, it is rather difficult to apply to the treatment of alcoholics, since it is not at all clear what the available alternatives are, or should be, for a given patient. Pending the solution of this problem, let us consider those treatment techniques in which punishment appears to have only a temporary suppression effect. Most of these offer the patient *no* rewarded alternative to the drinking. Experimental psychologists and learning theorists would not be surprised if the temporarily abandoned behavior occurs again. Therapists using aversive conditioning should take note of this and be less disappointed in their "treatment failures."

Another lesson to be learned from experiments on conditioning is that the attributes of effective punishment vary across species and *across stages in maturational development* within species—again a

---

* Animal trainers have recognized and used this principle for a long time. Whiting and Mowrer (1943) first rewarded one route to food, then punished it. When the subject ceased taking the punished route, they provided a new rewarded route. The old route was not traversed again.

Wolpe (1958) and Wolpe *et al.* (1964) have proposed treatment on the basis of reciprocal inhibition for which they claim great effectiveness. The principle is to oppose to the response that is to be extinguished one that is incompatible with it. In the case of anxiety responses, one of the best ways of achieving relief is to counterpose the response of relaxation, if necessary under hypnotic trance. We shall discuss this form of conditioning later on.

common-sense observation, but one rather easily overlooked in aversive conditioning. Of particular importance is the finding that *punishing* a response that was originally established by punishment (for instance, when drinking was the result of painful experiences) may be ineffective in eliminating the avoidance responses (giving up drinking) it is supposed to extinguish. Paradoxically, the punishment may *strengthen* the response. The implications of this laboratory finding have not been heeded sufficiently in the treatment of alcoholics; namely, that aversive conditioning is likely to be of no avail in alcoholics whose drinking was initiated by a trauma. The obverse may also hold: that there will be fewer or perhaps less tenacious problems associated with drinking in those instances where it is followed by benign consequences instead of painful ones. Anthropologists and social scientists who have studied drinking patterns in different cultures offer partial confirmation for this thesis.*

The eminent learning theorist Skinner (1953) has become quite pessimistic about the effects of punishment. He notes that response suppression is only temporary and that, in humans at least, side effects such as fear and neurotic or psychotic disturbances are sometimes the consequence, and not worth the short-term advantages. His position is that reward is a more effective means of controlling behavior. Other learning theorists have held the same opinion, notably Thorndike (1931).

Reviewing the early experiments on punishment, Bugelski (1956) infers that their purpose was to bring punishment into disrepute by demonstrating that it is ineffective in changing behavior. Various sentimentalists applauded this conclusion. Solomon (1964, p. 249) also observes that psychologists have not been particularly adventuresome in their search for experimentally effective punishments; he too feels that this might be due to soft-heartedness. In contrast to

---

* See R. and E. Blum, *Temperate Achilles* (1963).

A related problem arises when punishment reinforces the drive which instigated the undesirable behavior. Aversion conditioning can backfire under these circumstances. When the response to be eliminated is triggered by strong anxiety and when the conditioning itself arouses additional anxiety, that which was designed to extinguish the flames merely adds fuel to the fire. The neurotic behavior will be aggravated, either in intensity or frequency. It is with this possibility in mind that Franks (1960) counsels that the degree of neuroticism (anxiety) of prospective candidates for aversion conditioning be carefully assessed prior to deciding upon this form of treatment and that overly anxious patients be eliminated.

the experimenters in their laboratories, change-agents who treat alcoholics with debilitating, nauseating, or frightening drugs (succinylcholine chloride, for example*) can hardly be accused of being too
softhearted or sentimental. It is certainly curious that reward training
(positive reinforcement) has played up to now an insignificant part in
reconditioning alcoholics. Yet it would seem that treatment based on
relatively non-controversial learning principles ought to include and
emphasize positive reinforcement to a far greater extent than aversive
conditioning.

REWARD TRAINING

Shoben (1956), Conger (1956), Kingham (1958), and Ullman
(1958) have used learning principles to account for the etiology of
alcoholism. But only a few change-agents have written explicitly about
their experiences in applying learning principles, notably reward training, to the treatment of alcoholism. Of these few the most recent is
Kepner (1964). She views treatment of the drinking symptom as a
two-stage process: elimination of the old drinking response and acquisition of the new response, sobriety (abstinence). Sobriety is a
difficult task, since a pattern of responses established through many
repetitions must be abandoned to achieve it. She suggests setting a
series of graded tasks leading to sobriety. If successive and closer approximations to the final goal are consistently rewarded, the new
pattern of sobriety may eventually be established in the patient. She
proposes the following rewards: (1) The therapist should adopt an
accepting attitude. By that she means that the patient should be
valued as a human being rather than devaluated as a "drunk." The
drinking should be regarded as a serious but not a moral problem,
and the patient should not be made to feel sinful, willful, ashamed,
or guilty. (2) The post-intoxication distress should be alleviated; for
instance, by medication prescribed by a physician. (3) The therapist
should use the tools of encouragement, support, and understanding.
(4) The patient is to be helped to find substitute satisfactions to replace the drinking. When he engages in the recommended hobbies,
physical recreation, community activities, intellectual pursuits, em-

* Succinylcholine chloride (scoline) is used to induce a partial but
terrifying respiratory paralysis in order to bring the patient as close to an
experience with death as possible. Sanderson, Campbell, and Laverty (1963)
and Madill, Campbell, Laverty, Sanderson and Vandewater (1965).

ployment, or in relearning the art of being husband and father, or wife and mother, the therapist's approval as well as the intrinsic satisfactions of those activities will act as reinforcers of sobriety. That gained, the therapist should help the patient to feel a justified sense of accomplishment and should encourage persons in the patient's immediate environment to provide him with rewards for sobriety. Kepner is very hopeful that improvement will result when significant persons in the patient's environment "understand that if the patient experiences some gratification from his sober behavior, this more adjustive pattern can be learned in the same fashion as the old drinking pattern" (*ibid.*, p. 284).

She is equally hopeful that negative or aversive stimuli can be used to weaken and eventually eliminate the drinking response. Aversive stimuli are often informative; they let the individual know what the limits of acceptable behavior are and what will happen if he violates these limits. She notes, however, that friend, family, and even employers are often reluctant to define these limits, for creating a crisis involves a calculated risk. Nevertheless, it must be done, since the alcoholic will not become strongly motivated to give up drinking and make the new response of sobriety unless he is forced to face reality.* Notice that aversive stimuli can be either physical or psychological; they may simply require the patient to become aware of the consequences of his drinking behavior and the way it contributes to his daily problems.

We have purposely devoted a good deal of space to Kepner's philosophy and methods, for hers is perhaps the most recent and most explicit statement of what *early* learning theories offer the clinician concerned with changing his patient's behavior. The reader may well conclude that they offer less than one would hope in spite of their optimistic claim that relatively, or perhaps only seemingly, easy measures will lead to success and sobriety. Evidently this is not the case, or alcoholism should have been conquered long ago. It may be that a direct translation of the early learning theories into clinical practice has suffered from misunderstandings and inaccuracies. It is more likely that these early theories are, in themselves, inadequate to do what they

---

* Forcing the alcoholic to "face reality" is not a principle derived from learning theory per se, but from clinical experience. Alcoholics in industry and those brought into court have been motivated successfully by a crisis in the form of a confrontation with the consequences of their alcoholism.

set out to do: to predict behavior and to indicate how it can be made to change. Our hopes will have to rest on the burgeoning of sophisticated research in motivation to which we have alluded, and the resulting increased complexity of the newer learning theories. Until that progress and its *correct* translation into clinical practice have caught up with each other, all we can do for the moment is to recommend these developments to the reader's attention. Pending their validation by experience, we shall have to be content with the existing and most frequently employed learning principle: aversive conditioning. Good success has been reported for the various forms of aversion treatment. What these reports indicate about the effectiveness of one aversive treatment versus another, or about the relative correctness of the assumptions underlying conditioning on the one hand, and psychodynamically oriented treatment on the other hand are questions we are not prepared to answer. We wish to alert the reader from the outset that both obvious and subtle factors operate to becloud a fair and objective appraisal. The degree of success reported for any one method naturally depends not only on the particular characteristics of the patient, change-agent, and treatment setting, but also on the methods for measuring improvement, the stringency of improvement criteria, and the presence and adequacy of controls and of follow-up. All these factors must necessarily be held constant, or be controlled one by one when one compares one form of treatment with another. Not many studies of treatment outcomes meet these conditions; consequently, they remain isolated bits of evidence from which only the most tentative conclusions can be drawn. Controlled studies of treatment outcome under various treatment conditions are rare, and we shall come back to them later.

For the moment, we must mention another factor, a subtle one, that makes it even more difficult to choose which of the two major theoretical orientations seems to be more useful in alcoholism treatment. This factor is the confounding of the two orientations, psychodynamic and learning theory, within the same treatment situation. The reader will observe that, as various forms of aversive conditioning are described, their proponents mention a number of extraneous elements present and procedures employed concurrently that are totally irrelevant to pure conditioning. But from a psychodynamic point of view, these incidental features of aversion treatment must also be considered crucial for recovery. The nature of the relationship between patient and therapist is one example. If it happens to be seen as at all important in aversion treatment, this is not because in itself it plays any theoretical role, but rather because clinical experience has shown a good relationship to be useful.* Since psychoanalytic theory is derived from that very same clinical experience, it is no wonder that clinicians, of whatever theoretical bent, include psychodynamic considerations in their treatment. Whether they acknowledge them as such is another matter. Neither psychodynamics nor learning principles can be excluded from any human situation, especially the clinical one. We may look forward to considerable progress in treatment when a comprehensive theory of behavior that includes contributions from both has been developed.

BEHAVIOR THERAPY: RECIPROCAL INHIBITION AND DESENSITIZATION

Behavior therapists tend to ignore the patient-therapist relationship, perhaps because it is awkward to account for its effects within the traditional framework of conditioning. Just how awkward the attempt can be is seen in the argument of Wolpe *et al.* (1964). As he is one of the leading exponents of behavior therapy, which is coming into use in the treatment of alcoholics, let us examine his thesis. It proceeds as follows: Neurosis is learned; it results from faulty conditioning and can be unlearned by means of corrective conditioning or deconditioning, How is this done? Wolpe and some of his followers posit that anxiety-reduction is the key to success: "The most characteristic and common feature of neurotic habits is anxiety. There is persistent evidence, both experimental and clinical, that the great majority of neuroses are fundamentally conditioned autonomic responses. The individual has persistent habits of reacting with anxiety to situations that, objectively, are not dangerous" (*ibid.*). It follows that "if a response inhibitory of anxiety can be made to occur in the presence of anxiety-evoking stimuli, it will weaken the bond between these stimuli and the anxiety" (*ibid.*). The therapist, in this scheme, becomes a stimulus that evokes in the patient reciprocally inhibitory responses to anxiety; his function is the same as that of other reciprocal inhibitory stimuli, such as food

* Eysenck (1960, p. 11) states that "symptomatic treatment (by means of conditioning therapy) leads to permanent recovery, provided autonomic as well as skeletal surplus conditioned responses are extinguished. Personal relations are not essential for cures of neurotic disorder, although they may be useful in certain circumstances."

and sex, or stimuli that trigger respiration, assertive behavior, competitively conditioned motor responses, or deep muscle relaxation, and so forth. The benefits that might accrue from the patient-therapist relationship are said to be due to the relaxing effect of the therapist's presence. Wolpe accounts for the success obtained by traditional therapies by saying that "the reciprocal inhibition principle also affords an explanation for the therapeutic effects of interviewing as such . . ." (*ibid.*, p. 11).

But is reciprocal inhibition of anxiety really all that happens when behavior therapists see patients? We do not think so; but let the reader judge for himself in examining Wolpe's method more closely. Let us take as an illustration behavior therapy employed by Lazarus in the treatment of an alcoholic. Lazarus (1965, p. 738) holds that alcoholism can be equated with "compulsive drinking" and involves two processes: "(i) the conditioned autonomic drive (CAD), usually anxiety, from which (ii) the motor reactions develop. Fundamental therapy presupposes the extinction of both the CAD and the motor habits." To achieve these two ends, Lazarus instituted a multiple-pronged attack on the symptom in the case of a middle-aged married professional who had been "drinking with the boys" since he was a teenager but had become a solitary drinker in his late twenties. Treatment began in a nursing home to ameliorate somatic complications. During that time Lazarus obtained further details of the patient's life history and explained the behavior-therapy rationale to him. Aversion therapy was the first step in the program after the patient was discharged from the nursing home. It took place both in the consulting room and in the patient's own home and consisted of pairing the sight, taste, smell of alcohol and the desire to drink with strong faradic shocks to the patient's palm and forearm. While away from treatment, the patient was also equipped with a portable faradic unit and told to administer an electric shock to himself whenever he felt the need for a drink. The result was that the patient became "extremely sensitive to and anxious about the faradic shocks."* Lazarus utilized the anxiety to teach the patient how to avoid it by conditioning "anxiety-relief." He was told to lift a glass of brandy and to try to drink it, but as soon as he touched the glass a mild electric current was passed in his hand.

---

* We have mentioned earlier that there exists in aversive conditioning the danger of increasing anxiety so much that the treatment procedure itself becomes a stimulus for renewed or increased drinking.

The current increased in intensity the closer the glass came to his mouth and became noxious if the patient actually attempted to drink the brandy. The patient could get the current to stop by replacing the glass on the table and withdrawing his hand. In addition to the aversive conditioning and the anxiety-relief conditioning, interview sessions were conducted during which the patient was to recount all of the life- and work-situations during which he had felt anxious, unhappy, worthless, upset, regretful, guilty, unable to cope, and so forth. When a number of events which had caused him pain had been recalled, "systematic desensitization" therapy was initiated. The method has been described by Wolpe (1958) and consists of grading anxiety-evoking stimuli on a continuum of intensity. The patient is asked to imagine the least disturbing stimulus (event, feeling, fantasy, interpersonal situation) and to counterpose at the same time a relaxation response which is presumed to inhibit anxiety. This is done until the patient reports that he is no longer perturbed by the stimulus. At the next session the same procedure is repeated but with a more intense stimulus. Wolpe uses preparatory periods in which the patient is taught progressive relaxation, deep muscle relaxation, and relaxation during a hypnotic trance. Differential relaxation is suggested to the patient for daily use while he engages in activities that do not require the use of all his muscles. Specifically, the treatment consists of opposing incompatible responses to the response of anxiety in a protected setting where the amount of anxiety is "dosed"—that is, evoked only in an amount that the patient can tolerate comfortably and will be able to respond to with indifference at the end of the session.

Lazarus instructed his patient under deep hypnotic trance to re-experience all the events he had described as upsetting and leading to a desire to drink. Simultaneously, he was told to oppose the resulting anxiety, guilt, and remorse reactions with their "reciprocal inhibition" response afforded by relaxation. Hypnotic desensitization had the desired results after 20 such sessions. The patient wasn't "bothered" by any of the previously disturbing stimuli. To counteract his remaining "bottled up" feelings of resentment, which had been discovered in the interviews, he was told to express them directly but in a reasonable manner instead of suppressing them. In a special adaptation of role playing, "behavior rehearsal," the patient was helped to practice self-assertiveness in a variety of interpersonal encounters. After about two months of treatment during which the patient had remained abstinent, had gained weight, and had been free of tremors, he went on a one-month holiday and continued abstinent. While he was gone, his wife agreed to undergo desensitization treatment to inure her against her husband's past behavior. Upon the patient's return, he was given booster treatments of aversion conditioning once a month; at one time he was rehypnotized and received a post-hypnotic suggestion that if he were to do any solitary drinking, or have more than two glases of beer or wine, or more than two shots of liquor, he would immediately develop cramps, nausea and vomiting. Lazarus reports that he followed the patient for over 14 months during which he maintained himself successfully as a social drinker.

The excellent results obtained by Lazarus in a relatively short time merit further attention and discussion. We have repeatedly expressed the need for experimenting with new alcoholism treatment methods; certainly Lazarus, and for that matter Wolpe as well, claim that behavior therapy or the conditioning therapies constitute a novel approach. Wolpe (1964) claims, moreover, that behavior therapy is far more effective and effective in a shorter period than psychoanalysis. But is the method really new, and is it better?

The reader will have noted that Lazarus (following Wolpe) prescribes a great variety of therapeutic interventions in addition to the conditioning. These include a very careful history (Wolpe uses diagnostic testing in addition), discussion of upsetting events, teaching relaxation, role playing, environmental manipulation, hypnotic trance, post-hypnotic suggestions (Wolpe uses carbon dioxide inhalations*). All of these techniques have played important roles in psychodynamically oriented therapies and cannot be fairly subsumed under the title of *Conditioning Therapies—A Challenge in Treatment* (Wolpe *et al.* 1964). Furthermore, deep muscle relaxation as a precursor of the hypnotic trance and hypnosis itself are contingent upon a very special relationship of the patient to the hypnotist, based on trust, hope, dependency, and need gratifications. It contains many of the elements of a transference reaction, and its apparently beneficial effects are the same as those seen in the psychoanalytic situation

---

* Wolpe administers a mixture of 70 per cent carbon dioxide and 30 per cent oxygen to patients with pervasive anxiety. They are given one to four inhalations at full lung capacity per session. The proportion is potentially deadly; Meduna's 30 per cent carbon dioxide to 70 per cent oxygen has been considered dangerous, being the anesthetic dose. Wolpe reports great success in relaxing his patients and consequently reducing their anxiety by this method.

when the patient remains symptom-free for as long as he has substituted the transference neurosis for his disability. The difference
between the two techniques is that in psychoanalysis the patient
must work through the transference, examining and analyzing it
until it is resolved; whereas the relationship to the hypnotist (or
behavior therapist) remains unexamined and unresolved: witness,
for example, the therapist's influence embodied in the post-hypnotic
suggestions. These remarks are not designed to minimize the importance of hypnotically induced improvement; on the contrary,
they are designed to refocus attention on its essential feature—the
dynamic properties of the feelings which the therapist evokes in the
patient.

It would not matter what label is given to the dynamics of
the patient-therapist relationship—whether it be termed transference
resolved or unresolved, or classified as a reciprocally inhibitory response—were it not that the latter is limited to one single aspect of
the relationship, that of anxiety reduction with concurrent symptom
remission. There is nothing to be regretted in symptom remission,
even if it were to prove only temporary and dependent upon the
quality of the relationship. One problem does arise, however. As we
have described, there are many kinds of patient-therapist relationships,
some of them anxiety- or hostility-producing, all of them generating
strong feelings. It is frequently unwise to ignore them, both for the
patients' and the therapists' sake. Regarding the contention of behavior therapists that theirs is a new approach, we must conclude
that this is exaggerated; it is only their particular combination of
traditional psychodynamically oriented techniques (relabeled to be
sure) with conditioning techniques that is new. It is to be noted that
Lazarus' conditioning sequence has the special merit that it begins
with aversive conditioning (teaching the patient what not to do) and
is followed by operant conditioning (teaching him what to do).
Operant conditioning—rewarding the desired response, which the
patient is free to make or not to make—in contrast to aversive
conditioning, in which the response is forced, permits the shaping
of behavior to a desired goal by approximations. It has been only
rarely employed in the reconditioning of alcoholics* and deserves more
attention, inasmuch as it is a powerful educational tool. Another

* An attempt has been made to treat alcoholics by operant conditioning by Mertens and Fuller (1964).

point of interest is that Lazarus exerts great care in his conditioning procedures. His timing is precise; he uses electric current rather than any of the centrally depressing emetic drugs (apomorphine or disulfiram), which tend to make conditioning more difficult.

Wolpe's challenge that his and Lazarus' method is more effective and more rapid than psychoanalysis does raise a few doubts. He reports an 89.5 per cent improvement rate in a series of 210 cases to whom his method had been applied successfully. However, in examining these figures Stevenson (Wolpe *et al.*, 1964, p. 17) noted that certain patients who had begun Wolpe's treatment (initial interviews and testing) were not included in the evaluation of treatment outcome—Wolpe indicates this was because they appeared to be refractory to treatment. Recalculating the percentages on the entire series of cases, including those seen for testing, ($N = 295$), the recovery rate falls to 65 per cent. He points out that even though Wolpe had used the same criteria for rating improvement as had Knight (1941, as cited by Wolpe, *ibid.*, p. 14), one cannot evaluate one treatment method versus another without having matched control series. Without being sure that the statistical methods are the same, that the method whereby the evaluation criteria are applied is the same, we can draw no conclusions. We would add that there is a very great likelihood that the patient populations selected for treatment by the two methods are quite dissimilar. Wolpe states that he attempts to eliminate through his diagnostic testing psychotic and psychopathic individuals. Examining his case descriptions, one finds that, consonant with his theory that most neuroses are due to faulty autonomic conditioning resulting in inappropriate anxiety reactions, Wolpe selects for treatment persons suffering from diffuse, specific, or pervasive anxiety, from phobias, and only very rarely, from obsessions. No alcoholics appear in his reports. Thus it would seem that he sees the very patients who are most likely to obtain symptom relief by any method—faith-healing, hypnotism, placebo administration, suggestion, being placed on a waiting list—in other words, patients who easily form transference reactions that make the symptom unnecessary and result in apparent "cures."

It must also be observed that the treatment advocated by Wolpe is not inevitably as saving of time as he suggests. In his series of reported cases, the number of interviews ranges from one to 263. Wolpe states that he can sometimes determine whether a patient has had an adequate number of sessions within 40 trials. Most patients are seen between one to 30 times (35 patients) but some (13 patients) are seen over 80 times. The longest timespan over which treatment extended was 46 months—a not inconsiderable investment on the part of both patient and therapist in time, in effort, and in a reciprocal relationship!

AVERSIVE CONDITIONING THROUGH HYPNOSIS

Although not many change-agents use hypnosis, those who have employed it report considerable success in establishing a conditioned aversion response to alcohol. Its advocates recommend it over chemically induced conditioning because of its physiological safety. Many drugs that are capable of causing nausea and vomiting in response to the taste, smell, or sight of alcoholic beverages should not be employed in cases where there are gastrointestinal, hepatic, cardiac, or muscular disorders. These are the very conditions that are found in severe alcoholics. Further, certain characteristics of these drugs themselves suggest that other means of conditioning would be more effective. Apomorphine, disulfiram, and emetine have a depressant action that may make conditioning difficult. Moreover, as we have pointed out before, the interval between conditioned and unconditioned stimulus must be timed very precisely if the most effective conditioning is to occur. Apparently the best time interval between the administration of alcohol (conditioned stimulus) and the onset of nausea (unconditioned stimulus) should be approximately half a second. Such delicate timing is sometimes easier to achieve by hypnosis than by drugs.

The method for using only hypnosis* as the conditioning agent with alcoholics has been described in some detail by Abrams (1964).** The hypnotic suggestion of becoming ill acts as the unconditioned stimulus that in turn creates the unconditioned response of nausea

---

* That is, no group psychotherapy, concurrent individual counseling, or other treatment given in conjunction with aversive conditioning.

** For textbooks on hypnosis in which its history, its phenomenology, and the nature of related states are described; in which techniques of induction and management are given; and in which theories and applications are discussed, we refer the reader to the following: Brenman and Gill (1961, 1947), Erickson (1949), Estabrooks (1957), LeCron (1952), Meares (1960), Schilder (1956), Schneck (1959), Weitzenhoffer (1957), Wolberg (1948). For a brief review and critical evaluation of the recent use of hypnosis by American psychologists, see Moss (1965).

and vomiting. The conditioned stimulus—the alcoholic drink—is supplied immediately before the hypnotic suggestion. Treatment is considered successful when the conditioned reflex is so firmly established that the patient is *immediately* induced to vomit through the presence of the conditioned stimulus (alcohol), even when not influenced by the unconditioned stimulus (hypnotic trance). Abrams states that the negative aspects of the nausea and vomiting should be sufficient to create an aversive response to alcohol.

More specifically, his treatment takes the following course. In the first meeting, the procedure is explained and described. Treatment is continued only if the alcoholic is willing to undertake the discomfort and stress associated with it. If the patient assents, he is hypnotized and told to recall—or preferably, if the hypnotic state is deep enough, to relive—an occasion on which he was very ill after drinking. With the aid of hypnotic suggestion, the nausea, vertigo, and vomiting are re-experienced, and with continued repetition they become an automatic and immediate response to the hypnotic suggestion. The hypnotically induced hallucination of drinking an alcoholic beverage is then repetitively paired with the feeling of nausea and the emetic response, until the alcohol alone without hypnotic suggestion is sufficient to produce vomiting. Abrams suggests that treatment in a group setting is more effective than that of a single patient because, in his experience and that of others, the similar reaction of group members helps to strengthen the conditioned response. Conditioning by this method will generally occur within five to eight hypnotic sessions if the patients are seen approximately twice a week for 30 minutes. Abrams estimates that on the average from five to 20 sessions are necessary; and, in addition, when conditioning has been established, treatment should be repeated at three-month intervals during the first year to reinforce the aversion response to alcohol. We shall find that re-treatment after aversion has been created is recommended whatever the conditioning technique employed. This recommendation rests on a solid foundation of experimental studies on the extinction of conditioned responses when they are not reinforced.

Variations in the technique of inducing a vomiting response can be divided into two main classes. One class, using hypnosis alone, varies in terms of the setting (group is the most frequent treatment setting but individual treatment has also been reported) and the methods used for hypnotizing the patients; the depth of trance and the content suggested; the amount of preparatory history-taking and explanations; the presence or absence of post-hypnotic suggestions of remaining sober and of adopting a different style of life; the availability of concurrent auxiliary rehabilitation and re-educative measures or of some form of psychotherapy. It is not surprising in view of such possibilities of diversity that the permanence of sobriety and with it the reported effectiveness of hypnotically induced alcohol aversion is dramatically different in different hands.

A second class of variations adds to hypnosis the use of drugs that actually cause nausea and vomiting (apomorphine, emetine, and others). One way of doing this is to begin treatment by giving one of the emetic drugs for about two weeks, along with several hypnotic sessions each week. During hypnosis, suggestions are given that the patient has just taken the drug and will become nauseous and vomit. After several sessions, the patient begins to respond to the hypnotic suggestion and the drugs can then be discontinued. This has been found a successful technique by a number of investigators: Steck (1951), O'Hollaren (1947), and Gordova and Kovalev (1962).

Russian workers obtain their best results when the patient is able to go deeply enough into a hypnotic trance to hallucinate the drinking of alcoholic beverages. Beyond this depth, a further increase in trance is not necessarily related to a corresponding increase in the strength of stability of the aversion response (Tokarsky, 1938). This is not surprising from the standpoint of conditioning theory, for all that is required is to provide an opportunity for the unconditioned response (vomiting) to become associated with the conditioned stimulus (alcohol); the hypnotic suggestion constitutes the necessary link. There must be a sufficient trance achieved so the hypnotic suggestion can take effect, but more than that is irrelevant.

Contrary to the typical practice of aversive conditioning, when conditioning a patient against drinking alcoholic beverages through the use of hypnosis, one need not begin with the creation of a vomiting response. Direct suggestions can be made during the trance to the effect that alcohol tastes bad, or will taste bad in the future, that it is not to be touched again, or that sobriety will prove pleasant and intoxication frightening or painful. Any number of similar instructions can be given during hypnosis. A widely used practice is to suggest substitutes for the alcoholic beverage and simultaneously to suggest that it will give the patient the same lift or pleasure alcohol has given him in the past.

While these techniques are usually spoken of in the context of conditioning (and inasmuch as the patient learns new responses the term is appropriate), they are really better considered under the heading of symptom-removal and symptom-substitution, since they bear only a distant resemblance to aversive conditioning. To make it even more difficult to maintain the distinctions between these treatment modalities, they are frequently employed simultaneously, or in succession. Our difficulties in keeping the discussion within the frame of reference of conditioning and learning theory have just begun when symptom-replacement or substitution are being considered, for these concepts are most useful and achieve the greatest clarity of meaning within a psychoanalytic frame of reference. Inasmuch as they are simply descriptive of what goes on they can certainly be assimilated to learning phenomena such as "retroactive inhibition," "reciprocal inhibition," or perhaps "extinction" and learning of new responses. But the clinical importance of symptom-substitution lies not in mere description but in the implications for the patient's welfare.

Symptom-removal versus symptom-substitution has been the subject of much controversy. Its resolution is crucial in hypnosis; for with this technique rather dramatic and rapid effects can be achieved, some of them endangering the life of the patient if proper care in handling symptoms is not taken. The heart of the matter lies in the psychoanalytic assumption that symptoms are a compromise solution of unconscious conflict. If a symptom is removed before a new solution for the conflict has occurred, the consequences may be either a new or more crippling symptom (for instance, a psychosomatic one) to serve the same purpose as did the one that was eliminated, or an outbreak of intolerable anxiety or depression that could lead to psychosis, suicide, or murder. These possibilities are not merely academic; psychoanalysts cite cases in which they have become tragic realities. Consequently, there has been much apprehension over the untimely removal of symptoms that might play a part in maintaining conflicts in a tolerable state of equilibrium.

Deliberately and therapeutically induced formation of substitute symptoms of a benign kind has been proposed as an alternative to the more time-consuming and difficult procedure of resolving the conflicts through insight. Obsession with sobriety instead of with drinking, and dependence upon A.A. instead of alcohol have been advocated by some; others have suggested a *hypnotic substitution of symptoms* during the treatment processes. Estabrooks (1957) believes that a hobby will often be a sufficient replacement for the drinking because the alcoholic can develop an addictive-like interest in something of this nature. Steck (1951) substituted a non-alcoholic drink for the symptom by making this an especially pleasurable experience during the hypnotic state. Wolberg (1948) has also indicated the need for substitute symptoms.

Mann (1960) favors substitution to complete symptom-removal because he believes that patients can accept the goal of symptom-substitution more easily. He cites the case of an obese patient who under hypnotic trance revealed a history of alcoholism. Mann was successful in suggesting coffee or tea as a substitute that would provide the same stimulating effect as the previous breakfast of bourbon. He reports that together with the establishment of better eating habits, alcohol intake was eliminated within five weeks. Although the patient seemed to retain the need for an early morning boost, a benign one came to replace the detrimental one. Aside from the specific technique employed, Mann also recognizes the role of the ingredient that we consider basic in treatment success: "psychotherapy will continue to be practiced knowingly or unknowingly because the doctor-patient relationship often proves therapeutic in itself."

It seems likely to us that those investigators who report that they have not observed any adverse effects from symptom removal may have neglected to observe that the patient's relationship to the therapist can quite possibly have become the substitute symptom* whether the relationship corresponds to reality or is a fantasy or is compounded of both. For example, Wolpe *et al.* (1964) report no bad results in using hypnosis to remove symptoms in a variety of disorders. From what has been said previously about this approach, it appears more than probable that psychodynamics, such as the patient's relationship to and his dependence on the therapist, play a much more important role than Wolpe acknowledges. The reconditioning by itself, hypnotic or otherwise, cannot be regarded as pure and simple symptom removal. Since the very fact that the patient is amenable to hypnosis indicates that attachment to the hypnotist frequently constitutes a substitute symptom, we consider that hypnosis does not present the risk that disaster will follow upon symptom-removal. But there are other psychological hazards in the use of hypnosis. Meares

* In the section on "Psychoanalytically Oriented Hypnotherapy" (Chapter 14), we discuss these interpersonal factors in greater depth.

(1961), who shares our opinion that the hazards of symptom-removal have been overemphasized, mentions a number of cautions to observe. He would eliminate from hypnotic treatment patients who seek the pleasure of hypnosis for its own sake, rather than relief from their disabilities. He warns the hypnotist to avoid treating overdependent, masochistic patients, patients with unconscious homosexual fantasies, and patients who wish to prove that they are in control. If there is risk in treating such patients, it is surely a matter of degree. But since we can offer no further data, therapists will have to continue to rely upon their intuition and experience in these matters.

Writers describing hypnotic techniques are more helpful when it comes to dealing with the problem of the patient's increased suggestibility as a result of the "training" under hypnosis. The patient must be protected from possible bad effects of his acquired susceptibility to hypnotic influence. This can be done by hypnotic counter-suggestion designed to nullify efforts by unqualified hypnotists and exploitation by unscrupulous persons. Meares recommends a passive-induction method with patients who have trouble standing up to authority (psychotics, for example) so that their handicap will not be aggravated.

Another of the pitfalls of hypnotic treatment is the unfulfilled, or unfulfillable post-hypnotic suggestion. Meares recommends its use only sparingly and cautiously, for patients will suffer from anxiety or psychosomatic disturbances when they do not carry out the instructions. There is also a danger to the patient under hypnosis when he gains traumatic insight too rapidly. The likelihood of severe anxiety resulting from sudden awareness of unacceptable wishes is increased under hypnosis since the usual repressions (defenses) are not available to the hypnotized person. If the patient subsequently emerges from hypnosis in an acute panic stage, Meares advises that he be rehypnotized immediately and that amnesia for the disturbing insights be induced.

An emergency will also arise when an incipient psychotic potential is transformed into a full-blown psychotic episode. As in any form of psychiatric treatment where the same danger exists, diagnostic procedures must be instituted so that pre-psychotic individuals can be recognized. Meares recommends that neither those who have ideas of being influenced nor schizoid persons should be treated by hypnosis. Those who have great fears of close relationships, as indicated by their distance and formality, can be treated, but a passive-induction technique should be employed to safeguard them from anxiety. Disruptive anxiety can also arise when patients misunderstand the hypnotist. It is very important therefore that the hypnotist be careful in how he words his instructions. For instance, some persons may interpret that being told to go into a "deep sleep" means that they are to die; and foreigners or persons hard of hearing may simply not understand some of the communications. We would add that persons from a low educational and socio-economic background (as are many alcoholics) and persons who have been regressed to an earlier age level during trance may not understand abstract communications and should be spoken to in very simple, concrete, everyday language. Another practical caution is to make sure that the patient be fully awake before he leaves. It does happen that a patient will seem quite his usual self, although he is, in fact, still in partial trance. Under those circumstances, traffic and driving could become hazardous, and the patient would be incapable of making responsible decisions.

Dangers to patients in the use of hypnosis have been pointed out by other investigators; specifically when active induction methods popular with side-show hypnotists are used, like cracking the whip, slapping, and so forth. Kaim (1963) considers all such anxiety-inducing stimuli as potentially harmful. He cites sudden noises, sudden slaps, drugs and various methods of cerebral inhibition, "Hansen's hit," and other traumatic psychological methods; vagal stimulation by producing the oculo-carotid reflex (compressing the carotid sinus) and similar maneuvers for changing the circulation to the brain (Valsava's maneuver) that have been reported to cause damage. He states that he has even seen bad results from the use of stroboscopes and brain wave synchronizers—we assume that in such cases the hypnotic subjects are seizure-prone individuals in whom convulsions can be produced by visual stimuli synchronized with the alpha rhythm. Thus we cannot agree with some of the advocates of hypnosis, such as Abrams (1964), that the hypnotic technique is entirely free of physiological risks; and, as we have seen, there do exist psychological hazards in its use.

Aside from the question of potential hazards of hypnosis to patients, another question arises: are enough alcoholics hypnotizable to give this method broad applicability? The answer is yes, provided that necessary additional precautions, to which we shall address ourselves shortly, are taken. According to Hull (1933), only 10.48 per cent of the general population is refractory to hypnosis, and clinical experience has shown that alcoholics as a group have even less resistance. Perhaps not all of them are capable of entering a deep trance, but that is probably not even necessary.

Experimental studies of specific personality variables that can be used to predict whether or not a given individual will be hypnotizable have been by and large quite contradictory. Weitzenhoffer (1953), in reviewing the literature, found only one general variable: a positive attitude of the subject toward being hypnotized favors susceptibility. Deckert and West (1963) consider it unlikely that any consistencies will be discovered in personality, motivational, and attitudinal correlates of hypnotic susceptibility. And Dermen and London (1965) conclude that hypnotic susceptibility is not usefully related to personality (as measured by inventories and questionnaires) or to measures of "social and environmental perceptions"; nor does it seem to be related to measures of personal experiences, other than previous hypnotic experience.

Although the more rigorous experimental studies have failed to offer the clinician a helpful instrument in patient selection, clinical experience with alcoholics seems to have been consistent in finding the more dependent, passive person a likely hypnotic subject since he is amenable to hypnotic suggestion and able to profit from hypnotic treatment. For those relatively few alcoholics who have been treated by means of hypnosis, a respectable success rate has been reported. However, since these results were achieved by means of psychodynamically oriented group hypnotherapy (Paley, 1955; Friend, 1957; Reinert, 1965) they will be discussed more fully in Chapter 14. Here it is relevant to say only that if one combines the two variables diagnostic of success in hypnotic treatment and in aversion treatment studied by Wallerstein et al. (1957) at Topeka; namely, passive-dependence for the first and clinical depression for the second, one may perhaps obtain a group of patients optimally suited for hypnotic aversion treatment. We suggest that future research attend to patient assignment to this treatment modality on the basis of the syndrome "passivity-dependence-depression."

It certainly would seem that hypnosis, whether used to recondition the patient, to suggest an aversion to alcohol, or to assist in uncovering unconscious conflicts or traumata, could be used for a much larger proportion of alcoholics than is done currently. For instance, Gordova and Kovalev (1962) suggest that hypnosis should be employed alone with older subjects because of the physical contra-indications of drug use. With younger subjects who are less susceptible to hypnosis, this technique should be combined with apomorphine. They found that generally nine to 12 sessions were sufficient to develop abstinence, but with chronic alcoholics the number had to be increased to 15.

It now remains for us to specify the safeguards that should be maintained in using hypnosis with alcoholics. First of all, *we recommend that passive-induction methods be employed since they do not involve physiological risk and are not damaging to the dependent person, to those who have difficulties with authority figures, or to schizoid and pre-psychotic persons.* Persons with alcohol-related problems are quite likely to belong to one or the other of these groups. In addition, we subscribe to the cautions proposed by Meares. Finally, we urge that hypnosis be undertaken only by practitioners trained in psychodynamic principles and methods to avoid precipitous uncovering of unconscious materials and to recognize impending psychotic episodes before they occur. Hypnosis is not without psychological risks; it is therefore imperative that patients be protected from the unscrupulous and from the psychologically ignorant.

AVERSIVE CONDITIONING BY MEANS OF DRUGS

Apomorphine*

In 1899 C. J. Douglas demonstrated that apomorphine could be depended upon to produce sleep, even when patients are delirious. Subsequently Dent, a magnetic personality and a powerful therapist, introduced this drug for the treatment of addiction and alcoholism. His first impression of the effectiveness of apomorphine therapy was that results were due to the establishment of conditioned aversion

* Apomorphine is a nauseating substance legally defined as a narcotic. It is a non-addictive morphine derivative. For emesis one to five mg. are injected subcutaneously, or 6.5 mg. to ten mg. are taken sublingually. Average or large doses may cause CNS depression or, occasionally, euphoria, restlessness, and tremors. Excessive doses may cause violent emesis, cardiac depression, and death. It should not be given when a person is in shock or impending shock or when he is under the influence of opiates, barbiturates, and other CNS depressants. If a first dose fails to produce emesis, a second dose should *not* be administered.

reaction to alcohol (vomiting). As he gained more experience with the drug and became more convinced of its benefits, he attributed the results of the therapy to the tranquilizing and other regulatory physiologic properties of apomorphine. Many investigators have followed Dent's footsteps, some utilizing apomorphine as an agent for aversive conditioning, some in the same manner as Dent later had come to prefer, i.e., in sub-emetic doses taken by mouth. Whatever the merit of the drug itself, one must remember in evaluating Dent's enthusiasm for it, that it was once said of him: "Dent without apomorphine would be better treatment than apomorphine without Dent." His admiring colleagues report that Dent had a special brand of bedside manner that combined hypnotic suggestion and good humor. Modest about his own contribution, Dent himself regarded apomorphine therapy as purely chemical.

In the United States, apomorphine has rarely been used to produce an aversion response to alcohol. Lemere and Voegtlin (1955) have tried it out at Shadel Sanatorium but found its emetic action too short-lived for effective conditioning. Moreover, its sedative action interfered with effective conditioning. They discontinued its use after a number of severe shock reactions occurred as a consequence.

In Russia, Switzerland, and other European countries, apomorphine-induced alcohol aversion remains in vogue. Dent's later use of apomorphine as a tranquilizer is favored by the Swiss therapists to improve the patient's sense of well-being and to decrease his craving for alcohol (see Feldmann, 1959, 1958, 1953; Staehelin, 1952; Rüegg and Pulver, 1953).

Emetine Hydrochloride

Drug-induced aversive conditioning by means of the nausea and vomiting produced by emetine* is not very popular, probably

---

* Emetine is one of the alcoloids of ipecacuanha. In spite of reports that rabbits have died of small intravenous dosages of emetine, and in spite of the production of (usually minor and transient) electrocardiographic changes in humans, physicians treating alcoholics have, in general, felt that there is little risk involved in the use of emetine hydrochloride, *if* electrocardiograms are taken during the course of treatment and the patient is kept in bed. Aside from absolute bed rest during the course of treatment, daily recordings of the pulse rate at frequent intervals is recommended (tachycardia may be the first clinical sign of toxic effects). The patient

because of the considerable medical precautions that must be taken. Furthermore, it is difficult to evaluate the results because in the relatively few treatment centers (Shadel, for instance) where emetine is given, other psychological and psychodynamic methods are employed concurrently; this makes it impossible to consider drug-conditioned aversion in isolation. At Shadel, aversive conditioning has been employed since 1935. In 1940 Voegtlin presented the first report about the use of emetine. Lemere and Voegtlin (1955) describe the technique as producing nausea and vomiting at the sight, smell, and taste of alcoholic drinks by the administration of emetine. They, like others who use conditioning, consider correct timing essential: the alcoholic beverage must be drunk slightly before the onset of the nausea and vomiting due to emetine; otherwise true conditioning cannot be obtained. Each treatment session lasts for 30 minutes to one hour, and the number of treatments may vary from four to six, usually one every alternate day. The average length of hospitalization is ten days. The aversion to alcohol is reinforced by one or two reconditioning treatments whenever the patient is tempted to drink once again, or routinely at the end of six months and a year after the original treatment. Lemere and Voegtlin report that relapses are often treated with better success the second time; other change-agents have had the opposite experience, which seems to be the more general outcome of reconditioning by any method. The authors warn that it is essential to avoid absorption of any of the alcohol. If the patient feels even slightly intoxicated during the conditioning treatment, it will fail. If the patient does appear intoxicated, the stomach must be emptied immediately and that particular session discontinued. The writers insist on exact and meticulous attention to detail and flawless technique as mandatory conditions for the success of this method.

---

should be examined and questioned at least daily for diarrhea, fatigue, dyspnea on exertion, muscular tremors, weakness, or dizziness. Emetine should not be used in the presence of organic heart disease and should be used with the greatest caution in patients who are anemic and debilitated.

It is also contraindicated in kidney diseases. Emetine is a rather toxic drug which causes an acute fall in blood pressure, cardiac irregularities, degeneration of the heart muscle, weakness, pain, or paralysis of skeletal muscles. Aside from nausea and vomiting, it also causes severe diarrhea and, occasionally, dermatitis. In using emetine, it is *essential that the patient be maintained in bed and be depended upon not to make any physical exertions* since he may otherwise suffer a myocardial infarction.

What has been said in the introduction to the use of learning principles in treatment will serve to explain and confirm their insistence.

During a 13-year period, Lemere and Voegtlin obtained follow-
up data for over 4,000 patients treated by their method. Of these, 44
per cent have remained totally abstinent since their first treatment.
Of the patients who relapsed and were re-treated, 39 per cent have
remained sober since their last reconditioning treatment. The overall
abstinence rate of 51 per cent compares well with figures obtained by
other treatment, such as A.A. The results are even better when
only a one-year follow-up period is taken as criterion of success: 60
per cent of the patients remained abstinent.

The authors do not claim that the good results are due only
to the conditioning treatment; they accord a prime role to a beneficial psychological climate at the sanatorium. In the order of importance, they list first of all the effects of the conditioning sessions;
next the sympathetic attitude of the staff; then the therapeutic
effect of the patients on each other and the discussions with the
patients of their problems; and, finally, the practical efforts to rehabilitate the patient in his job, with his family, and in his recrea-
tions. Lemere (1955) states that the patients are taught that complete
abstinence is essential for recovery, and are educated to other methods
of escape from the stresses of living than drinking, like hobbies, sports
and relaxation. The entire staff attempts to create a positive environment; much of the psychotherapy consists of increasing the patients'
self-esteem. To be amongst themselves instead of being treated with
"mental cases" adds to the patients' feeling of worth. However, clearly
neurotic patients are also accepted at Shadel and do receive special
psychotherapy. In addition, pentothal treatment, with close follow-
up, has been made available and has proved helpful.

From the foregoing it is evident that the remission rates
at Shadel are a result of a combination of treatment procedures
and cannot be ascribed to any single one. Lemere himself points to
additional factors involved in the success of the aversion treatment
as practiced at Shadel. He believes that their patients are more stable
economically than those seen at other places; otherwise they would
not be able to pay the fees of several hundred dollars for the treatment. Patients, obviously with a sense of humor, speak of the "gold
cure" in which the main deterrent to drinking again is the thought of
wasting the money they have just spent for the treatment. Lemere
suggests that the best results are obtained at Shadel when groups of

alcoholics get together for discussion among themselves of their common problems. Another useful aspect of the total therapeutic situation is that patients see each other at the hospital in critical condition. This makes denial of the dangers of alcoholism impossible. To watch another patient come close to death from drinking may have a sobering effect, or at least a motivating one. Further help comes from relapsed patients who warn others, explicitly or merely by their presence, of pitfalls ahead. Patients who have remained abstinent when they return for reinforcement treatment can give new patients confidence that abstinence is possible; their example may act as an implicit suggestion that treatment will be successful. Lemere considers the follow-up to be the most important factor in the success of the conditioned reflex treatment. Hence the great value of the reinforcement procedure, which provides a method of keeping in touch with the patient for at least a year.

Another institution where aversion treatment using emetine has been given a long trial period is the Washingtonian Hospital. Thimann (1955) reports good results from its use, but treatment is not advised for patients who show lack of judgment and whose restlessness may prevent them from following the proper routine of bedrest for the necessary time. At the Washingtonian Hospital procedures to prevent mishaps consist of giving only six emetine injections initially, the dose being no more that 11.25 grains. Pilocarpine has been eliminated from the injectible emetine solution and the treatment is applied *only* to patients who accept bedrest and hospitalization for an additional four weeks after completing the initial series of treatment. The sessions last 20 to 30 minutes and are repeated daily for five or six days (provided no toxic symptoms ensue). The alcoholic drinks are offered straight and as highballs. The treatments are followed by six or seven preventive one-day reinforcement (reconditioning) sessions at four- to 12-week intervals. Treatment, together with reinforcement, lasts about a year. Some patients, if they wish, receive further reinforcements, four at three-month intervals, after the first year of treatment. Thimann warns that the technique requires adequate apprenticeship because the range of patients' reactions to the conditioned and unconditioned stimuli is so varied and the margin between under-dosage and over-dosage is so very narrow.

Many important auxiliary methods based on psychodynamic principles are used at the Washingtonian Hospital just as at Shadel Sanatorium. Group therapy has been organized, and a night hospital is available to permit patients to work in their normal environment during the day and retire to a protective environment for leisure time and during the night. The program is a graded one in which the patient is helped to become increasingly able to handle in a mature way all the usual daily problems of an adult.

The psychotherapeutic aspects of conditioned reflex treatment are discussed by Thimann in detail. He recognizes that "like any other physiologic or drug therapy, only even more so, the conditioned reflex therapy includes a considerable amount of dynamic psychotherapy."

With Thimann, we would emphasize the futility of attempting to evaluate the conditioned aversion response to alcohol achieved in clinical situations as though it were a unitary treatment modality. It is far from being that. Rather, it seems to function as an auxiliary in a complex psychotherapeutic environment where many other measures known to have a beneficial impact contribute to the overall results.

Disulfiram

Disulfiram* (antabuse) can be employed in several different ways. For the present, we shall describe its usefulness in creating a conditioned avoidance response to alcohol; later we shall present its

---

* Disulfiram (antabuse), or more precisely tetraethylthiuram disulphide, was first used in the rubber industry as one of the antoxidants. Its toxic effects when taken in combination with alcohol are due presumably to its inhibiting action on the aldehyde dehydrogenase (and oxidase), preventing thereby the oxidation of acetaldehyde, a toxic intermediary substance produced during the metabolism of alcohol and ordinarily converted immediately to acetic acid and, eventually, mainly into water and carbon dioxide, or into fatty acids. Formerly the symptoms of the disulfiram-ethanol reaction were attributed to a toxic increase of blood-acetaldehyde levels; recent evidence (Casier and Merlevede, 1962) casts some doubt on this contention. It may be that the toxic effects are due to a different substance, perhaps a quaternary ammonium base, which is formed in the presence of disulfiram and alcohol.

Disulfiram, when taken without alcohol, has side effects of its own. They may include dermatitis, abdominal cramps, nausea, peripheral neuritis, sedation, drowsiness, headache, and sometimes impotence and psychosis. The reader is referred to the bibliography compiled by Ayerst Laboratories (1961) on disulfiram toxicity and to the chapters by Harger and Hulpieu and by Himwich in Thompson (1956).

function as psychological "fence" or chemical barrier to drinking. Conditioning by means of disulfiram is based on the toxic effects of the disulfiram-ethanol combination. The symptoms are similar to those caused by acetaldehyde, known to be a potent sympathomimetic drug (acting like 1=epinephrine). At first there is a rise in blood pressure and sensations of warmth and deep flushing (peripheral vasodilation). Then the patient experiences sensations of air hunger (hyperpnea) and accelerated heart rate (tachycardia). Dizziness, nausea, and vomiting supervene, followed by pallor, a rapid fall in blood pressure, unconsciousness, and, with sufficiently high doses, death. The severity of the symptoms varies with the individual and is proportional to the amount of disulfiram and alcohol ingested. Because of its slow absorption rate, the reaction does not occur until about three to twelve hours after disulfiram has been taken. The usual procedure is to give disulfiram daily by mouth for several days (three to five), making sure that the patient has not had any alcoholic beverage for the 48 hours before the first dose is given. Between the third and fifth day, alcohol is given in a small test dose. The test drink should be administered in a setting where resuscitation equipment is immediately available—including oxygen, intravenous fluids, chlorpromazine and diphenhydramine (antihistaminics), and nor-epinephrine or ephedrine. These measures are necessary, for convulsions, cardiac arrhythmias and myocardial infarctions occasionally occur. EEG changes indicate that the drug has occasioned toxic effects on the brain (Himwich, 1956).

Sensitivity to disulfiram varies with individuals; some tolerate no more than .06 gm., while others may require as much as one gm. It is advisable to determine the *minimal* effective dose for each person and to discontinue treatment if adverse reactions occur. Because of the slow excretion rate of disulfiram, patients must be cautioned not to take alcohol in any form (including rubbing alcohol and alcohol used in cooking or in cough medicines) for at least two weeks after the last dose of disulfiram. Care has to be taken in the concurrent use of a barbiturate since disulfiram may potentiate it. In cases of *normal* pregnancy or in cases of *controlled* diabetes, the use of disulfiram is not counterindicated (Himwich, 1956). However, persons with brain damage and persons on the verge of a psychosis should not receive disulfiram (Gottesfeld *et al.*, 1951; Martensen-Larsen, 1951; Bennett, McKeever and Turk, 1951). There is some controversy about the safety of giving disulfiram to persons suffering from liver dysfunction:

Bennett and McKeever found that those patients who became psychotic during disulfiram treatment had either liver disease or brain damage. Himwich (1956), on the other hand, does not consider cirrhosis of the liver or gallbladder disease as counterindications. He suggests that cardiovascular disease and advanced age should rule out patients from this form of treatment although there is no consensus on this among investigators. Martensen-Larsen (1953) reports he has given disulfiram, upon special request, to alcoholics with cardiac decompensation. Conservative management would also rule out patients with malfunctioning kidneys and thyroid. In summary, if one takes a conservative view—and we do—then disulfiram aversion treatment should not be undertaken with the majority of chronic alcoholics, because, with the exception of pregnancy and advanced age, one or the other condition mentioned above is frequently found among them.

We proceed to a few examples. In a very careful study Bowman et al. (1955) report that one out of 100 patients who had no prior history of cardiac impairment suffered a severe myocardial infarction as a direct result of drinking part of a bottle of ale on the eleventh day of disulfiram medication. In two other patients, medication was discontinued because of abnormal electro-cardiographic findings during the first alcohol trial. Out of the 100, 16 cases of a shock-like state occurred during alcohol trials (in two patients no blood pressure readings could be obtained for five and ten minutes). Three cases of grand mal convulsions were observed, and ten patients had definite psychotic reactions. Six of these were severe depressions. One of these committed suicide; three made unsuccessful suicidal attempts. Two patients developed schizophrenic psychoses that were not evident prior to treatment, and one developed a paranoid reaction. One patient twice had a transitory manic-like reaction.

With increasing experience over the years, reduced dosage, and improved emergency care, the dangers of disulfiram psychosis have decreased. In reviewing the literature from 1948 to the time of his report, Angst (1956) noted the following untoward effects: death, epileptoid attacks, apoplexies and other neurological side effects, among them transient toxic psychoses. Out of a total of 3,722 cases treated by 54 investigators, 82 developed psychotic reactions (2.2 per cent). Angst regarded two-thirds of these as acute exogenous reactions of the Bonhoeffer type—clouding of consciousness, disorientation in time and space, delusions, delirium, stupor, hallucinations, mood changes, dementia; while one-third appeared to be schizo-phrenic and manic-depressive states. He noted that the investigator with the greatest experience, Martensen-Larsen, had only five inci-dences of psychotic reaction out of 2,550 patients treated (0.2 per cent). Calculating the percentage for the other 53 investigators brings the incidence of psychoses up to 6.5 per cent of the cases they had reported. Angst attributes the difference in part to patient selection factors; Jacobsen and Martensen-Larsen suggested in 1949 that over-dosage might play a role. Martensen-Larsen (1953, 1951), after careful follow-up of several years since his first report, recommends now that patients be observed during the first five days of disulfiram administra-tion to investigate and treat possible side effects as soon as they are noted. He suggests a recheck every five days after the initial period.

Since there are other, safer, and more effective methods of establishing a conditioned aversion response to alcohol, we cannot recommend the use of disulfiram for that purpose. We cite the disap-pointing experience of Lemere and Voegtlin (1955), who tried di-sulfiram experimentally at Shadel as a conditioning agent. They found that the response to it was not nearly so specific, deep, or lasting as that produced by emetine. They report that it was extremely difficult to induce patients to take the pills faithfully for any length of time, even when the medication was entrusted to an enthusiastic spouse.

Chemical Barriers or Psychological Fences: Antidipsotropic sub-stances like disulfiram that produce hypersensitivity to alcohol are used to create a chemical barrier against alcohol ingestion. This treatment does not deliberately set out to employ conditioning principles or psychotherapeutic methods (one can argue that learning is involved, although it is hoped that it will be one-trial learning). Psychological factors nevertheless do enter into the situation.

Hayman (1966), for example, who has unusually high remis-sion rates* using disulfiram has a clear awareness of these factors. He

---

* Careful studies of the outcome of treatment that uses the alcohol-disulfiram challenge in conjunction with psychotherapy usually report ap-proximately 50 percent remission rates. For instance, Lemere and Voegtlin (1955) report 51 per cent for a 13-year period during which 4,096 patients were followed, but for a one-year period as many as 60 per cent had re-mained abstinent. Wallerstein (1957) reports 53.2 per cent improvement in a sample of 47 alcoholics (averaging improvement figures for a period be-tween six to 24 months). Hoff (1963) reports a controlled study in which 1,020 alcoholics were treated for over a year with antabuse showing a 76.5 per cent improvement rate, while only 55 per cent of the 484 controls showed

describes, for example, how he requires his patients to make a one-year contract for care with prepayment of fees, which serves to motivate them to come for treatment regularly, to the weekly psychotherapy, and to the alcohol-disulfiram challenge repeated at intervals as warranted by the *"attitude of the patient, (and) the current relationship between patient and therapist."* *

When considering the use of disulfiram treatment one must, first of all, withstand a temptation. It would be easy to force the alcoholic to undergo disulfiram treatment against his wishes, somewhat like the required nalline testing of morphine or heroin addicts. We are opposed to this practice on the grounds that it removes all responsibility from a patient who should be sufficiently intact to judge for himself that he must abstain from alcohol under these circumstances. At least some remnant of choice and decision-making should be allowed to persons who have that much reality contact. As an example, we cite the method used at the Altanta Municipal Court, where chronic inebriates of the Skid Row variety were given the choice between jail and disulfiram (Bourne, Alford and Bowcock, 1965). Admittedly, this may not seem much of a choice at first glance; however, when it is remembered that quite a number of alcoholics become actually quite fond of their "quasi-permanent" jail companions and the security afforded by the institution, then freedom with disulfiram versus security and jail does after all constitute a genuine alternative.**

Another undesirable method of administration, which is, as Hoff (1963) warns, very dangerous to the patient, is to add disulfiram to food or drinks without his knowledge. Should the patient then drink, he would have a serious and perhaps fatal reaction, in addition to becoming justifiably angry at having been tricked. Hoff (*ibid.*, p. 195) advocates the use of disulfiram as a means of "self-enforcement" of the alcoholic's *own* motivation for day-to-day abstinence. Hoff recommends that "ideally the patient should monitor his own daily administration of disulfiram; that is, he should not delegate the responsibility for his taking the drug (and hence for his own sobriety) to any other person. Rightly used, disulfiram is not a kind of 'police-

---

improvement. Hayman's (1965, 1963) results, admittedly for a very small sample (12 patients), resemble more nearly those of the early investigators at the time when antabuse was first discovered.

* Italics are ours.

** The study does not report how many elected jail over disulfiram.

man' but becomes an adjunct by which the patient ensures his sobriety a day at a time while he works on his problems."

It is evident that this much responsibility can be assumed only by reliable, relatively intact and highly motivated patients. In practice, Hoff's advice is not often taken. Disulfiram has been used in a much more disciplinary fashion; frequently, the spouse is charged with overseeing the program and making sure that the patient has taken the medication. In hospital settings, disulfiram is of course generally given by a nurse as prescribed by the physician. If the patient views the receiving of disulfiram as a sign that he is being cared for, rather than coerced, frightened, babied, mistrusted, or dismissed, the "gift" of medication may have beneficial psychological side-effects. How disulfiram is dispensed, how the patient understands and interprets the intentions of the one who gives him the drug, will have an effect on the patient's willingness to continue treatment and to profit from it.

Other Antidipsotropics: The foregoing remarks also apply to citrated calcium carbimide (temposil), a drug which causes a similar —though milder—reaction in combination with alcohol. It has been employed in the treatment of alcoholics in much the same way, to provide a psychological fence against the impulse to drink; it has the advantage of not being as life-endangering as disulfiram should the patient imbibe while under this medication. Metronidazole (flagyl) has been reported to produce mild disulfiram-like reactions in combination with alcohol (Taylor, 1964). Flagyl has been used only with a few patients so far (53), and remains for the moment still in an experimental stage.

AVERSIVE CONDITIONING: CONCLUDING REMARKS

It is curious that in spite of its theoretical promise aversive conditioning has found only limited applications in the treatment of alcoholism. Perhaps the hazards in the use of emetine and disulfiram are one reason. The continuing experimentation with new and safer aversive methods would bear this out, were it not for the even more curious fact that at least one recently employed drug, scoline (succinylcholine chloride),* seems to be at least as profoundly frightening

* See Sanderson *et al.* (1963) and Madill *et al.* (1965) for preliminary reports on the effectiveness of the succinylcholine-induced apneic paralysis in creating and maintaining an aversion response to alcohol.

and potentially dangerous as disulfiram, if not more so. Scattered reports appear from time to time (Kantorovich, 1929; Lazarus, 1965)* of the successful conditioning of aversive responses to alcohol when electric shock of mild intensity is the aversive stimulus. While this technique—time-honored and successful in the animal laboratory as it is—does not present any risks, it is too early to draw any conclusions about its suitability for alcoholics in view of its anxiety-arousing potentials. Perhaps if it is followed by anxiety-reducing conditioning, as practiced by Lazarus, aversive conditioning by electric shock or by any other method might benefit the patient more generally than if it is employed alone. However, it would be surprising if any method for aversion conditioning could be found, however innocuous, that does not require a great deal of time and specialized skills from its practitioner and a personal relationship with the patient of some considerable depth. Aversive conditioning makes great demands on patient and therapist. Consequently, less hazardous and difficult treatment techniques that can be used by a greater number of change-agents with a larger population of patients than aversive conditioning have found more favor.

* In a preliminary report on electroconditioning therapy with alcoholics, using low voltage EST, Hsu (1965) notes that all of the 40 volunteer subjects became anxious during the treatment and indicated that the experience was extremely unpleasant. Since they were volunteers, they maintained a positive attitude toward the treatment, even though almost half (16) discontinued before the initial five EST sessions were completed; and only 16 out of the 24 who had completed the first five sessions returned for the two recommended two-day reinforcement series. No specific anxiety deconditioning procedures were employed by Hsu after the aversion conditioning. Had this been done, perhaps more of the alcoholics would have returned for the reinforcement series. Hsu reports no bad results, other than anxiety, with this form of aversive conditioning.

Chapter IX

~~~~~~

The Group Therapies

We shall now turn to a description of treatment modalities that are primarily based on empirical and clinical experiences and only secondarily derived from theory—whether psychoanalytic or learning. These treatment modalities, varied as they are, have three things in common: (a) They draw, borrow, and adapt freely—without concern for the niceties of logical and theoretical consistency—from any promising aspect of psychodynamics, aversive conditioning, reinforcement principles, and sociological speculations. (b) They are relatively easily applied by medical and paramedical personnel and do not require additional complex technical training and equipment. (c) They are usually one element only in a more complex system of treatment and rehabilitation, since the trend has been toward consolidation of the medical, psychotherapeutic, social welfare, and community resources to provide the alcoholic with a "total push program." It is only for the sake of convenience that we discuss the various modalities in separate chapters.

INTRODUCTION

There are probably as many different kinds of group therapies as there are different leaders, different patients, and different purposes

138   KINDS OF TREATMENT

for which a group convenes. Among the main types of group therapy
are those that are primarily for the purpose of *introducing the patient to the treatment program:* to orient him to treatment procedures
and to the respective roles of change-agent and patient. Sometimes
these groups are quite large, and, often, didactic material is employed successfully (films, lectures, discussion groups led by panels of
experts, discussions by the patients themselves, discussions led by
former alcoholics, and so forth).

Then there are groups formed for the purpose of helping the
patient learn how to occupy his time more constructively. These
groups are generally called *activity groups*: the patients engage in
common hobbies like painting, music, or dancing. Other groups of this
general type are designed to help *resocialize* the patient. These groups
represent another form of activity treatment, since the patients are
usually focused around something they do together and the resocialization happens as a by-product, even though it is the major aim
of the get-together. Another activity group is based on the *follow-up
discussions,* which are designed to keep track of cured patients in
order to help them maintain and consolidate their gains.

Another main type of group therapy is the one directed
expressly at the *symptom* of drinking. A.A. fellowships provide such
group treatment as do the Synanon organizations, which provide *live-
in* group treatment run by the addicts (many of them alcoholics)
themselves. Other live-in group therapies are the therapeutic communities in which the patients and the treatment staff work together
at running the treatment facility in a mutually beneficial fashion.
In addition, there are the programs provided by the Salvation Army,
also a live-in group arrangement, and the day-hospitals and night-
hospitals, which are facilities that have been initiated by community
mental health programs.

A further main type of group therapy is the organization that
provides group treatment sessions, which use some form of *psychodynamic* model. Patients come once or twice a week in order to discuss their problems and to gain insight into what they are doing. In
psychodynamically oriented group therapies, the methods vary considerably depending upon the theoretical orientation of the group
leader and on his psychological make-up (whether he is a forceful,
dynamic, and outgoing person, or a relatively passive person who
prefers to stay in the background).

In addition to variations in the setting and focus of different

types of group therapy, there also exist different techniques for conducting the group sessions. For example, one of these is role playing.
We shall examine the various group therapies and techniques one
by one, after presenting a very abbreviated overview of their background and principles.

BACKGROUND AND PRINCIPLES

Ever since its introduction, and especially since World War
II, group therapy has flourished in the United States. Much of its
popularity and growth was due to the fact that only limited personnel were available to meet the needs of persons who were seeking or
requiring some sort of psychological assistance. Another factor in its
rapid acceptance and expansion may have been its particular affinity
to a democratic temperament—witness the development of "leader-
less" groups.

Those historically inclined will be intrigued to learn that
the roots of group therapy go as far back as ancient Greece, to the
Dionysian chorus from which arose the Attic tragedies. These day-
long performances had a mass therapeutic effect, which Aristotle
described as emotionally cathartic. Moreno's psychodramatic techniques are a modern adaptation of the same principles that Aristotle
had found operating in classical drama: the spectator finds resolution
and purification of the same emotions and burdens of guilt and shame
as are portrayed on the stage by the actors, who interpret the
conflicts of family interrelationships.

Although not all group therapy is psychodrama, the basic assumption that patients who have similar medical, psychological, or
social problems can receive benefits from one another—as well as
from the change-agent in charge of their treatment—holds for the
various methods of group treatment, whatever the psychodynamic
explanation may be. One experienced group of investigators, Powdermaker *et al.* (1953), believes that the psychodynamics by which
improvement is achieved in group psychotherapy are by no means
clear, that they probably vary with the composition of the group, the
technique employed, and the aim and leadership of the members and
the group leaders. Without prejudicing this issue, let us return to
the evolution of group therapy in modern times. One may trace
formal group psychotherapy to the early 1700's when Anton Mesmer
conducted his group hypnotic sessions in France.

In the United States, at the beginning of this century, the credit for introducing a didactic form of group treatment goes to Pratt, a Bostonian internist who treated tuberculosis patients in a classroom like setting. By 1908 the clergy had become active in psychotherapy and was attacked for its efforts by an editorial in the New York Medical Journal (1908). Later on, some time after the first world war, another minister, Marsh, took up the cudgels for group psychotherapy once again; in the process he became a psychiatrist, an effective way of dealing with the opposition. We shall describe his eclectic treatment techniques presently. Returning to the time just before World War I, we find Moreno in Vienna beginning experimental group work with children, displaced persons, prostitutes and other underprivileged. He used a stage on which they enacted psychological situations, problems, and conflicts under his guidance. Later on, when he imported his method to America, his "Spontaneity Theater" became known as the method of *role playing*. Another Viennese, one of the early psychoanalysts, Adler, was the first to use the group method of treatment with working-class people. The evolution of group psychological treatment in the United States and England was a relatively slow one until World War II, benefiting from the influx of *émigré* psychotherapists after Hitler's rise to power. It was in those days that Marsh (1935) tells of his group method: He combined his treatment with everything that contributes to the psychological well-being of his patients including art classes and dance classes (activity groups), and so on.

Among the psychoanalysts who innovated group psychoanalysis was Trigant L. Burrow, who believed that behavioral disorders arise in a social situation from problems in social relatedness. Consequently, he suggested that attempts to understand and to ameliorate these disorders can best be carried out in a group setting. Burrow advanced the notion that the socially and emotionally disturbed individual can discover how his self-image is distorted by observing others and their reaction to him in a "safe" therapy group. This concept remains one of the basic elements of dynamically oriented group psychotherapy. It is closely related to Mead's (1934)* social

---

* We shall not detail the contributions of sociological theory to small and large group research. Among the writers basic to this field are Freud (1948), Le Bon (1922), Thrasher (1927), Moreno (1946, 1934), Lewin (1939), Lewin and Grabbe (1948), Asch (1952), Goffman (1957), Bales (1950), and Sherif (1948).

psychology and to Sullivan's (1947) psychiatric orientation.

Schilder and Slavson are other psychoanalytically oriented group psychotherapists in the United States who have been instrumental in establishing activity group psychotherapy with emotionally disturbed children. Slavson's work, particularly, is based on concepts derived from play-therapy; group leaders are taught to encourage the youngsters to work out their conflicts within a controlled play setting in a group. The interactions among the children and their relationship to the activity-group therapist are carefully studied (Slavson, 1954, 1940).

Psychoanalysis with groups of adults is described by Wolf (1950, 1949). He applies the principles of individual psychoanalysis directly to group treatment using transference, free association, dreams, and the patients' childhood problems. He encourages therapy groups to reenact the original family situation in order to afford patients with an opportunity to work through and resolve their difficulties.

Every school of psychotherapy in the United States has become involved in some form of group psychotherapy. The continuum ranges from the frankly repressive or inspirational, where group psychotherapy is used reconstructively to bring about a complete change (conversion) of behavior to the "client-centered psychotherapist," who employs group techniques for counseling situations. In offender rehabilitation, school adjustment, marriage problems, vocational guidance, and chronic illness management, group psychotherapeutic techniques have come into their own. With alcoholics these techniqes have proved particularly popular and now constitute perhaps one of the most extensively used treatment modalities. We shall therefore pay special attention to the variety of group therapy techniques and functions.

Group psychological treatment has one advantage over individual therapy in that it is helpful to a number of patients simultaneously. Are there other advantages besides? Murphy (1963) answers the question in detail, and many group therapists would applaud his statement. He says that a group "can supply the warmth and cohesion of a sort of family solidarity with which the suffering individual can identify; without any change of role the individual patient can immerse himself in, and become deeply identified with, the other group members. Secondly, the group can sometimes prepare members for life by giving opportunities in the group itself to the exemplified forms of social adaptation, such as love and friendly cooperation, which later can be directly carried over to other "real life" situations. Thirdly, the experience of giving as well as receiving help is made possible by the group. There is a direct and fundamental personal fulfillment of being capable of directed love and support of other group members."

Murphy considers that society itself can be a "therapeutic community." He believes that principles of group therapy are valid and should be the model for other types of group structures, because he foresees trends in our society toward an increasingly crucial importance of small groups safeguarding individualism and human values in an increasingly impersonal and technological world.

Chapter X

~~~~~~

Educational Group Therapies

DIDACTIC GROUPS

As the name implies, the function of education group therapy is to help patients acquire the necessary knowledge to maintain or to improve their physical and mental health. In the case of alcoholics, and many others, this often means that they must learn that *something* is wrong with their way of life, *what* that something is, and *how* they can change it. A didactic therapy group can serve to acquaint the alcoholic patient with the nature and management of his disorders, including his social and vocational problems; it can serve to orient him to the facilities of the community and its change-agencies and to the respective roles of patient and change-agent in the treatment process.*

* A recent experiment by Pattison *et al.* (1965) demonstrated that groups can also function as a diagnostic device. In seeking to enroll the wives of lower middle-class Negro and white alcoholics in a treatment-orientation class, the authors found that they were only partially successful in motivating the wives to participate in a treatment program. They nevertheless considered the group a valuable and efficient device for a diagnostic appraisal of the women's life situations, their potentials, and their problems. Among those

The great advantage of didactic therapy groups is the possibility of enrolling persons with alcohol-related problems (and that would include spouse and children) as students, rather than as patients—a boon to their damaged self-esteem. To do this, group treatment can be organized as a lecture course with active student participation in discussions, questions, and in deciding the content of the "course." Included in such a course may be the etiological role of personal and social factors in alcoholism, how to recognize danger signals, what to do about them, healthy and unhealthy personality development, concepts of what is "normal," and so forth. The purpose, methods, and rules of the change-agency (or agent) may be clarified.

If formal lectures are given (on mental health, for example), then one of the most important features is to provide ample time for a question and answer period, which should be guided along psychotherapeutic principles. The questions can be written anonymously in order to avoid initial embarrassment, but experience has shown that as the students become more at ease with each other and the lecturer, an open discussion can be held. It is possible to change the formality of beginning sessions very rapidly—first, by telling the "students" that the aim is to create a democratic "seminar"-type atmosphere and that they are expected to contribute their opinions as freely as possible; second, by explaining that the lecturer will be only a stimulus and moderator for their discussions. With middle-class and upper-class patients, such indoctrination is hardly necessary any more since most are well-read and know a good deal already about how group treatment functions. With persons of lesser educational background, these explanations remain necessary.

Marsh (1935) pioneered a group program that still has useful applications in many situations. He mentions that it is important to maintain optimism and a light touch, and to impress the "students" right from the start that they are not odd, and that the subject matter is not peculiar. To facilitate a pleasant atmosphere in the "classroom," he suggests that flowers be placed in it, and that there be music available so that somebody can play the piano or guitar or using either before or after class—preferably in a spontaneous fashion (initiative for the singing should come from the students

who have used group situations to facilitate rapid diagnosis of several persons at one time are Lewis (1954), Brown et al. (1962), and Weiss (1962).

and not necessarily from the instructor). He advises that "students" should have an opportunity to select a personal project—such as greeting newcomers, arranging chairs, caring for the flowers, cleaning the blackboard, writing the lecture outline, taking roll—to give them a sense of personal involvement in the class. Marsh encourages note-taking on the perhaps optimistic assumption that it will develop powers of attention and concentration.

He considers the development of peer support and control a useful device.* The instructor may assign one student the task of aiding or befriending some of his classmates. This assistant can be an individual who has a very serious and acute alcoholic problem. In helping a fellow student, he is thereby inspired to make an effort which he might not otherwise make. Helping each other to remain abstinent is a very prominent feature of the A.A. fellowships. Another example of the effectiveness of peer support is the Minnesota starvation experiment in which extensive use was made of the "buddy system" to prevent sneaking extra diet rations. Subjects undergoing starvation were never left alone; they always accompanied one another wherever they went. This was found to be the most effective single measure in preventing infringements of the starvation diet.

Among didactic techniques, Marsh recommends the following class exercises. The preparation of the subject's family case history, which should attempt to be objective rather than harpingly critical. Group discussions centered around (a) "earliest memory," (b) "ingredients of my inferiority complex," (c) "things I am afraid of," (d) "emotional monkey wrenches," (e) "disarmament conference of the human heart," (f) "social assets and liabilities," (g) "sources of inspiration and happiness," and (h) "night and day dreams." Senti-mental as some of these may sound, Marsh notes that they do pro-vide an opportunity for a good deal of laughter. Sharing the secret recesses of his heart allows a patient to realize that he is not as sinful, morbid, or abnormal as he imagined—that he is, on the contrary, quite like anybody else.

Other devices used by Marsh are tap-dance instruction for the whole group. He finds dancing most valuable to limber up an individual or a group. Folk dancing and social dancing are used by other group leaders. Recently, improvisational dancing also has found

---

* A.A. and Synanon make extensive use of this device to give new members a sense of accomplishment and belonging.

much favor among some freelance group leaders. We recommend that more attention be paid to its potentials by professional group leaders. In a few instances, Marsh's class is conducted as an informal dramatic group; he says that thereby the shyest person is encouraged to play the part of the gayest social lion, to give him the courage eventually to live something approaching his play-acting.

Homework can be given similar to the tasks listed earlier; one might ask class members to write a "mood history" to help them discover their favored emotional mechanisms. This would be the first step in planning and developing new and better mechanisms. The same can be done for emotional problems. One may ask class members to make an outline of their love-life history, their job history, and their physical development and illness history. As a transition to individual treatment the students may have private consultations. Marsh recommends they be called "tutoring" or "coaching," in a didactic setting.

We have given Marsh's approach considerable space, even though some of it may seem overly simple and optimistic. Marsh's handling of patients in a group situation is exemplary for dealing with the psychologically untutored, as alcoholics from deprived circumstances are likely to be. A program such as Marsh's can initiate treatment and lead later to deeper involvement in personality reconstruction for those patients who have an aptitude for the more demanding forms of psychotherapy. For the multitude of persons with alcohol-related problems, a course of didactic group therapy along Marsh's lines will provide them with temporary support which, in some cases, may be sufficient to allow a regroupment of forces and consequent improvement.

Since Marsh's day additional means of stimulating group discussion and self-assessment have come into limited use in alcoholism treatment. In some instances special films are shown that deal either with specific problems of alcoholism or with other problems in living. Any good portrayal of psychological issues (aggression, obsessions, typical problems in family interactions) can be made the starting point for a discussion that leads by degrees to some of the important concerns of class members.*

* An interesting use of film in the treatment of alcoholic offenders was reported by Jacobsen (1953). The film begins with a few pictures of the Copenhagen slums from which the majority of patients of the Copen-

Schilder (1939) suggests as basic problems for group discussion (1) body and beauty; (2) health, strength, efficiency, superiority, and inferiority in a physical sense; (3) aggressiveness and submission; (4) masculinity and femininity; (5) relationship between sex and love; (6) expectations for the future; and (7) meaning of death. (We would also include here the meaning of separation and loss, which psychoanalysts believe to be particularly significant to alcoholics.) Any one of these can be made a focal point for group discussion that will quickly reach into areas of concern and conflict. The direction and freedom of discussion will depend on where the group leader wishes to place the emphasis: on problems in living that are linked to the symptom of excessive drinking, or on problem areas in general, which leave it to the "students" themselves to discover the causal connections between their troubles and their habitual ways of escaping them.

RESOCIALIZATION GROUPS

It is possible to combine the didactic group treatment sessions with informal "student"-directed meetings, either immediately following the formal course or as an alternate meeting. Kadis (1956) identifies three principal types of coordinated meetings: the alternate, the pre-, and the post-meetings. The alternate meeting is considered particularly ideal. The pre-meeting held immediately before the regular group session can serve as a warming up process for post- and alternate sessions.*

---

hagen Institute of Forensic Psychiatry come. It shows one of the patients being arrested after stealing several bottles of liquor from a shop and follows him to an appearance before a court, where he is prosecuted as a suspected alcoholic. With his consent, he is examined by the chief psychiatrist of the Institute, as directed by the courts. His career at the Institute is followed. The present writers are not aware of any other films used to depict the career of an alcoholic from the beginning of his problem to his treatment at a given institution. Two documentary films of Synanon activities have been made (Mitchell, 1965; Cronkite, 1966). We suggest that there be more experimentation with film material. For a listing of educational film material used in group treatment of alcoholics, see Mullan and Sangiuliano (1966).

* It has been the experience of many group therapists who have not formally organized any coordinated meetings of this kind, that the patients congregate spontaneously after a session and discuss their problems at great length and with vivid interest. Psychoanalytically oriented therapists believe

Since group members require considerable experience with each other before the group becomes a cohesive unit and a code of behavior is developed, it is best to delay the formation of coordinated group until members have come to know each other sufficiently to be comfortable and share in the group spirit.

Other means of orienting and teaching patients by active participation to the nature of psychotherapy consist in the formation of patient clubs, hobby groups, the publication of an informative bulletin or newspaper for the change-agency, patient-organized entertainment using special radio programs, play productions and so forth.*

Informal group sessions with emergency ward patients have been found exceedingly useful in initiating treatment and, in particular, in motivating the patient to accept the idea that he needs treatment. As described by Brunner-Orne (1959), the goal is to enable the alcoholic to recognize his need for help and to establish a positive attitude toward future treatment. By means of discussing common problems with others in the same boat (the emergency ward, in this case), a positive relationship is more easily formed and psychiatric treatment is more readily accepted—especially when the patient on the emergency ward learns that the psychiatrist can help with immediate and pressing problems.

---

that subgroups (spontaneous gathering of two or more group members) should be discouraged because they are conducive to "acting-out transference resistances." To prevent these difficulties it is preferable to make a concerted effort to organize informal, group meetings, from which the therapist is absent.

* The reader is referred to an excellent description of various organizational techniques by J. W. Klapman, *Group Psychotherapy, Theory and Practice,* New York: Grune and Stratton, 1946.

Chapter XI

Live-In Facilities

Socialization depends on interactions during which a person learns how to respond to others. The first socialization occurs in the dyadic mother-child group; later it occurs between any other individuals in an intense dyadic relationship or in an emotionally charged larger group. Thus any kind of group treatment in which feelings are strongly aroused—regardless of the treatment's special purpose—will also have some socializing influence on its members. For the moment, we shall discuss only those groups that have come together expressly to resocialize the members of the groups. Activity groups, psychoanalysis with an educative aim, learning therapies, and all the other treatment forms that have a socializing influence as side benefits are described elsewhere.

In the live-in group facilities, one may expect dramatic resocialization effects, provided that a deep sense of involvement is felt by the participants. There are such a vast number of different kinds of live-in facilities that we can concentrate only on those that have been specifically designed with the alcoholic patient in mind (thus we shall not discuss treatment in psychiatric wards or in TB sanatoria—although there are many alcoholics to be found among patients in these facilities). The major live-in facilities where alcoholics may profit from the group experience are (a) jails and prisons, or the medical facility of a given state Department of Correction; (b) various therapeutic communities for alcoholics that exist in connection with psychiatric or mental health facilities; (c) Synanon, with its expanding facilities; (d) Halfway Houses; *and* (e) the Salvation Army Men's Social Service Centers.

CORRECTIONAL FACILITIES

The "drunk tank" is *not* the place for the alcoholic to learn new ways of dealing with his fellow men. Nevertheless it must be considered a group experience in which learning takes place—that is, old and disabling patterns of behavior are reinforced. Naturally, this is not the kind of learning one would recommend. It is our position that, as part of the therapeutic effort, a more effective way of resocializing the down-and-out alcoholic be employed than incarcerating him in the city jail time after time.

Myerson (1965) declares that his research has led him to the thesis that "in general the upper and middle class alcoholics may be treated as sick people whereas the alcoholics from the lower economic classes are disposed of as criminals." The usual procedure for handling "skid row drunks" is to arrest them and perhaps sentence them to jail. Myerson contends that jailing the destitute alcoholic is symptomatic of his and his family's failure to provide for him and that the police, courts, and jails are the only agents presently engaged in coping with his problems. Not that Myerson holds that jail is a solution to be desired; *but,* he points out, it is at least a beginning.

In comparing the backgrounds of skid-row alcoholics who elected to join a work-oriented halfway house and were subsequently able to re-establish themselves in jobs and family and to maintain sobriety, with those who did not change their hopeless and copeless ways, Myerson discovered that the former had the advantage of having learned a skill early in life and had come from smaller families with fewer problems. In view of these findings, Myerson recommends that there be a greater coordination between alcohol clinics, welfare and social agencies, and the police as early as possible in the life of the underprivileged youthful alcoholic. He suggests that there be developed an educational system for these youngsters that would focus on the development of adequate work habits to help them become self-sufficient later on. He considers work-oriented halfway houses a partial solution, but only for the alcoholic who already has some work skills.

What about the rest? There exist in some communities custodial care facilities, which are more or less self-supporting and which deal in a humane manner with the problems of the chronic alcoholic of the "skid row" type. We refer to the excellent program in Los Angeles County as one instance. There the alcoholics are rehabilitated physically and participate in farm labor which gives them (a) exercise to keep them in good physical shape and (b) a sense of purpose through their concrete contributions to the maintenance of the institution. This program, substituting for the "drunk tank" treatment, depends on an institution's close and excellent working relationship with the judges who hear the cases of chronic inebriates.

In Switzerland, similar programs of custodial care are operated for alcoholics, who attend voluntarily or are assigned to them by the courts. Many of these "drinker rehabilitation" facilities are located in the countryside. Some work on the principle that persons who are not able to get along with, or trust others, find it easier to relate to animals which make fewer emotional demands upon them than do people. At these "drinker rehabilitation" facilities alcoholics are assigned to farm labor and learn animal husbandry. They learn to care about the pigs, horses, and chickens they raise and perhaps thereby learn to care for people. These farm operations have the additional advantage of making the programs partially self-supporting. Unfortunately no useful figures on the success of these rehabilitation programs can be given. It is of interest to note that neither in Switzerland nor America is it deemed necessary to have a psychiatrist directing these resocialization efforts. In one of the first and most famous of the Swiss programs, a cobbler, Burckhardt, directed the institution.*

Within correctional facilities one finds another sort of group

---

* We are referring here to Ellikon, Canton Zurich, at that time under the supervision of Forel and Bleuler. The tale is that Burckhardt had become famous in Zurich for his success in curing alcoholics. Forel, who was at the time the superintendent of the Burghoelzli, the Zurich institution for the insane, asked him one day why it was that he, the poor cobbler, did so well in keeping the alcoholics sober when the famous psychiatrist (Forel) was such a failure with them. The cobbler is said to have answered: "Sir professor, I myself am abstinent, you are not." After this dialogue Forel too became abstinent and made Burckhardt superintendent of Ellikon.

psychotherapeutic effort whereby inmates attend regular vocational and educational classes and are taught arts and crafts in a group setting. Social recognition, in the form of public exhibits of their work, is often given. Organized sports, A.A. meetings, and meetings led by various service leagues (in California, the California Service League) are additional resources for resocializing alcoholics in detention facilities. Honor camps and work furlough programs are other examples of progressive live-in facilities that try to do more than to get the alcoholic off the streets.

We recommend that planning a group live-in treatment program should benefit from the experience of such advanced correctional facilities as, for example, the Vanderhoeven Clinic in Utrecht, pioneered by P. A. Baan. There an integrated correctional, rehabilitative, and psychiatric approach is employed. *One of the central features is that the inmates* are prepared from the beginning—step by step—for their eventual release.* They must earn their own money, with which they have to pay for food, lodging, treatment, education, and so on. Necessarily, the patients (inmates) must work. The clinic has its own workshop and sells its manufactured products to the community. Life at the clinic is made to approximate life on the outside. One example: patients (inmates) are not awakened by the staff in the morning. They must get up on their own. The director, Dr. Roosenberg, explains to a newcomer that if he is to earn the money for his keep and treatment, he will have to get up and work, and if he has no alarm clock to get him up in time, he must buy himself one, since upon his release he will be needing one in any case. The treatment focus is on the future reintegration of the inmate into society. Another unusual feature of the treatment program is that its psychiatric director and 50 per cent of the treatment staff (social workers) are women. While this is probably of no special significance with "normal" alcoholics, with very aggressive, violent patients the presence of women has a distinctly calming effect.**

In the California correctional system, widespread use of group treatment within prison and jail facilities has been made; this is

---

* The inmates are either court-referred offenders or come from other prisons where they have proven incorrigible or acutely psychotic.

** Experience with maximum security wards has demonstrated that the incidence of destructive behavior is greatly reduced when female attendants are introduced.

relevant to treatment of alcoholics since the inmate population has a very large number of offenders with alcohol-related problems. Kassebaum *et al.* (1963) surveyed 4,062 members of the staffs of institutions, camps, and parole offices throughout the state; 827 of these were engaged in group counseling. They found that nearly *all* respondents indicated that they felt the *idea* of group treatment was a sound one; but *only 28 per cent* of the counselors and *34 per cent* of the non-counselors felt that the program was being carried out *as well as could be expected.* In private conversations with group therapy leaders in these institutions it was noted that the officers in charge tend to exhibit little overt enthusiasm for the results obtained by group therapy.

There is no doubt, nevertheless, that such group treatments do achieve certain express aims; namely, to facilitate a less troublesome stay in prison by helping the prisoners adjust to the frustrations that are an unalterable part of life in an institution, and to improve the emotional climate of the institution. Whether some of the other stated aims of treatment are achieved in this setting cannot be asserted with conviction at this time. For example, further research must determine whether inmates are able to recognize that emotional conflicts underlie their alcoholism or criminality; whether they learn from their peers about the social aspects of their own personality; whether they gain a better understanding of fantasy and behavioral responses to the antisocial content of their daydreams; whether individual self-criticism, self-disclosure, and personality changes induced by pressures from other group members do occur; and finally, whether a reduction of symptoms (antisocial behavior, alcoholism, etc.) results from group treatment. Meanwhile, the counselors, if not the inmates, are working valiantly to realize these ends.

THERAPEUTIC COMMUNITIES

The concept of a therapeutic community was pioneered in 1947 by Maxwell Jones (1953) in England* and imported to the United States. It has many dedicated and convinced adherents. Therapeutic communities have been established in psychiatric wards—

---

* At the Industrial Neuroses Unit at Belmont Hospital. It was designed originally to deal with neurotic, unemployed individuals and with prisoners of war.

operating on the principle of the open door—and with in-patients of various kinds, notably alcoholics. Utmost therapeutic importance is attributed to the social structure of the treatment unit, and searching care is lavished to make its therapeutic impact maximally beneficial.

Jones considers the nurses the most important treatment personnel since they are numerically the largest group, and have the greatest intimate contact with the patients. (Jones includes attendants as well as people with degrees in the social sciences under the term "nurse.") At the Industrial Unit in Belmont there is no preliminary training school for these nurses. They enter the ward and are "affected" by the special atmosphere that has been established there. The nurses are expected to understand their own part in the structure of this community and help to make the structure an integrated one. The aim is to make the treatment facility the best possible place to resocialize the asocial, the antisocial, and the maladapted. Jones and his followers propose that friendliness and stimulation are essential ingredients of the therapeutic atmosphere. The nurses must attempt to understand the patients' problems without, however, interpreting them. When a patient wishes to discuss his problems, he is referred to the general discussion group that serves the main therapeutic function. The nurses' role is to interpret or transmit the therapeutic culture to the patients. This means that she not only encourages and supports patients when necessary, but that she also attempts to get patients to participate in the various community treatment activities, which include psychodrama.

Jones believes that in our culture the role of the "doctor" is still associated with a certain amount of magic and that he is more nearly a witch doctor than many people realize. To countract this tendency, the physicians at Belmont are deliberately informal; patients call them by their first names, and a great effort is made to treat everybody—patients, nurses, physicians and other staff—on an equal, democratic footing. The physicians do not wear the traditional white coat, nor do they display the stethoscope and the percussion hammer; instead, some wear quite casual clothes. Whenever possible the physicians participate rather freely in social situations and at social functions. Informal meetings and dancing with patients at the unit socials are common. The role of equal is continued after the patient leaves the hospital and attends the ex-patients club which meets weekly in the center of London. The purpose of this informality is to modify the patient's concept of the physician in the direction of a *benign* authority and to counteract unrealistic notions about the magical powers inherent in the physician's office. The role of the patient is to learn to accept his place in the treatment community. Various social therapy techniques are designed to help this process.

The social therapies include the following: *Unit Discussion Groups.* Each day the whole unit meets for a one hour discussion on such various topics as sociological problems, the programming of treatment for individual patients, and disciplinary measures. Reports from different administrative groups are heard, and various recreational activities are planned in common. Jones reported in 1953* that on two mornings a week a discussion group is held. Its leadership is usually taken by one of the physicians or by another staff member. Problems raised for discussion are always those that bear directly on the life of the ordinary working man; for instance, should marriage partners work, should husband and wife spend their leisure together, and similar concerns. The manner of handling these large group meetings and their content is left to the discretion of the particular group leader in charge on a given day. Aside from the intellectual and emotional stimulation these discussions provide, their aim is (a) to settle the various problems associated with group living; (b) to promote patient participation in the activities of the unit, such as the compulsory workshop detail, an assignment which raises a number of strains; and (c) to bring before the group as a whole those personal emotional troubles that have handicapped individual patients and that, in a differently oriented facility, would be the subject of one-to-one treatment sessions.

Psychodrama. At Belmont the procedure consists of dramatized episodes from a patient's past life. A patient volunteers to present his problem as he sees it, in a stage-play form. He chooses his cast among the patients or nurses; he may receive help in the writing of the play. After the play has been produced, it is discussed by the patients who are in the audience. The group leader, a physician, usually sums up what has been said and amplifies it to bring out any particular point he may wish to express.

Vocational Guidance and Follow-Up (including an *Ex-*

---

* Now that Jones is no longer associated with Belmont these procedures have probably changed to some extent.

Patients' Club). Everything is done to find social and vocational roles for the patients within the hospital and in the larger community. As far as possible the compulsory workshop simulates normal factory conditions, but with one important difference: conflicts associated with work roles can be solved while the patient is still in the hospital.

In the United States, several ingredients of Jones' methods have been retained in setting up therapeutic communities. One such ingredient is the establishment of an equalitarian atmosphere; another is the transmission of the therapeutic culture from staff to patient and to new arrivals; a third is the daily discussion involving the whole treatment unit—however large it may be.* The compulsory workshop idea has not found such general acceptance. However, here as in England, patients are given fairly large administrative responsibilities, commensurate with their state of mental health and their capacities.

SYNANON

A very interesting adaptation of the therapeutic community is the Synanon** group-living experiments started by an ex-alcoholic, Charles Dederich. Synanon differs from other therapeutic communities in that it is deliberately organized along the lines of a somewhat old-fashioned, autocratic family in which members are required to perform tasks that will benefit the whole group, and in which the persons *in loco parentis* (Synanon leaders) make a concerted effort to foster an ethic of self-reliance. Instead of the mass group meeting characteristic of therapeutic communities based on a democratic model, Synanon uses more or less informal discussion meetings of six patients (ideally, three male, three female) and one leader—who himself has been addicted, but who has remained symptom-free for an appreciable length of time. He acts as moderator using many unorthodox "weapons," such as insult, criticism, ridicule, cross-examination, and hostile attack. Dederich believes that the group moderator should not attempt to convince the others that he has no problems

* See Belden (1962, 1961) for a description of a therapeutic community at Napa State Hospital.
** Synanon is a coined word which originated in a member's mispronouncing the terms seminar and symposium. Aside from referring to the whole organization, it refers also to small, informal group meetings. (See *Time,* April 7, 1961.)

himself; on the contrary, it may very well be that the destructive drives of the recovered, or recovering, addict make him a good therapeutic tool—"fighting fire with fire," as Dederich put it.

Perhaps the goading and ridicule in which the members participate as attackers and attacked help to redirect hostilities more profitably from the intangible "They" of a scapegoat society to an immediate "Him" or "Her" with whom one can deal in the group. Dederich (1958) calls it "gut-level insights."

The basic techniques are to instruct the new member in what he is to expect (he is not asked to express a clear-cut desire to get well). He must come off the habit "cold turkey," *i.e.*, without any chemical help. Withdrawal takes place on a couch in a living room of the Synanon house, and older members are always on hand to help the initiate through the ordeal. Acts of kindness may occur but never sympathy—on the presumption that if nothing is gained by a show of suffering, withdrawal will tend to be shorter than it would be in a more sympathetic setting.* Alcohol, opiates, barbiturates, tranquilizers, psychic energizers may not be used at Synanon.

Synanon supplies a home and complete living for its members by soliciting cash and foods from sponsors and business firms. The families of applicants are contacted and encouraged to contribute from $500 to $1,000.

While the New York courts are sending offenders on probation to Synanon, in California a parolee may not belong to Synanon nor may parole officers attend meetings.** The state of Nevada paid Synanon to send its members into the prison to instruct the inmates in the use of Synanon techniques. New Jersey and Connecticut also work closely with Synanon. A beginning is being made to make Synanon self-supporting by means of commercial ventures known as

---

* Members of Synanon claim that their way of breaking the addiction is shorter and accompanied by fewer overt symptoms of distress than more conventional methods; they may be right. At least one should reserve judgment until more is known about all of the circumstances. It is quite possible that most of their members are not seriously addicted in the physiological sense, since many of the addictive drugs obtainable on the black market in this country (and especially in California) are considerably diluted (heroin, for instance) and may cause only a relatively mild physiological addiction. The problem would then be mainly one of psychological dependence and could be expected to yield to psychological intervention.

** The presumption is that, contrary to their stated policy, Synanon members do obtain and use illegal drugs.

"Synanon Industries." San Francisco and a few other California cities now have filling stations run by members of Synanon.

Since 1958, the date of incorporation of Synanon as a non-profit foundation, it has treated nearly 500 addicts and persons with severe social and psychological problems. The majority have been addicted to narcotics, dangerous drugs, and alcohol. Of 860 who have come to Synanon, 55 per cent have stayed and have kept free of addiction, even though the door is open at all times.* Whatever view one takes of this, it would seem that Synanon is an effort well worth studying in more detail.**

THE SALVATION ARMY MEN'S SOCIAL SERVICE CENTER

It is only in the last years that a few systematic reports of the Salvation Army's efforts to rehabilitate homeless, unattached alcoholic men have become available. Katz (1965, 1964), basing his study on the *Salvation Army Men's Social Service Handbook* (1960) and on his own work at the San Francisco Center and the Lytton Center, describes the approach and results. The centers provide residential care to its "beneficiaries," men who are chronically or temporarily "down and out." A spiritual program is offered—chapel and devotions; the "beneficiaries" are given work to do; they participate in a psychological program—individual and group therapy; psychiatric consultation and group discussions are available; they take part in a vocational-educational program—counseling and testing. Films are shown and the help of A.A. is enlisted. Ideally, the men stay from six to twelve months. Katz (1965) was able to locate about two thirds of the approximately 300 men on whom data had been obtained during their stay at the San Francisco and the Lytton Centers. The follow-up interviews on these men indicated that they felt able to remain abstinent more frequently; their earnings increased; and the length of time they spent in institutions as well as their residential mobility, decreased. Less than half reported an improved work pattern, although the overall evaluation indicated that

* As reported by W. Winslow in the 1964 Fall issue of *The Municipal Court Review, National Association of Municipal Judges.*
** For an enthusiastic description see Yablonsky (1964). See also Yablonsky (1962), Yablonsky and Dederich (1963), Casriel (1963), Cutter (1965), and Holzinger (1965).

about 40 per cent did show a measurable increase in gainful employment. Almost half experienced an improvement in their drinking pattern. Katz observed that these improvements were highly correlated with length of stay in the program and utilization of specific aspects of the program, particularly vocational counseling. We are not surprised that he found that improvement also seemed related to motivation and to prior socialization. As a matter of fact, he discovered in the analysis of the characteristics of the men served by the two centers that while their demographic characteristics were similar to those of other large samples of homeless and jailed alcoholics, their educational level and past occupational attainments were somewhat better than those of the typical homeless alcoholic. His findings are quite like those obtained by Myerson (1965) in his studies of results of a work-oriented halfway house program for homeless "Skid Row" alcoholics. It seems that a varied rehabilitation program in a residential or semi-residential setting does offer a hope of tangible improvement for at least those chronic inebriates who have some educational and vocational resources to draw upon.

When one considers that in 1961 there existed 124 such Salvation Army Centers in the United States with a capacity of providing for 10,388 men at any one time, and that there were 57,000 admissions—80 per cent of these with alcohol-related problems (as cited by Katz, 1964), then it is evident that their rehabilitation program makes quite a noticeable contribution to the amelioration of one of the most recalcitrant sections of the alcoholic population.

Chapter XII

Out-Patient Group Treatment
for Resocialization

ALCOHOLICS ANONYMOUS FELLOWSHIPS

Alcoholics Anonymous (A.A.), a self-help organization like Synanon, is run by alcoholics for alcoholics. It is like Synanon in the dedication and enthusiasm it engenders among its adherents and in the group spirit that pervades it. In the past, members looked upon themselves as an "outcast-elite"; whereas outsiders, "squares," were viewed with some suspicion and contempt—especially the professionals, the "headshrinkers" and "headcandlers." This division of their world into two, the "ins" and the "outs," has probably served useful functions. It has consolidated their group and has inflated their self-esteem by creating an aristocracy of the rejected.

To some extent these outcast-elitist feelings on the part of A.A. and Synanon members have changed. This may be due to a greater acceptance and recognition by professionals of the contributions of these groups to an increase in group self-confidence, and to a realization that self-help and professional help are not mutually exclusive—that a great deal can be accomplished and learned by cooperation.

A.A. differs fundamentally from Synanon in that it does not provide live-in facilities and that it is run on profoundly religious lines rather than on adaptations of psychodynamic and sociological principles. A.A. is only for alcoholics, although it does provide support for the families of members through the "Alanon" and "Alateen" subsidiary groups. A.A. has a much greater membership and a much longer history than Synanon. It originated in the early temperance and social reform movements—the Washingtonian Movement, the Oxford Group, and the Salvation Army. Its fellowship comprises more than 300,000 alcoholic men and women (including active members and "side-line" members, those recovered and inactive) dedicated to maintaining sobriety through total abstinence. Founded in 1935, it numbered about 9,000 active groups in 1962, of which about two thirds are in North America and the rest in 80 foreign countries.*

Fox, a psychoanalyst who has had a great deal of experience in treating alcoholics, states the case in favor of A.A.: "Probably the single most effective method of treatment we have is that of Alcoholics Anonymous. This is a fellowship of persons who have overcome, or are attempting to overcome, their problem drinking. It is the combination of help received and, later, help given to other alcoholics that seems to be the reason for its success, although many A.A. consider that religion is its main driving force. There are no dues and all work done is voluntary. No matter what other form of treatment is used, each patient should be urged to take part in the group life of A.A. as well" (Fox, 1957).

Trice (1959, 1957), basing himself on sociological surveys of A.A., presents a more guarded point of view. He says that A.A. has been eulogized and analyzed, but seldom have its "negative instances" been scrutinized. If one considers the five million alcoholics reported to exist in the United States (and these figures are based only on known cases, not on the undetected one that epidemiological surveys would identify) it is evident that however beneficial A.A. may

* In Europe similar treatment groups are called Blue Cross or Good Templars.

be, a membership of 300,000 does by no means reach significant proportions of patients, even though the reported 50 per cent* of cures (no relapses) and 25 per cent eventual recoveries are encouraging indeed. Unfortunately A.A. does not encourage scientific verification of these figures.

Whatever the merit of their claims of success,** it is a fact that many psychotherapists think very highly of A.A. and its potential and actual contribution to the treatment of the alcoholic. Fink (1959), a psychoanalyst who treats alcoholics, points out that an alcoholic who comes to a therapy session intoxicated will gain little or nothing from the session; whereas one who attends A.A. and cooperates with the program can become a fitting candidate for concurrent psychotherapy.

How does A.A. work? The "pigeon," a new A.A. member, receives encouragement from the "old timer," an older A.A. volunteer who has taken him under his wing and permits, or rather fosters, an interpersonal dependency that replaces the former dependence on the impersonal intoxicant. With the new satisfactions of friendship and reliance upon a "sponsor" for help in self-control, the "pigeon" can begin to cut down on his drinking. In this fashion he can be sobered up enough to be approached through psychotherapy if he is willing to accept this further step. A.A. prides itself on its program of effecting sobriety by itself without the help of psychotherapy. It accomplishes this in part through religion: a spiritual force is invoked to help counteract the patient's sense of failure and hopelessness. Optimism is engendered by the example of "old timers" who no longer drink and are proof to the "pigeon" that sobriety can indeed be achieved. A.A. members speak each other's language; the social barriers between professional "helper" and "drunk" do not exist. It is easier to listen to former alcoholics than to those who have never shared the stigma nor suffered from the problems of drinking. A very important feature is the fact that A.A. members who are

---

* Some estimates are as high as 75 per cent (Gellman, 1964).

** Equal if not greater remission rates are claimed for other treatment methods (notably LSD). The A.A. contention that it is the most effective method, if not the only one, does serve to enhance the morale of its actual and potential members. Useful as this propaganda is in helping alcoholics to accept A.A., it should not be overestimated at the expense of other facilities and treatment modalities that make fewer claims but attempt to validate those they do make.

helping newcomers spend all the time necessary to protect the newcomers from drinking impulses. They make themselves available at any time, even at night, in emergencies, and wherever the "pigeon" happens to be. Another tactic is the explicit program of *Twelve Steps*, which consists of the following: "(1) We admitted we were powerless over alcohol—that our lives have become unmanageable; (2) came to believe that a power greater than ourselves could restore us to sanity; (3) made a decision to turn our will and our lives to the care of God *as we understood him;* (4) made a searching and fearless moral inventory of ourselves; (5) admitted to God, to ourselves, and to another human being the exact nature of our wrong; (6) were entirely ready to have God remove all these defects of character; (7) humbly asked him to remove our shortcoming; (8) made a list of all persons we had harmed, and became willing to make amends to them all; (9) made direct amends to such people wherever possible, except when to do so would injure them or others; (10) continued to take personal inventory, and when we were wrong promptly admitted it; (11) sought through prayer and meditation to improve our conscious contact with God as we understood Him, praying only for knowledge of His will for us and the power to carry that out; (12) having had a spiritual experience as the result of these steps, we try to carry this message to alcoholics, and to practice these principles in all our affairs." *

Many psychoanalytically oriented psychiatrists regard abstinence achieved by these means as a substitute for drinking: a compulsion neurosis. Although substituting one disorder for another may not be the most desirable outcome, it certainly can be a vast improvement and is not to be considered as a criticism of A.A. On the contrary, it is often held that an anti-drinking compulsion is a very necessary psychological defense against the drinking compulsion, an antidote to be welcomed, nurtured, and encouraged as long as it is needed.

Tiebout (1961, 1944) states that to disregard A.A. because its practice does not follow accepted scientific procedures would be a short-sighted waste of clinical materials. In exploring A.A., he found the following A.A. concepts useful in understanding how it works: First, the alcoholic must *"hit bottom"* before he can be helped; second, he must develop and maintain *humility.* Tiebout has in-

* See *Alcoholics Anonymous Comes of Age* (1957), *Alcoholics Anonymous* (1960) and *Twelve Steps and Twelve Traditions* (1953).

corporated these principles into his own technique of treating alcoholics and identifies two closely related conditions necessary for alcoholism treatment; the first is termed "surrender" and the second *"ego-reduction."* In surrender the patient says "I can't go on as I please. You win, I lose." By ego-reduction is meant a re-evaluation of the self in realistic terms and a giving up of fantasies of omnipotence and infantile grandiosity. A succinct and insightful summary of A.A. psychodynamics can be found in Hayman (1966). The psychosocial factors operating in A.A. are presented in several excellent studies: Bales (1962), Jackson (1962), Maxwell (1962), Ripley and Jackson (1959). A recent sociological analysis by Gellman (1964) who participated as an observer in A.A. elucidates how personality changes can occur when one becomes a member of a new culture such as A.A. Gellman's work is particularly valuable in pinpointing the organizational factors that serve to facilitate group cohesion and the transmission of A.A. values and goals to new members. Another participant observer study of A.A. is that of the anthropologist Madsen (1965), which presents the concepts held by A.A. members about their work.

There is no doubt that A.A. fellowships offer an opportunity to lonely, humiliated, oftentimes socially inept and certainly defeated persons to come together and find in each other sources of hope and new ways of learning how to get along with each other and with people in the larger society. The technique of public confessions relieves guilt and removes at least this source of low self-esteem. Increased self-respect facilitates relations to others; new friends can be made; new horizons may open up.

Unquestionably, A.A. can be recommended. The question is, which type of patient will accept the program and who can profit from it? A number of studies have addressed themselves to finding an answer. Generalizing from the works of Maxwell (1962) and Trice (1959, 1957), we can draw a picture of the person most likely to succeed in A.A. He is probably lower middle-class, has completed high school, had religious training in his childhood and remains open to spiritual values. His drinking is in conflict with his ideals. He has had recent reverses: loss of job, or of drinking companions, or of family support of his drinking. He may even have been hospitalized for alcohol-related disasters (accidents, illness, emotional problems). Of course, the better adjusted and more ambitious person will profit most from A.A. Thus those most likely to succeed in A.A. may well be those with resources and ties presenting a generally greater success-after-defeat potential. Acceptance of A.A. of course requires initiation into it. Trice observes that it is easier to join A.A. if one has heard good reports about it (because it gives the discouraged alcoholic a glimmer of hope, says Maxwell); if one has a definite idea of what A.A. meetings are like; if one is introduced to the meeting by a sponsor with whom one has had previous acquaintance; and if the A.A. group takes the initiative in demonstrating an active concern in one.

We have mentioned that A.A. provides the alcoholic with a substitute compulsion for the one he is suffering from. It is not surprising therefore that it is the more compulsive individual, and the one who is able to submit to authority and has a liking for other people (see Machover, 1959a,b,c) who seems to get the most out of belonging to A.A. One should hesitate to recommend A.A. to a convinced and introverted agnostic or to an atheist who prefers to invent his own conduct codes and dislikes a rigid scheme governing his life.

It is to be understood that we are talking about averages. Personality studies, such as Machover's, are based on a sample, and are not necessarily a representative one of the gamut of personalities that make up the A.A. membership; nor can such studies be expected to describe the wide variety of individual A.A. group atmospheres. In recommending A.A. to a given individual, it is useful to keep these general guidelines in mind, while at the same time making allowances for the particular circumstances of the patient that may, against expectation, be appropriate to the particular conditions of his local A.A. group.

In conclusion we once again mention Hayman's (1966) chapter on A.A., addressed to the general practitioner, with its carefully thought out referral procedures. His suggestions will be found useful by other professional and lay persons—in particular his suggestion that family members be encouraged to join Alanon (a subsidiary group for spouses, relatives and friends of alcoholics), even if the patient himself refuses treatment or is unwilling to join A.A. We concur with this principle most heartily; it is one that has been fruitfully employed in child psychiatry and in family therapy. Underlying this principle is the assumption that any improvement from whatever source in the patient's life space will reflect substantial benefits upon him and, by interrupting whatever vicious cycle that may be operating, will pave the way for "spontaneous" improvement or the seeking of professional help.

RELEASED-OFFENDER GROUPS

In some correctional facilities group treatment has been made available to paroled and to released offenders. In California, inmates have been successful in obtaining from the legislature permission to congregate in groups after release while on probation (this had been previously prevented by law) for the purpose of forming their own A.A. fellowships. At the date of writing, it is not known to what extent this has proved successful in maintaining sobriety—instead of becoming a novel way for plotting other delinquent acts, as had been feared.

Experience with delinquents who come for group treatment without being under some form of legal compulsion has been rather discouraging. Within the confines of jail or prison, attendance and participation may have been quite satisfactory. Once on their own, group members tend to evaporate. In spite of pressure from probation and parole personnel, traditional group treatment—even if it addresses itself to concrete tasks of helping the released offenders to become more effective in finding jobs, in maintaining their marriages, in getting along with co-workers, and the like—has resulted in failure and frustration unless conditions of parole or probation have stipulated some form of post-release treatment. Novel approaches will have to be found. In the California correctional system, a "halfway-house" system is shortly to be tried out. If it is modeled on the therapeutic community, or if attendance at group psychotherapy is mandatory, as it is in the prison system itself, one may expect some results. Above all, group leaders will have to exercise their ingenuity to discover new incentives for holding the released alcoholics' interest in such groups once the compulsion to attend has been lifted.

We have no specific proposals, for we hold that the most effective techniques will be ones that have been adapted to the particlar conditions of a group—that take into careful consideration its socio-cultural composition, its stated goals, its implicit needs, and its actual capabilities. We shall, however, extrapolate from general social-psychological observations of alcoholic offenders* and from the experi-

---

* The reader interested in a description of the characteristics of

ence of A.A. and Synanon with addictive personalities, in order to describe several necessary ingredients for involving alcoholic offenders in a voluntary rehabilitation program.

Such a program must first of all be exciting to its members. The excitement must come from concrete, tangible (not intellectual) events and activities. For example, A.A. and Synanon mark special events, like the annual date of abstinence or staying "clean," with anniversary celebrations; and other happenings of organizational or personal significance are officially and ritually recognized. A.A. and Synanon make every effort to applaud, to congratulate publicly, those individuals who have achieved an important first goal—a public speech, a performance, or the like. Rewards must be *concrete, visible,* and *immediately understood.* The same goes for sanctions, which should not be devoid of humor when possible. We cannot say whether the method of shaving the head of Synanon members for rule infractions comes under the category of humor, but it certainly is a highly visible punishment. The social structure of the group must be inherently rewarding. The organization must be such that its members feel it to be their own; leadership should be theirs. The function of the (official) group leader should be that of the original catalyst who makes himself unnecessary as time goes on, while serving temporarily as a facilitator between his group and the community; later, he should delegate these and other responsibilities he may have had to assume in the beginning. The program must meet the group members at their emotional level, which is likely to be impulsive, intolerant of frustration, demanding of stimulation, dependent and at the same time rebellious, in need of structure, direction, and approval. Further, the program must be geared to the social, intellectual, and educational level of the group (frequently a culturally deprived one, requiring direct, simple, and picturesque techniques of communication). We consider it essential, in addition, that the group have an actual, constructive, and respected social role, recognized not only by members but by society at large, if any significant progress in resocialization is to take place. Once again we refer to the example of Synanon and A.A., and also to the Friend's Service Committee experiment in salvaging delinquent adolescents through the "Youth for Service" program.

---

chronic drunkenness offenders is referred to Pittman and Gordon (1962, 1958).

Chapter XIII

~~~~~~

Activity Groups and Psychodrama

ACTIVITY GROUPS

There are a variety of activities, enjoyable or valuable in themselves, which can be utilized by change-agents as therapeutic experiences. In this chapter we shall consider adult activity groups as a therapeutic device. The possibilities are legion—fishing trips for patients, outings for painting or photography, hikes or a day at the beach with provisions for sports and singing. Patients may be helped to organize weekly folk dancing or to set up a bowling league or a bridge-playing club. Expressive dancing, hobbies, crafts, and vocational and educational activities in shops or classrooms can also be used. In Switzerland the Blue Cross (Temperance Society) emphasizes camping and walking in the mountains, for their belief is that mental and physical health are thereby improved and that a sense of beauty and spiritual devotion is inspired. In the United States the emphasis has more often been on arts and crafts, as for example in occupational-therapy techniques and in the work of recreation leaders and vocational-rehabilitation personnel. Social clubs for dancing, bowling, playing chess and other games can be sponsored, rhythm bands have been found to be an enjoyable activity through which patients can learn to express emotions in safe and structured ways. A specialized and sophisticated activity therapy is psychodrama and its close cousin, sociodrama. Although it is a drama activity, psychodrama is unlike other activity therapies in that it is set up only to explore psychic and sometimes social problems. It provides no conventional activity such as dancing or hiking to serve as the primary purpose for getting together.

Underlying each of the activity group therapies is an effort to bring alcoholic patients out of their isolation; to provide positive reinforcement for acceptable social intercourse; and, from a psychodynamic point of view, to provide non-destructive and non-threatening outlets for aggressive and competitive drives, to stimulate the growth of affection, and to reduce fears of intimacy and tenderness. It is expected that good experiences in activity groups will not only provide new interests and teach new ways of self-expression but also develop self-confidence for each member as he succeeds in living in and enjoying society. Activity groups have in common the fact that the therapist can at his discretion exercise control over what is going on, for he can alter the structure of the organization either to foster spontaneity or to suppress emotional expressions that are getting out of hand. The therapist can also control the nature of activities, meeting times, and the composition of the membership. In psychiatric settings such as Belmont or other therapeutic communities, conduct and feelings arising out of recreational and vocational activities are made a focus of therapy-group considerations. In some places, small group meetings are held immediately after activity groups have completed their tasks. These sessions can be relatively informal or strictly orthodox in their psychodynamic approach.

It is our belief and our recommendation that a great deal more can be done for alcoholic patients by integrating activity therapies more closely with a psychodynamic approach. A great deal of experimentation needs to be done to find the best way of administering a judicious combination of psychotherapy with well-selected activity programs for a given patient. The integrated approach required by a rational, psychodynamically oriented activity group program will depend for its success on the cooperation of a number of different disciplines. The dynamically oriented therapist will have to learn precisely what the potential benefits are that can be derived from various activities. The potentials for sublimating aggressive drives in competitive sports have already been explored, for example, but less is known about the anti-depressant effect of informal, expressive group dancing.

In discussing activity therapy, the important practical and theoretical contributions of one of its American pioneers, Slavson, must be considered. Slavson (1943) describes activity therapy with children, but the application and extensions to alcoholic patients are equally useful. Generally his activity treatment consists in simple arts and crafts activities lasting from an hour to an hour-and-a-half, followed by a period in which patients and group leaders cook, serve, and eat together. Then they clean up the room. Sometimes trips, picnics and excursions are made. The group is to be a substitute family with the positive elements a family should have, counteracting the destructive or undesirable relations all patients have had with their own families. The aim of treatment is to *correct patient attitudes and perceptions* through a new type of experience and to enable them subsequently to enter into constructive relationships. Art materials and tools are provided the patients, and they are encouraged to vent hostility on the materials rather than on each other. Slavson affirms that this is an important phase of the treatment for it serves to *redirect aggression* and, in some instances, to sublimate it (transforming it into socially or spiritually significant activities). For children and for alcoholics, this acquisition of working skills and, hopefully, craftsmanlike attitudes toward work are exceedingly valuable benefits. Another asset of this kind of activity is that non-verbal individuals, persons who are inhibited in communicating their problems—the shy, the introverted, and the suspicious—need not resort to words but can express themselves through an activity. They can be with people, but need not relate to them until they are ready.

Clearly, this method has applications to the treatment of schizoid alcoholics, of alcoholics from different cultural backgrounds, and of alcoholics who have difficulties with the English language. It also has important application to the treatment of alcoholics with low intelligence and those who come from a social class not used to intellectualizing and verbal communication.

Slavson recommends that proper grouping of individuals be made a prime concern. He has observed that a very passive, withdrawn person will do poorly in aggressive, tumultuous groups and should be placed into a more protective group. A rejected individual should not be assigned to a group where he will be further persecuted.* The group must be planned in such a way that the inter-personal relations have positive value for every participant.

A major element of the group setting, according to Slavson, is its *permissiveness*; the patient must discover that the world is not necessarily frustrating, denying, and punitive. Because of the friendly and accepting attitude of the therapist, a patient learns to relate to people. Slavson believes that treatment consists of removing the patient's resistance to the world—of melting down his self-encapsu-lation. Once this is done, social living is presumed to release self-healing or adjustment-producing forces within the patient. The as-sumption that natural growth follows therapeutic release is consistent with a number of schools of psychotherapy.

Another advantage of activity group therapy is that for individ-uals who have difficulty dealing with authority—as many alcoholics have—the presence of participating members provides a number of sources of restraint besides the therapist himself. Power is diffused and, insofar as a democratic process is exercised by the membership, the patient is subject to group rather than therapist control. Since the group is involved in real tasks of genuine interest to its members, the exercise of authority is both vital and concrete. During the group's life, the patient learns to control his impulses and to adjust to the exercise of power. To maximize the group advantage, the therapist enhances group decisions. In social clubs, for example, parliamentary rules can be put in effect, regular elections held, and activity-planning made a group responsibility. The therapist functions in a catalytic, advisory, or intermediary fashion, delegating as many responsibilities as soon as possible.

We have emphasized that it is important to foster in patients intense involvement in their group, along with progressive, self-confident autonomy from the leader, and a sense that the group is theirs. We have also mentioned that group spirit is essential to bring about a change in attitude and behavior, since it is the emotions engendered in the group that supply the motive power for change. Thus, "group-cohesiveness" plays the same role as the emotional relationship between therapist and patient in individual treatment. It

---

* These suggestions are appropriate in settings where no attempts are made to help the patient become aware of the interpersonal techniques he has been using to provoke the rejection or persecution from which he suffers. Patient selection for psychodynamically oriented discussion groups will follow different principles from those employed in activity groups.

also mediates the transmission of shared implicit values and the enforcement of explicit rules of conduct. Frank (1955) considers group cohesiveness an important support for the self-esteem of the group members, since it increases their tolerance for unpleasant emotions and their ability to function as free and responsible persons.

Aside from the methods already described, what else can be done and how may one recognize that a common group spirit is being formed? Frank (and others as well) have pointed out that one of the first reliable signs of cohesiveness in hospital groups is common griping. Rather than being alarmed at the occurrence of griping, the group leader should encourage this activity as a first step towards bringing the members closer to each other by focusing hostility on objects outside the group, and providing a common enemy. Again Frank and many others (observers of A.A. and of Synanon, for instance) point out that a particularly effective binding force is a spirit of mutual helpfulness, of belonging to an in-group, and of participating in a special and rewarding kind of experience that is not shared by everyone.

PSYCHODRAMA

In 1911, in the gardens of Vienna, Moreno began to use psychodrama with children. He asked them to act out their fantasies as though they were staging fairy-tales. He named this method "Spontaneity Theater." In 1921 the first such "Spontaneity Theater" was opened in Vienna and came into use for the treatment of mental patients. Later, Moreno brought psychodrama to the United States; the original theater was built at Beacon, New York, in 1936.

Fox* reports that the first use of psychodrama in an all-alcoholic group was probably by Halpern (1951) in an outpatient setting. At Butner State Hospital, the technique was used by Haas (1958). Cabrera (1961) has used it to prepare alcoholic patients to leave Spring Grove State Hospital, Catonsville, Md. Increasingly the method has also been used with wives and children of alcoholics.

Underlying Moreno's practice of psychodrama is his belief that the individual develops independence and autonomy only gradually. The infant must have everything done for him; the "auxiliary

* Ruth Fox, in *Encyclopedia on Problems of Alcoholism* (article prepared 12/5/1962). Available in mimeograph from the Institute for the Study of Human Problems, Stanford University.

ego," the mother, assumes responsibility for all his needs. Only as the child matures can he progress to self-care and eventually to caring for and contributing to others. In psychodrama, the patient is weaned by gradual steps from helplessness and overdependence to attitudes consonant with his chronological age. The transition is facilitated by "auxiliary egos," the treatment personnel taking part in the psychodrama, who play the roles of the original "auxiliary egos": family members and other significant persons in the patient's life.

Immediately upon the arrival of the patient, doctors, nurses, and attendants, what Moreno calls the "non-specific treatment" begins. It consists of indoctrinating the patient to his treatment role, which is to live up to the expectations of the staff by becoming an interdependent person instead of a totally dependent one. Only when the patient is adequately motivated may he enter the psychodramatic theater itself. One sign of being ready is that he can offer a sufficient reason for wanting to enact a particular role.

There are three stages in the psychodramatic theater, arranged in concentric circles one above the other, with the largest at the bottom. A balcony is built to overlook the highest stage and constitutes itself an additional stage. The lowest stage of the three is near floor level and it facilitates the participation in the entire action by patients, members of the staff, and visitors. The lighting system responds to the mood changes. Verbatim reports are made, and slow-motion pictures are occasionally taken.

Spontaneity, not impulsiveness, is the goal although some planning of the scenes by the psychiatrist or his assistant precedes the action. A key person, a member of the staff, portrays as vividly as possible some life problem to which the patient responds. Suggestions for enhancing the action will come from the psychiatrist, who is on the overhanging balcony. During the stage presentation, the patient audience is expected to learn something of the psychological meanings and therapeutic implications of what they are witnessing. Although it is not necessary that they themselves participate in the dramatic action to profit from it, they often will warm up and get onto the stage. When no one does, the psychiatrist (auxiliary ego) will ask a patient or two to take part in certain scenes, usually on the basis of the psychiatrist's knowledge of a given patient's conflicts and needs.

Many variations of this technique have been employed since

Moreno introduced it. From the dynamic point of view, its benefits can be summarized as abreaction, catharsis, and, sometimes, insight. From a learning point of view, the gains may be described as those obtained by practicing new roles, rehearsing situations that previously were difficult to meet, and mastering new interpersonal skills.

Psychodrama has been used by various therapists, notably Ruth Fox, in treating alcoholics. Some of the difficulties encountered with many alcoholic patients in the use of this technique are their lack of imagination, disinterest in self-reflection and in verbal expression, and, in certain culturally deprived alcoholics, their lack of experience with the theater. With such patients it is useful to employ psychodramatic techniques to portray concrete and immediately practical situations, instead of focusing on subtle emotional conflicts. Rehearsing how to behave at a particular job interview, how to respond to an angry spouse, how to act when one is being questioned by an arresting police officer, how to explain an error to the boss, and any number of similar difficulties will be interesting and useful to patients with little or no verbal fluency and insightfulness. Group leaders can be quite content if their patients acquire a wider behavior repertoire by means of this technique. This in itself is no small gain, for it enables the patients to choose between alternatives; and, from a psychodynamic point of view, the capacity for deliberate choice is a token of greater frustration tolerance and a beginning of improved reality testing.

Psychodramatic techniques can be applied to the treatment of the alcoholic patient's immediate family. That his family is also suffering and is in need of help, there is no doubt. Fox (1962) calls alcoholism "*the* family disease"; it affects the family at all levels, social, emotional, and physical. Jackson's (1962)* evaluation of the impact of the alcoholic on his family, and Kogan and Jackson's (1965) description of personal difficulties in wives of alcoholics can give us many leads on how to focus the psychodramatic technique on typical problems facing the alcoholic's spouse. Common in alcoholic partnerships is a rapid and unpredictable role change. As the alcoholic partner shifts in level of adequacy, depending upon his state of inebriety and social disintegration, the sober one has to adjust with considerable flexibility to the new state of affairs. A sober wife

* A useful bibliography on the characteristics of the alcoholic spouse and the typical responses of families to crisis (depression, illness, alcoholism, and so on) is provided.

may have to become the breadwinner, assume a dominant role in the family, become more maternal, forgiving, and supporting to her husband and paternal to her children; while the sober husband may have to play a feminine, nurturant role. The sober partner will have to take responsibility (even for the drinking of the alcoholic spouse), put up with the mood changes and demands for exclusive attention, and handle his or her own responses to the ostracism, shame, lack of community prescription and help in managing the relationship and the problem. Psychodramatic re-enactment of characteristic scenes in family life can illustrate these role changes and the feelings engendered, which previously have been only dumbly perceived and reacted to with resentment, guilt, anxiety, and tension. Clearly recognized, new ways of coping with these feelings and these situations may emerge. The participants and the spectators of the episode can suggest a different ending for the one its author has proposed. Rehearsing the new techniques of coping and the happier ending on stage may pave the way for more constructive dealing with the same situation on the home front.

In any event, the spouse will gain a much needed experience in role changing and role-flexibility. This will stand him or her in good stead when the alcoholic makes a turn for the better; for that too will be a stress-point, requiring a drastic change in attitudes and realignment of family responsibilities and roles. The sober wife must learn to relinquish the authority she has had to acquire and return it to her recovering husband. In the opposite instance, the recovering wife must be reinvested with her maternal and wifely functions. The readjustment to a more capable, adequate, and respectable sober partner is not easy, especially when the marriage was based on the presumption of inadequacy. The wife who has chosen an alcoholic as life partner in order to make up for her own insecurity, dependence, and hostility may well sabotage her husband's efforts at sobriety in order to maintain her faltering self-esteem. To forestall a crisis that the disturbance of the family equilibrium would bring about, psychodrama can equip her to meet his improvement. This may be achieved by a two pronged approach: (1) in dealing with some of her fears and in giving her the actual experience of being herself a capable person, she can be helped to acquire a more optimistic self-image in the stage plays; (2) she can be prepared to handle successfully situations involving forceful males, without giving up her own integrity as a person or as a female.

In some instances the spouse groups are conducted without the patient being part of it; in others the patient and his family, including sometimes the children, are part of the treatment plan. The re-enactment of typical family situations and later of problem family situations usually arouses the interest of the group members and may lead to changes in behavior and more constructive handling of family tensions.

It is preferable that a group leader allow patients the choice of problems for reenactment, unless patients run out of ideas, are shy initially, or recapitulate the same problem situation unprofitably. This is to maintain maximum patient initiative and involvement. It has been found useful to reenact the same problem situation on several successive occasions, each time reversing roles. Thus, if the situation to be depicted is one where the husband comes home late for dinner and the wife is disappointed that her efforts of having a nicely cooked meal were in vain, then the therapist may first ask one of the women among the patients to play the role of the wife and one of the male patients to be the tardy husband. After this is done, the male patient takes the role of the disappointed wife and the female patient is the guilty party. One purpose of such role shifting is to provide the participants and audience with the experience of changing their allegiance and identification; another is to increase their capacity for empathy; a third is to practice taking the other person's point of view and to learn techniques for dealing with it.

The technique of role reversal as employed in psychodrama is especially useful in changing attitudes. Aside from getting to know the opposition's point of view, the patient gains insight into how his own behavior affects the opposition (and in this case the opposition is himself, so that the learning occurs as a result of direct experience). Research on modifying speaker's attitudes has shown that it is useful to ask each speaker to espouse the very point of view which he has originally debated against. As a result, speakers come to espouse the cause they had formerly opposed. Similarly, alcoholic patients who have had problems with authority figures may come to have a greater tolerance for the demands of boss, of probation officer, and even of psychotherapist or group leader.

Another useful technique is for the therapist to invite the patient audience to criticize the performance and require that others show how the roles should have been played to make the situation as realistic as possible. Finally, the audience may be invited to speculate why the problem arose and how it could have been prevented. If the analysis of such problem situations is carried one step further (admittedly a major one) to the underlying motivations stemming from childhood and to the parataxic distortions and the unconscious hopes and fears that motivated the behavior, then the psychodramatic technique is no longer a device to practice new behavior. It then advances to the level of insight therapy and becomes an adjunct of psychodynamic group treatment.

Chapter XIV

~~~~~~

Psychodynamic Group Therapies

Psychodynamic group therapies* in their many forms are primarily focused on the achievement of insight; the aim is to allow the patients' covert feelings to emerge into conscious awareness. It is presumed, as in individual psychoanalysis, that insight will permit the patient to control his behavior and to choose between alternative courses of action.

There are many methods and techniques designed to bring this about; as many as there are different schools of psychoanalysis, varieties of psychodynamic group therapies, and group leader personalities. Common to all is the presumption that the alcoholic is driven by feelings, motives, and urges of which he himself is not aware and which he therefore cannot direct to best advantage. From a theoretical point of view, there is no difference between individual and group psychotherapy in this respect. What *is* different is the fact that in the group situation no exclusive patient-therapist rela-

---

* For a general review of the literature and a study of the mechanisms of group psychotherapy, the reader is referred to Corsini and Rosenberg (1955) and to Mullan and Sangiuliano (1966).

tionship is established; the group's processes are mobilized to bring about insight, emotional growth, and ego-development.

The setting may be in the private practice of a physician (Martensen-Larsen, 1956), in a hospital, a clinic, a prison (Margolis, Krystal and Siegel, 1964); there may be groups for men, groups for women, and mixed groups. The Danish author does not permit women to participate in mixed groups if they are aggressive and exploit the weaker males. He treats wives of alcoholics and women alcoholics together.

ASSUMPTIONS

Whatever the particular group setting for insight therapy, whether it includes the alcoholic only, his spouse, or the whole family, the expectation is that if one encourages patients to express their feelings as freely as they can—without, however, injuring each other—insight into the nature and cause of the problem is gained and mature and self-controlled behavior will result.

Ackerman (1949) contends that the immediate therapeutic influence of the group is exercised through the role changes that the members impose upon each other by their remarks and interactions. The patients, in adapting to each other, allow the therapist gradual access to a variety of layers of their personality (similar to the "working through" process in individual psychoanalysis). In the two-person psychoanalytic relationship, earlier patterns of child-parent and sibling relations are relived and their destructive elements neutralized. The dynamics of a peer group situation can be enlisted to effect a similar neutralization and correction of the disturbed interpersonal relations. In the group there emerge old patterns of behavior typical of sibling-to-sibling and child-to-parent responses —some of which may be in harmony, others in conflict. The way in which the group forms, integrates, changes, and is affected by leadership determines the channels along which these emotions are released or restrained. In a group, a tangible social reality is present. Therapy moves back and forth between the social reality and the patient's inner emotional and fantasy life. This confrontation results in a continuous clash of the patient's image of his interpersonal relations and their actual nature, as perceived and interpreted by the leader and as illustrated by the characteristics of the group interactions.

PROCESSES

Ackerman proposes the following processes as operating in psychoanalytic group therapy: (1) The development of an emotional relationship between participants; (2) Mutual support; (3) Reality testing—modification of self-concepts in the direction of a more realistic perception of self in relation to others; (4) Release of pent-up emotion (catharsis); (5) Expression of conflict, both conscious and unconscious; (6) Change in patterns of resistance and defense against anxiety; (7) Diminishing of guilt and anxiety; (8) Growth of new insight and emergence of new and more useful patterns of adaptation.

These very general statements, which apply to individual psychoanalysis as well, have been more closely specified for the group analytic situation by Ezriel (1950). He contends—much as does Sullivan (1947)—that transference reactions (parataxic distortions) occur whenever one individual meets another. In the psychotherapeutic group, the manifest behavior of the participants contains features related to their attempts at solving unconscious tensions that arise from relations with unconscious fantasy persons (parents, siblings, significant others) and from residues of unresolved infantile conflicts. Each group member projects his unconscious fantasies upon the others and tries to manipulate them accordingly. A common group tension arises that leads to responses and interactions designed to diminish the tension. In particular, each member will try to reduce or resolve that part of the common tension that corresponds to his own contribution. The behavior of members acts as a stimulus that brings out in others responses that reveal their unconscious conflicts and strivings. Ezriel presents examples of how the group leader's interpretations* of the transference reactions allows the members to relinquish immature behavior and to respond eventually to the actual situation instead of to a fantasied one.

TECHNIQUES

It is possible to employ techniques directly adapted from psychoanalysis to the group psychotherapeutic situation, provided that

* The reader is referred to the excellent discussion by Strachey (1934) of how interpretations work. An interesting explanation of the effectiveness of inexact interpretations can be found in Glover (1931).

the patients meet the same strict criteria—high intelligence, ego strength, high frustration tolerance—as patients in individual psychoanalytic treatment. Alcoholics rarely possess these characteristics; however, Ezriel (1950) states that no definite criteria of patient selection are used at the Tavistock clinic.

Many experienced group leaders have expressed tentative opinions that patients with similar disorders should be grouped together; for instance, alcoholics should be seen separately from patients with other disorders. Wolf (1950) subscribes, in the case of alcoholics, to separate treatment.

It is commonly stated that the size of the group is important and should not number more than eight or ten in this type of therapy, in contrast to the large group discussions described earlier. The length of session varies. Some writers recommend 60 minutes, others prefer 90-minute sessions. The frequency of meetings varies from one to three times a week. Sometimes pre- and post-meetings are also recommended. Some psychotherapeutic groups have a definite time set for disbanding; others are self-perpetuating. Patients may join and leave groups after consulting with group members and the group leader. Very often patients are seen in individual treatment, either as a preliminary to entrance to the group or concurrently. Wolf prefers to prepare eight or ten patients by individual analysis for entry into a group. He asks them to reveal only their first names, partly to preserve anonymity and partly to create an easy atmosphere of informality. Patients are generally seated in a circle and informed of the procedures. Group-analytic theory and technique are described to them. Wolf assures his patients that he will not expose a specific historical event disclosed to him in confidence during prior individual sessions. Depending upon the setting in which group therapy takes place (it may occur in a prison setting), the matter of confidentiality will vary, of course, and *must be explained carefully* to the participants. Patients should also be warned *not to expose to outsiders mutual confidences* heard within the group.

In some psychotherapeutic settings, a female and a male leader are deliberately chosen so as to stimulate a mother and a father transference. However, this is by no means necessary, since patients are quite capable of using each other as parental substitutes.

We have already mentioned the technique and some of the functions of using alternate meetings after group cohesiveness has been established. At these meetings the therapist is not present. They serve to activate patients who are inhibited when the therapist is present and give the patients a chance to ventilate their feelings about the therapist more freely. Such frankness can accelerate treatment by bringing feelings and transference attitudes into the open at an early date.

If the therapist welcomes comments about what has been said during his absence, patients not only will be relieved of anxiety or guilt for criticizing him, but also will advance one step along the road of resolving their inappropriate anger—provided, of course, that the therapist demonstrates in his attitude and response that he is in fact neither the punitive nor the revengeful authority figure into which he has been cast.

Transference reactions can nevertheless become disruptive to a group. One way of handling these difficulties is to return patients to individual sessions when they show signs of becoming so anxious, hostile, or dependent that they are about to flee the group altogether. Other behaviors that threaten to disrupt the group are the various forms of resistance to treatment. Ezriel mentions the difficulties posed by the silent patient. Other problem patients are the patients who try to hide and submerge themselves in the group, those who show off and attempt to dominate the group, those who engage in a great deal of time consuming and irrelevant talk, those who are contemptuous, the latecomers, those who miss meetings or upset everybody by leaving the room dramatically at inopportune moments, and those who insist that the group leader solve their problem rather than working at the problem cooperatively with the other members. All these patients demonstrate by their idiosyncratic manipulations the particular unconscious fantasies and needs that strive for fulfillment at the expense of their own stated treatment goals. To the extent that the group leader is aware of the dynamics involved and succeeds in helping the patient to recognize and realign unconscious and explicit goals—or better yet, to the extent that he is able to get the patients themselves to deal constructively with the manifestations of treatment resistances—these resistances may become useful instruments in achieving insight into habitual patterns of impulse-control and of escape behavior.

One caution is appropriate here. Patients must not be allowed to indulge in deep interpretations of unconscious motivations ("wild analysis"). In the first place, they are likely to project their own fantasies. Second, when patients *do* give correct interpretations, they may well be achieving only intellectual, and not emotional, insight. While it may sound as if they are on the way to self-understanding to hear them apply psychoanalytic terms to describe their behavior, the chances are that their neurotic behavior will continue unabated in spite of the label. In the third place, deep interpretations often have a hostile and critical implication that the patient to whom they are addressed understands only too well. Sometimes, a deep interpretation prematurely offered—although correct and not designed to be subtly destructive—can frighten the patient and force him into a defensive position, even to the point of making it impossible for him to return to the group. Therefore, many psychoanalysts and psychodynamically oriented group therapists prefer to address themselves to problems of the "here and now,"* asking the group members to bring their current difficulties to the group and encouraging them to observe each other's behavior and to report their spontaneous responses to it rather than to speculate about the underlying reasons.

It is not always necessary or desirable to handle treatment resistances by psychoanalytic techniques. Wolf suggests that picnics, outings, and participation in social events can redirect disruptive behavior and effect an improvement. One cannot expect to succeed in every instance; patients who don't respond to additional private sessions with the group leader or to activity treatment and recreational opportunities may be allowed to transfer to another group or to interrupt group treatment, with the understanding that they are welcome back in the future. In those instances where a mutual decision is made to discontinue all forms of treatment, it is very helpful to patients if the therapist requests that they return for occasional private sessions and for planned recreational activities. It has been our own experience that even exceedingly uncooperative patients are pleased to retain some sort of tie to the group leader, will welcome post-treatment attention, and are quite willing to participate in treatment-related activities—including follow-up studies. Signs of interest on the part of the therapist may bring the inaccessible patient back

---

* Caplan (1956) and Parad and Caplan (1960) in a somewhat different context, advocate current crisis treatment and exploration of current problems for wives of alcoholics (as quoted by Pattison *et al.*, 1965) to ameliorate their adaptive functioning under circumstances of special stress.

to treatment and may also consolidate initial treatment gains.

While there are considerable theoretical differences and some differences of emphasis in practice, most of the psychoanalytically oriented group therapists will agree on basic elements of group treatment. Some few therapists are primarily concerned with the historical elements that may have caused alcoholism in the patients, while others emphasize unconscious feelings common to all group members; the majority recommend a so-called "situation analysis" (Powdermaker and Frank, 1953), which focuses on the momentary behavior patterns and verbalizations that occur in the group.

In the past, psychoanalytically oriented group leaders have sometimes assumed an objective, non-directive, uninvolved, non-judgmental role, consonant with the classical procedures of individual psychoanalysis of the neurotic person. It is being recognized more and more that a different approach must be made to the alcoholic—one that resembles the methods employed in child psychoanalysis, where the therapist works closely with the schools, the parents, and plays a parent-surrogate role, expressing affection for the patient and assuming to some extent an educational function. Much can be learned from the pioneering ventures in psychoanalytically oriented group treatment of extremely disturbed children by Bettelheim (1950) and by Redl (1963). Although the situation of the adult alcoholic outpatient and the asocial, delinquent or schizoid child in an institution are not comparable, the underlying assumptions of such treatment—and especially the judicious and inventive adaptation of psychoanalytic principles to the particular requirements of patients with emotional and personality maldevelopment or arrest—deserves attention from those who would use psychodynamic group therapy with alcoholics.

It has been emphasized throughout that the traditionally neutral and passive attitude of the therapist must be modified in treating alcoholics, whether by individual or by group therapy. Active involvement, environmental manipulation, and a multidisciplinary "total push" program are required, on the part of the therapist. Even with the relatively rare alcoholic patients who are able to achieve insight from psychodynamic group therapy, auxiliary techniques are necessary. We refer to the enlistment of "therapeutic assistants" (Margolis, Krystal and Siegel, 1964) to aid with certain treatment problems—assistants such as probation officers, welfare personnel, physicians, ministers, educators, relatives, and employers.

PSYCHOANALYTICALLY ORIENTED GROUP
HYPNOTHERAPY

In a previous section we have already discussed hypnotherapy groups employed to effect aversive conditioning to alcohol. Whether used as a facilitator for aversive conditioning or as a means for suggestion, indoctrination, or investigation, the special advantage of hypnotherapy is that it can be done easily in a group setting, thereby saving time and utilizing the suggestive power of the group itself. Inasmuch as it satisfies many dependent wishes, hypnotherapy is a considerable aid in promoting the development of therapeutic relationships. Most important is its value in decreasing resistances to the awareness of conflicts and in allowing unconscious material to be dealt with rapidly and early.

Abrams (1964) believes that ventilation and abreaction can be suggested directly in hypnosis and will result in not only an intellectual insight but a deep emotional understanding as well—provided neither is repressed immediately. He contends that personality changes can be reinforced through hypnotic suggestion and that long-standing inappropriate fantasies of parental ideals, demands, and values can be replaced with realistic conceptions. We would add that these are remarkable and difficult achievements; not everybody will be able to expect such results. But even lesser gains are welcome in the treatment of alcoholics.

Among the authors who have used hypnosis in the treatment of alcoholism are Brenman and Gill (1947), Copeland and Kitching (1937), and Wolberg (1948). Paley (1955, 1952) extended his experiences with individual hypnotic treatment to group treatment of alcoholics at the Winter Veterans Administration Hospital in Topeka.* Paley conceptualizes the group hypnotherapy modality as

* Paley's work was part of an experiment in which four different types of hospital treatment methods were compared (Wallerstein *et al.,* 1957). Disulfiram treatment in a group setting, conditioned reflex treatment using emetine as a conditioning agent, group hypnotherapy (under Friend's supervision) based on a combination of suggestive and abreactive techniques, and milieu therapy (as a control) were used. It should be noted that this experiment took place during a 69-day period, plus regularly scheduled follow-up appointments over a two-year period. The ward was a semi-closed one. Dynamically oriented total activities, weekly group-therapy sessions, and opportunity for as much individual psychotherapeutic contact with psychiatric residents as the patient wished characterized the therapeutic environ-

one that provides the patient with an experience of psychic surrender* and loss of control. He believes that this might evoke
positive responses in passive, shy individuals who are typically constricted and who find it difficult to establish relationships despite
their strong wish to do so. He also recommends this technique for
individuals who characteristically withdraw in the face of provocation
and stress. He postulates that hypnotherapy makes it possible to
overcome these barriers, enabling such persons to make a psychic
surrender—both desired and feared.

Friend (1957), who was responsible for the group hypnotherapy project in Topeka, discusses the psychodynamic features of
alcoholics that make them particularly amenable to hypnotic suggestion. He reports that as a group, the passive, dependent alcoholics are the most hypnotizable. They maintain a good record of
treatment completion (six out of eight); they show the best overall
improvement record (five out of eight with known good results);
and they are the most regular in follow-up contacts (only one out
of the eight was lost to the follow-up). The more aggressive alcoholics
tend not to complete this form of treatment.

It is instructive to consider some of the psychodynamic principles that seem to have operated in the effectiveness of the hypnotherapy method. Paley (1955) reports on an alcoholic patient with
whom hypnosis was attempted to secure effective material and
abreaction. Although the patient achieved a moderately deep trance,
hypnotic treatment was at first totally ineffective. Later, conditioning
under hypnosis (Wolberg's scheme) was partially successful but did
not prevent severe alcoholic episodes when hypnotherapy was termi-
nated. It was only after the patient had moved to a distant city
and a number of months had elapsed that his drinking stopped and
that the patient became capable of holding a responsible position,
was active in A.A., and had married. After 19 months of abstinence
from alcohol, the patient visited Paley and explained that he attributed the start of his change for the better to the hypnotic experience. However, the change began only *after* an interval of many

---

ment. The project was in operation for two and a half years during which
time a total of 178 patients were treated. Fifty-three per cent of them improved with disulfiram treatment, 36 per cent with hypnotherapy, 24 per
cent with conditioned reflex therapy (emetine), and 26 per cent improved
with milieu therapy (the control group).

* See the discussion of Tiebout's concept of "surrender" (p. 164).

months. At that time the conditioning returned in full force, so that he could not look at or smell alcohol without nausea. Paley suggests that the "surrender phenomenon" occurred in retrospect "perhaps after the homoerotic threat of hypnosis [close emotional ties to the therapist] had been mitigated by time and distance and the experiences of successful heterosexuality and masculine work achievement" (*ibid.*, p. 282). He states that one of the great advantages of group hypnotherapy over individual hypnotherapy is the dilution of positive as well as negative feelings towards the therapist, since these feelings can be directed at various members of the group instead. During the hospital study, Paley thought that the patients treated him for a considerable time as an outside consultant to his hypnotherapy group: he was respected and a little suspected.

It is of interest to note Paley's and Friend's methods: (1) suggestions to facilitate surrender in safe circumstances; *i.e.*, the group was asked to experience as personal and real the parables and direct suggestions about a group of men united by a common need under the aegis of a protective and helpful parental figure (the therapist); (2) suggestions for the relief of tensions, including an autohypnotic technique for facilitating sleep; (3) suggestions to fantasy pleasurable future situations, which were gradually associated with the idea of sobriety; (4) suggestions to fantasy more constructively on a more adult level, concerning jobs, family, plans; and (5) summarizing suggestions many times repeated, that satisfaction was permissible and would subsequently be equated with sobriety, while drinking would be equated with anxiety.

Others who have indicated that hypnotherapy can do a great deal for the alcoholic are Schneck (1959) and Van Pelt (1950). Bjorkhem (1956), who worked with patients demonstrating a real willingness to give up drinking and who were still able to function in the community, reports that he attained success with 80 per cent to 90 per cent of those he treated in this manner. Popham and Schmidt (1962) compared two groups of alcoholics, one treated by hypnotherapy and a control group treated by other methods. They found that patients treated by the former had a significant increase in their periods of abstinence and showed an improvement in some areas of social adjustment. Liechti (1948) concludes from his work that hypnotherapy is as effective as a psychoanalytic course and requires less time. He observed that when hypnosis deals *only* with the symptoms, the results are short-lived. Others who have employed this method are Schilder (1938), and Carver (1949),* although they describe this technique as severely limited. Abrams (1964, p. 1164) is less dubious and attributes the equivocal findings on the value of hypnotherapy with alcoholics to variations in the practitioner's skills and to differences in patient selection and methods employed. He recommends further research and clinical demonstration to determine the effectiveness of this treatment, to ascertain which particular hypnotic technique is most successful, and to determine what particular types of alcoholics respond best. Some of this preliminary work has been done on a limited scale at Topeka (Wallerstein *et al.*, 1957), but should be expanded to include many types of patients, methods, and variations in the group composition and group atmosphere.

GROUP-CENTERED TECHNIQUES

Probably the most non-directional and permissive leaders are to be found among the students of Rogers.** In their particular brand of group-centered therapy, the assumption is made that the permissive and protective climate of the group will offer the patients an opportunity to explore themselves, to change their perceptions about themselves, and to mature accordingly. They hold that each person has a basic urge to grow, to develop, and to expand his capacities and potentials as much as possible. Obstacles to "self-actualization" are removed by the therapist's and the group's "reflection of feelings." One hopes that this optimistic view of human nature as tending toward "self-actualization" will not prove to be a myth with the alcoholic patient, whom we view as a person in particular need of growth and change.

Rogers' students recommend the following treatment techniques as particularly appropriate to stimulate self-actualization: (1) acceptance of what is said by the client, (2) restatement of the content of what was said, and (3) clarification of the underlying feeling. (Insight is not considered to be essential in facilitating the process of maturation; transference attitudes are handled like all other emotion-laden expressions and not by interpretation, as in psychoanalysis.) In Rogers' opinion, group-centered therapy has the

---

* Additional references to reports on the hypnotherapeutic treatment of alcoholics can be found in Friend (1957).
** See Hobbs (1951).

advantage of providing emotional support in a situation where the patient is accepted and understood not only by a therapist but also by a number of other group members.* Another difference between the Rogerian approach and the psychoanalytic approach to group therapy is that the former is largely supportive and of limited duration, whereas the latter is uncovering and lasts for a much longer period (rarely less than a year).**

There are all shades and gradations of the degree of directiveness and the degree to which uncovering takes place in group psychotherapy. The amount of support given varies, as does the extent to which the analysis of perceptual errors and changes in self-image are emphasized. This is particularly true in the treatment of alcoholic patients, where a great deal of experimentation with variations in techniques must be made to meet their personal requirements.

NEW DIRECTIONS: EGO-PSYCHOLOGICAL TECHNIQUES

A meeting ground for Rogerian and Freudian points of view (the one focusing on the perceptual and the other on the instinctual potentials for change and growth) can be found in the newer development of psychoanalytic theory: ego-psychology. This expanded psychoanalytic frame of reference has practical implications, leading directly to experiments with new methods of group treatment of alcoholic patients. Using concepts derived from ego-psychology, Witkin *et al.* (1959) have designed experiments that indicate that the personality organization of the alcoholic is more immature and primitive than that of other adults. In particular, the alcoholic perceives his environment in a dependent ("field dependent") fashion that resembles a child's way of perceiving. The author's findings suggest that "field dependence" is a developmentally earlier mode of perception. Persistence in a field-dependent way of perceiving reflects limited progress toward self-differentiation. This relative lack of self-differentiation may be related to growth-hampering forces

* The reader is invited to compare the client-centered method with the one employed by Synanon, where the members are well understood by each other but not necessarily accepted—on the contrary, their maladaptive reactions and their excuses for their behavior are attacked and ridiculed.

** There do exist, however, psychoanalytically oriented, short-term, group psychotherapies, in particular Kotkov (1953a, 1953b).

during early development. The authors found non-alcoholic clinical groups who have been frequently characterized as dependent (for instance obese persons, ulcer patients) markedly field dependent in perceptual situations. The most recent study of Karp, Witkin, and Goodenough (1965) confirms that alcoholics, whether in remission (abstinent) or not, remain field dependent. The authors conclude that field dependence is a stable personality characteristic that arises prior to and contributes to the development of alcoholism.

Related observations have been made by Voth, father and son, working in separate hospitals. A. C. Voth (1965) used the autokinetic phenomenon* to discover a personality variable related to perceptual processes that could be expressed in ego-psychological terms, similar to field dependence. He tested 421 alcoholics hospitalized at the Mental Health Institute, Clarinda, Iowa, and compared their ability to perceive the autokinetic illusion with the ability of 560 normal controls. As predicted, he found that alcoholics were much less able to perceive the illusion than normals. His son, H. M. Voth, in 1962 and in collaboration with Mayman (Voth and Mayman, 1963), demonstrated that subjects who experience little or no autokinetic illusion are more reality-bound; are less prone to lose touch with their immediate surroundings; and show a state of "ego-closeness" (*i.e.*, they are stimulus-bound, think concretely, and have difficulty in shifting attention from one stimulus to another). Such subjects have difficulty in imagining events and giving their fantasy free reign; they are more dependent upon the external environment for support. They are also more dependent on the environment for maintaining self-esteem.

A. C. Voth infers that differences in autokinesis reflect basic differences in ego-structure, ego-autonomy, and styles or reality contacts. The greater the ego-autonomy (self-sufficiency, imperviousness to suggestions, intransigence, reflectiveness, enjoyment of solitude), the more extensive the autokinetic illusion. The less ego-autonomy (extroversion, suggestibility, distractibility, impulsiveness, exhibitionism, dependency, sociability), the more insignificant the autokinetic illusion. Alcoholics belong to the latter category, as demonstrated by their autokinetic performance and their behavior.

A. C. Voth thinks that the Witkin *et al.* (1959) studies of

---

* The ability to perceive and trace the illusory "movement" of a stationary pinpoint of light in a dark room.

field dependence in alcoholics are related to his own findings of low autokinesis correlated to low ego-autonomy and to H. M. Voth's concept of "ego-closeness," behavioral dependence, and unimaginativeness. The implication of low ego-autonomy in the alcoholic is that the type of group best designed to help him regain his composure and reality orientation is one that is clearly structured. Precisely described, unambiguous rules of conduct and specific, reliable routines should lead to more rapid improvement because of the alcoholic's dependency, his requirement of definite points of anchorage, and his inability to cope with abstractions.

Cantor (1964) has come to similar conclusions, having also attempted to describe the alcoholic—in this case the chronic "Skid Row" inebriate—from an ego-psychological point of view. He speaks of him as a "retarded" person—a person with a perceptual and cognitive retardation that leaves him poorly equipped to cope with the stresses of adult life. The kind of retardation to which Cantor refers is closely related to Witkin's concept of field dependence, to H. M. Voth's concept of "ego closeness," and to A. C. Voth's low ego-autonomy. Retarded cognition and perception correspond to the very early developmental stages of childhood, but they may also be present in adults with chronic brain syndrome. Paraphrasing Cantor, we find that the "retardate" is a person who is unable to assimilate and integrate incoming stimuli, and who is overwhelmed by any strong stimuli. Consequently he cannot cope with his environment, nor can he change his own behavior even when it is patently maladaptive. His reactions are rigid, constricted, stimulus-bound; he is frightened by novelty; in a choice situation he behaves in a stereotyped, perseverative manner, incapable of making a decision. Cantor suggests that such a person uses alcohol to "rid himself of the tension caused by overwhelming stimuli," and that he is neither bad nor lazy, but frightened because he is helpless and inadequate.

Cantor enumerates the consequences for group treatment of this type of alcoholic. He states that individual psychotherapy is too stressful for the inadequate alcoholic. *Choices should be made for him. Medication** should be made available to alleviate tension when alcohol has been forbidden or restricted. *Treatment procedures which take advantage of the chronic alcoholic's inability to switch should*

---

* Cantor emphasizes that such medication should be chosen from a non-addicting group of tranquilizers—in other words, no Miltown!

be employed. This means a very *routinized* and *highly reliable form of group meetings.* In the group treatment sessions, the retardate can be provided with *practice in choice-making* under non-stress circumstances. Cantor recommends that it might be possible to *develop a graded series of choice situations* that would develop tension tolerance for decision-making.*

Aside from the above recommendations, we are not aware of any other applications of the ego-psychological approach to the treatment of alcoholics. These are very new developments and we expect that the future will find a number of experiments in group treatment that incorporate these and related principles. At the present time we can only recommend that this promising approach be tried out and modified to suit the differing needs of various alcoholic patients.

* The reader is referred to Hauser's work in England (personal communication), which is also based on psychoanalytic ego-psychology. He trains his patients to become more observant in group situations and to be alert to discrepancies—even to the lies which, as the therapist forewarns them, he will deliberately introduce into the discussion. The purpose is to arouse attention in the patients and to strengthen the presumably weak cognitive functions of individuals whose frustration tolerance is low—as is the case with alcoholics and patients with behavior disorders.

Chapter XV

~~~~~~

Considerations in Drug Therapy

In this chapter we shall consider some management methods, and theoretical and practical issues that occur in connection with the use of drugs for the treatment of alcoholism. The scope of our discussion is limited because of two factors: first, this is not a medical or pharmacological guide offering advice to physicians on the administration of drugs per se: second, most of the drugs employed in the treatment of alcoholism are used behaviorally—that is, in aversive conditioning—and have already been considered in Chapter Eight.

There are a variety of ways in which drugs can be employed in treating alcoholics even though the primary practice is with aversive agents. One use is in the control of the concurrent physical disorders that frequently affect the undernourished, unhygienic or overstressed alcoholic. This is a medical matter beyond our scope. A second medical management problem for which drugs are employed is in the control of the abstinence syndrome—that is, the handling of the withdrawal period when the alcoholic is not only suffering severe psychological distress, but also facing severe medical risks including delirium tremens convulsions, coma, and death. Again this medical problem is beyond our scope. What is not outside our province is the warning to non-medical change-agents to be on the lookout for withdrawal signs in their clients and to be sure that competent physicians are on hand to treat these patients before it is too late. In many agencies educational efforts are necessary to call attention to abstinence syndrome dangers. For police and jailers, a splendid motion picture, *The Mask*, has been developed for just this purpose.

A third application of drugs is in the control of psychological symptoms that are associated either with the primary personality disorder present in the patient or with the consequence of his alcoholic career and subsequent low self-esteem, depression, or other reactions to his situation and conduct. Depending upon the symptomatology and personality, a number of psychoactive agents are available for prescription, including tranquilizers, anti-depressants, stimulants, and sedatives. Psychiatrists and other physicians will be familiar with these preparations the use of which is discussed by Hayman (1966). There are two cautions to be kept in mind in the administration of any psychoactive drug for symptom control or pain relief. One is the well-known propensity for the alcoholic to substitute one dependency-producing drug for another, or indeed, to employ several drugs simultaneously to potentiate the effects. Early clinical efforts to cure alcoholism with morphine, before morphine's addictive potentials were appreciated, were certainly successful in the sense that the drinker was capable of abandoning alcohol after his regime on the new pain-reliever was begun. On the other hand the shift in the addiction hardly proved to be a cure. These days one finds alcoholics using barbiturates and other sedatives either as alcohol substitutes or as potentiating substances. The same is true for tranquilizers. Recent cases (FDA Hearings, 1966) point to the danger of a shift from alcohol to meprobamate dependency. Other drugs such as marijuana, morphine, or belladonna are also used, especially by alcoholics who are rebellious or criminal. The use of other drugs in combination with alcohol offers added danger of toxic effects to the drinkers. A number of accidental deaths as well as probable suicides can be attributed to the use of alcohol in combination with sedatives.

A second consideration in the use of psychoactive drugs has to do with psychological features of case management. Routine prescriptions, often given by a physician who may not be the primary change-agent dealing with the alcoholic, tend to be automatic;

the patient passively receives what the doctor recommends. For the alcoholic the passive role is not a new one but merely repeats an unsatisfactory relationship to authority and responsibility. The question is, can the simple routine of prescribing medication also be brought into the psychotherapeutic endeavour by focusing on it and by trying to make the patient a more active partner in treatment? Problems of coordination of care, of available professional time, of patient capabilities, and of change-agent orientation are all involved here. Certainly one can argue that the patient's interests in the use of symptom-controlling drugs are a potentially fruitful area of inquiry in a psychodynamic sense; those interests must bear a close relationship to the alcohol-using pattern itself. Insofar as the patient can be encouraged to take on responsibility for discretionary use of such medications —not just "following doctor's orders" but abstaining from use even in the face of distress—there is hope for the growth of ego strength or character that will stand the patient in good stead in relationship to his alcohol use as well. It would, for example, be ironic if one change-agent were working hard to bring the patient around to a responsible self-control (including the capacity to withstand distress without resorting to the bottle), while a physician was at the same time encouraging the alcoholic to be a "good patient" by taking a tranquilizer each day. *We recommend that there be careful coordination of services between prescribing physicians and other change-agents. It is important not only to insure that the patient does not receive prescriptions from several different sources* (as he may well try to do in the best "addict" tradition), *but also that his prescription drug use comes under scrutiny as part of the therapeutic process. Insofar as possible the patient should be made a responsible treatment partner in his use of psychoactive drugs as much as in any other aspect of his living.*

There are two other uses of drugs that will occupy the remainder of this chapter. One employment purports to cure alcoholism by permanently relieving the personality or neurophysiological disorder that is presumed to underlie alcoholic symptomatology. In this category are the use of drugs for sleep treatment, the use of LSD to restructure the mind, or the use of powerful agents to simulate death and rebirth. The other drug application is for the future rather than the present. We refer to the development of a specific antagonist for alcohol that, unlike the aversive drugs now in use, would be a metabolic antagonist negating alcohol effects without producing illness. In the treatment of opiate addiction claims have been made for such antagonists—for example, methadone and cyclazocine. No such pharmaceuticals now exist for alcohol, but it is possible that one day they may. We shall comment on some problems that may attend the use both of these antagonists and of present and future personality-restructuring "cures."

SLEEP TREATMENT

Workers in various European countries, notably France and Russia,* have employed prolonged sleep treatment for a number of disorders. This method is not particularly in vogue in the United States. It is doubtful whether it can be recommended for alcoholics who have not yet completely gotten over the effects of acute intoxication, since this kind of treatment requires medication for long periods of time with sleep-inducing drugs, which may either potentiate remaining blood ethanol or aggravate nightmarish sensations attendant upon withdrawal.**

DEATH, REBIRTH, AND INITIATION INTO THE GROUP

The use of alcohol or hallucinogens during the rites of passage among non-literate peoples presumably enhances the sense of mystery and facilitates the occurence of sought-after experiences. Examples of these practices may be found among California and Southwest Indians (Gayton, 1958; Kroeber, 1918; Spier, 1918).

* In France the following researchers have reported on results of prolonged sleep treatment: Monnerot, Ey, and Faure, (1957); Monnerot, Puech, Benichen, Robin, and Langlois, (1957). In Canada: Azima and Vispo, (1960); Azima, (1958, 1955). As far as we know, there has been no wide application or even limited acceptance in the United States of prolonged sleep in the treatment of alcoholics.

** Burroughs (1957, pp. 119–131) writes in connection with the prolonged sleep cure that the theory sounds good: "you go to sleep and wake up cured." In his experience, chloral hydrate, barbiturates, and thorazine, only produced a nightmare state of semi-consciousness. Withdrawal of sedations, after five days, occasioned a severe shock. The end result was a combined syndrome of unparalleled horror. Since the cycle of sleep and wakefulness is always deeply disturbed during withdrawal, to further disturb it with massive sedation seemed a poor practice to him. Note that he is speaking of morphine addiction not alcohol addiction; however, it is possible that similar difficulties arise with prolonged sleep treatment of alcoholics.

One interpretation that can be placed upon the use of drugs during passage rituals is that symbolic death and rebirth to a new self take place. Using this concept, Weijl (1944) sets forth a parallel between drunkenness in a technological society and the death-rebirth-initiation experience among non-literate folk. Some alcoholics are said to re-enact a symbolic initiation ceremony in their periodic bouts of unconsciousness; their wish is to affirm their membership in adult male society, a society in which drinking itself is the token of manliness and where shared drunkenness can be the initiation. More than that, the drinker may be seen as killing off his old self and seeking a new one through alcohol—inebriety being the death and rebirth ceremonial.

Although it can be said that such a parallel is a rather romantic one, it does call attention to important features of some drinking behavior. It observes not just the self-destructive wishes of an alcoholic, but also the desire for self-change and betterment, which also exists. In addition, it implies at least the possibility of finding a more satisfactory channel for the drinker's fantasies and drug-use interests.

HALLUCINOGENS

Some therapists have sought to change the alcoholic "boy" into a man by substituting for alcohol some other drug that can provide a symbolic experience capable of facilitating change but that, at the same time, is devoid of toxic or addictive consequences. The hallucinogens have been considered by a number of investigators to fill this bill of particulars admirably. Such a use for hallucinogens is by no means a modern medical discovery; American Indians themselves used peyote specifically for the cure of alcoholism (Schultes, 1940). Other drugs as well, like succinylcholine and carbon dioxide, by their effects on the respiration center, bring patients close to an enactment of death, thereby promoting rebirth fantasies and eventual initiation into desired social groups or adult behavior. Insulin treatment has also been regarded as capable of stimulating these fantasies (Scott, 1950), especially if administered in a group setting where the "set" or instructions given lead the patient to expect the symbolic (or religious) rebirth experience.*

---

* Sandison (1959) reports that as the scope of the fantasy expanded

How splendid a hope that drugs can provide such an easy solution! We have the drugs; indeed, we have had them since time immemorial; but how have they stood up to the scientific test? A number of enthusiastic reports have recently appeared on the remarkable effectiveness of treating alcoholics with LSD. We list only a few of the most prominent: Osmond (1957), Smith (1959, 1958), Chwelos et al. (1959), O'Reilly (1962), Belden and Hitchen (1963), Hoffer and Osmond (1961), and MacLean et al. (1961). For a sophisticated but not entirely objective review of the general therapeutic effects of the hallucinogenic drugs, the reader is referred to Unger (1963).*

Ditman et al. (1962) state that LSD is perhaps unique in that it prompts so many claims, not only from the subjects and patients but also from investigators themselves (who frequently are their own best subjects). They investigated these claims among 74 persons who had taken LSD; of these 27 were alcoholics. After receiving LSD, a slightly higher per cent (67 per cent alcoholics versus 62 per cent non-alcoholics) of alcoholics claimed subjective improvement—feeling better and having increased self-understanding. A significantly greater proportion of alcoholics claimed improvement as judged by external factors—income, abode, and so forth (63 per cent alcoholics versus 23 per cent non-alcoholics). They also reported fewer problems (52 per cent alcoholics versus 17 per cent non-alcoholics) and less anxiety (56 per cent alcoholics versus 28 per cent non-alcoholics). The investigators attempted to reassess the alcoholic groups three and a half years after the LSD experience, but only 16 out of the original 27 responded—four having died in the meanwhile, three from alcoholism. The investigators found that after the longer time interval, claims decreased, especially those for sobriety; for none of the alcoholics had maintained sobriety at the time the follow-up assessment was made.

---

to perceive others in the group as also undergoing death and rebirth, clinical improvement occurred. Azima's (1958, 1955; Azima and Vispo, 1960) regression therapy employs a similar rationale, for it assumes that the patient must let his immature self vanish into oblivion before he can re-emerge from regression (symbolic death) ready to embrace a more full and healthy life.

* The debate on LSD is particularly instructive regarding the difficulty of avoiding experimenter bias. The proponents of LSD insist that the experimenter must have experienced it himself before he is qualified to speak; the opponents hold that the opposite is the case.

Although the Ditman study makes no pretension to be a controlled experiment, it is nevertheless most instructive with regard
to the authors' conclusions. They do not accept their subjects' (alcoholic *and* non-alcoholic) view of what happened to them as sufficient
evidence of real improvement; on the contrary, they point out that
the problem of adequate criteria remains to be solved, and they
deplore the fact that frequently the efficacy of treatment is judged
on the *unsupported* claims of patients. Ditman's work illustrates admirably how *little* one may have discovered when one has listened only to
the experimental subject, has no outside criteria for judging improvement, and has used no experimental controls. There are, of course,
many reasons why the subject's own evaluation is an insufficient measure of improvement. His judgment is affected by his own hopes; by his
relationship to the experimenter or therapist and his subsequent
understanding of what the latter expects ("experimenter effect" as
Rosenthal describes it); and, quite possibly, by the effects of alcohol,
LSD, or what-have-you, on subject sensitivity and accuracy per se.

The suggestibility of a subject receiving drugs is a disadvantage
in research, but in treatment it can be an advantage. A number of
workers recognize that suggestion can be applied with good effect
during LSD treatment. Some Canadian therapists deliberately suggest to the patient who is undergoing LSD that he will not drink
alcohol again. Others are not so explicit but manipulate settings and
post-treatment groups to achieve the same effect of producing desired
experiences or felt states of mind. Many patients comply, as studies
(Blum and associates, 1964) on differences in LSD effects show. Their
experiences depend upon initial expectations and kinds of settings for
drug administration.

Among the environmental effects that contribute to "suggestibility" is the enthusiasm of the therapist himself. Some treatment
agents have remarkable skills in creating situations conducive to
achieving desired subjective drug reactions in subjects. Leary seems
to be one of these (see Downing's observations at Zihuatanejo, 1964).
Leary contends that the establishment of a proper relationship between
patients and leader requires that the leader himself take the drug
with the patient.* When a "loving and accepting" group atmosphere

* This is not very different from the assertion by members of Synanon
and A.A. that only an addict or an ex-addict can understand and help
another one. Leary's method insures that patient and therapist are exactly on
the same footing, since all of them are undergoing the same drug experience.

is created—as Leary has done—among people seeking just such an atmosphere, it is very difficult to say how much of a positive response is due just to the drug itself. Certainly for individuals who are in need of a conversion experience—and it has frequently been said that this is precisely what is necessary for alcoholics—the messianic zeal of an enthusiastic LSD-using, LSD-giving therapist must have profound impact.

For an evaluation of the scientific merits of LSD in the treatment of alcoholism, the reader is referred to the penetrating criticism by Smart and Storm (1964). The authors state that it is necessary to determine whether the effects of the drug are attributable to its pharmacological properties, rather than to uncontrolled variables. The requirements for assessing pharmacological effects of a drug are set forth by the authors as follows: subjects must be divided into an experimental group receiving the drug and a control group receiving a placebo. Another method is to use a no-drug control. Unless the samples are matched, patients should be randomly assigned to the control and experimental groups. Neither treatment personnel nor patient must know which he receives. Objective measures or uncontaminated ratings of the treatment outcome are required. The authors recommend that these measures be made both before and after treatment so that accurate pre- and post-treatment comparisons can be made. These requirements were not met in *any* of the studies of LSD treatment for alcoholism that the authors have reviewed. Similar criticism can be addressed to the evaluations of other kinds of drugs used in individual and group therapy, such as the ataractics frequently employed in the treatment of alcoholics.

PLACEBO EFFECT

Clinical observation and psychopharmacological research have focused with interest on the "placebo effect," the fact that a person who thinks he is receiving a curative substance reports and shows changes even though he has only received an inert substance. In some studies an active instead of an inert placebo is given, the active agent being one which produces a recognizable physiological effect but which, nevertheless, is not known to have any effects in alleviating the symptoms or disorder that the patient presents.

The importance of the knowledge of the placebo effect itself and of the variables accounting for it is twofold for those interested in alcohol treatment. In the first place, we are warned to be exceedingly careful in the design of our research when that research seeks to determine the effect of a given drug on alcoholism treatment. Improvements observed may well be due to placebo effect alone or may reflect interactions between the specific experimental drug and variables that operate to produce placebo effects. The second consideration is that the very events that do contribute to a placebo response can be manipulated therapeutically—either simply to produce placebo effect; or, perhaps ideally, given sufficient knowledge of drug-person and drug-environment interactions, to deliberately enhance the curative effects of the drug, the person, and the environment, potentiating one with another. For examples of that potentiation, one looks at the work of Schacter and Wheeler (1962), of Lyerly *et al.* (1964), and of Klerman *et al.* (1959). These studies suggest that by doing the "common sense" thing of making suggestions to the patient conform to the most probable effects of the drug, and by combining these suggestions with outcomes compatible with the wishes and personality of the patient, one gets maximal treatment results.

The moral to be drawn from placebo work is that the self-confidence of the therapist, the expectations of other institutional personnel, the behavior of other patients, and the creation of a goal-consonant therapeutic milieu must all play a role in the strategy of psychotherapy with alcoholics—whether or not psychoactive drugs are employed. It also follows that if drugs are to be employed, whether because they have been shown to have specific "curative" effects with alcoholics or because they disorganize pathological personality patterns so that new and healthier structures may be imposed by the therapist (See Lindemann and von Felsinger, 1961) during the period when the patient is confused, anxious and dependent, the therapist cannot expect to sit back and let the drug do the work. To the contrary, drug, therapist, and setting combine to create the treatment milieu; if there is any prediction to be made about the future of pharmacotherapy with alcoholics, it is that no single drug by itself will heal anyone. It is the therapist's job to potentiate the drug, and it is the drug's job to assist the healing forces that exist within the patient himself. It is also the therapist's job to use the drug to potentiate himself as therapist, keeping in mind Balint's excellent maxim (Balint, 1957) that the most important tool the therapist has, is himself.

PROSPECTS AND DANGERS

In recent years, psychopharmacology has emerged as a new field; its clinical triumphs in the development of tranquilizers and energizers have carried it far forward. Accompanying that clinical advance there has been exciting biochemical and neurophysiological research. With the advent of synthetic hallucinogens and the study of their metabolism, coupled with observations on their very dramatic psychological effects, it is natural that further hopes would be generated. These hopes extend from the clinician's wish that pharmacological agents capable of affecting the personality of the alcoholic would be found (in contrast with specific agents such as disulfiram, useful only in conditioning and control approaches); to biochemist's expectation that anti-metabolites might be found capable of inhibiting alcohol absorption or speeding up metabolism without any damaging side effects. At the present time neither of these hopes has been realized. Although tranquilizers and anti-depressants have been employed medically to manage the alcoholic in withdrawal or remission, such drugs, although useful, are by no means specific curative agents. A discussion of their use is outside the domain of this book.

With reference to the hallucinogens, and LSD in particular, there is enough evidence now available to support a strong assertion that LSD itself is not an anti-alcoholic specific. Whether it is a useful agent in combination with "organizational" therapy and psychotherapy has not yet been determined. Most claims of success have been exaggerated; but that does not rule out the possibility of positive future findings. The enthusiasm of some experimenters and clinicians is understandable; the climate of psychotherapy suggests awesome advance, the needs of patients demand it, the therapist's own humanity—or boredom—stimulates it. But there are dangers. One is that the biased and uncontrolled study, while meeting the expectation of the researcher, raises false hopes in patients and their families and wastes the time of other researchers who must repeat—with better designs—the early work. Another danger is that the potential psychic toxicity of these drugs may be overlooked. That toxicity ranges from the production of psychosis or transient social disability to one or another form of drug-dependency, as for example in "multihabituation" (Cohen and Ditman, 1962). To substitute one drug for another is a convenient way to treat alcoholics, for the patient need shift only substances, not styles of life. But to substitute one damaging drug for another is not a treatment of choice. One is reminded that morphine was, at one time, thought to be a cure for opium addiction and that, later, heroin was thought to be a cure for morphinism. Freud had his own sad experience with cocaine. We think there is a lesson to be drawn. It counsels caution in hopes, care in research design, and safety in determining psychic as well as somatic toxicity.

Chapter XVI

~~~~~~

Total Push Programs

In the most progressive institutions for care of the mentally ill and also for the care of the alcoholic, "total push" treatment programs have been innovated with considerable success. Community mental health services and alcoholism clinics under public health and welfare departments are among those who provide many of the services we term "total push." Aside from bringing to bear all of the available techniques and facilities on an alcoholic's multiple problems, total push treatment is designed to re-establish and to maintain the patient in the community and to avoid the development of the "hospital syndrome," and undue and intractable dependence upon the institution.

Total push programs involve offering patients the services and skills of many professions; starting with a comprehensive medical, psychological, and social diagnosis, followed by the formulation of an equally comprehensive treatment plan. Alcoholics receive treatment and rehabilitation for their physical ailments, their vocational and educational shortcomings, and for personal, emotional, and recreational needs. Spouses and children are to be included in some form of treatment. Patients are assigned to individual, group, or drug therapy, or to a combination of all three. They are encouraged to take advantage of auxiliary forms of treatment: patient clubs, A.A. Fellowships, and so forth. Liaison is established between employers, parole or probation officers, welfare workers, and other interested persons.

As an example of a total push treatment effort, we cite the description by Hoover (1960) of the London, Ontario, program for alcoholics. There, many acute cases are managed; if necessary, they are admitted to the hospital. Chronic repeaters are encouraged to come for treatment at the clinic. The plan for many patients is to assist them during the hangover phase by means of drugs (sometimes a combination of disulfiram and chlorpromazine) and daily attendance at the clinic for a few days. It is only during this recovery phase that drugs and vitamins (B complex) are used extensively. After a patient has recovered, total push treatment begins to deal with his specific problems. Physical examination, medical referral if necessary, psychotherapy, cooperation with A.A., administration of disulfiram or citrated calcium carbimide (Temposil) where indicated as a psychological fence to protect the patient from the temptation to drink, and the use of social welfare agencies are part of the treatment plan.

The total push program is a promising new approach to alcoholics; therefore, we shall attend to it in more detail in the section on recommendations, under the title of *"progressive care"**—a term, borrowed from rehabilitation medicine, meaning that the patient is

---

* We refer the reader to the March 1966 issue of the *American Journal of Psychiatry,* which devotes a special section to what we have termed "total push" programs, under the heading of *Community Mental Health.* We recommend for special attention Yolles' detailed and informative comments on facts and problems arising from an integrated and comprehensive mental health program. He raises, among others, the issues of hospital liaison, difficulties attendant on the team approach, and the question of fees. Foley and Sanders apply concepts of ego-psychology and crisis theory (Lindemann, 1944; Caplan, 1964) to the structure of centers in which comprehensive and progressive care are administered. They suggest that one of the primary functions of such centers is to serve as a coordinating mechanism for all of the existing community facilities, so that a "well-integrated, broad spectrum of services" comes into existence, which acts as "a catalyst in filling gaps in services which exist, and preventing fragmentation and duplication of services which lead to discontinuity of care and antitherapeutic practices" (p. 987). Ives provides a description of the Yorktown Psychiatric Center organized as a community psychiatric clinic along the lines we have indicated. Simmons discusses methods of changing behavior through the therapeutic control of the milieu, citing psychoanalytic observations (Bettelheim, 1960); sociological theory (Goffman, 1963, 1957); and social psychiatric studies (Cumming and Cumming, 1962).

treated at each stage of his career according to his needs and progress and by means of any and all of the available resources within the change-agency and the larger community itself. In the case of total push efforts, group treatment extends over the whole range of possible situations in which the patient interacts with other people in a relatively protected, graduated series of therapeutically indicated interpersonal exchanges.

Conclusion to Part Three

Throughout Part III, we have attempted to indicate what type of patient *might* be likely to be receptive to which kind of specific treatment modality. Recapitulating, we can draw a very rough composite picture to indicate an approximate (and provisional) "best fit" of patient to treatment modality. Individual and group psychoanalytic methods seem most applicable to the upper-middle class, well-informed, reflective, secondary (neurotic) drinker. Aversive conditioning by any method, and chemical means to establish a psychological fence against drinking (disulfiram, temposil), have been said to be most successful with relatively well-organized, compulsive, probably clinically depressed, and probably middle-class persons. Hypnotherapy (along psychodynamic lines) appears to work best with passive-dependent alcoholics, possibly regardless of class membership. Until now, nothing much seems to have been effective with the homeless, "Skid Row" type chronic drinker, other than some form of custodial care (sometimes in jail or prison, sometimes in medical institutions, sometimes in halfway houses) in conjunction with drug treatment and, where available, activity programs such as the ones offered by the Salvation Army Social Service Centers. The more serious the social disintegration of the alcoholic, whatever the reason, the less likely that he can be reached at present by strictly psychological means. Instead, a maintenance regime (using medications and partial or complete institutionalization) is the last resort. Exceptional cases apart,

207

the most widely applicable and presently most effective method of dealing with a variety of alcoholics, regardless of class, is by means of one or another form of "organizational therapy"; that is, group therapy.

As for the selection of patients for group treatment to enhance their therapeutic effect upon each other and to minimize group disruption, we can offer once again only approximations, based on the suggestions of clinicians who have recounted their particular experiences in their particular treatment situations. By and large, therapists have not required any particular constellation of patient characteristics in the make-up of a group. Some group leaders advocate that the groups be homogeneous, but there is no consensus on this matter. Some have found it useful to have at least a few verbal patients in a group. Other therapists recommend that passive, weak, non-verbal males be placed in a group by themselves, rather than with aggressive, domineering patients; in particular, they should not have to contend with bossy women patients. Therapists with special skills in drawing out quiet patients find that it is not impossible to mix quite freely the shy and the inhibited with the exhibitionistic, outgoing, and perhaps even overweening patients. The very fact that they are so different, yet share the experience of being alcoholic or being in some sort of trouble, can be used therapeutically by some group leaders. The same can be said in the case of persons with paranoid trends, who have traditionally been considered unsuitable for group treatment—partly because they tend to take over the group and to play at being group leader themselves. It is usually recommended that they be treated in a situation where this predilection can be handled without losing the rest of the patients in the process. But if the group leader is comfortable enough and can handle the "auxiliary" group leader with firmness and some humor, it is possible to include even paranoid individuals. Indeed, they can become very valuable group members just because they are so frequently very insightful—at least into other people's motivations.

Thus, by using special precautions or special skills, it is often not necessary to exclude certain patients that one ordinarily would not consider good group candidates. If group therapy is supplemented by individual sessions for each group member (including exit interviews, as is done in industry), one can protect vulnerable patients, modulate the aggressiveness of others, or prevent potential drop-outs from making an irrevocable break with the group.

What are we to conclude? It is evident that no dogmatic state-ments can be made about the suitability of a given patient for a certain treatment or the inclusion into a particular group. Additional, prevailing circumstances—special skills of the group leader, unfore-seen potentials of the patient, unknown catalytic effects of the inter-action—can lead to unexpected improvement or failure. Our present state of knowledge must be described as limited to circumscribed treatment situations and patient samples from which it would be hazardous to generalize. We can speak of *controlled* experiments or controlled clinical studies in very rare instances only. In most cases, one investigation is not at all comparable to the next; no wonder the results are different, even if the "same" treatment is employed (or at least a treatment called by the same name). As a consequence, we have couched our composite picture of the "best fit" between patient and treatment in a hypothetical mood. We do not believe that one should recommend unequivocally one treatment modality or another for a given alcoholic. Treatment needs and resources will continue to vary from community to community and facility to facility. We assume that within each, therapists will be doing the best they can with what they have.

At this stage, we believe it preferable to recommend two steps. One is to do more and better research on treatment. This research should try to identify in a given situation the variables that are as-sociated with such practical and immediate matters as continuation in treatment, frequency of relapses, and the maintenance of the involvement of the treatment agents themselves. The longer-range research problem of evaluating treatment outcomes over time must also be the subject of continuing work, work that carefully isolates as many potentially influential variables as the available time and methods allow. The second step to be recommended is treatment innovation rather than blind adherence to traditional dogmas when those dogmas are unsupported by evidence. The therapist and administrator should seek creative clinical experiments using new methods for selecting and encouraging patients in treatment and for assigning patients to various forms of therapy. Change-agents should not worry too much about introducing innovations, for the literature suggests that new interven-tions are quite likely to lead to positive responses, if only just because they are "new"* and tend to elevate hope and interests. There are,

* Refer to industrial studies showing that work motivation (and out-

of course, limits on novelty and invention which, if they are not set, clearly lead to institutional disruption or patient confusion. Innovation must not be tried for its own sake, but must evolve from healing goals, reasonable theoretical inferences, basic knowledge of needed safeguards, and sensible assessment of institutional philosophies.

We have raised some of the questions that pose themselves when one considers what treatment modality to apply in a given case. One will also ask at what point in the career of an alcoholic is the chosen modality of greatest use, when does it become necessary to change the approach, and what will be the optimal course to follow as the patient improves, backslides, loses interest in treatment, and so forth.

In the next section we shall deal with the most frequently encountered problems.

---

put) are increased when innovations are introduced if the workers sense those changes as being an expression of management interest. The Westinghouse studies (Roethlisberger and Dickson, 1946) are the earliest and most famous example.

PART FOUR

TREATMENT PROBLEMS
FOR SPECIAL
CONSIDERATION

Chapter XVII

~~~~~~

Motivation and Expectations

Among the most frequently mentioned problems are how to get the alcoholic to come for treatment and, once there, how to get him to remain sufficiently long to obtain benefit from therapy. These problems are usually referred to as "how to motivate the alcoholic." Another less frequently mentioned but equally real problem is that of motivating the therapist. We shall begin with the latter.

MOTIVATING THE THERAPIST

Much has been said about the manpower shortage among alcohol treatment personnel, the reluctance of physicians and psychiatrists to undertake treatment of the alcoholic, the unwillingness of some physicians to recognize that alcoholism is a medical illness that requires medical treatment. Even among psychiatrists negative feelings toward treating alcoholics can be found (Hayman, 1963, 1956); although the more sophisticated may try to disguise their distaste, which nevertheless continues to exist. One of the early studies of physicians' activities and attitudes was by Riley and Marden (1946), who interviewed a sample (10 per cent) of the physicians in New Jersey. Of these, almost one half (43 per cent) considered their alcoholic patients as uncooperative and over one quarter of the physicians

213

(28 per cent) considered them as a nuisance, unmanageable, creating specific annoyances. Another study, undertaken by the Committee on Public Health of the New York Academy of Medicine (1946), noted a feeling of futility among the few physicians who reported that they accepted alcoholics for treatment. Straus (1952, 1948) adds further evidence of negative feeling: a community survey in Jackson, Mississippi, revealed attitudes on the part of physicians that range from frank rejection of the alcoholic patient, "I don't like to treat them . . ." and "disgusted . . ."; to more covert attitudes of rejection expressed as discouragement: "the usual alcoholic has no motivation for help, is unwilling to assume responsibility, deprives psychiatric patients of care by consuming the therapist's time in fruitless efforts." Another, similar feeling is expressed as the inability to do very much for the patient: ". . . my general feeling is a sympathetic one but I realize that I can offer little treatment to him." Physicians tend to categorize alcoholic patients as "uncooperative." (E. Blum, 1957)

By uncooperative may be meant that the patient pays poorly or not at all, aside from his other failings such as tardiness, neglecting to follow doctor's instructions, and dropping out of treatment before it is completed. An outspoken picture of physicians' attitudes is painted by Abrams and McCourt (1964). These authors admit that, "We were not immune to some of the attitudes we attributed to the physicians in the emergency ward. Feelings of hopelessness, anger, and disgust were not uncommon in ourselves in dealing with the homeless, jobless, Skid Row alcoholic. Seeing a comatose, unshaven, lousy, disheveled, dirty patient reeking of alcohol and vomitus can damage a doctor's therapeutic optimism. The antagonistic, rebellious combative, acutely intoxicated alcoholic, who (as happened to one of us) shows his contempt and anger by urinating on anyone who approaches, quickly makes a doctor doubt his desire to treat any alcoholic."

In spite of these feelings, the authors were able to treat alcoholics effectively. They attribute this to several factors, one of which was the enthusiasm aroused by the approach that was being tried out. Second was the fact that the psychiatrists were attempting to outdo each other in getting the patients to return to the treatment facility. Third, the interest in the alcoholic patient increased as the psychiatrists became aware of the serious social problems of the alcoholic and, as a result, became more eager to help. Instead of passing moral judgment, they looked upon the patients as sick, rather than as "bums." Finally, the physicians were reimbursed for their efforts (their salaries came from a grant which supported the study). The authors state, "Through such an arrangement we probably had a feeling of responsibility for the alcoholic and avoided the resentment of feeling insufficiently rewarded for the effort."

Let us consider one by one the difficulties encountered in treating alcoholics. As we have shown, one of the great obstacles in treating uncooperative patients in general is that they fail to pay their bills. We believe that many more treatment personnel would become available if this problem could be alleviated. The solution is not far to find: it requires simply that private physicians and professionals in appropriate specialties be reimbursed by public funds for the treatment of impecunious patients, and not only those whose problems are associated with alcohol use. Such a reimbursement scheme has found acceptance among physicians in San Mateo County, California, where it was found that outpatient psychiatric treatment was costing as much in the public-health facility per hour as private care would have cost. Consequently, it was deemed advantageous from the point of view of the relationship with the medical community and from practical considerations (staff limitations and space limitations at the facility) to make a contract with private psychiatrists for the care of clinic patients. In this way patients eligible for county psychiatric outpatient treatment could be referred to psychiatrists within their own community, who would treat them at their regular fee, payment of which was guaranteed by the county (Yolles, 1966). This scheme has been in effect and has been working to the satisfaction of all concerned for several years. There is no reason why a similar scheme cannot be adapted for the care of "uncooperative" alcoholic patients. As Yolles (1966) observes, psychiatrists in private practice are entering into contracts with public agencies to provide direct patient care. He mentions the Kerr-Mills Act, which provides for the services of individual psychiatrists to indigent patients (at present six visits are reimbursed) under a contractual arrangement with welfare departments, similar to the one we have described for San Mateo County, and the one that has come into existence in Texas as well.

The question of fees leads us immediately into the problem of medical services for individuals unable to pay for their care, primarily a matter of the economic administration of medical services. It cannot be divorced from a consideration of treatment as such, since there is no treatment possible unless there are trained professionals willing to

undertake it. Among the Western countries, the United States probably has one of the more backward programs of public medical care.
Viewed from the standpoint of the provision of services to the needy
(in psychological and economic terms), the several efforts that have
been made—county hospitals, group health programs, health insurance,
and the like—are all inadequate. (R. Blum, 1964) For models of
more adequate medical care programs, the reader is referred to the
English National Health Service; or in Canada, the Saskatchewan
program. As long as the medical profession in the United States
remains adamant in its stand against any similar provisions of medical
care for the general public, it is unlikely that those alcoholic patients
who need treatment most desperately will be reached. With the passage of Medicare legislation in 1965 providing services to citizens
over 65, the United States made a great step forward. Whether there
will be further progress toward insuring care for all, regardless of age,
remains to be seen.

What about other difficulties facing change-agents; for instance,
what about the feelings of futility and hopelessness engendered in so
many? We suggest several remedies that will provide at least a certain
bulwark against giving up so easily. One of these is additional training. This would include learning more about alcoholism; and, in
particular, learning that this "disease" counts among its victims relatively stable, even prosperous and respectably employed persons from
many walks of life—not just the irresponsible derelict, as a number
of physicians tend to believe. (See Blane *et al.* [1964] for a description
of the extent and the consequences of non-recognition of alcoholic
patients in medical practice.)

Additional training would also include skills in recognizing alcoholism in its early stages, when social and psychological disintegration
have not yet taken their toll. This means that physicians must become
alert to the possibility that alcoholism is a concurrent and complicating factor in many diseases and accidents other than those that are
obvious, as in the case of patients with a cirrhotic liver, gastritis, or
the Saturday-night syndrome of head injury or knife wound. As the
review of the literature and our own work with uncooperative patients
indicate (E. Blum, 1958), the medical schools' curricula and the
post-graduate alcoholism workshops that address themselves to this
very necessary task have so far reached only a few practitioners.
Early recognition and treatment of the more promising alcoholic
victim is a way of combatting the negative attitude of change-agents

by demonstrating that, given favorable conditions, alcoholism can be successfully treated. An exchange of views with experienced therapists will often serve to bolster the morale of personnel who have not yet had the opportunity to follow an alcoholic patient long enough to obtain any results. Personal reactions of therapists to their alcoholic patients have not been widely discussed in the literature, and so the beginner may not realize that there are indeed rewards if therapist and patient manage to work long enough together to overcome the first major hurdles.

Another way of improving therapist morale is to set realistic treatment goals, as we have recommended earlier. Psychoanalysts have commented that "treatment failure" is a blow to the therapist's pride; patients with "incurable" disease, chronic patients, even dying patients inspire many physicians to flee rather than to meet the challenge and the eventual defeat. Not many therapists are as unashamed to voice such sentiments as the one quoted by Fink (1959), who explained to an alcoholic patient whom he refused to treat: "I never had a failure and I don't intend to have one now!" Nevertheless, underlying many a more modest rationalization for excluding alcoholics from treatment is the fear of receiving a wound to the self-esteem. It must be added that this fear is well grounded in the fact that alcoholic patients—as well as any other patients with deep self-distrust and a bent for self- and world-destruction—test and frustrate their therapist, challenge him, attempt to provoke him to punish and reject them. The therapist must be proven to be as "bad" and as much a "failure" as the patient feels himself to be. It does not help the much tried therapist to tell himself that such behavior in the patient precisely reflects his illness and is as much a symptom thereof as any other more acceptable one.

What does help—and what is actually practiced in modern treatment facilities—is to deliberately support therapists by means of all the morale-building devices known to industry, administrative science, and psychology. What has been recommended in connection with creating a therapeutic group atmosphere for the benefit of patients holds for the therapist as well. Aside from morale factors inherent in the administrative structure of the treatment facility, the staff should be remunerated at a rate commensurate with the effort they have to make and adequate to bolster their self-esteem. In addition, an in-service training program should focus upon encouraging therapists to share their treatment experiences, to take a dispassionate view of the success-failure issue, to adopt instead an attitude of curiosity about their patients, to make learning about another human being the major personal gain that can be derived from treatment. The rewards should not come from getting the alcoholic to do something or to be something different from what he is but rather from the pleasure of a deeper understanding achieved in the joint venture. The administrative task is to bring about an atmosphere in which creative work can be done by staff and patients.

As we have proposed, the therapist himself is the most important medicine in the treatment of the patient; therefore, his well-being must be given prime consideration. Nor should it be forgotten that financial security, job security, and self-esteem are only three among the factors in high employee morale—perhaps not even the most important. Curiosity, novelty-seeking, love of adventure, dedication to a cause are motives that have prompted a great deal of enthusiastic perseverance and self-sacrifice. Effective administration will attempt to enlist these. Above all, boredom and stultifying routines must be avoided both in the treatment itself and in the management of the staff. Therefore, it is essential that full administrative and financial support be given to innovations, to innovators, to experimentation, and to research. Let the treatment of alcoholism become part of a socially significant and pioneering effort; the problem of motivating those who implement it will vanish. We recommend that from the highest levels on down, the fight against alcoholism be made prestigeful, remunerative, and exciting.

MOTIVATING THE PATIENT

A treatment problem of a different order is motivating the patient. In the past, it was thought that in order to help a patient he must want help. Traditionally, this meant that the patient must come of his own accord to the change-agent and convince him that he was indeed desirous of doing something about his problem. It is our opinion, shared by a number of others, that this definition of patient motivation serves as an effective barrier, if not a clever device, for keeping undesirable patients out of the treatment facility. The myth that only a patient so motivated can profit from treatment is a self-perpetuating one, a self-fulfilling prophecy. Since supposedly "unmotivated" patients are not seen by the change-agent, the change-agent never needs to test the validity of his assumption that they cannot be helped.

There are many therapists who refuse to accept alcoholics who are under some form of compulsion when they seek treatment (either from a probation or parole officer, from a judge, wife, or employer). Quite recently, Sterne and Pittman (1965) surveyed a number of welfare institutions, hospitals, and agencies in St. Louis. They interviewed the personnel about their attitudes toward policies and alcoholism treatment, paying particular attention to attitudes toward patient motivation. They found that change-agents by and large still consider motivation a prerequisite for treatment; indeed, one third or more of the institutions surveyed specify it as an eligibility requirement. Evidence of motivation is found in "(1) *Current behavior in relation to alcoholism,* including admission of the problem, indicating the desire to do something about it, taking the initiative in seeking treatment or in joining a sobriety-oriented organization, performance in treatment, and abatement or cessation of drinking. (2) *Socially approved concurrent behavior* in the areas of employment, family relations and personal grooming. (3) *Past behaviors or present attributes suggestive of personal resources* such as drinking history, occupational history, education, current level of physical and mental functioning, and capacity for insight. (4) *The social situation in which the alcoholic finds himself,* including the actual and perceived accessibility of various sources of interpersonal support in the form of responsive treatment agents or Alcoholics Anonymous personnel, and acceptance by family and friends. . . ."

Although not all respondents required all of these attributes and assets (the first category being the most popular), it is apparent that if these are used as selection criteria, most of the seriously disabled alcoholics are ruled out from treatment on the grounds that they cannot profit from it. The investigators suggest that many of the personnel they interviewed regard motivation as a static "given," subject to neither change nor influence and on a par with will power—this attitude effectively absolves the change-agent of any responsibility toward the alcoholic. Such an orientation on the part of treatment personnel is branded by the investigators as "moralistic"; they regard the proviso that patients must be motivated as a frequent "source of institutional and professional blockage in the treatment of alcoholics." Fortunately, reports in the literature are multiplying that spell the doom of the "patient-motivation" folklore.

The efforts of treating alcoholics in various industrial settings have done much to dispel the motivation criterion. Credit for this should go among others to Pfeffer (1958), a psychoanalyst, who was director of the Consultation Clinic for Alcoholism sponsored in 1952 by the Consolidated Edison Company of New York, and located at the University Hospital of New York University—Bellevue Medical Center. The Consolidated Edison Company procedure in alcoholism has proved a very effective means not only of recognizing employees with a drinking problem early in their careers but also of rehabilitating them.

The basis of the procedure is a firm, judicious probation policy. Probation is tentatively set at one year, with the understanding that it is really for an indefinite period. During the time that an employee is on probationary status, he may be denied increases in pay (for a year) as an incentive for his rehabilitation. If the employee relapses after the one-year probationary period, his case comes under immediate review. The patient is referred to the clinic, with his consent, by the medical department of the company. He pays the cost of his own clinic visit, even though he comes under what might be considered "duress." Pfeffer considers that probation is an extremely effective threat in motivating the desire for help because of the importance employment has for the particular group of alcoholics who are referred. The significance of work is not only salary, medical care, and pension, but also certainly the emotional and social ties established over a long period to other employees, supervisors, and the company (the average period of employment at Consolidated Edison Company is 22 years).

Pfeffer points out that the alcoholic usually denies the drinking problem and its consequences. It has been frequently said that the alcoholic must undergo some serious, meaningful, personal loss or impairment before he gives up this denial. Consequently, he comes for help only at the very last moment, when he has deteriorated physically, mentally, vocationally, and socially. Being placed on probation by his company serves as a warning that if he drinks again he will lose his job; this warning has the effect of making further denial of unpleasant reality impossible.

Of the 145 employees referred to the consultation clinic for alcoholism in this manner, 64 per cent were able to keep their jobs. Seventy-two per cent of those who continued treatment at the clinic maintained their jobs; only 45 per cent of those who discontinued treatment were able to keep theirs. Pfeffer reports that of those who continued treatment at the clinic, over 60 per cent are considered rehabilitated, or socially recovered, and 30 per cent much improved— a total of 90 per cent improvement! This is an impressive record for semi-compulsory treatment. It has important implications. First of all, these results throw in bold relief the enormous value of early detection of alcoholism; second, they illustrate what can be done when meaningful incentives and threats are employed to nullify the alcoholic's usual delusionary system of defense by denial. The implications are relevant not only for therapists who must think through once again the policy of not accepting patients unless they come of their own free will, but also for those who would bring a potential patient around to seek treatment—judges, probation officers, friends, and wives.

Threats and pressures judiciously selected and applied have another useful function besides forcing the alcoholic to show up at the therapist's door; they provide the alcoholic with an excuse for being there. A certain number of alcoholics have been described as counter-dependent. These are persons who cannot accept or express dependency needs. They cannot ever show themselves as needing or wanting something; they must not appear weak; and they are especially intolerant of help offered to them. It would be inconceivable for such counter-dependent individuals to seek help of their own accord, however much they may wish unconsciously to be nurtured and indulged. To force such patients in one way or another to seek treatment relieves them of the responsibility for having taken this distasteful step. Evidence from Davis and Ditman's study spells out this hypothesis (Davis and Ditman, 1963). Their study showed that at the end of six weeks, only ten per cent of court-referred and self-referred cases had dropped out of treatment. Davis *et al.* conclude "that alcoholic out-patients may not be less motivated for treatment than non-alcoholic psychiatric patients and that clinic attendance by court-referred patients can equal that of self-referred ones."

A cooperative program conducted by a court, an alcoholism clinic, and probation offices worked with remarkable success in Cincinnati (Mills and Hetrick, 1963). Their referrals increased until 88 per cent of them reached actual treatment. Similar conclusions are reached by Lemere *et al.* (1958). These authors remark that it is often assumed that duress is useless in the treatment of alcoholism but that their own experience did not support this presupposition. On the contrary, in their patient sample the decision to stop drinking was usually prompted by the threatened loss of a job, family, security, physical or mental health, or the respect of associates. They feel that pressure may help an alcoholic accept treatment sooner than he otherwise would, but they advise the therapist not to be identified with this pressure. The same recommendation is given by Pfeffer. In his experience, treatment of alcoholism can be successful even though considerable pressure may be necessary to initiate therapy. As treatment progresses, many patients become able to decide on abstinence on their own. The author concludes that "the well-meaning efforts of friends or relatives to protect the alcoholic from the consequences of his drinking may actually be of disservice to the patient. Shielding the patient may only postpone treatment beyond the point of optimum therapeutic effectiveness." (Pfeffer, 1958.)

Not all alcoholic patients are counter-dependent or need force to get them into treatment. Mindlin (1964) compared three groups of alcoholic patients, all court commitments to Mendocino Hospital and Napa Hospital (both California). One group consisted of patients who rejected help or had failed to seek help for their drinking problems. Another consisted of patients who had attended ten or more A.A. meetings but had never been in psychotherapy. A third group had had five or more previous sessions of psychotherapy, either group or individual. Mindlin found that motivation (or the recognition of the need for change and help) was much greater in both the A.A. and the psychotherapy groups than in the no-help group. Of great interest is her finding that self-esteem was comparatively lowest in the therapy group, average in the A.A. group, and highest in the no-help group. The author concludes that very low self-esteem, coupled with strong dependency feelings, favors an alcoholic's seeking psychotherapeutic help. (Stated in terms of the counter-dependency formulation, the findings confirm the notion that patients "motivated" to seek help are the ones who are willing to admit—on a questionnaire —their dependency needs and shortcomings. Such characteristics are conspicuous by their absence in the counter-dependent alcoholic.)*

* There are two other interesting findings in this study. One is that those alcoholics who had obtained help in the past were the ones who seemed better motivated to seek help and to wish change. It would seem that regardless of what the therapist thinks he might or might not have accomplished in treating an alcoholic, it is likely that over the long run some benefits will have accrued, even if it is nothing more than an increased readi-

The personality dimension of dependency versus counter-dependency is useful in considering what kind of treatment approach will minimize a patient's resistance to treatment. Interacting with the patient's feelings about dependency are the feelings of the therapist about "giving." Many of the approaches inspired by psychoanalytic insights have emphasized the need to give to the alcoholic as much as possible within the limits of reason, at least at first.* But what are the limits of reason? To alcoholics who are counter-dependent, who are fighting their hidden desire to be coddled and indulged, the prospect of obtaining the forbidden fruit is frightening. A generous attitude on the part of the therapist can lead them to redouble their defenses.

Wedel (1965), in a controlled study of 70 alcoholic clinic patients, found no significant difference in improvement ratings between patients who had received immediate supportive and helping relationships—including interviews with the family, assistance with current problems, and encouragement to return for missed appointments—and patients who had received the routine clinical treatment—evaluation, referral, or psychotherapy (group, casework or drug treatment). Wedel's patients were rated, on the basis of unspecified information received from their families, as being either generally receptive to help or not receptive to it. In the group that received extra support and help there were nine non-receptive patients and 24 patients rated as receptive or, as Wedel renames them, "highly motivated." In the group receiving only routine medical care, there were 20 non-receptive patients and 17 called receptive or highly motivated. Comparing treatment outcomes, the investigator found that none of the non-receptive patients who received only routine care improved. These findings reveal only a trend rather than a significant difference,

---

ness to seek help at some other time. The other finding of interest is that there was one factor that significantly differentiated alcoholics who sought treatment at A.A. Fellowships from those who had obtained psychotherapy. This was the factor of social ease versus isolation. Patients who felt and were isolated socially turned to psychotherapy, while those who only attended A.A. felt much more at ease socially. Mindlin recommends that in referring alcoholics to A.A. their capacity for integration with group activities needs special consideration.

* The reader is referred to the work of Chafetz (1959), Chafetz and Blane (1963), Chafetz, Blane *et al.* (1963); and to the writings of Abrams and McCourt (1964), Silber (1959), Sillman (1948), among others.

and they are based on "receptivity" ratings of uncertain reliability and validity. The "improvement" findings were based on "before" ratings made at the time of the post-treatment follow-up. Given these sources of error, one would be wise not to invest too heavily in the relationships reported. Nevertheless, should some later study confirm Wedel's initial observation, there would be reason to argue that in planning treatment, the extent of support or nurturance should be adjusted to the patient's capacity to accept proffered assistance. Help, just like gifts, must be appropriate to the recipient's state of mind. When "help" or giving is excessive, the generosity or kindness of the change-agent may defeat his intentions. When protectiveness becomes over-protectiveness, even patients who can accept their own dependency may feel smothered and hurry to escape.

One must also be cautious about the intentions of those change-agents who make a strong display of "helping." The patient who flees them may be quite astute in sensing something other than the milk of human kindness behind those loving protestations. "God save me from those people who keep telling me they want to help me," as one patient put it—and he may have been quite right. Price (1958) in her study confirms his feeling. Price analyzed the reaction of over-protectiveness in social workers and discovered that it was born not so much out of love and generosity but stemmed instead from their hostility to patients with social problems, particularly those who created difficulties in the environment. Over-protectiveness towards such patients served to cover up the feelings of annoyance and hostility. Thus, it appears that the seemingly giving attitude of the therapist might well have the deleterious effect on patients noted by Abrams and McCourt (1964), if it serves mainly to hide unconscious annoyance. And there is much in the alcoholic that can be annoying. He has been described as greedy, voracious in his demands, tricky, manipulative, impulsive and lying.*

* These same characteristics are described by therapists treating other drug-dependent patients. For example, Modlin and Montes (1964) found their morphine-dependent physicians to be just as prone to lying, sliding by, acting irresponsibly, and so forth. These findings add fuel to the debate over whether drug-dependent people are basically alike in their personalities or whether people using drugs illicitly or excessively suffer social disapproval so damaging that it makes them act in these devious and antagonistic ways. Both personality and social reaction factors can, of course, be operating simultaneously.

Perhaps one of the most trying aspects in treating the alcoholic with impartiality and good humor is his need to provoke the therapist into doing precisely what the therapist does not wish to do at all—namely, to set limits to his behavior, to punish and, worst of all, to reject him. The therapist has every reason to feel sorely beset; one who is trained to accept patient behavior, no matter what, will be hard put to admit being aggravated, even to himself. It is no wonder that these feelings may often be repressed and reappear as their opposite—in behavior that is overly nurturant, overly permissive—frightening the alcoholic away from treatment or forcing him into even more self-destructive behavior. As with the young child, firmness and discipline are required just as much as appropriate rewards in order to form a lasting, strong relationship between therapist and patient that can become a lever in personality change.

Chafetz (1964) has put the matter of therapist capabilities succinctly by calling attention to the need for the therapist to be active and supportive, to be able to offer help no matter how often the patient has lapses and returns to alcohol, to deal with counter-hostility toward the patient, to avoid excessive permissiveness, to be strong enough to introduce controls, but at the same time not to express hostility by being harsh and punitively controlling. An attitude of tolerant acceptance with consistent firmness should characterize the therapist's dealings with his alcoholic patients.

Among the writers who have been instrumental in bringing about the modern trend of being accepting, non-judgmental yet firm in treating alcoholic patients are the following: Glueck (1942), Powdermaker (1944), Haggard (1945), Kersten (1949), Brown (1950), Lolli (1955, 1953), Sapir (1957), and Wenneis (1957). Moore (1961), a psychoanalytically trained therapist, points out that it is very difficult for many therapists to maintain an accepting and non-judgmental role with the alcoholic patient.* Moore recommends that a treatment program for alcoholic patients should be frequently examined to see whether attitudes of the staff and the techniques employed are dictated by what is really best for the patients, or whether they are either overt expressions of hostility or covert defenses against such a feeling in the form of the opposite—an over-permissive attitude.

* See also M. L. Selzer, "Hostility as a Barrier to Therapy in Alcoholism," *Psychiatric Quarterly*, 1957, *31*, pp. 301–305.

PATIENT-THERAPIST CHARACTERISTICS

The last ten years have seen a number of studies on the relationship among social class membership, motivation for treatment, and length of stay in treatment. Findings show that middle-class patients remain in psychiatric treatment longer than lower-class individuals (Imber, Nash, and Stone, 1955; Schaffer and Myers, 1954). Schaffer and Myers ascribe this to different expectations on the part of patient and therapist and difficulties in communication between members of different social classes. Imber *et al.* (1956) tested another variable that may have a bearing on whether a patient accepts treatment, which they call "suggestibility." They view the psychiatric visit in the same light as the visit to any authority figure who plays an expert role. Whether the patient is ready to accept the expert's advice depends on the extent to which he is accessible to suggestion from authorities. The authors assume that suggestibility probably cuts across social class lines and their results confirmed their hypothesis. Patients who were suggestible tended to stay longer in psychotherapy; but if they were also members of the middle class the probability of acceptance of psychotherapy was greatly increased. No difference in suggestibility measured by the sway-test was found between middle- and lower-class patients. Lower-class patients who were not suggestible (did not sway) tended to reject treatment. In another study the same authors (Gliedman, Stone, Frank, Nash, and Imber, 1957) classified reasons put forward by patients for seeking treatment into two types. In one the reasons (incentives) were congruent with the expectations of therapists representing dominant schools of contemporary psychotherapy. (Included among these incentives were relief of psychological distress, improvement of interpersonal relations, increase in self-awareness and personality growth.) In the other group the incentives were not congruent with expectations of therapists. (They were primarily situational or environmental reasons for seeking treatment: family pressures, job pressures, pressures stemming from law-enforcement personnel, and the stigma of being labeled emotionally ill.) The authors found that incentives expressed by patients during their early contacts with the clinic were *not useful in predicting whether patients would or would not remain in treatment.* Two thirds of the research population (both remainers and non-remainers) expressed non-congruent incentives for seeking psychotherapy.

These findings show that it is not fruitful to try to assess a patient's motivation for treatment by the time-honored method of asking him why he has come to a therapist. What the patient answers will depend upon what he believes is proper for him to say in the patient role. His education and sophistication dictate his answer, and his answer will not predict what the ultimate course of his treatment will be. Reasons given for having come for psychotherapy are not necessarily related to motivation; more often, they serve the function of protecting the patient's self-esteem from the damaging admission that he needs psychotherapy, with its implicit social stigma. Insofar as the reasons offered do not in fact reflect what the patient expects of treatment, but perhaps only what he thinks is expected of him at that moment or what can be said with least awkwardness or distress, the patient's response to a question about "your reasons for coming here" must not be taken at face value by the change-agent. To do so, no matter how convincing or "insightful" or penitent the patient may be, is to prevent rather than encourage a consensus about expectations.

A study by Rosenthal and Frank (1958) was concerned with the finding that psychiatrists tend to refer for psychotherapy persons who are most like themselves. More white than Negro patients were referred to the Phipps Clinic, as were the better educated and those in the upper rather than the lower income range. Furthermore, clinic staff preferred the self-referred patient and those referred from other psychiatric sources, as compared to patients sent from other (medical) clinics. The authors consider this evidence for their thesis that psychiatrists consider as good candidates for psychotherapy those patients with whom they can easily communicate and who share their value systems. (See also Hollingshead and Redlich, 1958). Similarly, patients of lowest education and income level were most likely to refuse psychotherapy when it became available.* The authors conclude that rejection appears to be mutual.**

The findings of Rosenthal and Frank are relevant to the treatment of alcoholics inasmuch as many of the patients who come to alcoholism clinics come from a lower social class than the therapist. Once again we are confronted with the problems of motivating both

---

* As an aside, it is to be noted that none of the four court-referred cases in the sample refused treatment.

** See similar findings by Davis, Ditman, *et al.* (1963).

therapist and patient to overcome the cultural and social class gap that exists between them. The recent trend of enlisting sociologists and anthropologists as members of the treatment team may provide the bridge that is required. Enlisting ex-alcoholic patients as well as the proposed inclusion of trained lay volunteers in the treatment effort will also broaden the base for mutual understanding.

Chapter XVIII

~~~~~~

Getting Together

DIAGNOSTIC CONSENSUS

In his own eyes an alcoholic is not an alcoholic, nor does he drink too much; or if he should drink, it is not his fault but the fault of his wife, his boss, or his circumstances. We have discussed previously how such denial can be overcome by applying external pressure to force the alcoholic to recognize that something is indeed amiss or to frighten him into constructive action.

Moore and Murphy (1961) point out that although the degree of denial at admission has some significance, the more important prognostic feature is its relative rigidity or fluidity. In their experience, successful treatment is related to the patient's capacity for a decrease in denial. They consider that denial is part and parcel of the alcoholic's illness. It is their position that if only those alcoholics can be treated who admit that they are alcoholics and want to get well, the bulk of the very seriously disturbed people (the deniers) will not be seen. In their view, treatment must address itself directly to the problem of denial and the problem of the drinking behavior. They agree with Shea (1954), who recommends that alcoholism must be tackled directly and sobriety must become an obsession for the patient.

They believe that therapists who consider that drinking is only a symptom, and not the crux of the problem, add their own denial to that of the patient.

Aside from the emotional reasons that prevent the alcoholic from agreeing with the therapist's diagnosis that he is emotionally ill, social-class differences between patient and therapist bring about a considerable discrepancy in their respective views about what is emotional illness and health. Frank (1962) in particular has indicated some of the obstacles of reaching an agreement when patient and therapist are from different social classes. Lower-class patients tend to attribute their emotional problems (if they are aware of them at all) to physical complaints. They tend to cast the psychotherapist in the traditional medical role with which they are familiar. In one of his studies Frank found that the length a patient stayed in treatment was not directly related to the therapist's warmth but to whether his attitude was congruent with the patient's view of his illness. Patients who denied their illness were more likely to drop out of treatment if faced with a doctor who focused on the patient's interpersonal behavior and upon his subjective feelings; patients who accepted the diagnosis of emotional illness, on the other hand, showed the reverse tendency.

Freedman *et al.* (1958) explain that patients who deny emotional problems are likely to resent a physician's concern with their personal affairs. If the physician did not show this concern, the patient came back for more treatment; if he persisted in trying to be "therapeutic," they left. At the Phipps Out-Patient Clinics, the authors noted that failure to establish mutuality of expectation was related not only to early termination, but also to failure to improve in treatment. Those patients who least improved were the ones who saw their problem as medical while the therapist believed it to be primarily psychological.

According to Frank, therapy consists of getting the patient to accept the change-agent's view of his problem; therefore, the therapeutic effect of a therapist's interpretation depends not on its truths, but on whether *both* therapist and patient believe it to be true. The therapist's role is to apply an explanatory label to the patient's chaotic and inexplicable internal turmoil. If the patient can accept as valid the therapist's explanation, then this becomes the way he actually feels. Frank cites as an example a patient who discovers that his diffuse anxiety is really repressed rage at his mother; or that of another patient who's taught that the phobia he suffers from is an expression of fear of his own destructive impulses. These explanations also suggest certain lines of behavior that tend to lead to improved relationships with those against whom the symptom is said to be directed. Consequently, the patient feels not only less confused, but the actual social improvement gets the patient to feel better and to be better. While we do not necessarily subscribe to Frank's theory of healing as persuasion, we nevertheless consider his insight into the achievement of similar expectations, perceptions, and values between patients and therapist very helpful in understanding why it is so difficult for lower-class patients to establish rapport with their middle-class therapists and vice versa; why it seems that the lower-class patient does not improve as much or as rapidly as the middle-class patient, and why it is that he frequently fails to continue treatment, even though he has by no means gained maximum benefit.

INCOMPATABILITY

Personality clashes are another source of difficulty in patient and therapist interaction. How a patient and therapist hit it off depends not only on social class factors but also on the extent to which patient and therapist are compatible. Betz (1962) found, in her studies of differences in clinical style among psychiatrists, that it was possible to predict successfully* in advance of therapeutic performance that doctors with one kind of personality (interest pattern) saw a high proportion of their schizophrenic patients improve, whereas doctors with an opposite personality (interest pattern) had a lower improvement rate among their patients. What were the factors that made one set of doctors "better therapists"?

The "good therapist" expressed attitudes more freely on problems being talked about, set limits on kind and degree of obnoxious behavior, and more frequently grasped the personal meaning and motivation of the patient's behavior. They were the ones who selected personality-oriented rather than pathology-oriented goals in the treatment of a patient; that is, they were the ones who aimed at assisting the patient in definite modifications of adjustment patterns and more constructive use of assets, rather than mere decrease of "faulty" mechanisms. Betz's interpretation of her findings is that the "good

* Using, among other things, the Strong Vocational Interest Inventory.

therapists" were perceptive individuals who played responsible, individualistic roles in their own lives. The more ineffectual therapists' attitudes were dogmatic (black or white, right or wrong); they were likely to view the patient as wayward and needing correction. In them, the patient would find an emphasis on values weighted heavily towards deference and conformity.* If one extrapolates from these findings, one would say the difference between the "good" and "bad" therapists is along the dimensions of spontaneity versus rigidity, warmth versus coldness, exploration versus repression, activity versus passivity.

It is certainly of great value to test experimentally the common assumption that certain factors in the relationship between patient and therapist are crucial variables affecting the progress and the outcome of treatment. Recent investigations provide further information on the nature of these factors. In a laboratory setting, in an experiment on verbal conditioning, Sapolsky (1960) found that subjects were more rapidly conditioned if the experimenter had been introduced as a "congenial" person. The control group, to whom the experimenter had been introduced as "uncongenial," acquired the conditioned response more slowly—and, what is perhaps most relevant to analogous effects in the therapist-patient relationship, they learned better *after* the experimenter had left them. Similar results were obtained in a variation of this experiment, which tested intrinsic determinants of compatibility between subject and experimenter. Compatibility was established by matching subject and experimenter on the FIRO-B scale, described by Schutz (1958), which measures needs in interpersonal relationships. The assumption was that persons who express similiar interpersonal needs for "inclusion," for "affection," and for "control" would be compatible. Sapolsky checked this assumption by means of sociometric ratings; these bore out his contention that subject-experimenter pairs with high compatiblity scores would like each other, whereas the incompatible pairs would not. The main part of the experiment, the acquisition of a conditioned response, developed along expected lines. An experimenter with a compatible subject was more rapidly successful, while the incompatible

* It should be noted that Betz's study was of schizophrenic patients only. Consequently, her specific findings may not apply to alcoholic patients, especially if one considers the many varieties of persons with drinking problems that one encounters in clinical practice.

subject achieved the same level of learning only after the experimenter had left.

In a later study, Sapolsky (1965), using the same measuring device for compatibility as before, tested the hypothesis that the degree of interpersonal compatibility existing between patient and doctor would be a significant variable affecting the outcome of hospital treatment. He found this to be the case. Compatible patients felt that a similarity existed between themselves and their doctors and that their doctors understood them. They displayed more improvement in their condition than did patients who felt only low compatibility. There was some slight evidence that a similar relationship held true for the doctor, who felt that some likeness existed between himself and his more improved patient.*

What follows from such findings? We grant that these studies have marked only a beginning, that the number of persons tested has been small, and that all of the experimental subjects and patients have been women. Moreover, the situations of learning a conditioned response, and improvement in voluntary psychiatric patients with functional disorders, are not the same thing as unlearning long-established drinking habits by persons with alcohol problems. Nonetheless, a most important step has been made in pointing the way to a more effective assignment of patient to therapist: the isolation of some variables that are likely to contribute to treatment, and the description of how one might go about testing these and other variables that will strike the sensitive clinician as important and promising.

One of the important steps in psychotherapy is to overcome barriers to communication. If two persons are going to achieve together a common goal, they must be able to come to some sort of consensus about what that goal is—what is to be achieved through therapy. We believe that it is easier to bring about the necessary convergence in aim if patient and therapist learn to speak each other's language. Inferred compatibility, perceived similarity, actual similarity, and liking for each other facilitate such learning, at least in certain cases. We think that these positive emotional factors play a helpful part in the therapist's learning what the patient believes his problem to be and what he expects of the therapist in his role

* The reader is referred for further studies of the interaction between patient and doctor to Fiedler (1951, 1950); Fiedler and Senior (1952); Parloff (1961); Van der Veen (1965); Mendelsohn and Geller (1965).

of "doctor," so that he can meet the patient's beliefs and expectations appropriately and bring about necessary modifications.

The immediate practical application of research such as we have described would be to make patient assignment, when possible, a matter not only of psychodynamic considerations or convenience but also of the emotional preferences of patient and therapist for each other. We urge that before such "compatibility assignments" be undertaken, careful plans to evaluate their effectiveness be worked out. This caution is essential, particularly because there exists as yet no systematic information on the different kinds of attraction and repulsion between patient and therapist, some of which might be pathogenic. There are certainly sufficient theoretical grounds to presume that some kinds of attraction or perhaps certain degrees of attraction bode no good and therefore must be identified so that they can be avoided; conversely, it may also be found that an initial dislike of the therapist can be put to profitable therapeutic use. The problem is to specify and to predict which varieties of interpersonal emotions will be useful and which will be harmful, when, and to whom.

Chapter XIX

Other Problems

In this chapter we shall consider several other treatment problems that require special comment. The problems are not interrelated, but each poses an issue of concern to change-agents: we speak of the treatment of the homeless alcoholic, the handling of the dangerous alcoholic, and the question of total abstinence.

THE HOMELESS

A number of alcoholics, not necessarily only Skid Row types, are temporarily and sometimes permanently without family ties, friends, or contacts; they live wherever they happen to be. Many of them represent the last stages of alcoholism. Their prognosis has been viewed as among the least hopeful. We do not share this view, since we believe that one cannot set the same goals for all patients and that prognosis is dependent upon the treatment goal one has in mind. We also believe that using some of the newer concepts of character training, combined with progressive care, some positive gains can be made. Attention should be called to the possibility that the casual observer's estimates of the plight of the homeless alcoholic may exaggerate the disadvantageous features and fail to remark upon the positive aspects present in some environments, like rooming houses, resident hotels, and the Skid Row milieu. Palola, Dorpat, and Larson (1962), for example, have shown that suicide is less frequent among Skid Row alcoholics than among alcoholics from other different milieux settings. Reviewing studies of Skid Row, they comment that it is a congenial atmosphere where deviants find friends among their own kind. The down-and-out group provides acceptance and support in a well-developed sub-culture that demands little and yet offers a sense of belonging and opportunities for sociability.

Helping the Homeless

Rehabilitation on the Streets. As one considers means for the rehabilitation of the homeless alocholic, one thinks first of "community organization" or "street project" programs that work directly with the groups that constitute the Skid Row, "hobo jungle," and other rooming-house and hotel-district environments. In recent years street workers have gained experience with youth gangs in the big cities. In underdeveloped countries, community workers have organized city neighborhoods and villages. Recently, in the United States, persons working in anti-poverty programs have recruited self-helping personnel from among the ranks of the deprived. Among agencies in the alcohol-treatment field, the Salvation Army is perhaps most closely identified with Skid Row programs, but their Social Service Centers would only be a part of the street work that we propose for the homeless. *It is our recommendation that major efforts be made to reach urban homeless alcoholics by having street workers live in the sub-culture. Their job would be to establish confidence, to offer guidance that would channel the homeless to appropriate community agencies, and to accentuate the interpersonal resources of the naturally occurring groups somewhat in the way that activity-group therapists now work.*

Salvation Army Men's Social Service Centers. Important aid is extended by 124 centers to a large number of homeless alcoholics. More than 8,000 beds are provided to persons with alcohol-related problems. The program of work—spiritual and psychological rehabilitation—is demonstrably effective with those individuals who have a background of skill and who retain some personal resources.

Other Religious and Charitable Centers. A number of other religious denominations and charitable groups maintain support-providing missions, job opportunities, and chances for pastoral counseling among the homeless. The St. Vincent de Paul Society, Goodwill Industries, the worker priests among Catholics and Episcopalians: these are but a few. Unfortunately their efforts may receive very little community support and may not be well integrated with other community facilities that complement the work of these centers. In the past, some of these groups have emphasized help of the "hand-out" sort, which, while sustaining both life and the benevolent self-image of the charitable, does little to move the alcoholic along the road from passive receiving of alms to a more responsible partnership in his own rehabilitation. It is also unfortunate when activities are limited to religious exhortations without providing supportive groups and channels for actual self-improvement. *We recommend that among religious and charitable organizations working with the homeless there be increased coordination among themselves and with other agencies, that they take an active reaching-out role, and that from the very beginning the charitable effort involve a* quid pro quo *designed to move the alcoholic from passive to active participation in the work designed to help him.*

Synanon. Synanon has already been described. It is a resource for homeless alcoholics which is more likely to be acceptable to persons who cannot reconcile themselves to the strong religious emphasis of the A.A., the Salvation Army, and of other religious centers.

Community Hospital. According to Block (1962), communities should have a facility where the homeless alcoholic can be restored to physical and mental health. This should include a screening process for determining the proper agency to which the patient is to be referred for future help. If this is located within the hospital, the patient should be started right there on the road back towards physical, mental, and vocational rehabilitation.

Foster Home Placement. Candidates for foster home placement should be reasonably well-integrated and sufficiently reliable to attend an outpatient program either at a clinic or A.A. The patient must be either abstinent or sufficiently recovered not to go on a binge or otherwise offend his hosts. Block recommends that the family environment be such as to help the patient establish a satisfactory social contact, which would provide the necessary incentive for continuing treatment in a clinic and for complete rehabilitation. Preliminary investigations of these homes should be made to ensure suitability.

Halfway House. There should be a facility open to employable individuals who require supervision when not at work and a place to live where continuous treatment is available. The night hospital provides such treatment: some state hospitals have a work-furlough program whereby the patient may go out during the day and return to the hospital at night.

Rehabilitation Centers. The chronically ill alcoholic needs a place where he can be treated for a long period. Block recommends that such a facility should provide vocational therapy as well as physical and mental rehabilitation programs.

Permanent Supervision. Those patients who cannot respond to any other treatment need a completely sheltered or custodial environment. Block recommends a pleasant environment with recreational and occupational opportunities. If the alcoholic is psychotic as well, he will have to be cared for in a state mental hospital until sufficiently improved for transfer to one of the other facilities.

Halfway House for the Offender. The state of California (as already mentioned) will shortly be experimenting with such a facility for persons under the jurisdiction of the correctional system.

City Prisons and County Jails. Homeless alcoholics are quite likely to be arrested for public drunkenness or for other offenses associated with inebriety. As Pittman and Gordon (1962) have shown, a significant number of Skid Row alcoholics will have had non-alcoholic criminal careers prior to the onset of their alcoholism; being in jail will not be a novel circumstance. For many alcoholics the jail is the only home they have and a number of them seem to like it, getting along quite well in the highly structured prison routine. In Chapter Eleven we have stressed the importance of correctional facilities as treatment centers for alcoholics. We now suggest that jails are presently the most important community agency for the homeless, both because of the role of the police in identifying alcoholics through arrest and because of the potential value of jail programs for medical, vocational, and psychological rehabilitation.

An important agency is not necessarily a good one, and quite clearly most jails are not treatment centers. On the contrary, they are dreadful places that can do little but hold and harm people. Fortunately, there is a movement among local police administrators as well as state and national correctional authorities to improve the loathsome jail and to put in its stead a modern facility that, whether or not it ever cures, is at least humane and does not exacerbate misery, criminality, and pathology. For a review of the jail problem and modern trends the reader is referred to a recent article (R. Blum,

1964a). In some jails, as noted in Chapter 11, treatment as we define it is also taking place. Unfortunately, the number of jails offering genuine treatment can be counted on one man's fingers; a great effort is required to make more facilities into assets rather than liabilities for handling alcoholics.

In lieu of improvements in the majority of jails, a development of which many citizens despair, there is a movement to eliminate inebriety as a criminal offense. Should such changes in the laws occur, it will be necessary to provide some other live-in facility for the homeless alcoholic. In designing such facilities it will be important that planners break away from traditional notions for "total" institutions and follow the kind of schemes that constitute live-in facilities integrated with community-wide progressve care programs.

Whether or not changes in the law are made, many of the inmates of jails and prisons will nevertheless be persons with alcoholic problems. Many will be drawn from the ranks of down-and-out homeless persons who so often are the habitual and casual offenders. Consequently one cannot escape the importance of the jail as an institution to which many alcoholics will go, one which receives many cases not likely to be seen by other agencies. *We recommend that alcohol workers strongly support civic leaders and police and correctional administrations in their efforts to abolish the typical old-fashioned city prison and county jail and to replace these with humane facilities that incorporate genuine treatment programs. We further recommend that alcohol workers actively participate in planning new facilities and in providing services within them.*

HANDLING THE DANGEROUS ALCOHOLIC

Some change-agents, in their solicitude for their patients, may overlook the fact that many alcoholics are dangerous to others as well as to themselves. A review of the published data on crime and suicide (R. Blum, 1966) shows that alcoholics are more likely than ordinary people to commit suicide, to engage in violent crimes, and to cause traffic injuries and fatalities. In addition, as noted earlier, an important segment of the Skid Row society will be persons with records of criminal conduct prior to the onset of their alcoholism. As older men, some of them will continue to commit crimes.

The change-agent who is dealing with alcoholics will want to know whether his clients are likely to engage in damaging behavior.

He can base his predictions on two kinds of data: one is the record of past conduct and statements; the other is direct observation of present conduct and statements. If in the past an alcoholic has had a record of offenses, accidents, or suicide attempts, the wisest assumption is that he will repeat his behavior—at least until such time as his personality, drinking, or situation changes dramatically. Similarly, if a patient expresses an intent to commit suicide, speaks of homicidal intentions, or shows evidence of inability to control impulses, or if his conduct itself is combative, the change-agent must take heed.

Being alert to danger is not sufficient; nor can the change-agent assume that direct interpretations or warnings to the patient will prevent harmful conduct during a drinking bout. Controls must be instituted and these should be of a continuing sort, their nature geared to the particular circumstances of a client's life. As a major safeguard against traffic accidents, *all* alcoholic patients should be strenuously persuaded not to drive any vehicles or aircraft; if necessary, the change-agent must help the patient arrange for other transportation to work. Outpatients will require a motor pool, a volunteer driver, a family member who can take over driving, or a change of residence so that public transportation is available. If a patient is involved in an accident during treatment, it is not amiss for the change-agent in charge to ask the patient voluntarily to renounce his driver's license. If he refuses and if it is a court case, the therapist can inform the patient of his intention to ask the court to revoke the license. This is, of course, a very authoritarian and arbitrary act and will likely occasion much distress—including soul-searching on the part of the therapist himself. We think that the data on the accident risks of alcoholics are so compelling that the change-agent has a strong obligation to act in this way in order to prevent injury and loss of life.

Suicidal behavior, other than the chronic suicidal effort that alcohol use itself may represent, is always a risk. As we indicated in Chapter Fifteen, additional dangers of accidental death occur when there is concurrent use of barbiturates or tranquilizers. During periods of depression, when threats of suicide or veiled warnings of it are made, or during crisis periods when the patient feels disaster is near at hand, special suicide precautions must be taken. One set of precautions consists in the involvement of family members, employers, and others in a safety watch. A second precaution for clients who are not under observation or psychotherapy will be to inform them of the number of the local telephone suicide prevention service, if there be one. A third precaution is to insure that someone from the change-agency—a therapist, an expert lay person,* an A.A. colleague—is always on call should the patient need to talk to someone. A fourth precaution is to shift the patient from an unsupervised to a supervised environment, either placing homeless patients in a live-in center; admitting employed outpatients to night-care centers for the crisis period; or, as the risk rises, admitting the patient to the hospital. In a progressive care program of the sort described in Chapters 16 and 22, it will be relatively easy to move the patient in and out of care facilities depending upon the patient's condition.

Criminal behavior, especially the dangers of assault and homicide, are greatest in persons with prior histories of violence who have poor relations with their spouses or who in their leisure time consort with others who are violent. As Wolfgang (1958) has shown, most crimes of violence are the outcome of interpersonal conflicts in which both perpetrator and victim play a role. Risks are greatest in drinking situations; at taverns, for example, or in homes during drinking bouts. Since propensities to violence seem related to variables such as lower-class upbringing and living in delinquency areas as well as to personality and alcohol use per se, the change-agent will know which alcoholics are likely to hurt someone.

What to do about it? Try to keep the patient from being with people he dislikes or gets into fights with when he is drinking. If there is conflict with the spouse warn her—since women are more often victims—to leave before a fight starts; or, if one starts after drinking, to retreat immediately to a previously prepared safe position in someone else's house. If homicidal intentions are expressed by these patients, the objects of hostility should be warned off. If an obsessive intention is expressed, the police can be notified. Naturally, these actions can be taken only if the client has been told that as part of the treatment contract the change-agent will intervene. This means that at the time of intake the change-agency must have taken a history of criminality and have made a judgment of assaultive potential. For patients judged to be dangerous, the initial discussions must have included a definition of the change-agent's role as a person who will do all he can to protect the lives and safety of everyone and to prevent suicide and assault. The patient may protest, but the chances are he will be much relieved and that he will give ample

* See Chapter 5.

warning to the change-agent when his impulses are reaching the boiling point. It is very likely that the patient will also test out the therapist, giving him an early opportunity to do what he said he'd do. In any psychodynamically oriented therapy the therapist will be wise to explore these first tests without either rushing into action or backing off so that his bluff is called. The testing will easily be seen for what it is and will serve as a standard against which the genuine violent impulse can be measured.

The therapist must be cautioned against the patient's manipulating the interventions themselves as vehicles for upsetting or threatening the patient's enemies. A gullible therapist could easily find himself crying "wolf" daily to the great hidden amusement of his patient. On the other hand a therapist must feel free to act when a clear danger emerges. An important point here is that the therapist must not over-identify with the patient (or experience counter-transference) so that he fails to see the destructive components within the patient or fails to recognize the possibility of their release during drunkenness.

For clients who are on probation or parole while under treatment, the change-agent has an added measure of safety. He can have arranged with the patient and his supervising parole officer that when violence seems likely either may request a temporary revocation of free status. The revocation can be limited to a few days in jail if prior arrangements for such in-and-out custody have been made with the police and judicial authorities concerned.

Two final points must be made. One is that in spite of all his precautions, the change-agent is likely sooner or later to find his clients hurting themselves or others. The realistic goal is not to banish all dangerous behavior, but to reduce it as much as possible by intensive work with the client, by close cooperation with other agencies, by close communication with the client's family, and by willingness to intervene to warn others and to act to move the patient into supervised facilities as needs arise. The second point is that the change-agent must recognize that he is dealing with a particularly hazardous group of people. This is not to paint alcoholics as ogres nor to tar all patients with the violent brush. It is intended to point out the reality that many alcoholics do come from backgrounds where violence is common, do have destructive impulses, do experience impulse-release when drinking, do drive badly when drinking, and do maim and kill a goodly number of citizens each year using autos, guns, knives, and their fists. The change-agent cannot escape the critical nature of his role as citizen, which necessarily obliges him to protect others as well as his own clients.

THE TOTAL ABSTINENCE CONTROVERSY

The issue of total abstinence during treatment as a necessary condition for helping the alcoholic has been debated long and arduously. It is our position that total abstinence cannot be considered as a prerequisite if one adopts the broad definition of treatment we have proposed. A physician will not refuse treatment to the intoxicated alcoholic; nor should the psychotherapist reject a patient as soon as he has fallen off the wagon. We are not alone in this point of view; for example, Chafetz points out that an alcoholic who suffers a relapse (fails to remain sober) is not so different from a diabetic who relapses, slipping up on diet or insulin. If physicians were to argue from this case that treatment was a waste of time, few successfully treated diabetics would be around (Chafetz, 1963).

This is not to say that excessive drinking can be overlooked during treatment, nor that it is an easy problem to handle. What we would say, however, is that *lapses from sobriety should not be made an excuse for rejecting the alcoholic.* Lapses may be regarded and handled in the same way as other acting-out behavior (impulsive, self-destructive, or asocial behavior); namely, *treatment should be geared to reduce the incidence of such behavior, and its severity in actual manifestations and consequences.*

There is no agreement among therapists that total and permanent abstinence from alcohol should be considered as a necessary or even sufficient index of cure. The meaning of total abstinence varies for different types of alcoholics. For one type, abstinence is essential even though semi-pathological (since it substitutes one compulsion for another); for another type, abstinence represents an increase in self-control and inner freedom. In certain other alcoholics, abstinence may serve as an even more obnoxious way of relating to their environment than when they were merely habitually intoxicated. Menninger (1938) considered that the process of cure in an alcoholic had only begun when the alcoholic discovers that "getting drunk is not the only way that he makes himself disagreeable." Sobriety is not enough; a little inebriety may sometimes be preferable; indeed, some wives of alcoholics have expressed this very sentiment.

In 1962 a heated controversy arose, once again, about whether or not an ex-alcoholic could ever drink socially. The debate was precipitated by the report of Davies (1962) from the professorial unit at Maudsley Hospital in London, which stated that out of 93 treated patients, seven have become social drinkers for periods of seven to 11 years. Among the many comments that have appeared since this report in the pages of the *Quarterly Journal of Studies on Alcohol,* there were a few that indicated a similar treatment result—for instance, Thimann had reviewed the one and only case known to the Washingtonian Hospital in which a successfully treated alcoholic is now able to drink in a controlled manner. This patient was one of approximately 25,000 patients admitted during the past 22 years. Another comment describes Mukasa's results, which are obtained by giving small doses of temposil (citrated calcium carbimide) to his patients so that they will be able to drink in moderation; the toxic reaction produced by the drug in combination with alcohol is presumed to discourage the patients from drinking to excess (1965). Shea (1954), a psychoanalyst, reports that he has been able to carry the treatment of an alcoholic to the point where he was able to drink socially. Kendell (1965) describes the case histories of four alcoholics who have returned to normal social drinking for periods of between three and eight years. Kendell states that all four were addicts as defined by the World Health Organization Expert Committee and that they were not simply alcoholics, but addicts in the pharmacological sense ("gamma" alcoholics in Jellinek's terminology), showing "loss of control" over their drinking. There was no common feature among them, neither in age, sex, social class, duration and pattern of drinking, or personality; nor was there any common factor in the means by which they seemed to have regained control over their drinking. He points out that "the fact that many physicians with great experience in the treatment of alcoholism have never seen a normal drinker among their former patients is not strong evidence that such cases are rare," since these are only discovered in the course of a follow-up over a period of several years. Kendell's study indicates that some alcoholics are able to regain the pleasures of normal drinking without ever consulting a physician; others become social drinkers only after a long period of total abstinence outlasting the usual period of after care.

"Even the customary two-year follow-up, carried out to assess the efficacy of a particular therapeutic regimen, can hardly be expected to detect many normal drinkers, or to distinguish them confidently from those who relapse without social deterioration" (Kendell, p. 256).*

The lack of follow-up, or sufficiently long follow-up, would account for the comments on Davies' results from another therapist with a very large psychoanalytically oriented practice with alcoholics—Ruth Fox. She believes that of at least 800 patients whom she had treated, probably none could ever drink socially again. Her belief rests on an impressionistic basis, for no follow-up studies are reported on these cases.

Kendell agrees with the debaters that despite the possibility that some few alcoholics can return to normal social drinking, present therapeutic practices need not be changed. Glatt (1965) suggests that the concept of "loss of control" over drinking is best regarded as a progressive—not as a static or absolute phenomenon. It needs to be further investigated and its characteristic specified for various drinker types. He and most of the debaters, including Davies himself, believe it is necessary to continue to impress upon alcoholics the urgent need for permanent and total abstinence. Pending further therapeutic advances, we would provisionally agree with this position. In particular, we agree with Glatt's proposal that "loss of control" be carefully described in terms of its variations from one alcoholic to another.

---

* See the reports by Nørvig and Nielsen (1956), Selzer and Holloway (1957), de Morsier and Feldmann (1952), Moore and Ramseur (1960), as quoted by Kendell.

Chapter XX

~~~~~~

Social Issues Arising from Treatment Progress

With any powerful remedy there are dangerous side effects, and with any important change in social relationships there ensue problems in adjustment. Therefore, it is well to anticipate some of the problems that will arise as a consequence of current trends in treatment. We comment on three developments that hold great promise. Our objective is not to challenge that promise but merely to point up possible dangers so that risks may be forestalled.

TOTAL INSTITUTIONAL PROGRAMS

There are two contradictory developments in the administrative planning and clinical operation of institutions in which alcoholics reside for treatment. On the one hand, the community mental health movement (Bellak, 1964) and certain correctional programs (notably in California) are advocating and implementing the abandonment of large institutions situated far from the homes of patients or inmates in favor of smaller local facilities, which are not only physically nearer to the "real world" but operationally provide for freer movement of inmates in and out of the institution. For example, efforts are

246

being made to implement work-furlough programs in jails (see R. Blum, 1964a), earlier and more flexible paroles from prisons, and—for hospitals—increased emphasis on day-only or night-only care, weekend passes, and the like. It is not these developments that concern us, possibly because our own bias in favor of these changes and commitment to their spread is so strong. They do, of course, reduce the possibility of comfortable institutionalization for those inmates who make a home in an institution, for they try to force the person to stay in the ordinary world and deny him a permanent haven where his responsibility is less. In our culture, where institutional dependency is considered burdensome to the community and narrowing or limiting for the life of the inmate, we do not think it excessively cruel to gear institutions toward the release rather than the retention of their charges. On the other hand, the contradictory trend is an emphasis on more efficient "total" institutions. A "total" institution, to use Goffman's term (1963), is one in which almost all aspects of the inmate's life are directed by the institution. People are moved in the mass, their individuality is submerged, their self-identifications are altered. Institutions become "total" when there is a need to hold large numbers of people with relative administrative ease, when there is reason to separate certain kinds of individuals from the parent society, and when there is a desire to control or alter the conduct of people. Although most institutions of the sort usually described as "total"— chronic disease hospitals, orphanages, the army, convents, prisons, and the like—are large, it is also quite possible to have small numbers of people as inmates. Whether large or small, such institutions are successful in their functions; they are quite effective in containing and directing conduct.

In some regions one finds medical or correctional administrators planning larger institutions that will house alcoholics; these facilities may be general medical centers, mental hospitals, jails, prisons or some sort of combined medical-correctional facility. The modern general hospital, which is increasingly being encouraged to develop wards for the treatment of alcoholic and psychiatric cases, is itself growing larger in size and more efficient and "total" in its milieu. Goffman (1963), Lewis and Coser (1958), and R. Blum (1960, 1958) have considered their development with some alarm. Plans for more advanced regional medical centers, hospitals-in-the-round, and other medical facilities that further centralize and concentrate the treatment apparatus necessarily stress more complex specialization, automation, and administrative ease, so that an increasing number of patients can be processed. As a result, effective individual psychological and rehabilitative care are made subordinate.

Increases in institutional size are made in response to social changes. Urban populations are growing, and the increasing level of education and public concern about deviancy means that larger numbers of alcoholics will be identified as cases and/or persuaded to define themselves as patients. Moreover, with stricter requirements for high-level technical and interpersonal performance, individuals with conduct defects of the sort associated with alcoholism and other behavior disorders—which in earlier days might have been tolerated—will more and more be considered in need of institutionalization. And, of course, the greater financial resources of families, including aid under Medicare Social Security, necessarily will bring more people into hospitals. Finally, with the further development of industrial society and the ever-advancing requirements for technical skills in performance, there will be large numbers of persons who either lack the skills to become employable or whose skills become obsolete as production methods change. Titmuss (1959) has said that "the dominating characteristics of industrial conditions . . . have been, from the point of view of the worker, irregularity and impermanence." Those without work are also, for the most part, without status or other resources and must be expected to constitute our population of "inadequates," a definition applied by others and quite beyond the control of the person so described. Among this group all manner of miseries—including alcoholism—will be found in proportions higher than among the fortunate. As the number of failing and rejected persons increases, due to increasing population growth, more rapid automation, and associated skill redundancy, one must anticipate that more alcoholics will be generated, that their presence will be defined as a social problem and a public health problem, and that the demand for institutional services for their control or treatment will grow. This demand, when occurring in regions where large institutions are not out of favor, will likely be met by administratively efficient but quite possibly therapeutically ineffective institutional care.

In Chapter One we set forth our belief that insofar as alcoholic deviation is intensely disapproved by society, there will be demands for control rather than treatment—that is, the welfare of the individual alcoholic will be subordinated to community welfare. We also indicated earlier that complete abstinence and total cures are not reasonable treatment goals, at this stage of our knowledge, for most alcoholics. Consequently, what the therapist seeks and what the community insists upon will be at odds. The community demands can be met by "total" institutions, for these are the means best known for effecting conduct control and immediate change—even if the change in behavior is limited to the period of confinement. When such community demands prevail, medical and correctional facilities will emphasize control rather than providing for the slow changes and freedom for individual growth and backsliding which characterize the treatment orientation.

We shall not argue, at this point, for treatment as against control. Our present point is that large institutions that effectively subordinate the individual to administrative and community demands do in fact create real troubles. The inmate, made passive and dependent, finds it most difficult to return to active responsible life. That dependency so commonly found among alcoholics is encouraged. The possibilities for returning the alcoholic to the community as a better integrated and healthier person are reduced. Certainly no one who has seen the successful jail or chronic-ward adjustment of the alcoholic inmate and then watched his disability speedily recur upon release will be surprised to learn that social failure is to be expected among inmates forced to be dependent but not rehabilitated by typical mass institutions. Those who have been active in combating the hazards of such institutions—especially the pioneers in community psychiatry, home care, modern penology, and the like—have much to teach those efficiency-oriented but naive planners who presume that by saving costs and centralizing facilities only benefits can accrue to either the community or the recipients of care.

Not all new institutions, of course, will be merely larger, space-age-equipped repetitions of the dreary places already so well known and so demonstrably insufficient in their human qualities. Some of the new institutions may well be really modern in the sense that they seek to do more than control or direct inmate behavior; they will in fact aim to change post-institutional conduct by means of the careful management of total environmental control. They will use the most sophisticated knowledge of group dynamics, of learning theory, of the implications of findings on sensory deprivation, critical periods, and the like. They will ultimately become, in short, complete and successful examples of what modern treatment hopes to accomplish, except for one failing: they will not be doing treatment at all. For their purpose will be the reduction of deviancy without regard for individual wishes.

These institutions would take as their model the special environments created by the Chinese Communists for the purposes of thought reform, settings well described by Lifton (1963). We must expect such developments whenever a community insists upon conformity and whenever behavior-manipulation methods are available that assure "reform" via no-holds-barred total environments. A person is an especially vulnerable target whenever he has a personality structure particularly suited to all-or-none belief systems. Lifton describes that personality as "totalistic." Certainly many alcoholics might be so described. As in the ideological efforts of the Chinese, the thought reform of alcoholics would allow little freedom for individuals to find their own private paths to joy or to elaborate the material of their own resources and dispositions to reach some individually pleasing state of being. Total environmental manipulation to produce alcoholic reform as dictated by the community will no doubt reduce alcoholism, and the citizens who demand such achievements (for good reasons, we grant) will be pleased. The anti-alcoholic zealots who would be turned out by these reform facilities might not regret that they themselves had not been given the freedom to choose a different goal—since for the alcoholics "freedom" had meant only hours filled with compulsive suffering and indignity. The question is, is it any worse to be forced into abstinence than to be free to suffer alcoholic symptomatology?

That issue will not be resolved here. We call attention to the fact, however, that total environmental control places a powerful tool in the hands of any "true believer" (Hoffer, 1951); and that the use of the tool is always morally justified in the eyes of the convinced. Righteousness in the name of either reform or "helping" does not dispel the obligation which any change-agent in a free society has to ask *who* it is that benefits from his efforts. One must always be sure that an individual is not lightly deprived of the right to seek his own destiny.

The trend toward large, complex impersonal treatment centers, medical or correctional, creates still another problem. Because these well-equipped and well-financed facilities undoubtedly will provide increasing opportunities for combining research with treatment, and because individual professional reputation and economic advancement increasingly depend upon one's research activity and subsequent publication, clinicians may be tempted to abandon or modify treatment work in favor of participating in research. Thus, hospitals may have fewer and fewer professional personnel with any self-identification or interpersonal interests that will be immediately beneficial to the patients. Furthermore, if we can assume that personal interest in the patient is important for treatment effectiveness as well as for patient satisfaction, these "cold-blooded" research orientations, even if they are presumably directed toward "cures," could conceivably negate actual treatment success.

As this unquestionably necessary professional commitment to research increases, one must expect that the paramedical personnel will more and more take charge of actual contact with patients. As these personnel (nurses, technicians, and the like) in turn become more and more fragmented and specialized—and more technically oriented— the patient as a person may be lost from their view as well. It may happen, as some observers fear, that the only staff members who will take time out to say "hello" to patients and to introduce themselves will be those least touched by professional status and least ambitious for it: the charwoman, the janitor, and others whose modes of relating remain personal rather than professional.

Furthermore, as private practice moves toward group practice and as small hospitals become larger centers, respon bilities for care of patients become diffused among a variety of specialists and even among several individuals within the same specialty; as a result, it becomes more difficult to find any single person who in fact takes responsibility for what is done to the patient. What with conferences and committees, groups rather than individuals render the decisions. The advantages here are obvious: patients are protected from careless decisions and have the benefit of a variety of informed opinions. The disadvantages are less obvious but as great: group agreement and group approval become more important to the participants than the fate or welfare of the patient; views that are extreme but nevertheless correct are modified to meet group standards. And, of course, with the boredom and loss of professional time resulting from the growth of committee work, the professional has less time for patients and comes to feel, realistically, less involved with any patient. Contact and responsibility generate continuing concern and involvement; their absence can only serve to remove professionals further from actual patient care.

There is a final point to be made about large and efficient, or even small and finely geared, facilities: when the people in them have no opportunity to enjoy one another's company, both staff and patients suffer. When change-agents must work in settings that are empty of personal significance because the people there are anonymous and estranged, the change-agents become just as regimented and de-individualized as do the inmates. When this happens, treatment—as we understand it—is crippled. It follows that those responsible for building and running institutions in which treatment can take place must emphasize opportunities for interaction between therapist (or change-agent) and alcoholic patient, so that the staff will themselves feel human enough to impart energy and concern to their therapeutic effort.

ADVANCES IN DRUG TREATMENT

Psychopharmacology is something of a wonder child: its recent development has been rapid, it has been accompanied by exciting findings in neurophysiology and biochemistry; its contributions to reducing the size of hospital populations are splendid; the hopes for what may emerge in the future are high. It is not sheer fantasy to hope one day for drugs that are specific anti-alcohol agents—not mere conditioning agents (such as disulfiram) but drugs that act meta-bolically to block or modify alcohol effects as such.

As the search for chemical prophylaxis continues, we must not overlook an important phenomenon. Research on drug effects shows that at least in psychopharmacology, drug-therapy success is still dependent on the therapist's structuring the situation adequately.* Thus, those who use drug therapy must not be bent only on the identification of new agents; they must also identify the characteristics of the setting (including, of course, matters of expectation, personality, and group composition) that can most advantageously be used to maximize gain. Assuming that these determinants are identified, it will behoove the physician, or other change-agents associated with treatment, not to forget their application once the antialcohol wonder drug is found.

* Here we refer to that range of dosage that allows for variability of behavior to emerge (as opposed to higher dosages, which among the stronger psychotropic drugs reduce variability by producing sedation, agita-tion, psychosis, coma, or death). See the discussion in Chapter 15 on the placebo effect.

There is still a larger problem. Our reliance on drug therapy is a cultural convention, albeit one derived from its demonstrable utility in alleviating pain and in healing. That reliance, based on medical experience, expresses an optimism that technological products, pharmaceuticals, are a means to the control of illness and—as one sees in aversive conditioning—of deviation as well. As the medical use of drugs increases, so does the larger cultural interest in them, an interest hardly limited to the sick. Nowadays drugs are employed to search for God and the soul, to expand the self, to unleash hidden potentials, to express social protest, to alleviate normal anxiety, to prevent normal sleep, to provide an escape from reality. Like magic, a drug in itself is neither good nor bad; it is the purpose for which it is used that matters.

Ironically the most powerful drug now known to man, LSD—itself prematurely claimed to be a cure for alcoholism—is becoming the basis for drug abuse among some of the change-agents who would use it to cure or "expand" others. Drug abuse, fortunately, is an infrequent outcome of the use of any drug, even opiates. (R. Blum, 1966c) Drug dependency, for example, is the result of a number of antecedent events. However, we do suggest that the absolute number of drug-abusing persons increases as the optimism over what drugs can do grows, as powerful mind-altering agents become increasingly available, as institutional sanctions or opportunites for culturally integrated use fail to arise, and as the larger environment breeds conditions where drug dependency becomes preferable to alert involvement in ordinary events. What we fear is that more and more change-agents, bored or unhappy with their work or themselves, will become victims of their own optimism about drugs and of their opportunities for nonmedical use. We do not subscribe to the notion that only a reformed addict can cure an addict; we could hardly support a derivative of that adage—namely, that only a drug-dependent therapist is fit to treat a drug-dependent patient.

At the present time the excessive use of drugs by change-agents is not a big problem, nor is there known to be a widespread abuse problem for drugs other than alcohol in the general population. But the use of drugs as treatment tools is most certainly widespread, and that is also of concern to us here. Why? Because drug use in the care of behavior disorders and mental distress may well be more widespread than the evidence for the efficacy of these psychotropic agents would itself warrant. Some physicians feel more like "real doctors" when they can give their patients tangible things such as pills, and many patients feel more like real patients when they receive a pill. Also, it is simply less time-consuming to administer pills. Certainly one can understand how the busy physician—beleaguered by larger patient populations and facing the bleak prospects of insufficient professional "reinforcements," since the training schools in medicine, psychology, and other treatment fields are not keeping up with demand—will rely heavily on pharmaceuticals.

We must anticipate further rapid increases in the demands for available treatment time, and we must expect physicians and their paramedical allies to continue to respond with time-saving and cost-saving—and therefore largely technological—innovations. But although this economically imperative action can be justified on practical grounds, it should *not* be rationalized as a therapeutic one. We suggest that medical therapists use drugs by all means—either because there is clinical evidence that they work or because they are the only resort left to harassed staff for maintaining contact between the alcoholic and a professional helping hand. But don't let the force of events create an ideology of justification unpenetrable by new facts. We ask that drug dispensing not become a substitute for more satisfactory treatment methods—even if these latter are more difficult and are time-consuming.

Intervention through Conditioning, Electrical Stimulation of the Brain, and Surgery

A third major area of advance, past and future, lies in the direct manipulation of behavior—either externally, by the applications of learning theory (as exemplified by operant conditioning) or internally, by the introduction of electrical, chemical, or mechanical (surgical) changes into bodily tissue. At present the tissue operated upon is primarily the brain.

Conditioning of the patient, however, need not be limited to environmental stimuli. Soviet work on interoceptive conditioning (Razran, 1961) involves the stimulation of internal organs such as the bladder or stomach whereas the great advances in electrical stimulation of the brain (ESB) (Olds, 1958), show what remarkable conditioning effects may be achieved through direct stimulation of the brain itself. Similarly, aversive conditioning with disulfiram involves complex cues, some of the more dramatic of which are internal.

In addition one now has agents which can be applied externally but which diffuse through the skin to affect internal processes. One imagines that DMSO (dimethylsulfoxide), the agent in question, might be used in conditioning. What is significant about these developments is not the distinction between internal or external conditioning or between direct interventions which permanently affect behavior as opposed to conditioning efforts; but rather that one now has sufficient knowledge of anatomy, physiology, and genetic and learning processes reasonably to expect that human behavior can be controlled by discreet interventions applied at particular moments in time to particular structures in the body.

Common to each intervention actual or imagined and excepting intrusions on genetic materials is the requirement that one human operate with or upon another human to produce the results. The human subject must allow himself to be acted upon so that his behavior is changed. If the subject does not allow it, the intervention must be accomplished by force. Immediately we face the problem of deciding under what circumstances one person may invade another's body to create behavior changes not sought by the subject himself. It is not a new problem; psychotic patients often object to electric shock treatment; and not only patients but many lay people and professionals as well have objected to lobotomies and leucotomies.

The alcoholic, like many other drug users, presents a chronic dilemma even with present relatively modest interventions. He may not agree that he is sick, he resists being "cured," he may state that he enjoys his drug use and that he wants no part of being changed. When the community insists that its standards and not those of the drug-dependent person will prevail, then the protesting patient is subject to severe sanctions such as jail, coercive disulfiram therapy, or mental hospital commitment. The citizens who make the decisions to control the alcoholic in spite of himself can do so with a relatively clear conscience, for neither incarceration, aversive conditioning, nor commitment are considered to produce irreversible effects in the sense that the mind itself is invaded and altered. That assumption can, of course, be questioned; for institutionalization of any sort will have an impact which permanently affects lives. Nevertheless, to put a man in an institution is not the same order of invasion or alteration as to lobotomize him, to castrate him, or to practice the new interventions which hold such promise for behavior control.

What will occur when citizens must decide whether or not

to intrude upon the drug user with means much easier than institutionalization but with effects far more dramatic? There will be no long-term infringement on liberty; once operated upon, the altered and now *ex*alcoholic would be free to return to the normal world. On the other hand, the one-time invasion of privacy that is required to insert the electrodes in the skull or to conduct the conditioning series with a gavage or catheter (to be fanciful about what might be used) will be a profound step however quick it may be. It is easy to say that what we do for the deviant is for his own good as well as for our protection. No doubt the professionals who make the decisions would be, like lobotomy boards in the past, humane and responsible men. If the judiciary are involved, for one might conceive of a system of court appeals by the patients or their families, it is possible that the judges might easily be made glad that such simple measures exist to convert the truculent drunk to a mild-mannered abstainer. Certainly the community can be expected to influence its doctors, judges, psychologists, and others to employ whatever humane and efficient devices are at hand to insure the tranquility of the citizens who desire that disapproved deviancy cease to be a menace. To return a man to "normal" cannot be so bad, nor can it be evil to save an addict from himself. Furthermore, as it always has, the community reserves the right to use whatever sanctions it can to enforce its moral values as well as to protect its safety. Nevertheless it is no simple thing to deprive a man of even the myth that his mind is his own and that responsibility for what he does is his.

Our society is heterogeneous. It offers a variety of alternatives for ways of life and things in which to believe. It provides alcohol and other drugs. It has many paths to pleasure, too; some open and easy, some—the "vices"—more devious and private. At the same time that the society offers these opportunities, it seeks to deny some of them. A society, besides inventing satisfactions for personal needs and making a market place of goods and services, also has within it forces of convention and cohesion. For each kind of possible conduct moral standards emerge which define who is behaving properly and who is not. On the basis of these standards some individuals are marked as deviants. Some deviants are relatively acceptable—poets, mystics, eccentric inventors; whereas others are unacceptable—Skid Row "bums," rapists, militant Communists.

This is the broad stage upon which the conflict over the handling of drug use and drug abuse occurs. Historically it is not a new problem. Greeks in ancient times reviled Greeks for being sots: "dog-eared wine sacks" they called them. When the first recorded drug epidemic occurred, that of the spread of tobacco in the fifteenth and sixteenth centuries, rulers and moralists responded to the "stinking chimney-pots" with edicts ranging from prohibition to cutting off ears and heads. In China one of the cures for opium use was also head chopping; in the United States we have restricted that remedy to opium sellers. The conflict involves a variety of drugs: marijuana, LSD, amphetamines, and, of course, alcohol.

However the issues of this conflict are posed, we believe that one underlying component is an organic social process in which all of us as individuals are engaged. That social process has two elements. On the one hand, as social animals we must, in order to survive, maintain the conditions which are necessary for continued social interaction and effective cooperation. Such activity is group-centered and sensitive to the standards and needs of others. On the other hand, as individuals we seek experiences and gratifications which are personal, some of which are achieved at the expense of or without regard to the interests of others. When these aspects of social process are contrary, one has a conflict of values: community welfare versus individual liberty.

In the future, when, presumably, we shall have very effective and superficially humane means for reforming alcoholics regardless of their own desires, how shall we balance the exercise of community power against individual freedom, even the freedom to be unpleasant or sick? Speaking for ourselves, we cannot argue that alcoholism itself is any kind of a personal or social good. We do not subscribe to the romantic notion that alcoholism is a necessary condition for some creative people. We believe, for instance, that Dylan Thomas would have been a poet without having been an alcoholic and that the poet and the world would have been better off had he not died so young. Nevertheless we do not believe that any of us who are interested in the treatment of alcoholism can be insensitive to the constitutional dangers which our methods pose, especially as we demonstrate—as has been done—that successful treatment can occur without the initial willingness of the patient to be treated. Given new methods of direct electrical, chemical, or surgical intervention or of total institutional or psychopharmacological care, it will not only be alcoholics who can be changed against their will, but anyone. Once an apparatus exists for the manipulation of human behavior, the apparatus itself will be of the same order as magic—that is, power neutral in itself but made good or bad by the intentions of those who use it. Too often in this century scientists and clinicians have applied their skills without regard for such issues. We would hope that those who are developing methods for the control of drug-use behavior will not proceed without consideration and foresight.

PART FIVE

TREATMENT EVALUATION

Chapter XXI

~~~~~~

Evaluation Difficulties and Solutions

". . . perhaps the greatest weakness of all alcoholism treatment programs, whether in North America or Europe, is the lack of a critical evaluation of their success or failure with alcoholic patients. Anecdotal material, patient material about how much they liked the facility, poems which patients write extolling the virtues of the program and the staff, and clinical statements of physicians and psychiatrists about their success tell us little, if anything, about the success of the facility. This statement also applies to A.A., for we have no clinical investigation of the success or failure of alcoholics who joined this group . . . As yet, the field of alcoholism has had no carefully controlled experiments which would attempt to compare the success and failure rates of treated and non-treated patients who had originally been seen in the same facility." (Pittman, 1963)

Since the above statement was made, the situation—perhaps under the influence of similar criticisms—has changed for the better. Pittman is one of the very active investigators who address themselves to improving the status of treatment-evaluation research. Several extremely interesting programs are under way at the Alcoholism Treatment and Research Center, Malcolm Bliss Hospital (Washington

University School of Medicine, St. Louis). A demonstration comprehensive community-centered program with inpatient hospital treatment and systematic referrals to community agencies was started in early 1962 by Pittman, Ulett, and Stauffer. A controlled experiment on the effect of treatment upon the natural history of alcoholism is also in progress, conducted by Pittman, Catanzaro, and Vago. Patients are divided into long-term and short-term care groups. The assignment is on the basis of specific criteria (using a prospective interview for candidates for long-term treatment) on a random basis. Twenty-five per cent of the patients who meet the criteria for long-term care are discharged immediately; these form the control group. Both the study and control group have an exit interview before final discharge. Follow-up interviews are conducted for 12 months after discharge and for two to five years after that. Treatment results are evaluated in terms of adjustment prior to and after treatment; they are compared to that of the control patients. Although the results are not available at present, the method is described nevertheless, since it is exemplary.

Some excellent work attempting to measure treatment outcome is in process in various state alcohol-rehabilitation programs; special mention must be made of Florida, Massachusetts, California, Illinois, Virigina, and Georgia. In this connection one must also note the careful studies conducted by Metneki and Balint under the auspices of the Hungarian Ministry of Health. These studies compare alcoholics who have undergone a tapering-off cure as outpatients or inpatients to those who have not had social post-care. A similar study is in progress in Oslo under the direction of Alveberg, Larsson, Sande and Skram. The results have not yet become available.*

Also to be cited for careful design is the demonstration and research project in the vocational rehabilitation of alcoholics, sponsored by the National Council on Alcoholism. It includes three patient groups of ten members each who receive group psychotherapy and vocational guidance, and three control groups receiving group therapy only. Clinical evaluations and follow-up studies of the results are planned.

Results of treatment at the Salvation Army center in San Francisco with Skid Row alcoholics are being evaluated currently by W. McCord and J. McCord. In order to distinguish which type of

* More information will become available from the National Institute for Alcohol Research, Statens Institute for Alkohol Forskning, Munthes Gate 31, Oslo, Norway.

client is "curable" by the center's methods, a similar study is being done by Rubington at a halfway house. Mention should be made also of the Alcoholics Rehabilitation Service of the Georgia Department of Public Health, which is studying the effect of visual exposure to alcohol on sober alcoholics. No conclusions have been drawn as yet about what the long-range effects of such visual exposure are; but an increase of anxiety was found during the time the alcoholics were looking at the bottles, as compared to patients just sitting in a room with the observer. The investigators, Agrin and Callaway, used 30 patients with 30 controls. In that same service, various drug treatments including treatment for vitamin B6 deficiencies have been in progress under the direction of V. Fox and Chelton. Much of this research was still unpublished at the time of this review.

SELECTION OF VARIABLES

Aside from the criticism that evaluation of outcome studies has neglected to include control groups, there are other difficulties that beset such research: uncontrolled, environmental factors that influence treatment outcome have, for the most part, not been taken sufficiently into consideration. In general, there is little information in the literature about such important variables as (a) how the patient was referred; (b) why he came to a particular change-agency at a particular time and under whose aegis; (c) the nature of his first contact at the treatment agency—frustrating, encouraging, rejecting, disappointing; (d) to what extent his expectations of treatment were met and to what extent he was made to feel even more miserable upon his first encounter; (e) the degree of compatibility or congruence between patient and therapist and the extent of possible misunderstandings for reasons of differences in class or other factors; (f) the home and job environment during treatment and afterwards; (g) the various inter-current events that affect outcome, such as being placed on the waiting list, therapist-assignment, shifts in therapists, reason for termination, or changes in the family situations, home environment, and job environment to which the patient eventually must return; (h) the nature of the patient's problem, his drinking and sobriety patterns, his diagnosis and the concomitant medical problems.*

* For a comprehensive discussion of and references to the problem of

Some outcome studies take into consideration a few of these factors, but it is hardly practical to consider them all in any given study. Yet to the extent that critical variables are uncontrolled or fail to be randomly distributed among populations being compared, one loses knowledge. The purpose of a control is, of course, to provide a base-line measure of what happens to an alcoholic patient who does not receive the form of treatment under scrutiny but who is also evaluated for change before and after. Clearly, then, the goodness of a study depends on having control and treatment groups that are alike on all characteristics that might produce change independent of or in interaction with a particular treatment method. It is not sufficient to have alcoholic controls who are generally rated as having good social skills, high intelligence, and considerable ego resources if these controls are to be compared with a treatment population rated as socially inadequate, not very intelligent, and having few ego resources or strengths. It would take a miracle, not treatment, to produce significant gain in the latter group over the former.

Insofar as one chooses to match controls and treatment groups on a given variable, one is expressing the belief that it is a variable related to change and treatment outcome. Insofar as one fails to match on a variable, one assumes that it has no effect on outcome. If that assumption is not based on experimental evidence, the clinical researcher is in jeopardy of wasting his experiment. Because investigators are unwilling to assume they know everything about the variables that ought to be matched, or because it is overwhelmingly difficult to match several variables at once, research workers prefer the random-assignment system whereby a sample of alcoholics is randomly distributed both to treatment and to no-treatment groups. The assumption there, usually tenable, is that the populations under comparison will not differ significantly on most variables of interest. (It does happen that the risk of significant differences arising by chance increases the more variables one compares the groups on.)

In any event, although the random-assignment procedure is far preferable to the method of matching variables, even this relatively uncomplicated procedure is not often used. The nature of things in

selecting significant variables in treatment-evaluation research, we refer the reader to the proceedings of a conference on research on psychotherapy (Strupp and Luborsky, eds., 1962). This conference also included a presentation of research methods and research designs useful in treatment evaluation.

many treatment facilities precludes research design from taking precedence over administrative or clinical routines. In consequence, much evaluation research takes one of two paths. The first is to follow the course of particular patients who in the ordinary run of things are identified as having one or another characteristic predicted to be relevant to treatment outcome. The second is to try to control after the fact by comparing in terms of improvement populations who have received different forms of treatment, running averages or some such measure on presumably important variables (age, sex, and so on) and reporting how the populations did in fact differ from one another, or failed to differ.

A third common procedure is to assign patients selectively to one form of treatment or another (rarely to non-treatment control groups, since clinicians are most reluctant not to treat anyone coming to them with disability or pain) based on characteristics described at intake and in an attempt to do either patient-to-patient or group average matching. For example, if in the normal run of intake one patient, Sarah, female and age 43, is sent to group therapy, then the next female in the 40 to 50 age range, Jane, might be assigned to a social rehabilitation unit instead, presuming those two treatments were being compared. The difficulty is immediately seen: Jane might be a chronic alcoholic from a non-supportive socio-economic environment, whereas Sarah might have an acute drinking problem arising from an exacerbation of anxiety in turn associated with an impending divorce. If treatment outcome does in fact depend on personality, situational stress, and environmental resources, it is certainly not a fair comparison to conclude at the end of the study period that Jane's marked improvement proves that the group psychotherapy she experienced was superior as a treatment method to the social rehabilitation that Sarah had, and which produced in Sarah only a bit of learning on how to get along with people and to use her leisure time better.

In spite of research disadvantages, investigators will continue to have to work within frameworks of opportunity. In doing so they will have to exercise caution in accepting their own findings whenever work is done without no-treatment controls or whenever there is a failure to match on outcome-determining variables. As an illustration of what some of these variables are that are predictive of outcome *regardless* of what treatment method (or non-method) is employed, we shall discuss a few of the intake-characteristic and outcome-success findings.

Age. Many studies have reported that older patients, especially those over the age of 30, have a higher rate of abstinence at the time of follow-up than the younger ones.* This has been observed among drug addicts in general and has been termed the "burning out" or "maturing out" phenomenon.

Employment Status. In general, alcoholic patients who have been in their jobs for one year or longer tend to do better in treatment than those who have held their jobs for a shorter time. This is also confirmed in studies of treatment outcome with patients in medical treatment.

Social Factors. A number of authors have addressed themselves to the predictive value of factors such as occupation, social history, class, and so forth. Among the investigators are Mindlin (1959). She found in particular that success and failure groups were differentiated by the following: marital status, present economic resources, usual occupation, and arrest record, (as well as by psychological factors such as motivation, current intellectual functioning, and diagnostic category by Rorschach signs). In doing an evaluation study it would be wise to use a weighted prognostic index such as Mindlin's in order to have an even representation of patients in the experimental and control groups ordered according to their scores on such an index.

Factors Related to Length of Treatment. A number of studies have shown that the above variables are predictive of length of stay in treatment. There may or may not be a relationship between length of treatment and outcome. Factors found to influence length of stay are education, age at which the drinking problem started, family history, and sex.

Other Factors. Among the other variables that are known to have a great effect on outcome of treatment, regardless of the type of illness, are job opportunities for the discharged patient and type of home environment encountered after discharge. Studies have shown that offenders who did best on parole were the ones who had a family to return to; whereas among schizophrenic patients, those who did best in maintaining emotional adjustment were patients who had found acceptance in a foster home and did not have to return to the disturbed nuclear family that had brought on the breakdown (Meyerson, 1958). It is not known what type of home environment is most

---

* This is contrary to the folk belief that only younger patients are a good treatment risk.

conducive to maintaining treatment gains after discharge for the alcoholic patients. Experience in rehabilitating Skid Row alcoholics has shown that those who maintained some kind of continuing relationship to the treatment center were also the ones who remained comparatively healthiest. Those who returned to their home in the Skid Row environment deteriorated most rapidly.

Population Density. Moving from fact to speculation, we recommend as particularly interesting another environmental variable for consideration, even though it is difficult to control or manipulate. Population density and the changes in population density are at present only hypothetical determinants, but evidence from Calhoun's work on rats (Calhoun, 1962) has shown that increased population density —over some presumably optimal point—leads to behavior disorganization, what he calls a "behavioral sink." His line of research has been taken up by Rodgers and Thiessen (1964) in their work with alcoholics. If it were to be found that long-term results of treatment do differ according to the population density of the neighborhood to which the discharged alcoholic is exposed, the implications are that city planners and town authorities would become necessary partners in alcoholic treatment and prevention programs.

Previous Treatment Experience—Faith. Another speculative variable for consideration is the number of times a patient repeats the same kind of treatment. It may well be that this number is an inverse measure of patient faith in the efficacy of the method. It has been found that patients who may have done comparatively well following their initial treatment (aversive conditioning) do not appear to benefit after a relapse from treatment by the same method (reconditioning) as much as they did originally. A similar decrease in effectiveness has been observed in hormone treatment: Voegtlin (1955) noted that once the patient has relapsed after treatment with adrenal steroids, continued treatment of the same sort appears to have less effect in helping to maintain abstinence. The same may be said for many new treatment methods. It has been frequently remarked that they seem to work very well for the first year; after that their effect wanes with the decrease of the therapist's conviction and the patient's faith. Frank (1962) has remarked how little we know about the role of patient faith in influencing the treatment process and outcome.

In this regard we suggest that patient faith has its corollary in the therapist's conviction; both are likely to reinforce each other. The implications for treatment research are considerable. If the therapist's belief in the efficacy of his method shapes the outcome of his work, then his conviction that absence of treatment (for the control group) will fail to bring about changes is also a determinant in bringing about the expected results. It has been demonstrated that this is indeed the case,* making it clear that regardless of the treatment method employed, the patients in the experimental group will benefit, and those in the control group will not. This means that when designing evaluation studies the greatest care has to be exerted in assigning therapists matched for enthusiasm to the treatment groups that are to be compared, and in assigning patients with matching exposure to treatment—if they cannot be matched on faith.

How the experimenter guards against suggesting to the control group that its members will not get better, is left to his ingenuity; however, one may profit from the experience of Powdermaker *et al.* (1953) and of Wallerstein's group (1957) mentioned previously, whose control groups improved partly as a protest in one case; and because they received attention, in the other case.

PROCESS VERSUS OUTCOME

Aside from comparing one kind of treatment with a different kind of treatment or with no treatment at all, a number of different possibilities present themselves to the investigator. Luborsky and Strupp (1962, pp. 308–329) describe the trends of present-day research as accenting the *interaction* among the main treatment variables: patient, therapist, life situation, and the treatment itself. Another accent falls upon *methodological clarification* and better *definition of variables.* What holds for research in psychotherapy is particularly relevant to research on treatment of alcoholism, since in both cases the interest has been mainly in doing something for the patient rather than looking at what is being done and asking whether it serves the purpose for which it was intended. In the past psychologists have been more interested in studying the process of psychotherapy rather than its outcome. In the summary of the 1958 conference on research in

---

* We refer the reader to the interesting studies of Rosenthal (1964), Uhlenhuth *et al.* (1964, 1959) Fisher *et al.* (1962) and Joyce (1961). Consider also the industrial research finding that merely paying attention to or showing concern for workers increases their productivity (Roethlisberger and Dickson, 1946).

psychotherapy, Parloff and Rubinstein (1959, p. 277) remark that "the tenor of the discussion strongly suggested that 'outcome' research was generally scorned as being 'applied,' in contrast to the other two aims (process and personality theory), which had the more lofty designation of 'basic' research." Unsophisticated improvement ratings characterize the typical outcome study, while the analysis of the psychotherapeutic process has had the advantage of the more challenging problem of developing process-scoring systems, which have been getting better from year to year as more systems have been developed. Analysis of psychotherapeutic processes has additional interest in that it may serve to validate the theory upon which a particular therapy is based (learning theory, theory of social processes, and psychoanalytic theory are the most popular). Fortunately, by 1961, when the second conference was held, the issue of outcome versus process studies had all but vanished. Strupp and Luborsky (1962) comment that the greater sophistication of recent outcome studies has made them equally respectable. We may expect that this development will prove of practical help to the therapist who needs to know what will work, not how it works.

FOLLOW-UP

Outcome studies have a number of disadvantages. They require a very careful follow-up, preferably over a number of years; and the follow-up is complicated by the fact that a number of extraneous circumstances, quite apart from the effects of psychotherapy per se, have crucial bearing upon the patient's maintaining his progress or deteriorating. In essence, outcome studies require the same patience and dedication from the experimenter as do longitudinal studies. They require a tremendous commitment on the part of the investigator, who must in addition face the fact that longitudinal studies have lately been unpopular with the granting foundations. Under those circumstances, it is understandable that less attention has been paid to this aspect of psychotherapeutic research.

With chronic patients (which most alcoholics are) follow-up is an integral part of treatment. We urge, therefore, that more attention be paid to this final part in treatment, both for the sake of the patient and for the sake of evaluating the effectiveness of a given treatment method. This is in line with our overall recommendation that research and treatment should be closely integrated; in fact, the experimental research-directed attitude should inform the treatment endeavor. Wherever possible, one of the major treatment goals is for both patient and therapist to learn more about alcoholism.*

DATA STORAGE AND RETRIEVAL

As more sophisticated research and data-collecting methods come to be employed, there will arise the problem of what to do with all the material that has been gathered. For maximum communication between investigators working in the same area, a device must be made available so that research results (and data as well) can be rapidly disseminated. Several central data storage and retrieval systems are already in operation.** We refer in particular to the Classified Abstract Archive of the Alcohol Literature at Rutgers University, the Psychopharmacology Abstracts published by the U.S. Public Health Service, and the abstracts being developed at the Ontario Addiction Research Foundation. We recommend that in addition to existing systems, another be developed based upon a system of uniform record keeping for alcoholic patients. Basic data would then be nationally available and nationwide population selection for research might become feasible, providing that the data were stored in a way that made quick retrieval possible. Electronic data storage and retrieval systems recommend themselves. Needless to say any such system depends upon the adequacy of initial recordkeeping by clinicians and agencies (See R. Blum and Ezekiel, 1962).

PSYCHOLOGICAL OBSTACLES IN EVALUATING TREATMENT

There are several socio-psychological obstacles to doing evalua-tion research. One is resistance to change and to innovation (R. Blum and Downing, 1964). That obstacle is particularly acute in the larger treatment facilities, where the research effort is usually coordi-

* The reader is referred to the discussion on how to help the counter-dependent patient accept psychotherapy. The "helping attitude" is prob-ably out of place with this type of patient; the model of the research enter-prise shared by patient and therapist will probably be more welcome.

** The reader is also referred to Keller's (1964) discussion of the problem of coping with the information explosion, in which a description of the Classified Abstract Archive of the Alcohol Literature is presented.

nated with a simultaneous effort at improving the operations of the facility. The implicit assumption of evaluation, which is that treatment as it is may not be effective, is of course immediately threatening to the participants. Any administrator who has tried to evaluate the efficiency of practices in his facility knows how difficult this is, and how many precautions must be taken to insure personnel cooperation, to minimize their being made to feel inadequate or unappreciated, and to prevent their becoming resentful and rebellious in consequence. Their reaction comes as no surprise to the psychologically sophisticated. It is not just neurotics or inadequate persons for whom description is a threat activating barriers and defenses; for most of us, there is nothing more disagreeable than to have our behavior and its consequences described in detail. For that reason a psychoanalytically oriented therapist will not describe or interpret until the patient has himself shown evidence that he no longer needs to defend against awareness. Researchers evaluating treatment need to show the same sensitivity, since their work entails a description of the operation of a treatment facility and of the roles and activities of its therapists.

The other obstacle to inaugurating a program of research on psychotherapy is that it may interfere with the process of treatment, as therapists have frequently asserted or feared. Throughout this chapter we have indicated that we believe the therapist to be the most important factor in the treatment success. As Pullar-Strecker (1945) has said so well in discussing the history, method, and philosophy of insulin treatment for alcoholics: "All treatments give good results in good hands." Frank maintains that the "good hands" are the hands the patient has faith in. We propose that they are those that inspire confidence because they are confident themselves. Perhaps therapists are right; research may very well undermine this confidence and interfere with treatment. It stands to reason that the self-critical attitudes required of the investigator do not make for the self-confidence and faith the therapist needs to be maximally effective. It is well known that it is only the rarest individual who combines therapeutic and research outlooks at the same time. Certainly the newest ideas that have come out of treatment research on how the therapist influences the patient for better or for worse have been by no means flattering to the therapist's self-image. Strupp and Luborsky (1962, p. 316) observe that therapists do not like to think of themselves as "manipulators or controllers; they do not enjoy being compared with brainwashers or faith healers." They also note that the participants in the conference on research and psychotherapy "felt strongly that the language of conditioning, manipulation, and control was out of place in psychotherapy. They preferred to think instead of assisting healing potentialities, allowing a person to choose for himself, and to help him find new purposes by releasing him from the bonds of his biography." Commitment to such a self-image augurs badly for dispassionate reappraisal. How to overcome their resistance? One answer lies close at hand—following the psychoanalytic technique.

What we recommend is that some of the research in treatment address itself to analysis of the therapist's resistances to treatment evaluation. We believe that such an effort will not only yield fascinating results but will also go some way towards removing the resistances to the research itself; further, it will provide guidelines to facilitate future treatment research as more is learned about the therapist's reactions to it. For instance, we have stressed the need for follow-up studies. To do such studies adequately, the extra-treatment environment in which the discharged patient lives must be assessed. The investigator will have to go to the home, to the patient's place of work, and to the places where he congregates for recreation and pleasure, including the bars. There are, at the present time, very few therapists who can be induced to do so. The reasons are no doubt varied and to a large part unknown or only speculative. If a follow-up is to have any therapeutic benefit for the patient, as we believe it should have, it would behoove the therapist to move out of the office from time to time and visit the discharged patient in his home environment. Why he has by and large failed to do so is an interesting question for research and can become a first step in setting up a program of follow-up studies. It is admirably suited to the interests and emphasis of the new methods in community psychiatry.

PART SIX

RECOMMENDATIONS

Chapter XXII

Recommendations for Care

COMPREHENSIVE CARE

In the 1961 report of the Surgeon General's Ad Hoc Committee on Planning for Mental Health Facilities (1961) the following recommendations were made:

"A comprehensive treatment program of the alcoholic should include consideration of his family and his immediate social environment. A total framework of community care utilizes such resources as the general practitioner, clinics, general hospitals, public health services, courts, correctional institutions, and facilities for acute and long-term treatment. Programs include case finding, diagnosis, treatment, and follow-up care. Attention should also be directed toward aspects of nutritional deficiency and reeducation.

"Among the facilities and programs which have proved particularly effective are outpatient services in clinics, day and night hospital programs, halfway houses, vocational counseling and rehabilitation services, group therapy programs, and follow-up care by public health nurses.

"The Skid Row population is a segment of the problem of alcoholism closely associated with mental illness, mental retardation, and social and economic failure. Special community services must be developed to aid this group."

How these recommendations can be implemented is set forth below.

TREATMENT FOCUS

There does not exist reliable information showing which treatment method is most appropriate and effective with which kind of alcoholic. To get that information we need comprehensive studies comparing a variety of different treatments tried out on the full range of alcoholic populations, thereafter identifying which patient, situational, and therapist characteristics were associated with given treatment outcomes. Since no such studies have been conducted, no one is yet in a position to recommend, with a high probability of accuracy in prognosis, particular therapies for particular patients. But not knowing everything is not equivalent to knowing nothing, or so we hope. It does appear established that conventional psychotherapies are best used with neurotic and "reactive" alcoholics of the upper and middle classes. For the vast majority of alcoholics, one-to-one dynamic psychotherapy will not be the treatment; rather, there will be reliance on the more available, flexible, and easily applied methods encompassed in community psychiatry. There is also likely to be an increasing use of mass applicable techniques such as totalistic institutions, drug therapies, and direct neurophysiological interventions; which, as we have mentioned, hold out both promise and risk. Because of the vulnerability of the alcoholic to physical illness and to environmental threats (whether accidents or drunk-rolling), there must be attention to protective environments or the imposition of activity limitations. Because of the threat the intoxicated person poses to others (assault, traffic accidents, petty crime, and so on), there must also be some form of supervision or restraint, at least during periods of excess drug use. Necessarily, then, the great emphasis in treatment will be, following adequate case identification, the provision of environmental, group, and brief-contact programs. Typically, these programs will provide opportunities for the alcoholic to maintain contacts with physicians to assure health care, with professionals to allow for crisis resolution, and for the utilization of critical periods, or brief contacts as "starter" periods for inducing change, and will offer environments that assure safety, protect health, offer support, and the chance to consolidate gains, and protect others from danger.

In pursuing these broad aims, we must assume that there will never be sufficient professional personnel either to offer therapy or to staff the needed programs. Most of the alcoholic's experience will be with people who are part of these safe environments but who do not possess professional healing skills. Since large numbers of alcoholics are involved, the safe environments must be either institutions of one sort or another—public health, residential, recreational, or work centers—or "total" facilities such as hospitals, jails, and addict centers. In these environments professional intervention in the form of psychotherapy or medical care can take place, but it is not to be assumed that—except for acute cases—such intervention will be the central activity of the facility. The emphasis on modifiable environments is, one must recognize, more a response to pressures of patient and community demand than an indictment of psychotherapy. Nevertheless, by making the most of what one is forced to do, one can reap advantages as well as frustrations. The greatest advantage is the possibility that by working with environments we can begin preventive work not possible in individual clinical intervention.

TREATMENT GOALS

The goals to be listed here are derived from modern forms of community psychiatry.*

1. The first goal is to *maintain the person in the community* as long as possible by means of *maximal flexibility in the form and administration of therapy; and of maximal involvement of the community itself*. This involvement includes case finding and supportive programs (neighborhood clubs, recreational facilities, volunteer associations for child care, nursing care, welcome wagons, and similar programs). Further, the community-psychiatry approach to alcoholism provides a number of different kinds of services along which people may be passed, depending upon their diagnosis (physical health,

* (See in particular Bellak, 1964; Titmuss, 1959; Simmons, 1958; French, 1952; Cumming and Cumming, 1962; Sigerist, 1960; Belknap, 1956; Stanton and Schwartz, 1954; Simmons *et al.*, 1954; Balint, 1957; and Jones, 1953.)

social assets and liabilities, psychological status, and the like) and upon their needs.

2. Another goal is *the provision of services by a large number of people with different skills, beginning with involved laymen* (experts by virtue of having suffered in one way or another, directly or indirectly, from alcoholism; or having had experience—professional or personal—with alcoholics) and preferably *requiring the fewest proportionate numbers from the most highly trained and least available professionals*. The goal is to get a cadre of involved citizens who will take the lower-echelon yet highly responsible posts of case finding and supervision. They will be part of the new environment created for the patients. It is possible that involving lay personnel in such work may have a preventive (inoculative) effect as an extra benefit. Such a cadre of volunteers, themselves not victims of alcoholism, must be created.

None of this is part of an expensive program of hospitalization, nor does it require new facilities. Hospitalization is needed only for the mentally ill alcoholic or the physically ill alcoholic; for both we have present facilities for treatment.

3. *The goal is a diversity of services and techniques easily accessible to the alcoholic, coordinated by a minimum number of agencies, and run by the fewest possible bureaucratic personnel.* Only the most extreme types of alcoholics (to be discussed) will need additional facilities.

4. The over-all plan (to be outlined below) is intended to provide *maximal utilization of presently existing mental-health and public-health facilities* and *integration of these* for the benefit of persons with alcohol-related problems. In the setting up of integrated programs of progressive care, particular attention must be given to facilitate *continued and constant contact by one significant change-agent* with a given patient assigned to him throughout his treatment career—regardless of locale of a particular treatment facility at any particular moment in time. The observance of this caution is essential in assuring that the patient does not come to feel lost in the shuffle.

PROGRESSIVE CARE

Progressive care is a concept and a system of treatment that has been applied in the hospital care of general medical and surgical patients. When this scheme is applied to the treatment of alcoholism, it implies a total program that can be discussed in terms of four features. One feature of progressive care focuses on facilities. Essentially it aims to provide a variety of facilities, each one of which is suited for a particular phase of an individual patient's treatment. A second feature is organization. Here one is concerned with the administrative and staff structures that exist to insure the integration of services and the utilization of personnel and facilities in accordance with the premises of progressive care. A third feature centers on patient evaluation. Evaluation is critical since upon it depend all dispositions of the patient to the available facilities. A fourth focus is upon patient treatment or treatment stages—that is, it is concerned with the processes whereby a patient is correctly assigned to the facilities and personnel best fitted for treating him at each stage in his treatment career. Necessarily it attends to the nature of these stages.

As a treatment scheme, the progressive care concept anticipates four general and two subsidiary stages. These are (1) *intensive care* (crisis or emergency) in special recovery units; (2) *extra care*; (3) *normal care*; (4) *post-hospitalization care* for chronic patients; (5) *post-hospitalization after-care*, including continuous-treatment clinics for recovering patients, and (6) visiting nurse programs and educational programs for *preventive care*. In such a scheme the patient is placed into the program at any point appropriate to the particular stage of his disability, and he progresses to the next stages according to his particular needs.

The program must be based upon a very careful *diagnosis* of each patient to determine his assets and liabilities. (Such an assessment includes his social and employment resources, his physical-health status, his personality, and the nature and history of his drinking.) The *diagnosis at the initial contact* serves to place the patient in a treatment situation suitable to the severity of his disabilities. *Periodic reassessment* is undertaken in order to keep moving him into treatment situations of progressively greater independence or, if need be, to return him to a more protected situation. The focus is not on curing alcoholism per se; rather, the avowed aim of treatment is to avoid the deleterious side effects of alcoholism.

The progressive care scheme requires a management cadre that includes psychiatrists, ministers, social psychiatrists, expert group-leaders, psychologists, research staff, and other available persons with special skills who will organize the over-all treatment situation. Their tasks include the provision of (a) training, supervision, and guidance for the expert lay and volunteer workers; (b) psychotherapy for those patients who seem to need it and seem to be able to profit from it; (c) the maintenance and improvement of community relations; (d) the initiation of research and assessment; and (e) the planning of new programs.

Outpatient Care

This program, in effect in some areas, allows for the greatest degree of patient freedom. The alcoholic patient is controlled only insofar as his dietary, health, and housing needs are concerned. As an addition to outpatient care, we recommend that the services of a visitor (a trained lay person) be available to patients who are able to hold a job. The visitor or guide can help solve practical and personal problems that arise. If a responsible family member is available, he may take over this type of supervision.

Day and Night Centers

There are groups of drinkers whose pattern of periodic excessive drinking is identifiable in the period of diagnosis. These patients can be referred to activity centers, where there will be available substitute activities designed to forestall binge drinking. Psychotherapy is made available for those who seek it, but this is not the central purpose of such centers. There will be a need for day centers, night centers, and undoubtedly also for weekend and holiday centers. The model for such centers is drawn from modern community mental health programs and from penology. In such centers (as in the outpatient clinics) food, vitamins, and medication can be available for self-maintaining, presently nondrinking alcoholics.

Continuous-Treatment Clinic

(In conjunction with either of the two preceding). Patients who need no more than an occasional reassuring discussion, or medication in conjunction with such interviews, are seen whenever they drop in at the continuous-treatment clinic for a brief, unscheduled session (20 to 30 minutes), preferably with the same worker or workers as their contact person.

Extra Care

This program is intended for patients who cannot hold a job. It aims to enable them to subsist outside an institution. They can obtain at outpatient clinics food, medication, vitamins, and a certain amount of alcohol (perhaps to be consumed in the clinic to assure safety). Home-visiting service is also provided. Parallels to the extra-care program are the English plan for treating drug addicts and the New York City methadone treatment experiment; in both cases the drug addict is supplied with a daily maintenance dose of a drug in a medically supervised environment. The Salvation Army, halfway houses, and similar organizations already provide important services for the type of patient needing "extra care"—although they do not, of course, supply drugs.

Pioneer-Care Units

This facility is the only one here suggested that requires a new program. It should be (like all the others) under the administrative direction of the chief mental health officer of the county or the state. In a sense this program combines an indigency program with a voluntary commitment program for those patients who cannot maintain themselves outside an institution of some sort. It is modeled upon the modern honor farms, which safeguard those prisoners for whom no security measures are necessary. As in the honor farm program, the patient participates in a review of his case and agrees that he is to be a ward of the state for a *determined* period of time. Once he has entered upon such an agreement, he may live—together with his family (a concept evolved from Soviet and Mexican penal experience) —in a sanatorium or colony where limited drinking is allowed. The sanatorium is to be administered, along the lines worked out by Maxwell Jones at Belmont, and Roosenberg at the Vanderhoeven Clinic in Utrecht, as a *patient-run therapeutic community*. The state provides the setting, the housing, and part of the food. The inhabitants of the community either work competitively or provide state services to contribute to their keep and to earn a salary. Stay can be for either six months or a year, with a graded system of releases. The old-timers, returnees, and those graduates who wish to return at a more responsible level of employment are trained to be supervisors of the community, under the guidance of expert personnel. Police, parole boards, unions, industrial employees, and an educated community assist in *case finding* and *referring*. Depending upon the interest and capacity of the expert in charge of the program, psychotherapy for experimental purposes may be undertaken. We conceive of this new type of intensive care unit as an exceedingly important one for those many alcoholics, homeless, poor, or otherwise without resources, who are willing to enter into voluntary self-commitments. It is very likely that many of the occupants of jails and prisons charged simply with alcohol-use offenses would be amenable to participating in voluntary rather than criminal commitment programs.

Maximum-Control Units

These facilities will be compulsory residence centers for alcoholics who require, for their own or others' safety, maximum supervision. They will be for persons who refuse to cooperate at any level either in defining themselves as in need of change or in protecting others from danger when they become intoxicated. They will have a history of dangerous conduct, either violence, suicide attempts, or traffic injuries while using alcohol. They will have been processed either through the courts on criminal charges or perhaps, if new codes are developed, on medical-civil commitments where there is an opportunity for a court hearing. These dangerous alcoholics constitute a major menace and a serious social problem.

The development of coordinated programs of progressive care for these involuntary cases poses many difficulties. There is a need to modify the procedures used in jails and prisons to which dangerous alcohol offenders are committed. There is a need to develop new facilities better suited to the practice of progressive care. There is a need to alter present statutes and to devise new laws so that sentences are compatible with treatment needs and so that civil as well as criminal commitment can be practiced more widely. Ideally, indeterminate sentences with maximum limits set by law will be made possible. Ideally, alcoholic offenders responsible for traffic injuries or fatalities will more often be subject to criminal charges which will offer an opportunity for compulsory treatment in institutions *if and when* the drivers refuse voluntarily to enter treatment and to turn in their operator's licenses. Implicit here is a system whereby dangerous alcoholics eligible for probation are offered the opportunity for out-patient care or for self-commitment to intensive-care units.

Several other safeguards are necessary. There must be regular and mandatory judicial review of the inmate's status as well as periodic reviews by institutional staff. The judiciary would be expected to release inmates deemed insufficiently improved by the staff but whose period of incarceration had approached the maximum limit set by law for incarceration for the offense. There must be adherence to the progressive-care concept: inmates must constantly be offered opportunities to learn and to try out responsibility, moving as fast as they can through graded freedoms until they can be released, on the basis of evidence of actual conduct change, to less controlling environments. The staff must be able to exercise options in matters such as reductions in degrees of security or transfers to other facilities. Modern correctional programs include these same options; the task is to provide them for all maximum-control units for alcoholics.

There is nothing new in any of the foregoing suggestions. Attorneys and judges working on new commitment laws for narcotics offenders will recognize that what they are developing can be applied to alcoholics. Personnel in medical programs of progressive care, in community psychiatry programs, in modern correctional endeavours, and clinicians and citizens concerned with both reducing dangerous behavior and protecting the rights of offenders will all recognize how they can make contributions to a coordinated effort to control and to treat alcoholics.

Supplementary Procedures for Progressive Care Programs

Telephone Care. In some communities emergency telephone centers are available for the emotionally ill; the suicide-prevention service is the best known. Newspaper advertisements and other mass media tell the community of the possibility of calling for someone to talk to at any hour. A similar procedure has been developed by A.A. for its members. When an alcoholic is agitated and fears he will begin drinking, he calls another A.A. who comes over to help him through the crisis period. It is likely that any community alcoholic-treatment program will do well to advertise a similar telephone service and to staff it with trained workers, either professional or lay, who can offer counsel and who can encourage the alcoholic to come in for personal care or who can go out to meet the alcoholic. For the safety of counselors invited into unsavory neighborhoods or uncertain situations, two-person visiting teams or a police liaison partner will sometimes be advisable.

Consultants for General Hospitals. Any community health service will offer consultants to other agencies. Community psychiatry programs have shown the value of offering such services. One institution of particular importance for alcohol programs is the general hospital. Traditionally resistant to psychological and social aspects of patient care, hospitals greatly need alcohol personnel who can serve as case finders and as aides to the staff. Large numbers of patients pass through routine outpatient medical care without having their drug use problems identified (Wolf *et al.*, 1965; Schremly and Solomon, 1964). In addition, many hospitalized patients will have case histories taken and care provided with their alcohol problems overlooked. Finally, there will be recognizable alcoholics admitted, quite often to the repugnance of hospital staff, whose care may be substandard. Professional alcohol workers can offer great service first by educating medical and nursing staffs and second by providing direct services to patients with alcohol problems. One important task is to assure referrals so that upon release from medical and surgical care the now identified alcohol-problem patient will not be lost but will be recruited as a patient for an appropriate alcohol program.

Alcohol Consultants in Other Institutions. In setting up consultation services specifically for persons with developing or full-blown alcohol problems, it is well to focus upon institutions whose patients are particularly vulnerable to alcohol problems. Knowledge of vulnerability can be gained either by using the findings from past surveys of the social characteristics of problem drinkers or by conducting special epidemiological studies within a community or within organizations. Considering the high risk run by poor urban males who are Negro, Fundamentalist, or Catholic, one can conceive, for example, of setting up consultation services with the aid of civil rights workers, anti-poverty workers, ministers, priests, and church missions located in poor neighborhoods. Given the ethnic risks of Irish and Puerto Rican Catholics one might plan consultation programs with the help of Puerto Rican leaders and Knights of Columbus fraternal officers. Because of the particular importance of the police in working with alcoholics and because of the concentration of Catholics in some big city police departments, special emphasis could be given to consultation services established within police departments.

Consultation with the emphasis on alcoholism prevention should be made available to high schools and colleges. One envisions educating students directly about how to drink; advising administrators and health staff and helping them to identify and handle students who already have drinking problems; and direct services to students who already exhibit alcoholism vulnerability. Straus and Bacon (1953) have shown that it is possible to identify college students whose drinking behavior suggests very considerable risk for increasing troubles. Such students would be prime targets for clinical work. Given the presently expanding use of mind-altering drugs on campuses, one would expect alcohol prevention and treatment services to be made part of general programs for drug-abuse control. Similarly, were one working with teen-age gangs in poor and delinquent neighborhoods whose members appear to have high risks of later alcohol dependency (an inference from Cisin and Cahalan, 1966), one must plan to integrate efforts to control drug abuse as such, whether the drug be tobacco, glue or gasoline (sniffing), methedrine, LSD, heroin, or alcohol. We make a general point here. It is that consultation services must themselves be coordinated among mental health, public health, alcohol, or other drug workers—indeed, whenever different consultants are working with the same populations. It is also critically important that programs directed at alcohol abuse be an integral part of programs directed against drug abuse per se.

DIAGNOSIS AND SECONDARY PREVENTION

Fitting the Patient to the Treatment Method

The success of progressive care depends upon an accurate diagnosis at each stage in the patient's treatment career. The determination of whether the patient can participate in society fully, to some extent, or not at all—that is, the intensity of care needed—hinges upon both adequate and continuing evaluation. Below are listed some of the aspects of the patient's life and personality that must be considered.

A careful *social diagnosis* determines environmental resources and liabilities that any given program must consider in order to obtain maximal benefit for the patient in the most efficient manner.

A sophisticated *dynamic diagnosis* of the patient's personality determines the particular emotional needs a given program will have to provide to ensure maximum personality growth of the patient.

A *medical evaluation* is essential to make sure that complicating physical problems can be taken care of before they become over- whelming. Patients who arrive for treatment of medical difficulties in connection with excessive drinking receive some such diagnosis auto- matically; but it may be overlooked when a patient presents himself (or is under pressure to present himself) in a sober state and without blatant physical ailments.

There must be included a realistic evaluation of *treatment goals* at each stage in the patient's career, including an assessment of his own stated and implicit goals and the degree to which these are congruent with those of the change-agent.

Identification of Patient's Drinking and Sobriety Patterns

The drinking characteristics of the patient must be studied, described, and categorized: when, with whom, how much, and to what purpose or effect. While such a study is part of the initial diagnostic work-up, it also must be periodically revised—not only to assess progress (or backsliding, as the case may be) but also to institute necessary safeguards at time of maximum stress and vul- nerability and to direct treatment efforts to crisis periods (times when the patient is in particular need, at which times he may be most willing to participate in therapy).

A sophisticated differential diagnosis is needed, one that dis- criminates among the various forms of drinking described in the literature (see Bowman *et al.*, 1955; Esser, 1952; Jellinek, 1946; Knight, 1937a). Some of these are: maintaining peer esteem versus solitary drinking to forget troubles; family-abetted drinking versus drinking to gain ascendancy or revenge over friend or foe; drinking as preventive or self-curative measure versus self-destructive drinking. The role of contributing factors must be defined in order to counteract them by appropriate therapeutic and environmental maneuvers. Techniques adapted from welfare casework, from probation, from medical care, and from psychology and psychiatry will have to be drawn upon.

The purpose is not to label the patient but to evaluate the operating circumstances which precipitate excessive drinking as well as the environmental and internal assets that can help to inoculate him and to increase his resistance to the "disease."

Chapter XXIII

Recommendations for Administration

RECRUITING LAY WORKERS

It is necessary to enlist more personnel in alcoholism prevention and treatment services. Many of these workers can and should be non-professionals. Laymen can make great contributions at many levels of service. The goal is to interest laymen in working with alcoholics or populations vulnerable to alcoholism, to recruit those laymen for service, and to train them. Once they are on the job, the administrator must be sure that his professional staff is willing to accept their contributions. One wants no snobbishness or conceit that sets one staff group against another and splits a potential treatment team into a group of warring factions.

Where is one to look for interested laymen? We suggest volunteer bureaus, the Junior Leagues, women's clubs, men's fraternal organizations, senior citizen groups, VISTA volunteers, church auxiliaries and the like. We should also try to involve those who have had personal experience with problem drinkers; for example, the wives of A.A. members, families of alcoholics who have died from the illness, and recovered alcoholics themselves. Some of these informed citizens will have strong reasons for wanting to combat alcoholism, and their own tribulations can stand them in good stead. Another place to look for recruits is among the ranks of economic, ethnic, and religious groups themselves especially vulnerable to alcoholism. These will be people who speak the right language, know the problems, and can operate as lay experts to educate, find cases, and consult and treat their brethren. Their use also opens possibilities for research—for example, one can test to see which combinations produce comfortable relations and which ones are too close for effectiveness. One might, for instance, explore using Negro teenagers as group leaders for groups of Negro alcoholic juvenile-offenders, comparing their results with results achieved by adult leaders both Negro and Caucasian.

MAINTAINING STAFF INTEREST AND MORALE

Every administrator faces the problem of keeping up staff interest and efficiency. Since alcoholism treatment is a trying business and since many professionals do not enjoy working with alcoholics—or those who do enjoy it become despairing—it is particularly important to keep the staff stimulated, to provide supports to get them through their trying times, and to keep the administrative house in order so that bureaucratic tangles and personnel mismanagement do not foul up the works.

Realistic Goals

One way to provide work satisfaction is to be sure that the treatment goals fostered by the administration are those which a staff can achieve. This means that the hard-to-achieve "cure" is not required but rather, as we discussed in earlier chapters, emphasis is on caring activities per se and upon improvements rather than miracles. It has been amply demonstrated (R. Blum, 1960) that the omnipotent doctor is a threat to himself as much as to his patients. Do not let the institutional milieu seduce or coerce the staff into omnipotent self-demands which can only lead to a sense of failure. It must be the day-to-day activities and the relationship with the patient, his family, and other persons in the community that is made worthwhile; for the change-agents' pleasure cannot be limited to those occasional high points when something remarkable happens.

Research

A source of work stimulation will be found in emphasis upon discovery and learning as well as upon helping. Formal research is but one way to discovery. A staff that is curious but not too rigorous can nevertheless be encouraged to have a scientific outlook, to seek to identify new phenomena or new relationships, to come to enjoy the realization that uncertainty surrounds much human conduct, to take delight in surprise, and to profit from errors. An institution which stimulates curiosity and learning about drugs, about people, and about situations which produce alcohol abuse will sponsor lectures, offer book seminars, hold clinical conferences, open laboratory facilities to eager laymen as well as professionals and will encourage new avenues of research or action.

Rotation of Workers

Workers should be rotated through various services. Each time this is done, opportunities for increased personal and professional growth must be made available. New professional and community contacts, possibilities for trying new techniques, opportunities to continue contact over time—after rotation—with particular patients: all might be considered.

Hours

An enormous amount of time can be consumed by a staff member as he attends to the needs of a patient. Job arrangements, family problems, physical health matters, and welfare demands are just some of the tasks that occupy the active change-agent. Chafetz, Blane, *et al.* (1962) estimate that a professional worker requires eight hours of coordinating these services for every one hour of interview time. As long as the change-agent is doing his job, the administrator must acknowledge the time required and try not to intrude upon it with demands for more visible services. One aid is to provide extra lay support for the auxiliary tasks and for many of the primary ones as well. Whether lay personnel are volunteers or not, their time costs less than professionals and is well applied to many outside tasks.

The other side of the coin is that some professionals within institutions become loafers; or, if not patently that, they use a screen of red tape and so-called conferences as a substitute for work involving patients. One study in a mental health service (R. Blum and Downing, 1964) showed that personnel not engaged in outside work on behalf of patients might spend only one third their time in patient care. Attempts to increase efficiency are met with typical responses to "rate busters"—rebellion, anger, and the like. The wise administrator will keep watch on how time is actually spent.

Management Skill

Administrative methods and the atmosphere of the organization influence the feelings and conduct of all personnel and, through them, patients and the outside community. As social psychiatric research has shown (Stanton and Schwartz, 1954), the way that the staff members get along with one another affects what goes on in their therapy with patients. What is happening at administrative levels also gets transmitted to patients. Since alcohol-treatment facilities have extra problems in recruiting and maintaining staff and in helping their patients, it is imperative that the institution be run in a sophisticated fashion. It is shocking and surprising to see individuals who are highly sensitive in their own interpersonal or therapeutic relations become utterly insensitive to psychological factors when they are elevated to management positions. It is equally shocking to find a professional narrowness that leads some people to equate knowledge of clinical dynamics with knowledge of the complex social determinants affecting organizational behavior. The psychiatrist who would abhor an untrained man practicing psychiatry may be quite willing to practice a new specialty himself—administration—without feeling the need for further training. Like the lay practitioner, the sensitive man may succeed without training, but the risks are high. A wise course is to assume the need for further knowledge as one takes on administrative tasks. Courses in administration such as those taught at Berkeley's Center for Training in Community Psychiatry are very much recommended. Such work can forestall the disasters that occur when administrative methods themselves set up impediments and irritations that destroy staff motivation. Each institution must be run so as to offer clients, change-agents, supporting staff, and the administrators themselves daily work satisfactions, opportunities for career growth, ego support, and simple joy in human relationships.

When human relations falter seriously, it is usually because of unspoken features; one goal of psychodynamic treatment is to bring these into awareness so that they may be dealt with. Organizations also have troublesome or disruptive features which are unspoken or unrecognized but which, if brought to light in a constructive, gentle way, can be handled and made the basis for improvement. In the treatment of alcoholics it is very likely that antagonisms can arise among the staff (including administrators, professionals, lay experts, and all the others), reflecting issues unresolved in the culture or community itself. It would seem worthwhile to provide for periodic discussion, itself expertly handled, during which these issues can be brought out. Typical issues for debate are also issues which recur throughout the pages of this book; for example:

Personality-development goals. Do we want to promote personality change? If so, do we wish the alcoholic to become more mature and have greater ego strength—the kind of change a psychoanalyst would sanction? Do we want him simply to be happier, to get rid of incapacitating symptoms, to self-actualize himself, as some psychologists and existentialists would wish?

Conduct goals. Do we want the alcoholic to be totally abstinent, to be able to drink moderately, to stop anti-social behavior (illegal activities, drunk driving, unemployment, public nuisance), or to learn discretion?

Value goals. Should the alcoholic be converted in spirit and in action to the Protestant Ethic (work hard, delay pleasure, plan for the future, be constructive), and in these ways resemble his therapist? Should he learn to abandon arrogance and embrace humility? Should he practice putting the welfare of others before his own, helping them in order to help himself, as A.A. would have it?

Attraction or revulsion for the alcoholic as a person can be reflected in uncertainty about goals. This common ambivalence is manifested in the reluctance to treat the alcoholic; in the low status of alcoholism as a problem worthy of treatment, and in the conflict over help or punishment, control or treatment. These feelings also emerge in arguments over voluntary or compulsory treatment and perhaps in unwillingness to evaluate the results of treatment.

Conflicting cultural themes underlie some of the attraction and revulsion felt toward the drug-dependent person. Is pleasure to be indulged or restrained? Is work the only estimable way of life? Dare a man enjoy being dependent? Is escape always a sin? Is only the God-given state of mind acceptable, or may a man tamper with mind's alteration? What are a man's rights to be different, to hurt himself, to annoy others? Is any form of conduct really a "disease"?

Practical issues. When the time comes to debate the composition of special treatment teams, professional rivalries and self-interest should be "de-fanged" if possible. Try to agree on what specialists are to be included and from what fields in order to handle the multiple somatic, social, and psychological difficulties of the patient. Clarify referral and inter-agency relationships to ensure maximum treatment efficacy. What jealousies and prejudices must be resolved? Who will be responsible when trouble comes—for example, when patients lapse or relapse? How can the staff adjust to the facts of failure—for example, who will bear the brunt of handling chronic and apparently incurable alcoholics? When does progressive care reach a dead end?

PATIENT-CARE MONITORING

When other people besides a single therapist or other change-agent watch, talk to, and otherwise work with an alcoholic, opportunity arises for true staff involvement, quality control, and increased knowledge about what is going on. Observations by other professional staff are to be welcomed; lay helpers or lay experts (whatever one calls them) should be encouraged to be with the patient and offer their impressions to all concerned change-agents. In addition, more formal contact and monitoring should be set up for patients on waiting lists (should there still be any) and for those referred out. The lay agents can do this work.

Observing the patient and shared involvement in his treatment career are not enough. Administration, excellence of care, patient safety, and research require that *clinical records be kept—and kept well.* Immodestly we suggest a particular book as a guide, R. Blum and Ezekiel, 1962.

Institutions are already too full of committees; yet we find ourselves recommending them, or at least special ones. To supervise the work of physicians in hospitals there exist review groups of respected physicians who go over what the doctors do. Tissue committees, medical audit committees, and record committees are watchdogs, at least if they take their responsibilities seriously and can overcome understandable reluctances to criticize or restrain colleagues. Alcohol-treatment facilities need similar watchdogs. Case conferences and staff meetings sometimes serve this purpose, but they are not sufficient. Each individual worker—professional or lay—should have his "control," a colleague of equivalent or greater training and experience, with whom he regularly discusses each person under his care. When care includes interventions of a specific and potent sort—for example, aversive conditioning, electric shock, hypnotherapy, drug treatment— a review committee covering each form of treatment should be established. Each committee should meet regularly; review each case; keep records indicating the frequency with which patients under the care of each professional suffer an unexpected bad result or have complaints filed on their behalf; and, when a given professional appears responsible for an undue number of harmful results due to the treatment method itself, take preventive measures. Such measures may include the requirement that the professional have further training, the requirement that he seek approval from a consultant before using a potent technique, or a reduction in his freedom to engage in certain kinds of treatments within the facility.

AGENCY EVALUATION

Within the various kinds of treatment facilities there are numerous problems that need evaluation and study to improve operations. Among the practical concerns of an agency that may be met by agency-oriented studies are the following:

Motivating Personnel. The question is how to interest personnel in the problems of diagnosis and treatment and how to train personnel so that they are not driven away from the problems that face them in meeting and treating alcoholics, especially those whose behavior runs counter to the usual conceptions therapists have of the patient role. From therapist surveys one might learn to identify factors associated with personnel turnover and with job dissatisfaction, to pinpoint the sources of frustrations in the treatment of alcoholics, and—very important—to examine attitudes of revulsion or disdain or mechanisms whereby people project their own negative ego-image upon the "alcoholic scapegoat." We already know that only a few people do care about the problems of alcohol and that most people wish to avoid thinking about them. Hence, a prime research endeavor might well be to learn more about the dynamics of this indifference and methods to counteract the real psychic and social barriers to the handling of the alcoholic.

Improving training. How effective is the in-service training offered to staff? Are people learning, within the limits of what is presently known, the basis and techniques of psychotherapeutic medicine, the preventive management of social misconduct, crisis intervention, the identification of prodromal signs associated with bouts of excessive drinking, epidemiological methods applicable to case finding and preventive work, or even simple facts about community resources and how their own facility works?

Improving the organization. What is actually going on in the facility? What are the lines of communication? What are the covert or informal procedures whereby things get done or small groups protect their integrity from outsiders or superiors? What kind of informal "training" of new staff by "old hands" goes on, and does this counteract agency goals or professional ideals? Who in fact is being seen and by whom? What shape are the records in? Why *that* bad? These are typical questions to which an agency self-survey (whether called operations research, program evaluation, or systems analysis) can address itself. What is learned must be fed back into the system slowly and with greatest care, for organizations are even *more* sensitive and defensive about receiving "interpretations" of what is going on than are solitary individuals. Perhaps the reason is that in psychotherapy the patient knows the therapist intends no harm and may even be his friend. No member of an organization is likely to believe the same about researchers who are evaluating his role therein. As with the premature interpretation, the organizational study is useless unless the findings are presented in such a way that acceptance and cooperative implementation can ensue.

Surviving in the community. Not all social research is an elaborate business of design, controls, statistics, or even questionnaires and flow charts. Sometimes it simply means gathering ordinary facts in an orderly way; so much of what constitutes agency-oriented research is already S.O.P. for the sophisticated administrator. Anybody who plans to do anything new in any organizational framework or anyone who sees he has problems with people in any aspect of the work setting is well advised to seek out the facts that bear on his plans or his troubles. A good politician or a good manager knows this already; sometimes professionals must be taught to be good politicians and managers before they can be at all effective in organizational work. Consider, for example, the problem of getting other agencies to work in alcohol programs. Why should they? Unless the alcoholic worker

can tell them why, the other agency will not "buy" cooperation. And
the selling requires knowledge of the other agency's mandate, its
real interests, its troubles, its capabilities, its sources of support, and
other relevant features. These are facts that have to be gathered before
one tries to sell programs to anybody else. The other agency is not
usually a hostile camp; one of the easiest ways to find out about
it is to ask the people there. However, people don't know, or won't
say, some of the most relevant things about themselves or the settings
they work in; so one also has to ask about these matters from those
who deal with them. These fact-finding missions are part of the job
of anyone who has to or wants to enlist the cooperation of others.

Alcohol programs have special problems. Sometimes it isn't
a matter of getting other people and facilities to cooperate; sometimes
it is a matter of just staying alive. In California in the last several
years, and no doubt other places, worthwhile alcohol programs have
been executed or threatened with the axe. To survive in a community
one must know the community. One must know where the centers of
power are, the factions, the sore spots. One must know where the
money is, how hard it is to get, who is for and who is against its
being spent on the poor, the sick, the outcasts, and the trouble-makers.
These are political facts, and it is not enough that a program chief
worry about them; if his staff and lay experts (trained lay volunteers)
are really part of things, they will worry too—and will take action
in the community. Sometimes one may have to conduct a community
survey to assess public concern about alcoholism or to determine public
willingness to be taxed for treament of alcoholics. Often the fact-
finding can be less formal—inquiries to see what supervisors or town
councilors think about alcohol programs, to see what they fear if they
do endorse them, to learn what they think they may gain by supporting or opposing them. Elected officials hold power at the pleasure
of all the people, but ordinarily officials listen closest only to some
of the people. One who wishes to survive in a community, to serve
it better, had best learn who are the listeners and who are the talkers.
Academically it may be considered a matter of community organization or dynamics. Politically it is a matter of going out into the
community to see what individuals and interest groups exist and
how they can be "sold" on the need for alcohol programs; or, if
they are unalterably opposed to either helping or spending, what
counterforces may be enlisted to educate or neutralize them.

For some professionals, political realities seem distant, dull, or tawdry. As dedicated people they want to help their patients, not worry about the mercurial swells of public opinion or the log-rolling world of politicians. But for any patient population that is essentially indigent, there can be no treatment unless someone other than the patient pays for it; even the most detached professional demands his fee. It is the public who pays, and it will be their representatives who decide how the money is spent. Those are the facts of alcoholism treatment. Consequently, one must learn as much as he can about the community in which he is working.

Chapter XXIV

~~~~~~

Recommendations for Related Research

It is increasingly popular these days to be critical of contemporary methods of treatment, to point to all that needs to be learned and all that *must* be done by way of research, and then smugly to sit back and wait until someone else does it. The clinician or other change-agent who reads the research-oriented descriptions of his operations and needs may well feel devastated by what is declared to be his ignorance and overwhelmed to the point of paralysis by what he is told he ought to do by way of research. The clinician knows that if one were to wait until all the research findings were in, it would be another five hundred years before anyone dared lift a finger to treat an alcoholic. He also knows that if it were not for the treatment and clinical study he has been conducting, many of the questions the researcher raises would never have come to awareness; for the questions have arisen out of clinical work.

No wonder the treatment world seems divided into two parts; one composed of clinicians and other doers who forge ahead—sometimes with their eyes shut to the needs for research and evaluation to avoid feeling badly about what they are doing; the other part consisting of researchers who, happily detached from patient responsibility, fret about clinician resistance, wonder whether anything that's being done in therapy can be justified, and worry if they can ever finish in one lifetime even one tenth of the investigative effort they have set out for themselves.

The plague, if one there be, is on both their houses, yet to avoid the limitations inherent in either point of view is difficult. Many readers are aware of this and we know they will be sympathetic as we set ourselves to the task of suggesting areas for study that are, to us, the most pertinent to alcoholism treatment needs. There is no intention here to draw up any kind of master plan for research in alcoholism or to touch upon the many unanswered questions about its etiology, correlates, and consequences. In defense of our avoiding those rich and complex regions we can only say that (a) this is a book about treatment, and (b) in considering the addictions (dependency on any drug), it seems to be the case that the factors leading to initial drug use can be quite different from those associated with continuing drug use and those in turn different from factors associated with disability from use. What one needs to know to treat a disorder is likely to be quite different from (but certainly not independent of) what one needs to know in order to prevent it.

At present it appears to us that three kinds of research hold promise for those interested in doing something about alcoholism in the near future. None of these areas will offer the promise of finding what causes alcoholism or what can cure it; they do offer hope for those who want to limit and treat it. The endeavours we recommend are (1) studying interaction between alcoholics and change-agents; (2) analyzing "gate-keeper" responses to alcoholics; and (3) initiating epidemiological surveys.

INTERACTION STUDIES

Who is the best match for an alcoholic of given background, personality, and situational characteristics? What kind of psychiatrist should attend to his inner life and medication? What social worker should work with his environment? What physician can best handle his person as well as his neuritis? Whitehorn and Betz (1960, 1957, 1954); Klerman (1960); Uhlenhuth and Park (1964); Joyce (1962); and others have made strong beginnings, asking what kind of therapist gets what kind of result. Whitehorn and Betz, it will be recalled, found that therapists with "personality," in the popular sense of vitality and outgoing interest, were better able to treat regressed schizophrenics than were uninvolved detached people—the classical psychoanalytic notion of the ideal therapist. There seems little question that early and valuable results could be produced if similar studies were done on the optimal characteristics of persons treating alcoholics. As one became more refined, one could identify subclasses of therapists and match them to kinds of alcoholics.

The results of interaction studies should be put to use in two ways; one in treatment assignment at intake based on the diagnostic characteristics of both the alcoholic and the change-agent; the other in training programs. Why training? Because the kind of change-agent *behavior* that leads to patient cooperation or recovery may be discovered by examining the characteristics of change-agents associated with successful and unsuccessful outcomes. It is not the social class of the doctor that affects the patient; it is how the social class expresses itself in looks and conduct to which the patient reacts. Therefore, one may well hope to find critical kinds of behavior, which, it is presumed, can be changed. If behavior can be changed, then it can be taught. It can be taught in training programs that aim to give each change-agent a wider repertoire of skills so that he may successfully be assigned to a greater variety of patients. The versatile change-agent will use his skills differentially depending on the patient, just as any therapist does now. The only difference is that he will have more skills and will know which ones lead to improvement in given classes of alcoholics.

At the very least, research that simultaneously takes account of patient, therapist, and treatment-method variables must have some kind of a Latin Square design. This calls for a great number of cases to whom all possible major forms of treatment are applied, all matched and controlled, composed of heterogeneous elements. Only thus can the role of background characteristics, age, social status, and diagnosis be determined, both in patient and in therapist.

One may take the past research describing treatment method, patient characteristics, and outcomes (and where available, therapist characteristics) and build an after-the-fact Latin Square. One might begin to build into the checkerboard all those dimensions about which information is given, to see which squares are empty. The result would be a graphic picture of what kind of research needs yet to be done; what kinds of patient populations have yet to be offered; and which kinds of treatment methods should complete the design.

What is suggested is a Completion Square. For example, let us imagine that a full literature review revealed that disulfiram treatment evaluation had been reported on lower-class males and middle-class males and females. No lower-class females and no upper-class persons of either sex would have been followed. In that simple Completion Square there are three empty squares for those unevaluated groups defined by sex and social class. One can do the same for each type of treatment and for as many population variables as one suspects play a role in treatment outcomes. The method offers one way of contributing to general knowledge via treatment studies in institutions.

GATE-KEEPERS AND AUXILIARY HEALERS

Any person who is in a position to identify an alcoholic and to refer him to a treatment agency is a gate-keeper, to use the terminology of Kurt Lewin. If the person recognizes the alcohol problem of another and gets the alcoholic into care, he has opened a gate. If he does nothing, he keeps the alcoholic's possible road to recovery closed. A gate-keeper can be, for example, a college dean, a teen-age-gang street worker, a work foreman, a probation officer, a physician, a minister, a policeman, a social case worker, or a family member. Since these people do play critical parts in patient treatment careers—not only in case finding and referral but later too as resources in treatment—one wants to learn all one can about how to maximize their gate-opening capacities. For instance, members of families of alcoholics have been the object of worthwhile research (Jackson, 1956; Freeman and Simmons, 1958) and parallel studies of the families of mentally ill persons throw additional light on family dynamics (Clausen and Yarrow, 1955). Even so, a number of questions remain. One can ask what the circumstances are that lead family members to resist admitting that a relative is alcoholic or to resist his being treated once illness is admitted. What roles do family members play in one case to keep the drinker on the wagon and in another case to encourage him subtly to resume his drinking? Consideration of psychodynamics should not lead one to ignore hypotheses based on a family's inadequate information about alcoholism or its false premises about the requirements for or nature of treatment itself. The reader will think of many hypotheses to test; much worthwhile work beckons.

Another step is to study how one may train families to assist in treatment. The family does have a part in diagnosing trouble, in getting the patient to a change-agency, and in giving support and auxiliary treatment to enhance the professional treatment—even if it is as simple as decreasing the number of drinks he has per day or being with him as a safety factor when he is intoxicated. If, as many suspect, the family has a role in participating, prolonging, or aggravating the illness, then how can we instruct and guide families to handle their alcoholic member so that he will obtain proper care and cooperate with treatment, and so that they will give him the necessary emotional backing? One may experiment with didactic methods, especially when the family is given a supervisory role (see Chapter 5). It is not to be assumed that family interactions are inevitably pathogenic for the patient. That assumption may stem from therapists' predilection to overidentify with the patient, a therapeutic weakness commonly seen in therapy with children, where the therapist comes to view the evil parents as the source of all the child's sorrows. Family members unable to make the alcoholic feel their more sensible point of view may just be frightened of his potential for violence; they would be quite able to deal more positively with him had they adequate instruction in just what to do and what resources to call upon in a crisis. The information needed may be as simple as knowing that the police or sheriff's department can be called in to help take the patient to the hospital (it may be useful to point out that in some departments the police receive special training and act in a kind and considerate way). Were one to evaluate the effects of education and work with families, and were one to find even five to ten per cent improvement in their recovery rates over those of control cases, one would be pleased.

Experiments in bringing the family into the treatment situation can be done in night schools and in adult-education centers; different methods should be tried and *evaluated*. Guidelines for experiments in reaching and teaching families more effectively can be sought from psychotherapists experienced in family dynamics and family therapy. One would also hope to involve these therapists directly in the education of families with alcoholic members. Ministers too should be involved; they should be taught how successfully they can assist families in preventing, identifying, and referring alcohol problem patients, and participating in treatment. One means for more involvement of pastors would come through their being invited to participate in a variety of alcohol programs; for example, in a Community Alcoholism Research Training Center. One can conceive of fascinating action-research programs of a three-step nature—working with parish priests who in turn would work with Irish working men's groups and women's groups with the goal of producing in these groups and in families awareness of how to handle incipient and actual alcoholism. A variety of other possible efforts will no doubt come to the reader's mind.

EPIDEMIOLOGICAL APPROACH

We do not embrace the disease concept of alcoholism in its entirety. Nevertheless, it has distinct advantages in certain research formulations of alcohol problems. In treatment research particularly, the disease concept offers the advantage that the epidemiological approach becomes particularly appropriate. As Morris (1957) points out (and we have quoted him liberally below), epidemiology informs of the health of the community and, by historical study, of the *rise and fall of a disease*. With reference to the changing patterns of alcoholism in a population, it provides a community diagnosis of the *present nature and distribution of health and disease* among the population, the *dimensions* of these and, in particular, disease *incidence, prevalence,* and *mortality* due to it. It takes into account that society is changing and that health problems, including the addictions and alcoholism, are changing as well. It studies the *workings of healh services*. This begins with the determination of *needs* and *resources,* proceeds to the *analysis of services in action,* and finally attempts to *appraise the success* with which these services meet the needs of the community it presumably serves. *It helps to complete the clinical picture* by including all types of cases in proportion and by relating clinical disease to the sub-clinical, including secular changes in the character of the disease and its picture in other countries. It leads to the discovery of *identifying syndromes* from the distribution of clinical phenomena among sections of the population. It engages in a *search for causes* of health and disease, starting by discovering groups having high and low rates of disease, then studying these differences in disease patterns in relation to differences in ways of living. Finally, it tests these notions of causation in actual practice by introducing preventive measures among populations.

The epidemiological method is a primary method for studying the *social* aspects of health and disease and linking these to biological

and clinical features. Since epidemiology focuses on natural populations, it will often wish to establish the distribution of various forms
of a disease in these populations. By comparing cases identified "at
large" to cases that come to clinics or to other specialized agencies,
one can learn not only which forms of an illness constitute clinical
problems, but also what social and psychological factors account for
some types of cases being seen while others exist without becoming
clinically identified. The method also allows for the identification of
syndromes that may include social as well as biological features, and
it assists in finding factors providing immunity from as well as vulnerability to illness. Morris writes, "Epidemiology . . . helps to complete the clinical picture and natural history of disease . . . (and)
by identifying harmful ways of living and by pointing the road to
healthier ways, helps to abolish the clinical picture. One of the most
urgent social needs of the day is to identify rules of healthy living
that might reduce the burden of metabolic, malignant, and degen-
erative diseases which are so characteristic of features of our society."*

In order to treat a patient, one needs to know something about
what has caused his condition in order to be able either to remove
the causative factors or to circumvent them. Nutrition, climate, sea-
son, geography, geological factors, occupational hazards, and the like
should be considered among causal factors. When groups to be studied
are characterized by their environment and special ways of life, one
can begin to unravel "causes" of disease, causes about which it may
be possible to suggest and do something by way of control and prevention. In epidemiology, crucial aspects of ways of life include the
satisfaction of elementary human needs and the presence and kinds
of growth hazards and trauma.

Epidemiologists are only at the beginning of identifying such
"causes" in the environment, in mass habits and social customs, which
may be related to the main contemporary problems of public health.
Cultural factors including eating customs, poverty, ignorance, and
unhygienic practices are some of these. One needs to think of a pattern
or complex of causes, very likely of differing importance and directness,
adding together, possibly compounding each other; and again very
likely, varying in different situations—as seems indeed to be the case
with alcoholism. Morris thinks that *for such problems of "multiple*

---

* Among alcohol authorities who have advocated epidemiological
studies of the kind outlined above is Chafetz (1963).

causality" the epidemiological method is particularly suited to identify causes and to disentangle their relations. For example, in studying any contagious disease one would be concerned to understand the effects of belonging to a given sex and age; the psychological causes contributing to the incidence of the disease; the economics of a disease (as will be described in the case of alcoholism and alcohol industry relationships); the way of life of the patient (for instance, denial of family life, working as contract migrant labor, etc.)—all are to be taken into account.

When one tries to unravel the relationship existing among these etiological factors, one should consider these categories: *chain of events, predisposing genetic susceptibilities, provoking trauma, precipitating factors* and possibly *perpetuating causes,* and, finally, *chain reactions,* which bring about a spiraling of pathogenic effects. The notion of multiple causality implies that postulated causes must be experimentally crossed with each other to determine their relationships and their relative importance. Are the different causes merely one and the same thing under different guises? If not, do they add together to produce the disease? Or do these causes multiply each other in some way? Particularly important for alcohol treatment research is the question of the *dynamic* relationship of causes. If one cause or more perform a homeostatic function, it must not be assumed that simple interference will have simple results.*

In alcoholism research, geographical pathology is especially relevant. This includes the *local peculiarities* of the disease and factors that aid or interfere with recovery from the illness. For instance, the manner in which the clinical picture and the mortality differ may yield important etiological clues. Very interesting contributions have already come from anthropologists who have studied drinking in different regions; however, the clinician in the United States should be equally sensitive to such research opportunities insofar as we have populations from widely different geographical, ethnic, and racial backgrounds, who may exhibit different forms of the alcoholism syn-

---

* As we have said earlier, psychoanalysts have often voiced the fear that when one interferes with a symptom, one may produce a very undesirable reaction. A psychotic episode may be precipitated if problem drinking is stopped (and the patient becomes suddenly abstinent without being relieved of his underlying conflict, which the drinking had alleviated). See the reports on psychoses precipitated by disulfiram therapy (Bowman *et al.*, 1955).

drome. The principle is that if poverty or affluence, obesity or mal-
nutrition, hard work or indolence, warm weather or cold, moisture
or aridity, crowding or isolation, altitude or deficiency diseases, nervous
strain combined with physical inactivity, exercise combined with freedom from anxiety, or other micro- or macro-climates breed different
clinical pictures of the same disease, the exact details of each specific
situation must be investigated. This is where clinicians and epidemiologists can collaborate to best advantage to bring about a clarification. This is particularly true for our rapidly changing patterns of
drinking behavior. We may expect a shift in the rates of incidence
and the character of alcoholism both in a qualitative and a quanti-
tative fashion.*

Alcoholism as a disease should be viewed as a *biological process*.
Its eradication by eliminating alcohol ingestion altogether, as a re-
former might sweep the world free of sin, is not enough for a rational
approach to the problem. The research-oriented therapist must analyse
dispassionately his geographic locale to see what is happening to his
patient decade by decade, and how this compares with what is
happening elsewhere. What are the differences in manifestations of
alcoholism that beset Negroes living in Harlem as compared with
those in rural Alabama? To what extent is alcoholism actually a
man-made disease? For anyone in our society, what impact does the
prolongation of the average life-span have upon the prospect of his
contracting alcoholism?

Of prime importance in clinical research is the examination of
a sick individual *in the setting* where he became ill and where, after
his recovery, he may also become ill again. We wish to emphasize
this point because in modern practice the effort tends to be concentrated on measurement and observations of patients in an examining
room or in a clinic setting. For various reasons, the therapist isolates
himself from the patients' surroundings by this procedure. As Paul
(1958) points out, "hospital care is not the end of all modern clinical
medicine, particularly if the science of preventive medicine is to be
developed, which, in turn, depends a great deal upon its basic science
—epidemiology."

Modern practice calls for a relatively prompt medical intervention to alleviate immediate symptoms and quick discharge of the

_____

* See Hirsch (1860), who called attention to the fact that diseases in
the past have not always been similar to those in the present.

patient to his home. Such practice is often extremely beneficial, but at the same time it can also obscure the causative events that have led up to the acute breakdown, and which may affect other members in the household, prolong the disease, or complicate eventual recovery. While this has been recognized for infectious diseases, it is particularly relevant to alcoholism. Clinical investigation of the patient's household will correct the tendency to ignore his pathogenic setting. Paul, to whom we are indebted for much that follows, describes charts and diagrams that can be used in such research: family charts and community charts in which relevant events in patients' histories are listed, such as hereditary, growth, and environmental factors including working conditions that may have had some bearing on health.

Paul reminds the reader that the farmer requires good seed, good soil, and a proper climate if his crops are to be plentiful. The same may be applied to alcoholism: there has to be alcohol, there has to be a susceptible organism, and there have to be proper environmental circumstances to precipitate this disease in an individual. All three factors must be considered as causes: *genetic factors and ways of living must eventually be included as important variables in research design.*

The "single-cause idea" was very popular after Pasteur had discovered the germ theory of disease. However, it has come to be regarded, by sophisticated investigators at least, as an oversimplification. "It takes more than a microbe to produce a disease, just as it takes more than a seed to produce a plant" (Paul, p. 65). Similarly, the clinician who would do research in alcoholism and treatment of alcoholism must differentiate direct precipitating causes from supplementary causes and assign them priority. These other causes are to be found in the characteristics of individual members of the population attacked, as well as in the environment in which both host and disease agents find themselves. It is the sum, or interaction, of these influences that give rise to alcoholism. It is up to the researcher to discover the valences or weights proper to each. This will yield knowledge about the contributory factors that determine whether a severe case, a mild case, or no alcoholism at all will be the result of drinking.

In all these conditions the *individual's resistance,* conditioned probably by both hereditary and environmental factors, occupies a dominant position. His susceptibility and his ability to "cope with or to succumb" to addiction, injury, or insult, are relevant research variables. In clinical medicine it is recognized that these characteristics are often impossible to treat, or even to measure; nevertheless, they should not be ignored. As stated before, prophylactic measures, designed to increase man's resistance to alcohol addiction, insofar as they are effective will be the proof of the correctness of the research hypotheses.

Other important causal variables are the macro-climate and the micro-climate. The first includes temperature, rainfall, humidity, seasonal variations, and so on;* the second consists of the sum of those intimate living conditions in which a given individual finds himself. It includes the nature of rural or urban living, housing, temperature and humidity within the home or working place, living space (crowding or isolation), food; it includes also the life satisfactions and frustrations and all the circumstances of poverty or affluence. It is evident that macro-climate and micro-climate are interrelated. For instance, if one assumes that excessive drinking is frequently associated with loneliness and social isolation, then such geographic or climate factors as affect socialization become extremely important. A pleasant sunny climate, such as prevails in the Southern countries, facilitates gregariousness enormously; and in fact, alcoholism is hardly a problem in those countries where people congregate day in and day out at the taverns to drink and to socialize for long hours at a time (R. and E. Blum, 1963; see also Sadoun, Lolli, and Silverman, 1965).

Another important factor is change in the population. We know from studies of the epidemiology of infectious diseases that within a small homogeneous population an infectious disease may flare up for a while and then burn itself out, once all the susceptible cases have contracted the disease and have either died from it or recovered. The situation is quite different in a population in which a constant influx of immigrants provides new fuel for the epidemic to continue. For example, Bartlett (1962) has shown how a stochastic model applied to epidemics allows prediction when actuarial methods do not; the difference is that population changes over time and population characteristics in terms of the number of susceptible individuals at any one point in time determine critical threshold values. Below these values the incidence of the infection will decline; above them epidemics will occur. The "susceptible immigrant" is a useful concept in alcoholism research. San Francisco, for instance, has one of the highest alcoholism rates in the country. It also has a high rate of immigrants.

---

* The striking North-South dichotomy in alcoholism incidence, both in the U.S.A. and in Europe, is an example.

It would seem that San Francisco provides an environment where alcoholism is either endemic and those individuals who enter this area without previous immunization fall prey to the diseases, or where the immigrants are themselves transmission vectors. While such analogies suffer from the faults of all analogies, nevertheless, some interesting possibilities can be derived from them: for instance, the influence that previous exposure to alcohol will have. "Immunity" to alcoholism can be found in populations where children are exposed from a very early age to drinking practices that are integrated into their way of life. Conversely, we also know how badly populations disintegrate who are exposed to alcohol for the first time and who have had no previous experience with other intoxicating substances. Indeed, from cross-cultural studies (Child, Bacon, and Barry, 1965) we know that societies with the least integrated drinking (and presumably most abuse) are those where alcohol has been recently introduced, not where it was aboriginally present. Detailed clinical observations and research such as can be made during the treatment of people from various ethnic background (those who have been inoculated against alcohol and those who have not) will yield more precise information on the mechanisms underlying resistance or immunity to alcoholism. We still do not know very much of what makes some people more vulnerable than others to alcoholism or to other addiction. To what extent is this vulnerability genetic or inherent? To what extent has it been acquired through exposure and training? What alternatives are there to becoming addicted to one particular poison, to one compulsive behavior, or to one single form of satisfaction? Perhaps it is a consolation to alcohol researchers to know that these questions are largely unanswered in the study of infectious diseases as well; and that even there, the problem of measuring the degree of resistance looms large.

As in many somatic diseases, alcoholism prevalence rates (and other drug addiction rates) all over the world are different for men than for women. It is interesting to note that, just as with a duodenal ulcer (Wolff, 1953), and perhaps even in the case of coronary thrombosis, these relative prevalence rates seem to be changing as the socio-economic position of women changes. The Swiss, for example, are concerned that alcoholism rates for women will increase if women are given the vote. Strange as this may seem, perhaps they are right. In any event, it will be well to pay close attention to the factors that so far have protected women from alcoholism in order to discover why men are more susceptible to this disease. Here again is an area where research concern and preventive efforts go hand in hand with treatment.

When dealing with the problem of genetic make-up, which predisposes one individual and protects another, one must bear in mind that just because one is faced with a high prevalence of alcoholism in one family, this by no means establishes a hereditary tendency to acquire this condition. Other things may "run" in families that actually are determined by unchanging so-called "domiciliary" factors, or local customs, not heredity. These domiciliary variables include dietary deficiencies, which in turn may be determined by economic or cultural factors. Even the method of controlling for genetic factors by using identical twins is not altogether foolproof. It may be argued that the intra-uterine environment shared by identical twins was sufficiently traumatic (inasmuch as not enough oxygen, food, or space were available) to make twins more susceptible to any number of pathogens than a single child would be, including more susceptible to becoming dependent upon substances such as alcohol.

SUMMARY

We propose the following research priorities to provide the clinician with information that will enable him to apply the most effective and rational methods where they will be of maximum benefit: (a) *Methodological research* to determine if and what instruments exist that are capable of identifying cases of alcoholism. See R. Blum (1962). At present it is certainly open to question whether we have the necessary tools. Thus, the first step will be to evaluate our case-identifying instruments and to add to our diagnostic armamentarium. (b) Assuming the availability of methods for case finding, case identification, and case designation, *studies to determine the particular characteristics of cases with reference to provision of care (i.e.,* is the identified alcoholic treatable, what treatment methods are most appropriate to him and at what stage is he, or is he at least amenable to some community action or influence). (c) *Actuarial-descriptive studies* that describe the prevalence and incidence of alcoholism to indicate the magnitude of the problem by group and region; and which are correlated to the treatment and rehabilitation facilities available in that region. (d) *Etiological studies* to learn more about how alcoholism comes about; for example, what is the association of alcoholism with given biological or social characteristics; what is its association with vulnerabilities to other chemical substances and to other emotional problems. Case identification and case designation studies could be undertaken with the aim of a revision of pathological concepts.* For example, one may ask what is the association of various alcoholism syndromes with other physical disorders or diseases; one may ask whether it is possible to modify current classifications of alcoholics into useful categories. (e) *Studies to implement the provision or administration of facilities.* Such studies would answer questions regarding the location of various needed facilities, what the expected clientele will be, and so forth. (f) *Studies set up to evaluate services* to alcoholics in terms of (1) utilization; (2) effects on rates of prevalence (are there a greater number of rehabilitated alcoholics as a result of the services provided by the facilities in question); (3) rates of incidence (are there fewer alcoholics as a result of preventive efforts made by the facilities in the area under investigation).

(g) Among the other research that will benefit clinical practice, and which is not based upon a strictly epidemiological approach are, among others, longitudinal studies dealing with the problems of early sensitivities, dynamically oriented studies of child alcoholics within their families, and animal research focusing on situational determinants associated with the self-selection of alcohol (see Masserman, 1943) and with genetic factors in addiction liability (see Rodgers and McClearn, 1962), the goal being not just the isolation of alcohol predisposing variables but the study of the effect of environmental interventions in prevention and treatment. An illustration of this kind of work is the fine study by Thompson and Warren (1965) showing how environmental settings affect re-addiction rates in morphine-using rats.

---

* See Opler's criticism of present-day nosology (Opler, 1963).

Chapter XXV

Final Comment

In the United States many citizens are temporarily or permanently disabled—psychologically, socially, or physically—by alcohol. Their disabilities bring immense distress and danger to other citizens in the community. No citizen can be sure that his own life will not suffer some unanticipated pain or disaster brought about by others acting under the impact of alcohol. No wonder, then, that there must be public as well as private efforts directed toward the control and reduction of alcohol-related problems.

The effort to reduce distress and danger arising from alcohol abuse includes a variety of methods that are psychological in nature. Some of these efforts are educational, some manipulative, and some simply refined forms of coercion; we do not consider them psychotherapeutic since their aims are set without regard for the wishes and well-being of the alcoholic himself. There are, on the other hand, a number of techniques that are genuinely therapeutic, for they are employed in cooperation with the patient and with full regard for his dignity and welfare. These therapeutic efforts have here been the subject of our concern.

Reviewing the variety of psychotherapeutic endeavours, including a number of promising programs conducted by non-professionals, one concludes that although there is as yet no "sure cure" for alcoholism, there are treatments that lead to improvement and, in some cases, full remission. Contrary to past pessimism, there is sufficient evidence now at hand to say that the rate of improvement for alcoholics approaches that for treated mental illness in general—a reasonable across-the-board figure being 50 per cent improvement. The adherents of some methods, almost always new techniques but with short-term follow-up evaluations, claim as high as 80 per cent improvement, but we feel that these claims must be viewed with great caution. As with the many methods of psychotherapy, the rate of success in alcoholism treatment—inasmuch as it can be estimated—seems about the same even when treatments are different. This state of affairs should lead, we suggest, to further attempts to isolate the sources of healing common to the several treatments, and to some reduction in the partisanship shown by the more dogmatic claimants for particular methods.

With reference to treatment goals, it is our position that moderate rather than extreme changes should be sought. Improvement can occur in practical matters such as reducing the amount and frequency of alcohol ingested, in reducing the dangers and despair attending drinkers and those about them, and in making provision for the reduction of undesirable side effects. Such goals can be met by present treatment means. These same means are not so likely to achieve complete abstinence or a reorganization of personality such that psychopathological features predisposing to drug abuse disappear. Alcoholism itself is best considered a chronic condition requiring life-time care.

The emphasis of limited goals is reflected in several important principles. One is that many persons besides professionals in medicine, psychology or social work are found to be qualified to participate in alcoholism treatment. These change-agents can make splendid contributions to individual, family, and community well-being and should be encouraged to do more. A second principle is that complete abstinence is not required as a treatment goal; instead, one expects to achieve a reduction of the abuse of alcohol, although one may also occasionally achieve normal social drinking without abuse. A third principle is that by setting limited goals one prevents discouragement in the healer, in other change-agents, in the family, and in the alcoholic himself, that can lead to premature abandonment of treatment efforts. Those efforts must not be abandoned.

The effort to heal alcoholics has suffered from defects that are, we believe, capable of remedy. One defect has been the grossly insufficient manpower devoted to treatment endeavours. A very few dedicated people, non-professionals as well as professionals, have borne a great burden of care. Their ranks must be enlarged.

A second defect, perhaps not unrelated to the first, has been the striking apathy and almost willful disinterest that has been seen among citizens, professionals, and public authorities when it comes to the support of *treatment* for alcohol-related problems. People involved in prevention and treatment have been lonely and unappreciated. Fortunately, it appears that times are changing and that, aside from the perennial moralizing and clamor for punitive programs (which have never been in short supply, thanks to at least some vocal segments of the public), there now appears to be a rising interest in the humane and effective prevention and treatment of alcoholism.

A third defect, quite opposite to apathy but much related to the vociferous demands for punishment and control, has been zealotry among healers and change-agents themselves. Perhaps a dedicated few are driven to bias and self-righteousness in order to maintain their endeavours; so much the sadder. In any event, zealotry—admittedly among only a few, but an important few—have confounded certain treatment efforts and have acted to make moderation and objectivity unpopular in some circles. We know too little to allow dogmatism to bind us; let moderation in thought as well as in drinking hold sway.

A fourth defect is related to the third; some portion of our lack of facts must be attributed to poor research rather than none at all. It is a tired complaint that clinicians have been lax in their research methods and that experimentalists have devoted themselves to trivia. An unfair charge, we would say, in many cases, but still fair enough too often. The solution is both simple and difficult: better training for research, more supervision in research, more emphasis on evaluation during treatment, and more communication between clinicians and experimenters so that one can teach the other.

As a fifth defect we would list the failure on the part of most concerned people—citizens and professionals—to consider alcoholism within the larger framework in which it belongs. Alcohol is but one drug among many mind-altering drugs; alcoholics are but one group suffering the effects of drug dependency and abuse. What is needed is not isolation and provincialism among those concerned with each of the drugs abusable or the classes of abusing users, but a community of interest and effort—regardless of whether the special interest be the opiates, alcohol, tranquilizers, stimulants, sedatives, hallucinogens, or carcinogenic tobacco. We see the problem as a general one—defined either in terms of people who use drugs and who suffer and cause suffering thereby; or, pharmacologically, in terms of drugs that have potentials for damage as well as for helping and giving pleasure. Everyone involved in the study of drug effects and drug abuse and everyone involved in experiments on prevention and treatment should consider himself a member of a community of interest; in this community we all have much to learn from one another.

Our final point: the treatment of alcoholism is a slow business, a demanding business and, in terms of patient numbers, an overwhelming business. It is easy to become discouraged. The knowledge that treatment works should help to keep the change-agent going. But knowledge is not enough; healers are people and need supporting environments in which to work. We think the creation and maintenance of those environments is critical. Consequently, the art of competent administration becomes a necessity, the pleasure of good working conditions becomes a requirement, and the excitement of a close-knit, fully alive work group becomes a *sine qua non* for treatment and research.

Bibliography

ABRAMS, H. S. AND MC COURT, W. F. "Interaction of physicians with emergency ward alcoholic patients," *Quart. J. Stud. Alc.*, 1964, *25*, 679–688.

ABRAMS, S. "An evaluation of hypnosis in the treatment of alcoholics," *Am. J. Psychiat.*, 1964, *120*, 1160–1165.

ABRAMSON, H. "Lysergic acid diethylamide (LSD-25): III. As an adjunct to psychotherapy," *J. Psychol.*, 1955, *39*, 127–155.

ACKERKNECHT, E. "Primitive medicine and culture pattern," *Bull. hist. Med.*, 1942, *11*, 503–521.

ACKERMAN, N. W. "Psychoanalysis and group psychotherapy," *Group Psychother.*, 1949, *3*, 214–215.

ADAMS, H. B. "Mental illness, or interpersonal behavior?," *Am. Psychologist*, 1964, *19*, 191–197.

AGRIN, A. "Who is qualified to treat the alcoholic? A discussion," *Quart. J. Stud. Alc.*, 1964, *25*, 347.

AICHHORN, A. *Wayward Youth.* New York: Viking, 1936.

Alcoholics Anonymous. New York: Alcoholics Anonymous World Service, 1960. [1st ed. 1939.]

Alcoholics Anonymous Comes of Age: A Brief History of A. A. New York: Alcoholics Anonymous Publishing, 1957.

317

ALEXANDER, F. *Psychoanalysis and Psychotherapy: Developments and Training.* New York: Norton, 1956.

ANGST, J. "Zur Frage der Psychosen bei Behandlung mit Disulfiram (Antabus). Lieterarübersicht und kasuistischer Beitrag," *Schweiz. Med. Wschr.,* 1956, *86,* 1304–1306.

APPLE, D. (ed.). *Social Studies of Health and Sickness.* New York: McGraw-Hill, 1960.

ARIETI, S. (ed.). *American Handbook of Psychiatry.* Vol. II. New York: Basic Books, 1959.

ARMSTRONG, R. G. "A review of the theories explaining the psychodynamics and etiology of alcoholism in men," *Psychol. Newsl.,* New York Univ., 1959, *10,* 159–171.

ASCH, S. E. *Social Psychology.* New York: Prentice-Hall, 1952.

ASH, P. "The reliability of psychiatric diagnosis," *J. abnorm. soc. Psychol.,* 1959, *44,* 272–276.

Associate of the British Society of Addiction. "The nursing of alcoholic patients," *Brit. J. Addict.,* 1947, *44,* 75–78.

Ayerst Laboratories. *"Antabuse" Toxicity.* Bibliography compiled by Ayerst Laboratories. New York: 1961.

AZIMA, H. "Prolonged sleep treatment in mental disorder: Some new psychopharmacological considerations," *J. ment. Sci.,* 1955, *101,* 593–603.

AZIMA, H. AND VISPO, R. H. "The problem of regression during prolonged sleep treatment." In G. J. Sarwer-Foner (ed.), *The Dynamics of Psychiatric Drug Therapy.* Springfield, Ill.: Thomas, 1960.

AZIMA, H. "Sleep treatment." In J. H. Masserman and J. L. Moreno (eds.), *Progress in Psychotherapy.* Vol. III. New York: Grune and Stratton, 1958.

AZRIN, N. H. AND HOLZ, W. C. "Punishment during sixth-interval reinforcement," *J. exp. Animal Behav.,* 1961, *4,* 343–347.

BAILEY, M., HABERMAN, P., AND SHEINBERG, J. "Identifying alcoholics in population surveys," *Quart. J. Stud. Alc.,* 1966, *27*(2), 300–315.

BALES, R. F. "The therapeutic role of Alcoholics Anonymous as seen by a sociologist." In D. J. Pittman and R. R. Snyder (eds.), *Society, Culture and Drinking Patterns.* New York: Wiley, 1962.

BALES, R. F. *Interaction Process Analysis.* Cambridge: Addison-Wesley, 1950.

BALINT, M. *The Doctor, His Patient and the Illness.* New York: International Universities Press, 1957.

BANNERJEE, S. *Psychotherapy,* 1957, *1, 2*; as cited by Sandison, R. A., "The role of psychotropic drugs in group therapy." In M. Rosenbaum and M. M. Berger (eds.), *Group Psychotherapy and Group Function.* New York: Basic Books, 1963.

BARTLETT, M. S. *Essays on Probability and Statistics.* London: Methuen, 1962.

BARZUN, J. *Darwin, Marx, Wagner: Critique of a Heritage.* [2nd ed.] Garden City, N.Y.: Doubleday-Anchor, 1958.

BELDEN, E. "A therapeutic community for hospitalized alcoholics," *California's Health,* 1962, *20,* 89–90.

BELDEN, E. AND HITCHEN, R. "The identification and treatment of an early deprivation syndrome in alcoholics by means of LSD-25," *Am. J. Psychiat.,* 1963, *119,* 985–986.

BELKNAP, I. *Human Problems of a State Mental Hospital.* New York: McGraw-Hill, 1956.

BELL, R. G. "Who is qualified to treat the alcoholic? Comment on the Krystal-Moore discussion," *Quart. J. Stud. Alc.,* 1964, *25,* 562–568.

BELLAK, L. (ed.). *Handbook of Community Psychiatry and Community Mental Health.* New York: Grune and Stratton, 1964.

BENNETT, A. E., MC KEEVER, L. G., AND TURK, R. E. "Psychotic reactions during tetraethylthiuramdisulfide (antabuse) therapy," *J.A.M.A.,* 1951, *145,* 483–484.

BERNSTEIN, A. "The psychoanalytic technique." In B. B. Wolman (ed.), *Handbook of Clinical Psychology.* New York: McGraw-Hill, 1965.

BETTELHEIM, B. *The Informed Heart.* Glencoe, Ill.: Free Press, 1960.

BETTELHEIM, B. *Love Is Not Enough.* Glencoe, Ill.: Free Press, 1950.

BETZ, BARBARA J. "Experiences in research in psychotherapy with schizophrenic patients." In H. H. Strupp and L. Luborsky (eds.), *Research in Psychotherapy.* Proceedings of a conference, Chapel Hill, North Carolina, May 17–20, 1961. Baltimore: American Psychological Assoc.; French-Bray Printing Co. 1962.

BJORKHEM, J. "Alcoholism and hypnotic therapy," *Brit. J. med. Hypn.,* 1956, 7 (4), 23–33.

BLANE, H. T. AND MEYERS, W. R. "Behavioral dependence and length of stay in psychotherapy among alcoholics," *Quart. J. Stud. Alc.,* 1963, *24,* 503–510.

BLANE, H. T. AND MEYERS, W. R. "Social class and establishment of treatment relations by alcoholics," *J. clin. Psychol.,* 1964, 22, 287–290.

BLANE, H. T., OVERTON, W. F., AND CHAFETZ, M. E. "Social factors in the diagnosis of alcoholism. I. Characteristics of the patient," *Quart. J. Stud. Alc.,* 1963, *24,* 640–663.

BLOCK, M. A. "A program for the homeless alcoholics," *Quart. J. Stud. Alc.,* 1962, *23,* 644–649.

BLUM, EVA M. "Psychoanalytic views on alcoholism," *Quart. J. Stud. Alc.,* 1966, 27(2), 259–299.

BLUM, EVA M. "Who is qualified to treat the alcoholic? A discussion," *Quart. J. Stud. Alc.* 1964, *25,* 350.

BLUM, EVA M. "The uncooperative patient in medical practice." In R. H. Blum (ed.), *Supplementary Studies in Malpractice.* Medical Review and Advisory Board, California Medical Association, confidential report, 1958.

BLUM, R. H. "Mind altering drugs and dangerous behavior: Alcohol." A report to the President's Commission on Law Enforcement and the Administration of Justice, 1966. (Xerox)

BLUM, R. H. AND ASSOCIATES. *Utopiates: The Use and Users of LSD-25,* New York: Atherton, 1964.

BLUM, R. H. "Jailers' revolt," *The Progressive,* 1964(a), *28,* 40–43.

BLUM, R. H. *A Common Sense Guide for Patients to Hospitals and Medical Care.* New York: Macmillan, 1964 (b).

BLUM, R. H. "Case identification in psychiatric epidemiology: Methods and problems," *Millbank Mem. Fund Quart.,* 1962, *40,* 253–288.

BLUM, R. H. *Management of the Doctor-Patient Relationship.* New York: McGraw-Hill, 1960.

BLUM, R. H. *Hospitals and Patient Dissatisfaction.* San Francisco: California Medical Association, 1958.

BLUM, R. H. AND BLUM, EVA M. *Health and Healing in Rural Greece.* Stanford: Stanford University Press, 1965.

BLUM, R. H. AND BLUM, EVA M. "Temperate Achilles, A study of drinking practices and beliefs in rural Greece." Stanford: Institute for the Study of Human Problems, 1964. See also "Drinking practices and controls in rural Greece," *Brit. J. Addict.*, 1964, *60*, 93–108.

BLUM, R. H. AND DOWNING, J. J. "Staff response to innovation in a mental health service," *Am. J. pub. Health*, 1964, *54*, 1230–1240.

BLUM, R. AND EZEKIEL, J. *Clinical Records for Mental Health Services.* Springfield, Ill.: Thomas, 1962.

BOCHNER, A. K. "The ABCD of alcoholism," *News, Cleveland Center on Alcoholism*, 1962, *4*, 1–4.

BORTZ, EDWARD. "Who is qualified to treat the alcoholic? A discussion," *Quart. J. Stud. Alc.*, 1964, *25*, 351.

BOURNE, P. G., ALFORD, J. A., AND BOWCOCK, J. Z. "Treatment of skid-row alcoholics with disulfiram," (prepublication abstract) *Quart. J. Stud. Alc.*, 1965, *26*.

BOWMAN, K., SIMON, A., *et al.* "A clinical evaluation of tetraethylthiuram disulfide (antabuse) in the treatment of problem drinkers." In E. Podolsky (ed.), *Management of Addictions.* New York: Philosophical Library, 1955.

BRENMAN, MARGARET AND GILL, M. M. *Hypnosis and Related States. Psychoanalytic Studies in Regression.* New York: International Universities Press, 1961.

BRENMAN, MARGARET AND GILL, M. M. *Hypnotherapy.* New York: International Universities Press, 1947.

BROWN, B. W., ESQUIBLE, A., GRANT, M., AND PICKFORD, E. M. "Health department alcoholism program in Prince Georges County, Md.," *Public Health Rep., Washington*, 1962, *77*, 480–484.

BROWN, C. L. "A transference phenomenon in alcoholics: Its therapeutic implications," *Quart. J. Stud. Alc.*, 1950, *11*, 403–409.

BRUNNER-ORNE, M. "Ward group sessions with hospitalized alcoholics as motivation for psychotherapy," *Int. J. Group Psychother.*, 1959, *9*, 219–224.

BUGELSKI, B. R. *The Psychology of Learning.* New York: Holt, 1956.

BUNZEL, RUTH. "The role of alcoholism in two Central American cultures," *Psychiatry*, 1940, *3*, 361–387.

BURROUGHS, W. "Letter from a master addict to dangerous drugs," *Brit. J. Addict.*, 1957, *53*, 119–131.

BURROW, T. "The basis of group-analysis, or the analysis of normal and neurotic individuals," *Brit. J. med. Psychol.*, 1928, *8*, 198–206, Part III.

CABRERA, F. J. "Group psychotherapy and psychodrama for alcoholic patients in a state hospital rehabilitation program," *Group Psychother.*, 1961, *14*, 154–159.

CALHOUN, J. B. "Population density and social pathology," *Sci. American*, 1962, *206*, 139–148.

CANTOR, J. M. "The role of motivation in the rehabilitation of the domicile alcoholic." Paper presented at a symposium on *Approaches to Rehabilitation and Research in Alcoholism* at the American Psychological Association meeting, Los Angeles, 1964.

CAPLAN, G. *An Approach to Community Mental Health.* New York: Grune and Stratton, 1961.

CAPLAN, G. *Principles of Preventive Psychiatry.* New York: Basic Books, 1964.

CAPLAN, G. "Patterns of parental response to the crisis of premature birth," *Psychiatry*, 1960, *23*, 365–374.

CAPLAN, G. "An approach to the study of family mental health," *Public Health Rep., Washington*, 1956, *71*, 1027–1030.

CARVER, A. E. "Modern trends in the treatment of alcoholism," *Med. Pr.*, 1949, *222*, 49–53.

CASIER, H. AND MERLEVEDE, E. "On the mechanism of the disulfiram-ethanol intoxication symptoms," *Arch. int. Pharmacodyn*, 1962, *139*, 165–176.

CASRIEL, D. *So Fair a House.* Englewood Cliffs: Prentice-Hall, 1963.

CHAFETZ, M. E. "Who is qualified to treat the alcoholic? Comment on the Krystal-Moore discussion," *Quart. J. Stud. Alc.* 1964, *25,* 358–360.

CHAFETZ, M. E. "A contemporary view of the problem of alcoholism," *Acad. of Med. Bull.,* 1963, *9,* 125–135.

CHAFETZ, M. E. "Practical and theoretical considerations in the psychotherapy of alcoholism," *Quart. J. Stud. Alc.,* 1959, *20,* 281–291.

CHAFETZ, M. E. AND BLANE, H. T. "Alcohol-crisis treatment approach and establishment of treatment relations with alcoholics," *Psychol. Rep.,* 1963, *12,* 862.

CHAFETZ, M. E., BLANE, H. T., ABRAMS, H. S., GOLNER, J., LACY, ELIZABETH, MC COURT, W. F., CLARK, ELEANOR, AND MYERS, W. "Establishing treatment relations with alcoholics," *J. nerv. ment. Dis.,* 1962, *134,* 395–409.

CHAFETZ, M. E., BLANE, H. T., AND HILL, MARJORIE. "Social factors in the diagnosis of alcoholism," *Quart. J. Stud. Alc.,* 1965, *26,* 72–79.

CHEIN, I., GERARD, D. L., LEE, R. S., AND ROSENFELD, EVA. *The Road to H. Narcotics, Delinquency and Social Policy.* New York: Basic Books, 1964.

CHERKAS, M. S. "Synanon Foundation—A radical approach to the problem of addiction," *Am. J. Psychiat.,* 1965, *121,* 1065–1068.

CHERKAS, M. S. "Synanon Foundation." In *A.M.A. Scien. Pro., 120th meeting of the Am. Psychiat. Assoc.,* 1964.

CHILD, I. L., BACON, M. K., AND BARRY, H. A. "A cross cultural study of drinking," *Quart. J. Stud. Alc.,* Supplement #3, 1965.

CHWELOS, N., BLEWETT, D. B., SMITH, C. N., AND HOFFER, A. "Use of d-lysergic acid diethylamide in the treatment of alcoholism," *Quart. J. Stud. Alc.,* 1959, *20*(3), 577–590.

CISIN, I. H. AND CAHALAN, D. "American drinking practices." Social Research Project, George Washington University. Presented at a symposium on "The Drug Takers" at UCLA, June 12, 1966.

CISIN, I. H. AND CAHALAN, D. "Social research project: National survey of drinking," George Washington University [unpublished].

CLARK, W. "Operational definitions of drinking problems and associated prevalence rates." Berkeley Drinking Practices Study, 1966 [unpublished].

CLAUSEN, J. A. "The sociology of mental illness." In R. K. Merton,

L. Broom, and L. S. Cottrell, Jr. (eds.), *Sociology Today: Problems and Prospects*. New York: Basic Books, 1960.

CLINEBELL, JR., H. J. "Who is qualified to treat the alcoholic? Comment on the Krystal-Moore discussion," *Quart. J. Stud. Alc.,* 1965, *26,* 124–127.

COFER, C. N. AND APPLEY, M. H. *Motivation, Theory and Research.* New York: Wiley, 1964.

COHEN, S. AND DITMAN, K. S. "Complications associated with lysergic acid diethylamide (LSD-25)," *J.A.M.A.,* 1962, *181,* 161–162.

Committee on Public Health Relations of the New York Academy of Medicine. "A survey of facilities for the care and treatment of alcoholism in New York City," *Quart. J. Stud. Alc.,* 1946, *7,* 405–438.

CONGER, J. J. "Reinforcement theory and the dynamics of alcoholism," *Quart. J. Stud. Alc.,* 1956, *17,* 296–305.

Connecticut, State Dept. Mental Health, Alcoholism Division. "Alcoholism treatment digest," *Conn. Rev. on Alcoholism,* 1962, *14,* 5–8.

COPE, T. P. AND PACKARD, F. A. *A Second Appeal to the People of Pennsylvania on the Subject of an Asylum for the Insane Poor of the Commonwealth.* Philadelphia: Waldie, 1841.

COPELAND, C. C. AND KITCHING, E. H. "Hypnosis in mental hospital practice," *J. ment. Sci.,* 1937, *83,* 316–329.

CORIAT, I. H. "Some statistical results of the psychoanalytic treatment of the psychoneuroses," *Psychoanal. Rev.,* 1917, *4,* 209–216.

CORIAT, I. H. "The psychopathology and treatment of alcoholism," *Brit. J. Inebr.,* 1912, *9,* 1–10.

CORSINI, R. J. AND ROSENBERG, BINA. "Mechanisms of group psychotherapy: Processes and dynamics," *J. abnorm. soc. Psychol.,* 1955, *15,* 406–411.

COSER, ROSE. "The Role of the Patient in a Hospital Ward." Unpublished Ph.D. dissertation, Columbia University, 1957.

COSER, ROSE. "A home away from home," *Soc. Prob.,* 1956, *4,* 3–17.

COWGILL, ELVYN. Personal communication; manuscript in preparation, 1965.

CRAWLEY, A. E. *Dress, Drinks and Drums: Further Studies of Savages and Sex.* London: Methuen, 1931.

CROWLEY, R. M. "Psychoanalytic literature on drug addiction and alcohol," *Psychol. Rev.,* 1939, *26,* 39–54.

CUMMING, J. AND CUMMING, ELAINE. *Ego and Milieu: Theory and Practice of Environmental Therapy.* New York: Atherton, 1962.

CUTTER, F. "Drug addiction and Synanon," *Calif. Dept. ment. Hyg. Newsl.,* 1965, *5,* 4–5.

DAIN, N. *Concepts of Insanity in the United States 1789–1865.* New Brunswick: Rutgers University Press, 1964.

DAVIES, D. L. "Normal drinking in recovered alcohol addicts," *Quart. J. Stud. Alc.,* 1962, *23,* 94–104.

DAVIES, D. L., TIEBOUT, H. M., WILLIAMS, L., SELZER, L., BLOCK, M.; FOX, RUTH, ZWERLING, I., ARMSTRONG, J. D., ESSER, P. H., BELL, G. R., SMITH, J. A., THIMANN, J., MYERSON, J., AND LOLLI, G. "Normal drinking in recovered alcoholics: Report, comments, and response by D. L. Davies." New Brunswick: Rutgers Center of Alcohol Studies, n.d.

DAVIS, M. AND DITMAN, K. S. "The effect of court referral and disulfiram on motivation of alcoholics," *Quart. J. Stud. Alc.,* 1963, *24,* 276–279.

DECKERT, G. H. AND WEST, L. J. "The problem of hypnotizability: A review," *Intern. J. clin. and exper. Hypn.,* 1963, *11,* 187–200.

DEDENROTH, T. E. A. "Some newer ideas and concepts of alcoholism and the use of hypnosis (Part I)," *Brit. J. med. Hypn.,* 1965, *16*(2), 27–31. Part II, 1965, *16*(3), 39–43.

DEDERICH, C. "Synanon Foundation." Paper read before the Southern California Parole Officers meeting, October, 1958.

DEMONE, JR., H. W. "Experiments in referral to alcoholism clinics," *Quart. J. Stud. Alc.,* 1963, *24,* 495–502.

DENT, J. Y. "Discussion on the management of the alcoholic in general practice," *Proc. R. Soc. Med.,* 1954, *47,* 331–333.

DENT, J. Y. "Apomorphine in the treatment of anxiety states, with especial reference to alcoholism," *Brit. J. Inebr.,* 1934, *32,* 65–88.

DERMEN, D. AND LONDON, P. "Correlates of hypnotic suggestibility," *J. consult. Psychol.,* 1965, *29,* 537–545.

DEVRIENT, P. AND LOLLI, G. "Choice of alcoholic beverage among 240 alcoholics in Switzerland," *Quart. J. Stud. Alc.*, 1962, *23*, 459–467.

DITMAN, K. S. "Alcoholism," *Am. J. Psychiat.*, 1956, *121*, 677–681.

DITMAN, K. S., HAYMAN, M., AND WHITTLESEY, J. R. B. "Nature and frequency of claims following LSD," *J. nerv. and ment. Dis.*, 1962, *134*, 346–352.

DOLLARD, J. AND MILLER, N. *Personality and Psychotherapy.* New York: McGraw-Hill, 1950.

DORCAS, R. M. *Hypnosis and Its Therapeutic Applications.* New York: McGraw-Hill, 1956.

DOWNING, J. J. "Zihuatenejo: An Experiment in Transpersonative Living." In R. Blum and Associates, *Utopiates: The Use and Users of LSD-25.* New York: Atherton, 1964.

DUBOS, R. *Mirage of Health: Utopias, Progress and Biological Change.* New York: Harper, 1959.

Editorial. "The Emmanual church movement in Boston," *N.Y. med. J.*, 1908, *87*, 947–1048.

EFRON, V. AND KELLER, M. *Selected Statistical Tables on the Consumption of Alcohol, 1850–1952, and on Alcoholism, 1930–1960.* New Brunswick: Rutgers Center of Alcohol Studies, 1963.

ERICKSON, M. H. "Hypnosis in medicine," *Brit. J. med. Hypn.*, 1949, *1*(1), 2–8.

ERIKSON, E. H. "The problem of ego identity," *Quart. J. Stud. Alc.*, 1956, *4*, 56–121.

ESSER, P. H. "Drinker types," *Folia psychiatrica, neurologica et neurochiurgica neerlandica*, 1952, *55*, 161–179.

ESTABROOKS, G. H. *Hypnotism.* New York: Dutton, 1957.

ESTES, W. K., KOCH, S., MAC CORQUODALE, K., MEEHL, P. E., MUELLER, JR., C. G., SCHOENFELD, W. N., AND VERPLANCK, W. S. *Modern Learning Theory: A Critical Analysis of Five Examples.* New York: Appleton-Century, 1954.

EY, H., AND FAURE, H. "Sleep therapy and the use of chlorpromazine," *Intern. Rec. Med.*, 1957, *170*, 1–10.

EYSENCK, H. J. (ed.). *Behavior Therapy and the Neuroses: Readings in Modern Methods of Treatment Derived from Learning Theory.* New York: Pergamon, 1960.

EZRIEL, HENRY. "A psychoanalytic approach to group treatment," *Brit. J. med. Psychol.,* 1950, *23,* 59–74.

FARBER, I. E., HARLOW, H. F., AND WEST, L. J. "Brainwashing, conditioning and DDD (debility, dependency, and dread)," *Sociometry,* 1957, *20,* 271–285.

FEJOS, P. "Man, magic, and medicine." In. I. Galdston (ed.), *Medicine and Anthropology.* New York: International Universities Press, 1959.

FELDMANN, H. "The ambulatory treatment of alcoholic addicts: A study of 250 cases," *Brit. J. Addict.,* 1959, *55,* 121–127.

FELDMANN, H. "A propos du traitement ambulatoire des alcooliques: Étude de 250 cas," *Méd. et Hyg., Genève,* 1958, *16,* 530–531.

FELDMANN, H. "Le traitement de l'alcoolisme chronique par l'apomorphine: Étude de 500 cas," *Sem. Hôp. Paris,* 1953, *29,* 1481–1491.

FENICHEL, O. *The Psychoanalytic Theory of Neurosis.* New York: Norton, 1945.

FIEDLER, F. E. "A method of objective quantification of certain countertransference attitudes," *J. clin. Psychol.,* 1951, *7,* 101–107.

FIEDLER, F. E. "A comparison of therapeutic relationships in psychoanalytic, non-directive and Adlerian therapy," *J. consult. Psychol.,* 1950, *14,* 436–445.

FIEDLER, F. E. AND SENIOR, K. "An exploratory study of unconscious feeling reaction in 15 patients-therapists pairs," *J. abnorm. and soc. Psychol.,* 1951, *7,* 101–107.

FINK, H. K. "Treatment of the alcoholic," *Acta psychother.,* 1961, *9,* 183–192.

FINK, H. K. "To accept the alcoholic patient or not: Problems in psychotherapy with alcoholics," *Samiksa,* 1959, *13,* 47–74.

FISHER, S., COLE, J. O., RICKELS, K., AND UHLENHUTH, E. H. "Drug set interaction: The effect of expectation on drug response in outpatients." Paper presented at the Collegium International. Neuropharmacolegium, Munich, 1962.

FISKE, D. W. AND MADDI, S. R. *Functions of Varied Experience.* Homewood, Ill.: Dorsey, 1961.

Florida State Alcoholic Rehabilitation Program. "Motivating the alcoholic," *Professional,* 1962, *8*(4), 1. "Prolonged group therapy," *Professional,* 1962, *8*(5), 1–4.

FOLEY, A. R. AND SANDERS, D. S. "Theoretical considerations for the development of the community mental health center concept," *Am. J. Psychiat.,* 1966, *122,* 985–990.

FOX, RUTH. "Children in the alcoholic family." In W. C. Bier (ed.), *Problems in Addiction: Alcoholism and Narcotics.* New York: Fordham University Press, 1962.

FOX, RUTH. "Psychodrama with alcoholics." Article prepared for the *Encyclopedia on Problems of Alcoholism.* Stanford: Institute for the Study of Human Problems, 1962. (Available in mimeograph.)

FOX, RUTH. "Treatment of alcoholism." In H. E. Himwich (ed.), *Alcoholism: Basic Aspects and Treatment.* Washington: Publication #47 of the Am. Assoc. for the Advancement of Science, 1957.

FRANK, J. D. "The role of cognition in illness and healing." In H. H. Strupp and L. Luborsky (eds.), *Research in Psychotherapy.* Baltimore: French-Bray Printing Co., 1962.

FRANK, J. D. *Persuasion and Healing: A Comparative Study of Psychotherapy.* Baltimore: Johns Hopkins Press, 1961.

FRANK, J. D. "Some effects of expectancy and influence in psychotherapy." In J. H. Masserman and J. L. Moreno (eds.), *Progress in Psychotherapy.* Vol. III. New York: Grune and Stratton, 1958.

FRANK, J. D. "Group therapy in the mental hospital." Monograph Series #1, *Am. Psychiat. Assoc., Mental Hospital Service,* 1955, 1–17.

FRANK, J. D., GLIEDMAN, L. H., IMBER, S. D., NASH, E. H., AND STONE, A. R. "Why patients leave psychotherapy," *A.M.A. Arch. Neurol. and Psychiat.,* 1957, *77,* 283–299.

FRANKS, C. M. "Behavior therapy, the principles of conditioning and the treatment of the alcoholic," *Quart. J. Stud. Alc.,* 1963, *24,* 511–529.

FRANKS, C. M. "Alcohol, alcoholism and conditioning." In H. J. Eysenck (ed.), *Behavior Therapy and the Neuroses: Readings in Modern Methods of Treatment Derived from Learning Theory. Part IV: Aversion Therapy.* New York: Pergamon, 1960.

FREEDMAN, N., ENGELHARDT, D. M., HANKOFF, L. D., GLICK, B. S., KAYE, H., BUCHWALD, J., AND STARK, P. "Drop-out from outpatient psychiatric treatment," *A.M.A. Arch. Neuro. and Psychiat.*, 1958, *80*, 657–666.

FREEMAN, H. E. AND SIMMONS, O. G. "Mental patients in the community: Family settings and performance levels," *Am. soc. Rev.*, 1958, *23*, 147–154.

FRENCH, T. M. *The Integration of Behavior.* Vol. I, *Basic Postulates.* Chicago: University of Chicago Press, 1952.

FREUD, ANNA. "Problems of technique in adult analysis," *Bull. Philadelphia Assoc. for Psychoanal.*, 1954, *4*, 44–70.

FREUD, S. *The Standard Edition of the Complete Psychological Works of Sigmund Freud.* In 23 vols., J. Strachey (trans. and ed.), with Anna Freud. London: Hogarth and Institute of Psychoanalysis, 1953–1964.

FREUD, S. *Group Psychology and the Analysis of the Ego.* London: Hogarth, 1948.

FRIEDMAN, H. "Patient-expectancy and the reduction of symptom intensity," *Arch. gen. Psychiat.* [In press.]

FRIEND, M. B. "Group hypnotherapy treatment." In R. S. Wallerstein, et al., *Hospital Treatment of Alcoholism.* New York: Basic Books, 1957.

FROMM-REICHMANN, FRIEDA. "Recent advances in psychoanalytic therapy." In P. Mullahy (ed.), *A Study of Interpersonal Relations.* New York: Heritage, 1949.

GAYTON, ANNA H. *Yokuts and Western Mono Ethnography.* Berkeley: University of California Press, 1948.

GELLMAN, I. P. *The Sober Alcoholic: An Organizational Analysis of Alcoholics Anonymous.* New Haven: College and University Press, 1964.

GLATT, M. M. "Normal Drinking in recovered alcohol addicts: Comment on the article by D. L. Davies," *Quart. J. Stud. Alc.*, 1965, *26*, 116–117.

GLIEDMAN, L. H., STONE, A. R., FRANK, J. D., NASH, E. H., AND IMBER,

S. D. "Incentives for treatment related to remaining or improving in psychotherapy," *Am. J. Psychother.*, 1957, *11*, 589–598.

GLOVER, E. "The therapeutic effect of inexact interpretation: A contribution to the theory of suggestion," *Intern. J. Psychoanal.*, 1931, *12*, 397–411.

GLUECK, B. "A critique of present day methods of treatment of alcoholism," *Quart. J. Stud. Alc.*, 1942, *3*, 79–91.

GOFFMAN, E. *Asylums.* New York: Anchor-Doubleday, 1963.

GOFFMAN, E. "Characteristics of total institutions." In *Symposium on Preventive and Social Psychiatry.* Washington: United States Government Printing Office, 1957.

GOODERHAM, M. E. W. *Manual of the East Toronto Branch, Alcohol and Drug Addiction Research Foundation,* 1966. (Mimeograph.)

GORDOVA, T. N. AND KOVALEV, N. K. "Unique factors in the hypnotic treatment of chronic alcoholism." In R. P. Winn (ed.), *Psychotherapy in the Soviet Union.* New York: Grove, 1962.

GOTTESFELD, B. H., LASSER, L. M., CONWAY, E. J., AND MANN, N. M. "Psychiatric implications of the treatment of alcoholism with tetraethylthiuram disulphide," *Quart. J. Stud. Alc.*, 1951, *12*, 184–205.

GREENSON, R. R. "The classic psychoanalytic approach." In S. Arieti (ed.), *The American Handbook of Psychology.* Vol. II. New York: Basic Books, 1959.

GRUNWALD, H. "Group counseling in a case work agency," *Intern. J. Group Psychother.*, 1954, *4*, 183–192.

GUTHRIE, E. R. *The Psychology of Learning.* New York: Harper, 1935. [Rev. ed., 1952.]

HAAS, J. Paper read at the North Carolina conference of the *Am. Soc. of Group Psychother. and Psychodrama,* 1958.

HAGGARD, H. W. "The physician and the alcoholic," *Quart. J. Stud. Alc.*, 1945, *6*, 213–221.

HALPERN, B. Paper read at the *Connecticut State Conference on Alcoholism,* New Haven, 1951.

HARGER, ROLLA N. AND HULPIEU, H. R. "The pharmacology of alcohol." In G. N. Thompson (ed.), *Alcoholism.* Springfield, Ill.: Thomas, 1956.

HARTMANN, H. *Essays on Ego Psychology.* New York: International Universities Press, 1964.

HAUSER, A. Personal communication, London, n.d. Institute for Group and Society Development.

HAYLETT, CLARICE H. AND RAPOPORT, LYDIA. "Mental health consultation." In L. Bellak (ed.), *Handbook of Community Psychiatry and Mental Health.* New York: Grune and Stratton, 1964.

HAYMAN, M. *Alcoholism: Mechanism and Management.* American Lectures in Living Chemistry #645. Springfield, Ill.: Thomas, 1966.

HAYMAN, M. "Treatment of alcoholism in private practice with a disulfiram-oriented program," *Quart. J. Stud. Alc.,* 1965, *26,* 460–467.

HAYMAN, M. "The general practitioner and the alcoholic," *Mind: Psychiat. in Gen. Practice,* 1963, *1,* 198–222.

HAYMAN, M. "Attitudes toward alcoholism of psychiatrists in Southern California," *Am. J. Psychol.,* 1956, *112,* 485.

HENGSTMANN, H. "Hypnotherapy with alcoholics," *Brit. J. med. Hypn.,* 1964, *2*(2), 10–17.

HESS, E. H. "Imprinting in birds," *Science,* 1964, *146,* 1128–1139.

HESS, E. H. "Imprinting," *Science,* 1959(a), *130,* 133–141.

HESS, E. H. "Two conditions for linking critical age for imprinting," *J. comp. physiol. Psychol.,* 1959(b), *52,* 515–518.

HESS, E. H. "Effects of meprobamate on imprinting in waterfowl," *Ann. N.Y. Acad. Sci.,* 1957, *67,* 724–733.

HESS, E. H., POLT, S. M., AND GOODWIN, E. "Effects of carisoprodol on early experience and learning." In J. G. Miller (ed.), *The Pharmacology and Clinical Usefulness of Carisoprodol.* Detroit: Wayne State University Press, 1959.

HILGARD, E. R. *Theories of Learning.* New York: Appleton-Century, 1948. [Rev. ed. 1956.]

HILTNER, S. "Who is qualified to treat the alcoholic? A discussion," *Quart. J. Stud. Alc.,* 1964, *25,* 354–357.

HIMWICH, H. E. "Alcohol and brain physiology." In G. N. Thompson (ed.), *Alcoholism.* Springfield, Ill.: Thomas, 1956.

HIRSCH, A. *Handbook on Historical and Geographical Pathology.* Erlangen: Enke, 1860.

HOBBS, N. "Group centered psychotherapy." In C. R. Rogers (ed.), *Client-Centered Therapy.* New York: Houghton Mifflin, 1951.

HOFF, E. C. *Alcoholism.* New York: Science of Human Behavior Library, 1963.

HOFFER, A. AND OSMOND, H. "Double blind clinical trials," *J. Neuropsych.,* 1961, *2,* 221–227.

HOFFER, E. *The True Believer.* New York: Harper, 1951.

HOLLINGSHEAD, A. B. AND REDLICH, F. C. *Social Class and Mental Illness.* New York: Wiley, 1958.

HOLZINGER, R. "Synanon through the eyes of a visiting psychologist," *Quart. J. Stud. Alc.,* 1965, *26,* 304–309.

HOOVER, M. P. "Management of acute alcoholic intoxication," *Canadian M. A. J.,* 1960, *83,* 1352–1355.

HSU, F. L. K. "Electroconditioning therapy of alcoholics," *Quart. J. Stud. Alc.,* 1965, *26,* 449–459.

HSU, F. L. K. "A cholera epidemic in a Chinese town." In B. D. Paul (ed.), *Health, Culture and Community: Case Studies of Public Reactions to Health Programs.* New York: Russell Sage Foundation, 1955.

HULL, C. L. *Principles of Behavior.* New York: Appleton-Century, 1943.

HULL, C. L. *Hypnosis and Suggestibility.* New York: Appleton-Century, 1933.

IGERSHEIMER, W. W. "Who is qualified to treat the alcoholic? Comment on the Krystal-Moore discussion," *Quart. J. Stud. Alc.,* 1965, *26,* 118–127.

IMBER, S. D., FRANK, J. D., GLIEDMAN, L. H., NASH, E. H., AND STONE, A. R. "Suggestibility, social class and the acceptance of psychotherapy," *J. clin. Psychol.,* 1956, *12,* 341–344.

IMBER, S. D., NASH, JR., E. H., AND STONE, A. R. "Social class and duration of psychotherapy," *J. clin. Psychol.,* 1955, *11,* 281–284.

IVES, G. A. "The Yorkton Psychiatric Centre," *Am. J. Psychiat.,* 1966, *122,* 1017–1020.

JACKSON, JOAN K. "Alcoholism and the family." In D. J. Pittman and

C. R. Snyder (eds.), *Society, Culture and Drinking Patterns.* New York: Wiley, 1962.

JACKSON, JOAN K. "Sociological view of Alcoholics Anonymous." Article prepared for the *Encyclopedia of Problems of Alcohol,* 1962.

JACKSON, JOAN K. "The adjustment of the family to alcoholism," *Marriage and Family Living,* 1956, *18,* 361–369.

JACOBSEN, E. "A new form of treatment for delinquent alcoholics as applied in Denmark," *Brit. J. Addict.,* 1953, *50,* 7–11.

JACOBSEN, E. AND MARTENSEN-LARSEN, O. "Treatment of alcoholism with tetraethylthiuram disulfide (antabuse)," *J.A.M.A.,* 1949, *139,* 918–922.

JAHODA, MARIE. "Current concepts of positive mental health." *Joint Commission on Mental Illness and Health.* New York: Basic Books, 1958.

JAMES, W. *The Varieties of Religious Experience.* New York: Doubleday, 1954.

JANIS, I. *Psychological Stress.* New York: Wiley, 1958.

JELLINEK, E. M. *Government Programs on Alcoholism: A Review of Activities in Some Foreign Countries.* Dept. of National Health and Welfare, Ottawa, 1963.

JELLINEK, E. M. *The Disease Concept of Alcoholism.* New Haven: Hillhouse, 1960.

JELLINEK, E. M. "Estimating the prevalence of alcoholism: Modified values in the Jellinek formula and an alternative approach," *Quart. J. Stud. Alc.,* 1959, *20,* 261–269.

JELLINEK, E. M. "Recent trends in alcoholism and in alcohol consumption," *Quart. J. Stud. Alc.,* 1947, *8,* 1–42.

JENSEN, S. E. "A treatment program for alcoholics in a mental hospital," *Quart. J. Stud. Alc.,* 1962, *23,* 315–320.

Joint Commission on Mental Illness and Health. *Action for Mental Health: Final Report.* New York: Basic Books, 1961.

JONES, MARY C. "Personality antecedents of drinking patterns in adult males," *J. consult. Psychol.,* 1967. [In press.]

JONES, MARY C. "Drinking patterns in the context of the life history: A developmental study." Monograph prepared for the Cooperative Commission on the Study of Alcoholism. Stanford: Institute for the Study of Human Problems, 1965. (Available in mimeograph.)

JONES, MARY C. "Review of studies in the field of alcohol using psychometric methods." Article prepared for the *Encyclopedia of Alcohol Problems*. Stanford: Institute for the Study of Human Problems, 1962. (Available in mimeograph.)

JONES, MAXWELL. *The Therapeutic Community: A New Treatment Method in Psychiatry*. New York: Basic Books, 1953.

JOYCE, C. R. B. "Differences between physicians as revealed by clinical trials," *Proc. R. Soc. Med.*, 1962, *55*, 776–778.

JOYCE, C. R. B. AND SWALLOW, J. N. "The controlled trial in dental surgery: Premedication of handicapped children with carisoprodol," *The Dental Pract.*, 1964, *15*, 44–47.

JOYCE, C. R. B. AND SWALLOW, J. N. "The controlled trial in dental surgery," *The Dental Pract.*, 1961, *15*, 44–47.

KADIS, A. L. "The alternate meeting in group psychotherapy," *Am. J. Psychother.*, 1956, *10*, 275–291.

KAIM, B. "Some dangerous techniques of hypnotic induction," *Am. J. clin. Hypnosis*, 1963, *5*, 171–176.

KANTOROVICH, N. V. "An attempt at associative reflex therapy in alcoholism," *Nov. Refl. Fiziol. Nerv. Sits.*, 1929, *3*, 436–447. [Psychol. Abstr. #4282, 1930.]

KARP, S. A., WITKIN, H. A., AND GOODENOUGH, D. R. "Alcoholism and psychological differentiation: Effect on achievement of sobriety on field dependence," *Quart. J. Stud. Alc.*, 1965, *26*, 580–585.

KARP, S. A., WITKIN, H. A., AND GOODENOUGH, D. R. "Alcoholism and psychological differentiation: Effect of alcohol on field dependence," *J. abnorm. Psychol.*, 1965, *70*, 262–265.

KASSEBAUM, G. G., WARD, D. A., AND WILNER, D. M. "Group treatment by correctional personnel." *Board of Corrections Monograph, 3*, Sacramento, Calif., 1963.

KATZ, L. "The Salvation Army men's social service center: I. Program," *Quart. J. Stud. Alc.* 1964, *25*, 324–332. "The Salvation Army men's social service center: II. Results," *Quart. J. Stud. Alc.*, 1966, *27*, 636–647.

KELLER, M. "Documentation of the alcohol literature: A scheme for an interdisciplinary field of study," *Quart. J. Stud. Alc.*, 1964, *25*, 725–741.

KELLER, M. "The definition of alcoholism and the estimation of its prevalence." In D. J. Pittman and C. R. Snyder (eds.), *Society, Culture and Drinking Patterns*. New York: Wiley, 1962.

KENDELL, R. E. "Normal drinking by former alcohol addicts," *Quart. J. Stud. Alc.*, 1965, *26*, 247–257.

KEPNER, ELAINE. "Application of learning theory to the etiology and treatment of alcoholism," *Quart. J. Stud. Alc.*, 1964, *25*, 279–291.

KERSTEN, P. M. "Changing concepts in alcoholism and its management," *Quart. J. Stud. Alc.*, 1949, *9*, 423–531.

KIEV, A. (ed.). *Magic, Faith, and Healing*. New York: Free Press, 1964.

KIEV, A. "The psychotherapeutic aspects of primitive medicine," *Human Org.*, 1962, *21*, 25–29.

KINGHAM, R. J. "Alcoholism and the reinforcement theory of learning," *Quart. J. Stud. Alc.*, 1958, *19*, 320–330.

KLAPMAN, J. W. "The case for didactic group psychotherapy," *Dis. nerv. Syst.*, 1950, *11*, 35–41.

KLAPMAN, J. W. *Group Psychotherapy Theory and Practice*. New York: Grune and Stratton, 1946.

KLERMAN, G. "Staff attitudes, decision making and use of drug therapy in the mental hospital." In H. C. B. Denber (ed.), *Research Conference on the Therapeutic Community*. Springfield, Ill.: Thomas, 1960.

KLERMAN, G. L., DIMASCIO, A., GREENBLATT, M., AND RINKEL, M. "The influence of specific personality patterns on the reactions to phrenotropic agents." In J. Masserman (ed.), *Biological Psychiatry*. New York: Grune and Stratton, 1959.

KLERMAN, G. L., SHARAF, M. R., HOLZMAN, M., AND LEVINSON, D. J. "Sociopsychological characteristics of resident psychiatrists and their use of drug therapy," *Am. J. Psychiat.*, 1960, *117*, 111.

KNIGHT, R. P. "Evaluation of psychoanalytic therapy," *Am. J. Psychiat.*, 1941, *98*, 434–446.

KNIGHT, R. P. "The dynamics and treatment of chronic alcohol addiction," *Bull. Menninger Clinic,* 1937(a), *1,* 233–250.

KNIGHT, R. P. "Psychodynamics of chronic alcoholism," *J. nerv. ment. Dis.,* 1937(b), *86,* 538–548.

KNIGHT, R. P. "The psychoanalytic treatment in a sanitorium of chronic addiction to alcohol," *J.A.M.A.,* 1938, *111,* 1443–1446.

KNUPFER, GENEVIEVE. California Drinking Practices Study. Report #3, "Characteristics of abstainers." State of Calif. Dept. of Public Health, Div. of Alcoholic Rehabilitation, 1961.

KNUPFER, GENEVIEVE AND ROOM, R. Drinking patterns and attitudes of men in three American ethnic groups: Irish, Jews, and white Protestants." Drinking Practices Study, Mental Research Institute, Berkeley, 1966. (Unpublished.)

KNUPFER, GENEVIEVE, FINK, R., CLARK, W. D., AND GOFFMAN, A. S. California Drinking Practices Study. Report #6, "Factors related to the amount of drinking in an urban community." State of Calif. Dept. of Public Health, Berkeley, 1963.

KOCH, S. *Psychology: A Study of a Science.* Vol. II. *General Systematic Formulations, Learning Processes.* New York: McGraw-Hill, 1959.

KOGAN, KATE L. AND JACKSON, JOAN K. "Some concomitants of personal difficulties in wives of alcoholics and nonalcoholics," *Quart. J. Stud. Alc.,* 1965, *26,* 595–604.

KONOPKA, G. "Social group work: A social work method," *Soc. Work,* 1960, *5*(4), 53–61.

KOTKOV, B. "Analytically oriented group psychotherapy of psychoneurotic adults," *Psychoanal. Rev.,* 1953(a), *40,* 333.

KOTKOV, B. "Experiences in group psychotherapy with the obese," *Psychosomatic Med.,* 1953(b), *15,* 243.

KOVACH, J. K. AND HESS, E. H. "Imprinting: Effects of painful stimulation upon the following response," *J. comp. physiol. Psychol.,* 1963, *56,* 461–464.

KRASNER, L. "The therapist as a social reinforcement machine." In H. H. Strupp and L. Luborsky (eds.), *Research in Psychotherapy.* Proceedings of a conference, Chapel Hill, North Carolina, May 17–20, 1961. Baltimore: American Psychological Assoc., French-Bray Printing Co., 1962.

KROEBER, A. L. *Handbook of Indians of California.* Berkeley: California Book Co., 1953.

KRYSTAL, H. AND MOORE, A. "Who is qualified to treat the alcoholic? A discussion," *Quart. J. Stud. Alc.,* 1963, *24,* 705–720.

KUBIE, L. S. *Practical Aspects of Psychoanalysis.* New York: Norton, 1936.

LANE, R. E. AND SEARS, D. O. *Public Opinion.* Englewood Cliffs: Prentice-Hall, 1964.

LAZARUS, A. A. "Towards the understanding and effective treatment of alcoholism," *S.A. med. J.,* 1965, *39,* 736–751.

LEAKE, C. D. AND SILVERMAN, M. *Alcohol Beverages in Clinical Medicine.* Chicago: Year Book Medical Publishers, 1966.

LE BON, G. *The Crowd: A Study of the Popular Mind.* London: Unwin, 1922.

LECRON, L. M. (ed.). *Experimental Hypnosis.* New York: Macmillan, 1952.

LEIGHTON, A. H., CLAUSEN, J. A., AND WILSON, R. N. "Introduction: Some key issues in social psychiatry; Orientation." In A. H. Leighton, J. A. Clausen, and R. N. Wilson (eds.), *Explorations in Social Psychiatry.* New York: Basic Books, 1957.

LEMERE, F. "Who is qualified to treat the alcoholic?" *Quart. J. Stud. Alc.,* 1964, *25,* 558–560.

LEMERE, F. "Psychological factors in the conditioned reflex treatment of alcoholism." In E. Podolsky (ed.), *Management of Addiction.* New York: Philosophical Library, 1955.

LEMERE, F., O'HOLLAREN, P., AND MAXWELL, A. "Motivation in the treatment of alcoholism," *Quart. J. Stud. Alc.,* 1958, *19,* 428–431.

LEMERE, F. AND VOEGTLIN, W. L. "An evaluation of the aversion treatment of alcoholism." In E. Podolsky (ed.), *Management of Addiction.* New York: Philosophical Library, 1955.

LEVINSON, D. J. "Psychotherapists' contributions to the patient's treatment career." In H. H. Strupp and L. Luborsky (eds.), *Research in Psychotherapy.* Proceedings of a conference, Chapel Hill,

North Carolina, May 17–20, 1961. Baltimore: American Psychological Assoc., French-Bray Printing Co., 1962.

LEWIN, K. *et al.* "Patterns of regressive behavior in experimentally created social 'climate,' " *J. soc. Psychol.*, 1939, *10,* 271–299.

LEWIN, K. AND GRABBE, P. "Conduct, knowledge, and acceptance of new values." In Gertrud W. Lewin (ed.), *Resolving Social Conflicts.* New York: Harper, 1948.

LEWIS, L. AND COSER, ROSE. "The dangers of hospitalization." In R. H. Blum (ed.), *Hospitals and Patient Dissatisfaction.* San Francisco: California Medical Assoc., 1958.

LEWIS, M. L. "The initial contact with wives of alcoholics," *Soc. Casework.*, 1954, *35,* 8–14.

LIECHTI, A. "Bemerkungen zur Hypnotherapie bei Alkoholkranken," *Gesundheit und Wohlfahrt,* 1948, *28,* 183–199.

LIFTON, R. *Thought Reform and the Psychology of Totalism.* New York: W. W. Norton, 1963.

LINDEMANN, E. "The Psychosocial Position on etiology." In H. D. Kruse (ed.), *Integrating the Approaches to Mental Disease.* New York: Hoeber-Harper, 1957.

LINDEMANN, E. "The meaning of crisis in individual and family living," *Teachers' College Rec.*, 1956, *57,* 310.

LINDEMANN, E. "Symptomatology and management of acute grief," *Am. J. Psychiat.*, 1944, *101,* 141–148.

LINDEMANN, E., CHAFETZ, M. E., AND BLANE, H. T. "Alcohol-crisis treatment approach and establishment of treatment relations with alcoholics," *Psychol. Rep.*, 1963, *12,* 862.

LINDEMANN, E. AND CLARKE, L. D. "Modification in ego structure and personality reactions under the influence of the effects of drugs," *Am. J. Psychiat.*, 1952, *108,* 561–567.

LINDEMANN, E. AND VON FELSINGER, J. M. "Drug effects and personality theory," *Psychopharmacol.*, 1961, 2, 69–92.

LOLLI, G. "On therapeutic success in alcoholism." In E. Podolsky (ed.), *Management of Addictions.* New York: Philosophical Library, 1955.

LOLLI, G. "On 'therapeutic' success in alcoholism," *Quart. J. Stud. Alc.*, 1953, *14,* 238–246.

LOLLI, G. "Alcoholism, 1941–1951: A survey of activities in research, education and therapy. V. The treatment of alcohol addiction," *Quart. J. Stud. Alc.*, 1952, *13*, 461–471.

LUBORSKY, L. AND STRUPP, H. H. "Research problems in psychotherapy: A three-year follow-up." In L. Luborsky and H. H. Strupp (eds.), *Research in Psychotherapy.* Proceedings of a conference, Chapel Hill, North Carolina, May 17–20, 1961. Baltimore: American Psychological Assoc., French-Bray Printing Co., 1962.

LUSTMAN, C. R. (ed.). *Social Work with Groups.* Pittsburgh: Veterans Administration Hospital, 1963.

LYERLY, S. B., ROSS, S., KRUGMAN, A. D., AND CLYDE, D. J. "Drugs and placebos: The effect of instructions upon performance and mood under amphetamine sulphate and chloral hydrate," *J. abnorm. soc. Psychol.*, 1964, *68*, 321–327.

MAC GREGOR, FRANCES C. *Social Science in Nursing.* New York: Russell Sage Foundation, 1960.

MAC LEAN, J. R., MAC DONALD, D. C., BYRNE, U. P., AND HUBBARD, A. M. "The use of LSD-25 in the treatment of alcoholism and other psychiatric problems," *Quart. J. Stud. Alc.*, 1961, *22*, 34–45.

MACHOVER, S., PUZZO, F. S., AND PLUMEAU, F. "An objective study of homosexuality in alcoholism," *Quart. J. Stud. Alc.*, 1959(a), *20*(3), 528–542.

MACHOVER, S., PUZZO, F. S., AND PLUMEAU, F. "Clinical and objective studies of personality variables in alcoholism. I. Clinical investigation of the 'alcoholic personality,' " *Quart. J. Stud. Alc.*, 1959(b), *20*, 505–519. "Clinical and objective studies of personality variables in alcoholism. II. Clinical study of personality correlates of remission from active alcoholism," *Quart. J. Stud. Alc.*, 1959(c), *20*, 520–527.

MADDOX, G. L. "Teen-age drinking in the United States." In D. J. Pittman and C. R. Snyder (eds.), *Society, Culture and Drinking Patterns.* New York: Wiley, 1962.

MADILL, MARY-FRANCES, CAMPBELL, D., LAVERTY, S. G., AND VANDE-WATER, S. L. "Aversion treatment of alcoholics by succinylcholine-induced apneic paralysis: An analysis of early changes in drinking behavior," *Quart. J. Stud. Alc.*, 1965, *26*, 684–685. [Prepublication abstract.]

MADSEN, W. *Alcoholics Anonymous as a Subculture.* [In press.]

MANN, H. "Hypnotherapy in habit disorders," *Am. J. clin. Hypn.,* 1960, *3,* 123–126.

MARGOLIS, M., KRYSTAL, H., AND SIEGEL, S. "Psychotherapy with alcoholic offenders," *Quart. J. Stud. Alc.,* 1964, *25,* 85–99.

MARSH, L. C. "Group therapy and the pyschiatric clinic," *J. nerv. and ment. Disorders,* 1935, *82,* 381–392.

MARTENSEN-LARSEN, O. "Group psychotherapy with alcoholics in private practice," *Intern. J. group Psychother.,* 1956, *6,* 28–37.

MARTENSEN-LARSEN, O. "Psychotic phenomena provoked by tetraethylthiuram disulfide," *Quart. J. Stud. Alc.,* 1951, *12,* 208–216.

MASSERMAN, J. H. *Behavior and Neurosis.* Chicago: University of Chicago Press, 1943.

MAXWELL, M. "Alcoholics Anonymous: An interpretation." In D. J. Pittman and C. R. Snyder (eds.), *Society, Culture and Drinking Patterns.* New York: Wiley, 1962.

MC CONNELL, E. D. "Treating the problem drinker," *Med. World,* 1940, *58,* 201–303.

MC CORD, W. AND MC CORD, J. "A longitudinal study of the personality of alcoholics." In D. J. Pittman and C. R. Snyder (eds.), *Society, Culture and Drinking Patterns.* New York: Wiley, 1962.

MC GOLDRICK, JR., E. J. "Who is qualified to treat the alcoholic? A discussion," *Quart. J. Stud. Alc.,* 1964, *25,* 351–354.

MEAD, J. H. *Mind, Self and Society.* Chicago: University of Chicago Press, 1934.

MEARES, A. "An evaluation of the dangers of medical hypnosis," *Am. J. clin. Hypnosis,* 1961, *4,* 90–97.

MEARES, A. *A System of Medical Hypnosis.* Philadelphia: Saunders, 1960.

MEERLOO, J. A. M. *The Rape of the Mind: The Psychology of Thought Control, Menticide, and Brain Washing.* New York: World, 1956.

MENDELSOHN, G. A. AND GELLER, M. H. "Structure of client attitudes toward counseling and their relation to client-counselor similarity," *J. consult. Psychol.,* 1965, *29,* 63–72.

MENNINGER, K. A. *Man Against Himself*. New York: Harcourt, Brace, 1938.

MENNINGER, W. C. "The treatment of chronic alcohol addiction," *Bull. Menninger Clinic*, 1938, *2*, 101–112.

MERTENS, G. C. AND FULLER, G. B. *Manual for the Alcoholic*. Minnesota: Wilmar State Hospital, 1964.

MEYER, F. M. "The psychology and treatment of alcohol addicts," *Brit. J. med. Psychol.*, 1943, *19*, 381–387.

MEYERSON, D. "A three-year study of a group of skid-row alcoholics." In H. E. Himwich (ed.), *Alcoholism: Basic Aspects and Treatment*. Publication #47 of the Am. Assoc. for the Advancement of Science, Washington, 1958.

MILLER, N. E. "Learning resistance to pain and fear: Effects of over-learning, exposure, and rewarded exposure in context," *J. exptl. Psychol.*, 1960, *60*, 137–145.

MILLER, N. E. "Learnable drives and rewards." In S. S. Stevens (ed.), *Handbook of Experimental Psychology*. New York: Wiley, 1951.

MILLS, R. B. AND HETRICK, E. S. "Treating the unmotivated alcoholic: A coordinated program in a municipal court," *Crime and Delinquency*, 1963, *9*, 46–59.

MINDLIN, DOROTHY F. "Attitudes toward alcoholism and towards self: Differences between three alcoholic groups," *Quart. J. Stud. Alc.*, 1964, *25*, 136–141.

MINDLIN, DOROTHY F. "The characteristics of alcoholics related to prediction of therapeutic outcome," *Quart. J. Stud. Alc.*, 1959, *20*, 604–619.

MITCHELL, D. *House on the Beach*. Documentary film on Synanon made by the Rediffusion Company, 1965. (Available by request to Synanon.)

MODLIN, H. C. AND MONTES, A. "Narcotics addiction in physicians," *Am. J. Psychiat.*, 1964, *121*, 358–365.

MOLTZ, H. "Imprinting: Empirical basis and theoretical significance," *Psychol. Bull.*, 1960, *57*, 291–314.

MONNEROT, E., PUECH, J., BENICHEN, L., ROBIN, C., AND LANGLOIS, H. "La cure de sommeil conservet-elle des indications psychiatriques?

Considérations personnelles portant sur 700 cas," *Ann. Médico-Psychol.*, 1957, *11*, 845–880.

MOORE, R. A. "Reaction formation as a counter-transference phenomenon in the treatment of alcoholism," *Quart. J. Stud. Alc.*, 1961, 22, 481–486.

MOORE, R. A. AND MURPHY, T. C. "Denial of alcoholism as an obstacle to recovery," *Quart. J. Stud. Alc.*, 1961, 22, 597–609.

MOORE, R. A. AND RAMSEUR, F. "Effects of psychotherapy in an openward hospital on patients with alcoholism," *Quart. J. Stud. Alc.*, 1960, *21*, 233–253.

MORENO, J. L. "Psychodrama and group therapy," *Sociometry*, 1946, *9*, 249–253.

MORENO, J. L. *Who Shall Survive? A New Approach to the Problem of Human Interrelations.* Washington: Nerv. and Ment. Dis. Publishing Co., 1934.

MORRIS, J. M. *The Uses of Epidemiology.* London: Livingstone, 1957.

MORSIER, de, G. AND FELDMANN, H. "Le traitement de l'alcoolisme par l'apomorphine: Étude de 500 cas," *Schweiz. Arch. Neurol. Psychiat.*, 1952, *70*, 434–440.

MOSS, C. S. *Hypnosis in Perspective.* New York: Macmillan, 1965.

MOWRER, O. H. *The New Group Therapy.* Princeton: Van Nostrand, 1964.

MUKASA, H. "Cyanamide against alcohol." Reported in *Med. News, London*, 1965, 120, 15. [Abstr. in *Quart. J. Stud. Alc.*, 1965, *26*, 715.]

MULLAN, H. AND SANGIULIANO, IRIS. *Alcoholism: Group Psychotherapy and Rehabilitation.* Springfield, Ill.: Thomas, 1966.

MURPHY, G. "Group psychotherapy in our society." In M. Rosenbaum and M. Berger (eds.), *Group Psychotherapy and Group Function.* New York: Basic Books, 1963.

MYERSON, D. J. Speech given at the National Conference on Legal Issues in Alcoholism and Alcohol Usage. Swampscott, Mass., June 17, 1965. (Available in mimeograph.)

MYERSEN, D. J., MACKAY, J., WALLENS, ANNE, AND NEIBERG, N. "A report of a rehabilitation program for alcoholic women prisoners," *Quart. J. Stud. Alc.*, 1961, Supp. #1, 151–157.

MYERSON, D. J. "Clinical observations on a group of alcoholic prissoners, with special reference to women," *Quart. J. Stud. Alc.,* 1959, *20,* 555–572.

MYERSON, D. J. "The study and treatment of alcoholism: A historical perspective," *New Eng. J. Med.,* 1957, *257,* 820–825.

NØRVIG, J. AND NIELSEN, B. "A follow-up study of 221 alcohol addicts in Denmark," *Quart. J. Stud. Alc.,* 1956, *17,* 633–642.

O'HOLLAREN, P. "Pentothal interview in the treatment of chronic alcoholism," *Calif. Med.,* 1947, *67,* 382.

OLDS, J. "Self-stimulation of the brain: Its use to study local effects of hunger, sex, and drugs," *Science,* 1958, *127,* 315–324.

OLDS, J. AND MILNER, P. "Positive reinforcement produced by electrical stimulation of the septal area and other regions of the rat brain," *J. comp. physiol. Psychol.,* 1954, *47,* 419–427.

OPLER, M. K. "The need for new diagnostic categories in psychiatry," *J. Natl. med. Assoc.,* 1963, *55,* 133–137.

OPLER, M. K. "Social psychiatry: Evolutionary, existentialist, and transcultural findings." In *Proceedings of the Third World Congress of Psychiatry.* Toronto: University of Toronto Press, 1962.

O'REILLY, P. O. "Lysergic acid and the alcoholic," *Dis. nerv. Syst.,* 1962, *23,* 331–334.

OSMOND, H. A. "Review of the clinical effects of psychotominetic agents," *Ann. N.Y. Acad. Sci.,* 1957, *66,* 418.

PALEY, A. "Hypnotherapy in the treatment of alcoholism," *Bull. Menninger Clinic,* 1962, *16,* 14–19.

PALEY, A. "Hypnotherapy in the treatment of alcoholism." In E. Podolsky (ed.), *Management of Addictions.* New York: Philosophical Library, 1955.

PALOLA, E. G., DORPAT, T. L., AND LARSON, W. R. "Alcoholism and suicidal behavior." In D. J. Pittman and C. R. Snyder (eds.), *Society, Culture and Drinking Patterns.* New York: Wiley, 1962.

PARAD, H. J. AND CAPLAN, G. "A framework for studying families in crisis," *Soc. Work,* 1960, *5*(3), 3–15.

PAREJA, C. A. "El suero humano alcoholizado. Informe sobre ciento once casos tratados," *Med. Publ. Univ. Guayaquil, Ecuador,* 1947, *35,* 1–8.

PARLOFF, M. B. "Therapist patient relationships and outcome of psychotherapy," *J. consult. Psychol.*, 1961, *25,* 29–38.

PARLOFF, M. B. AND RUBINSTEIN, E. A. "Research problems in psychotherapy." In E. A. Rubinstein and M. B. Parloff (eds.), *Research in Psychotherapy.* Washington: American Psychological Assoc., 1959.

PATTISON, E. M., COURLAS, P. G., PATTI, R., MANN, B., AND MULLEN, D. "Diagnostic-therapeutic intake groups for wives of alcoholics," *Quart. J. Stud. Alc.,* 1965, *26,* 605–616.

PAUL, B. (ed.). *Health, Culture and Community: Case Studies of Public Reactions to Health Programs.* New York: Russell Sage Foundation, 1955.

PAUL, J. R. *Clinical Epidemiology.* Chicago: University of Chicago Press, 1958.

PEARLIN, L. I. "Treatment values and enthusiasm for drugs in a mental hospital," *Psychiatry,* 1962, *25,* 170–179.

PFEFFER, A. Z. *Alcoholism.* Modern Monographs in Industrial Medicines, A. J. Lanza (ed.). New York and London: Grune and Stratton, 1958.

PITTMAN, D. J. AND STERNE, M. "Concept of motivation: Sources of institutional and professional blockage in the treatment of alcoholics," *Quart. J. Stud. Alc.,* 1965, *26,* 41–57.

PITTMAN, D. J. AND TONGUE, A. (eds.). *Handbook of Organizations for Research on Alcohol and Alcoholism Problems.* Lausanne: International Bureau Against Alcoholism, 1963.

PITTMAN, D. J. "The role of sociology in the planning and operation of alcoholism treatment programs," *Brit. J. Addict.,* 1963, *59,* 35–39.

PITTMAN, D. J. AND GORDON, C. W. "Criminal careers of the chronic drunkenness offender." In D. J. Pittman and C. R. Snyder (eds.), *Society, Culture and Drinking Patterns.* New York: Wiley, 1962.

PITTMAN, D. J. AND GORDON, C. W. *Revolving Door: A Study of the Chronic Police Case Inebriate.* Monographs of the Yale Center of Alcohol Studies #2. New Haven and Glencoe: Free Press, 1958.

PIXLEY, J. M. AND STIEFEL, J. R. "Group therapy designed to meet the needs of the alcoholic's wife," *Quart. J. Stud. Alc.,* 1963, *24,* 304–314.

PLATO. *Symposium.* In *Dialogi* (in 6 vols.), H. and M. Wohlrab (eds.). Bibliotheca Scriptorum Graecorum et Romanorum Teubneriana, Lipsiae: In Aedibus B. G. Teubneri, 1890–1909.

PLAUT, T. F. A. *A Report to the Nation by the Cooperative Commission on the Study of Alcoholism.* New York: Oxford [in press].

PLAUT, T. F. A. "Epidemiological aspects of alcoholism and alcohol problems." Paper presented at annual winter meeting of Mass. Publ. Health Assoc., Boston College, Jan. 25, 1962.

PLINY. *Natural History.* In ten volumes, Latin with English translation by H. Rackham. The Loeb Classical Library, T. E. Pate, E. Capps, W. H. D. Rouse (eds.). Book 27.40, 121–124. London: Heinemann, 1938.

POPHAM, R. E. AND SCHMIDT, W. *A Decade of Alcoholic Research.* Toronto: University of Toronto Press, 1962.

POSER, E. G. "The effect of therapists' training on group therapeutic outcome," *J. consult. Psychol.,* 1966, *30,* 283–289.

POWDERMAKER, FLORENCE. "The relation between the alcoholic and the physician," *Quart. J. Stud. Alc.,* 1944, *5,* 245.

POWDERMAKER, R., POWDERMAKER, FLORENCE B., AND FRANK, J. D. *Group Psychotherapy: Studies in Methodology of Research and Therapy.* Cambridge: Harvard University Press, 1953.

PRIBRAM, K. H. "Reinforcement revisited: A structural view." In M. R. Jones (ed.), *Nebraska Symposium on Motivation,* Vol. II. Lincoln: University of Nebraska Press, 1963.

PRICE, GLADYS. "Social casework in alcoholism," *Quart. J. Stud. Alc.,* 1958, *19,* 155–163.

Psychopharmacology Service Center Bulletin, "Behavioral research in preclinical psychopharmacology: Issues of design and technique." U.S. Dept. Health, Education and Welfare, Washington, Sept. 1961.

PULLAR-STRECKER, H. "The use of insulin in the treatment of alcoholism and alcoholic addiction," *Brit. J. Inebr.,* 1945, *43,* 14–38.

RAZRAN, G. "The observable unconscious and the inferable conscious in current Soviet psychophysiology. Interoceptive conditioning, semantic conditioning, and the orienting reflex," *Psychol. Rev.,* 1961, *68,* 81–147.

REDL, F. *The Aggressive Child.* Glencoe, Ill.: Free Press, 1963.

REDL, F. AND WINEMAN, D. *Controls from Within.* Glencoe, Ill.: Free Press, 1952.

REES, T. P. "Back to moral treatment and community care," *J. ment. Sci.,* 1957, *103,* 303–313.

REIK, T. "Die Pubertätsriten der Wilden," *Imago,* 1915, *4,* 125–144, and 1916, *4,* 189–222.

REINERT, R. E. "The alcoholism treatment program at Topeka Veterans Administration Hospital," *Quart. J. Stud. Alc.,* 1965, *26,* 674–680.

RICHARDSON, H. B. *Patients Have Families.* New York: Commonwealth Fund, 1948.

RILEY, JR., J. W. AND MARDEN, C. F. "The medical profession and the problem of alcoholism," *Quart. J. Stud. Alc.,* 1946, *7,* 240–270.

RIOCH, MARGARET J. "Changing concepts in the training of therapists," *J. consult. Psychol.,* 1966, *30,* 290–291.

RIPLEY, H. S. AND JACKSON, JOAN K. "Therapeutic factors in Alcoholics Anonymous," *Am. J. Psychiat.,* 1959, *116,* 44–50.

RODGERS, D. A. AND MC CLEARN, G. E. "Alcohol preference of mice." In R. C. Bliss (ed.), *Roots of Behavior.* New York: Hoeber-Harper, 1962.

RODGERS, D. A. AND THIESSEN, D. D. "Effects of population density on adrenal size, behavioral arousal, and alcohol preference of inbred mice," *Quart. J. Stud. Alc.,* 1964, *25,* 240–247.

ROE, ANNE. "Alcohol and creative work. I. Painters," *Quart. J. Stud. Alc.,* 1946, *6,* 415–467.

ROETHLISBERGER, F. J. AND DICKSON, W. J. *Management and the Worker.* Cambridge: Harvard University Press, 1946.

ROGERS, C. R. (ed.). *Client-Centered Therapy.* New York: Houghton Mifflin, 1951.

ROGERS, C. R. AND DYMOND, R. *Psychotherapy and Personality Change.* Chicago: University of Chicago Press, 1954.

ROSENBAUM, M. "Some comments on the use of untrained therapists," *J. consult. Psychol.,* 1966, *30,* 292–294.

ROSENBAUM, M. AND BERGER, M. *Group Psychotherapy and Group Function.* New York: Basic Books, 1963.

ROSENTHAL, D. AND FRANK, J. D. "The fate of psychiatric clinic out-patients assigned to psychotherapy," *J. nerv. and ment. Dis.,* 1958, *127,* 330–343.

ROSENTHAL, R. "Experimenter outcome-orientation and the results of the psychological experiment," *Psychol. Bull.,* 1964, *61,* 405–412.

ROSENTHAL, R. "On the social psychology of the psychological experiment," *Am. Scientist,* 1963, *51,* 268–283.

ROSS, N. AND ABRAMS, S. "Fundamentals of psychoanalytic theory." In B. B. Wolman (ed.), *Handbook of Clinical Psychology.* New York: McGraw-Hill, 1965.

ROTH, J. A. "Ritual and magic in the control of contagion." In E. Jaco (ed.), *Patients, Physicians and Illness.* Glencoe, Ill.: Free Press, 1958.

RÜEGG, R. AND PULVER, W. "Die Durchführung medikamentöser Alkoholentwöhnungskuren in einer medizinischen Abteilung," *Schweiz. med. Wschr.,* 1953, *83,* 889–892.

RUSSELL, CLAIRE AND RUSSELL, W. M. S. *Human Behavior—A New Approach.* Boston: Little, Brown, 1961.

SADOUN, R., LOLLI, G., AND SILVERMAN, M. *Drinking in French Culture.* New Brunswick: Rutgers Center of Alcohol Studies, 1965.

Salvation Army. *Salvation Army Men's Social Service Handbook.* New York: Salvation Army, 1960.

SANDERSON, R. E., CAMPBELL, D., AND LAVERTY, S. G. "An investigation of a new aversion conditioning treatment for alcoholism," *Quart. J. Stud. Alc.,* 1963, *24,* 261–275.

SANDISON, R. A. "The role of psychotropic drugs in group therapy," *Bull. World Health Org.,* 1959, *21,* 505–515.

SAPIR, JEAN V. "The alcoholic as an agency client," *Soc. Casework,* 1957, *38,* 355–361.

SAPIR, JEAN V. "Relationship factors in the treatment of the alcoholic," *Soc. Casework,* 1953, *34,* 297–303.

SAPOLSKY, A. "Relationships between patient, doctor compatibility, mutual perception, and outcome of treatment," *J. abnorm. Psychol.,* 1965, *70,* 70–76.

SAPOLSKY, A. "Effect of interpersonal relationships upon verbal conditioning," *J. abnorm. soc. Psychol.*, 1960, *60*, 241–246.

SAUNDERS, L. *Cultural Differences and Medical Care.* New York: Russell Sage Foundation, 1954.

SCHACTER, S. AND WHEELER, L. "Epinephrine, chlorpromazine, and amusement," *J. abnorm. soc. Psychol.*, 1962, *65*, 121–128.

SCHAFFER, L. AND MYERS, J. K. "Psychotherapy and social stratification: An empirical study of practice in a psychiatric outpatient clinic," *Psychiatry*, 1954, *17*, 83–93.

SCHILDER, P. *The Nature of Hypnosis.* New York: International Universities Press, 1956.

SCHILDER, P. "Results and problems of group psychotherapy in severe neuroses," *Ment. Hygiene*, 1939, *23*, 87–98.

SCHILDER, P. *Psychotherapy.* New York: Norton, 1938.

SCHNECK, J. M. (ed.). *Hypnosis in Modern Medicine.* (2nd ed.) Springfield, Ill.: Thomas, 1959.

SCHREMLY, J. AND SOLOMON, P. "Drug abuse and addiction reporting in a general hospital," *J.A.M.A.*, 1964, *189*(6), 512–514.

SCHULTES, R. E. "The aboriginal uses of Lophophoria Williamsii," *Cactus and Succulant J.*, 1940, *12*, 177–181.

SCHULTZ, J. H. "Hypnotherapy with alcoholics," *Brit. J. med. Hypn.*, 1964, *15*(2), 2–8.

SCHUTZ, W. C. *FIRO-B: A Three Variable Theory of Interpersonal Relations.* New York: Rinehart, 1958.

SCOTT, E. M. "Who is qualified to treat the alcoholic? Comment on the Krystal-Moore discussion," *Quart. J. Stud. Alc.*, 1964, *25*, 561–562.

SCOTT, R. D. "The psychology of insulin coma treatment," *Brit. med. J.*, 1950, *23*, 15–44.

SECHEHAYE, MARGUERITE A. *Symbolic Realization: A New Method of Psychotherapy.* New York: International Universities Press, 1951.

SELYE, H. *The Stress of Life.* New York: McGraw-Hill, 1956.

SELYE, H. "Stress and Disease," *Science*, 1955, *122* (3171), 625–631.

SELZER, M. L. "Hostility as a barrier to therapy in alcoholism," *Psychiat. Quart.*, 1957, *31*, 301–305.

SELZER, M. L. AND HOLLOWAY, W. H. "A follow-up of alcoholics committed to a state hospital," *Quart. J. Stud. Alc.*, 1957, *18*, 98–120.

SHEA, J. "Psychoanalytic therapy and alcoholism," *Quart. J. Stud. Alc.*, 1954, *15*, 569–605.

SHERIF, M. *An Outline of Social Psychology.* New York: Harper, 1948.

SHOBEN, JR., E. J. "Views on the etiology of alcoholism. III. The behavioristic view." In H. D. Kruse (ed.), *Alcoholism as a Medical Problem.* New York: Hoeber-Harper, 1956.

SIGERIST, H. E. *On the History of Medicine.* New York: M. D. Publications, 1960.

SIGG, B. W. *Le cannabisme chronique: Fruit du sous-developpement et du capitalisme,* 1963. [No publisher given.]

SILBER, A. Personal communication, 1963.

SILBER, A. "Psychotherapy with alcoholics," *J. nerv. ment. Dis.*, 1959, *129*, 477–485.

SILLMAN, L. R. "Chronic alcoholism," *J. nerv. ment. Dis.*, 1948, *107*, 127–149.

SIMMEL, E. "Psychoanalytic treatment in a sanitorium," *Intern. J. Psychoanal.*, 1929, *10*, 70–89.

SIMMONS, L. W. "Impact of social factors upon adjustment within the community," *Am. J. Psychiat.*, 1966, *122*, 990–998.

SIMMONS, L. W. AND WOLFF, A. G. *Social Science in Medicine.* New York: Russell Sage Foundation, 1954.

SIMMONS, O. *Social Status and Public Health.* New York: Social Science Research Council, 1958.

SKINNER, B. F. *Cumulative Record.* New York: Appleton-Century, 1961.

SKINNER, B. F. *Science and Human Behavior.* New York: Macmillan, 1953.

SKINNER, B. F. *The Behavior of Organisms: An Experimental Analysis.* New York: Appleton-Century, 1938.

SKOLNICK, J. H. "A study of the relation of ethnic background to arrests for inebriety," *Quart. J. Stud. Alc.*, 1954, *15*, 622.

SLACK, C. W. "Experimentive-subject psychotherapy: A new method of introducing intensive office treatment for unreachable cases," *Ment. Hygiene,* 1960, *44*, 238–256.

SLAVSON, S. R. *An Introduction to Group Therapy.* New York: International Universities Press, 1954.

SLAVSON, S. R. "Group therapy," *Ment. Hygiene,* 1940, *24,* 36–49.

SLAVSON, S. R. "Group therapy special section meeting," *Am. J. ortho. Psychiat.,* 1943, *13,* 648–690.

SMART, R. G. AND STORM, T. "The efficacy of LSD in the treatment of alcoholism," *Quart. J. Stud. Alc.,* 1964, *25,* 333–338.

SMITH, C. "Some reflections on the possible therapeutic effects of the hallucinogens," *Quart. J. Stud. Alc.,* 1959, *20,* 202–301.

SMITH, C. M. "A new adjunct to the treatment of alcoholism: The hallucinogenic drugs," *Quart. J. Stud. Alc.,* 1958, *19,* 406–416.

SOLOMON, R. L. "Punishment," *Psychologist,* 1964, *19,* 239–253.

SPENCE, K. W. "Theoretical interpretations of learning." In S. S. Stevens (ed.), *Handbook of Experimental Psychology.* New York: Wiley, 1951.

SPIER, L. *Yuman Tribes of the Gila River.* Chicago: University of Chicago Press, 1933.

SPIER, L. *Klamath Ethnography.* A University of California publication in American Archeology and Ethnology, Vol. 20. Berkeley: University of California Press, 1930.

STAEHELIN, J. E. "Über den Alkoholismus in der Schweiz; einige ätiologische und therapeutische Probleme," *Schweiz. Med. Jahrb.,* 1952, 21–30.

STANTON, A. H. AND SCHWARTZ, M. S. *The Mental Hospital.* New York: Basic Books, 1954.

STECK, H. "Quelques remarques sur la prophylaxie et la thérapeutique de l'alcoolisme," *Schweiz. Med. Wschr.,* 1951, *81,* 535–537.

STERNE, MURIEL W. AND PITTMAN, D. J. "The concept of motivation: A source of institutional and professional blockage in the treatment of alcoholics," *Quart. J. Stud. Alc.,* 1965, *26,* 41–57.

STEVENSON, I. "Discussion of J. Wolpe: 'The conditioning therapies and psychoanalysis.'" In J. Wolpe, A. Salter, and L. J. Reyna (eds.), *The Conditioning Therapies: The Challenge in Psychotherapy.* New York: Holt, Rinehart, and Winston, 1964.

STRACHEY, J. "The nature of the therapeutic action of psychoanalysis," *Intern. J. Psychoanal.*, 1934, *15*, 127–159.

STRAUS, R. "Medical Practice and the Alcoholic." In E. Jaco (ed.), *Patients, Physicians and Illness.* Glencoe, Ill.: Free Press, 1948.

STRAUS, R. "Community surveys, their aims and techniques," *Quart. J. Stud. Alc.*, 1952, *13*, 254–270.

STRAUS, R. AND BACON, S. D. "The problems of drinking in college." In D. J. Pittman and C. R. Snyder (eds.), *Society, Culture and Drinking Patterns.* New York: Wiley, 1962.

STRAUS, R. AND MC CARTHY, R. G. "Nonaddictive pathological drinking patterns of homeless men," *Quart. J. Stud. Alc.*, 1951, *12*, 601–611.

STRUPP, H. H. AND LUBORSKY, L. (eds.). *Research in Psychotherapy.* Washington: American Psychological Assoc., 1962.

SULLIVAN, H. S. *Conceptions of Modern Psychiatry.* Washington: William Alanson White Psychiatric Foundation, 1947.

SYME, L. "Personality characteristics and the alcoholic," *Quart. J. Stud. Alc.*, 1957, *18* (2), 288–302.

Synanon in Prison. Documentary film narrated by W. Cronkite on CBS-TV, March 13, 1966.

"Synanon House, Reno, Nevada," *Time,* March 1, 1963.

[Synanon] "S.S. Hang Tough," *Time,* April 7, 1961.

SZASZ, T. "The myth of mental illness," *Am. Psychologist,* 1950, *15*, 113–118.

TAYLOR, JO ANN T. "Metronidazole—A new agent for combined somatic and psychic therapy of alcoholism: A case study and a preliminary report," *Bull. Los Angeles neurol. Soc.*, 1964, *29*, 158–162.

The Twelve Steps and Twelve Traditions. New York: Alcoholics Anonymous, 1953.

THIMANN, J. "Conditioned reflex-treatment of alcoholism." In E. Podolsky (ed.), *Management of Addictions.* New York: Philosophical Library, 1955. "Constructive teamwork in the treatment of alcoholism." In E. Podolsky (ed.), *Management of Addictions.* New York: Philosophical Library, 1955.

THIMANN, J. "Conditioned reflex as treatment for abnormal drinking:

Its principal technique and success," *New Eng. J. Med.*, 1943, *228*, 333–335.

THOMPSON, CLARA. *Psychoanalysis, Evolution and Development.* New York: Heritage, 1950.

THOMPSON, G. N. (ed.). *Alcoholism.* Springfield, Ill.: Thomas, 1956.

THOMPSON, T. AND WARREN, O. "Susceptibility to readdiction as a function of the addiction and withdrawal environments," *J. comp. physiol. Psychol.*, 1965, *60*, 388–392.

THORNDIKE, E. L. *Human Learning.* New York: Appleton-Century, 1931.

THRASHER, F. *The Gang.* Chicago: University of Chicago Press, 1927.

TIEBOUT, H. M. "Alcoholics Anonymous—An experiment of nature," *Quart. J. Stud. Alc.*, 1961, *22*, 52–68.

TIEBOUT, H. M. "Therapeutic mechanisms of Alcoholics Anonymous," *Am. J. Psychiat.*, 1944, *100*, 468–473.

TITMUSS, R. M. *Essays on the Welfare State.* New Haven: Yale University Press, 1959.

TOKARSKY, B. A. "Therapy of Alcoholism," *Sovetsk. vrach. Zh.*, 1938, 1033–1050 [no. Vol. No. given].

TOLMAN, E. C. *Purposive Behavior in Animals and Men.* New York: Appleton-Century, 1932.

TRICE, H. M. "The affiliation motive and readiness to join Alcoholics Anonymous," *Quart. J. Stud. Alc.*, 1959, *20*, 313–320.

TRICE, H. M. "A study of the process of affiliation with Alcoholics Anonymous," *Quart. J. Stud. Alc.*, 1957, *18*, 39–54.

UHLENHUTH, E. H., CANTER, A., NEUSTADT, J. O., AND PAYSON, H. E. "The symptomatic relief of anxiety with meprobamate, phenobarbitol and placebo," *Am. J. Psychiat.*, 1959, *115*, 905–910.

UHLENHUTH, E. H. AND PARK, L. C. "Experiments outcome—Orientation and the results of the psychological experiment," *J. Psychiat. Res.*, 1964, *2*, 101–122.

ULLMAN, A. "Sociocultural backgrounds of alcoholism," *Ann. Am. Acad. pol. soc. Sci.*, 1958, *315*, 48–54.

UNGER, S. M. "Mescaline, LSD, psilocybin, and personality change," *Psychiat.*, 1963, *26*, 111–125.

U.S. Department of Health, Education and Welfare. "Surgeon General's Ad Hoc Committee on Planning for Mental Health Facilities." Public Health Service, Publication No. 808, 1961.

VAN DER VEEN, F. "Effects of the therapist and the patient on each other's therapeutic behavior," *J. consult. Psychol.*, 1965, *29*, 19–26.

VAN PELT, S. J. "Hypnosis and alcoholism," *Brit. J. med. Hypn.*, 1950, *2*, 25.

VAN PELT, S. J. "Hypnotherapy in medical practice," *Brit. J. med. Hypn.*, 1949, *1* (1), 8–13.

VOEGTLIN, W. L. "The treatment of alcoholism with adrenal steroids, ACTH." In E. Podolsky (ed.), *Management of Addiction.* New York: Philosophical Library, 1955.

VOEGTLIN, W. L. "The treatment of alcoholism by establishing a conditioned reflex," *Am. J. med. Sci.*, 1940, *199*, 802–809.

VOTH, A. C. "Autokinesis and alcoholism," *Quart. J. Stud. Alc.*, 1965, *26*, 412–422.

VOTH, H. M. "Ego autonomy, autokinesis and recovery from psychosis," *Arch. gen. Psychiat.*, 1962, *6*, 288–293.

VOTH, H. M. AND MAYMAN, M. "A dimension of personality organization, an experimental study of 'ego-closeness'-'ego-distance,' " *Arch. gen. Psychiat.*, 1963, *8*, 366–380.

WALLERSTEIN, R. S. "The problem of the assessment of change in psychotherapy," *Intern. J. Psychoanal.*, 1963, *44*, 31–41.

WALLERSTEIN, R. S., et al. *Hospital Treatment of Alcoholism.* New York: Basic Books, 1957.

WARKOV, S., BACON, S. D., AND HAWKINS, A. C. "Social correlates of industrial drinking," *Quart. J. Stud. Alc.*, 1965, *26*(1), 58–71.

WEBER, MAX. *The Sociology of Religion.* Trans. Fischoff. Boston: Beacon, 1963.

WEDEL, HAROLD L. "Involving alcoholics in treatment," *Quart. J. Stud. Alc.*, 1965, *26*, 468–479.

WEIJL, A. "Theoretical and practical aspects of psychoanalytic therapy of problem drinkers," *Quart. J. Stud. Alc.*, 1944, *5*, 200–211.

WEIJL, A. "On the psychology of alcoholism," *Psychoanal. Rev.*, 1928, *15*, 103–104.

WEIJL, A. "Zur Psychologie des Alkoholismus," *Intern. J. Psychoanal.*, 1927, *13*, 478.

WEISS, V. "Multiple-client interviewing as an aid to diagnosis," *Soc. Casework*, 1962, *43*, 111–114.

WEITZENHOFFER, A. M. *General Techniques of Hypnotism.* New York: Grune and Stratton, 1957.

WEITZENHOFFER, A. M. *Hypnotism: An Objective Study in Suggestibility.* New York: Wiley, 1953.

WENNEIS, A. C. "Responding to the emotional needs of the alcoholic," *Soc. Casework*, 1957, *38*, 189–193.

WHITEHORN, J. C. AND BETZ, BARBARA. "A study of psychotherapeutic relationships between physicians and schizophrenic patients," *Am. J. Psychiat.*, 1954, *111*, 321–331. "Further studies of the doctor as a crucial variable in the outcome of treatment with schizophrenic patients," *Am. J. Psychiat.*, 1960, *117*, 215–223.

WHITEHORN, J. C. AND BETZ, BARBARA. "A comparison of psychotherapeutic relationships between physicians and schizophrenic patients when insulin is combined with psychotherapy and when psychotherapy is used alone," *Am. J. Psychiat.*, 1957, *131*, 901–910.

WHITING, J. W. N. AND MOWRER, O. H. "Habit progression and regression—A laboratory study of some factors relevant to human socialization," *J. comp. Psychol.*, 1943, *36*, 229–253.

WILLIAMS, L. "An experiment in group therapy," *Brit. J. Addict.*, 1948, *54*, 109–220.

WILLIAMS, L. "Who is qualified to treat the alcoholic? Comment on the Krystal-Moore discussion," *Quart. J. Stud. Alc.*, 1965, *26*, 118–120.

WILLIAMS, R. J. "Who is qualified to treat the alcoholic? Comment on the Krystal-Moore discussion," *Quart. J. Stud. Alc.*, 1964, *25*, 560–561.

WINSLOW, W. "Synanon: An application of the reality principle," *The Municipal Court Review, Natl. Assoc. Municipal Judges*, Fall, 1964.

WITKIN, H., KARP, S., AND GOODENOUGH, D. "Dependence in alcoholics," *Quart. J. Stud. Alc.*, 1959, *20*, 493–504.

WOLBERG, L. R. *Medical Hypnosis: The Principles of Hypnotherapy.* New York: Grune and Stratton, 1948.

WOLF, A. "The psychoanalysis of groups," *Am. J. Psychother.*, 1949, *3*, 525–558. "The psychoanalysis of groups," *Am. J. Psychother.*, 1950, *4*, 16–50.

WOLF, I., *et al.* "Social factors in the diagnosis of alcoholism. II. Attitudes of physicians," *Quart. J. Stud. Alc.*, 1965, *26*, 71–79.

WOLFF, H. G. *Stress and Disease.* Springfield, Ill.: Thomas, 1953.

WOLFGANG, M. E. *Patterns in Criminal Homicide.* Philadelphia: University of Pennsylvania Press, 1958.

WOLFGANG, M. E. AND STROHM, R. B. "The relationship between alcohol and criminal homicide," *Quart. J. Stud. Alc.*, 1956, *17*, 411–425.

WOLMAN, B. B. (ed.). *Handbook of Clinical Psychology.* New York: McGraw-Hill, 1965.

WOLPE, J. *Psychotherapy by Reciprocal Inhibition.* Stanford: Stanford University Press, 1958.

WOLPE, J., SALTER, A., AND REYNA, L. J. (eds.). *The Conditioning Therapies: The Challenge in Psychotherapy.* New York: Holt, Rinehart and Winston, 1964.

YABLONSKY, L. *The Tunnel Back.* New York: McGraw-Hill, 1964.

YABLONSKY, L. "The anticriminal society: Synanon," *Fed. Probation,* 1962, *26* (3), 50–57.

YABLONSKY, L. AND DEDERICH, C. E. "Synanon: As a program for training ex-offenders as therapeutic agents." In *Experiment in Culture Expansion.* Report of proceedings of a conference held at California Rehabilitation Center, Napa, July 10–12, 1963.

YARROW, M. R., CLAUSEN, J. A., AND ROBBINS, P. R. "The social meaning of mental illness," *J. soc. Issues,* 1955, *11*, 33–48.

YOLLES, S. F. "Community mental health: Issues and policies," *Am. J. Psychiat.*, 1966, *122*, 979–985.

ZILBOORG, G. *A History of Medical Psychology.* New York: Norton, 1941.

Subject Index

Citrated calcium carbimide (Temposil), 135, 205, 207, 244
Cocaine, 203
Commitment, voluntary, 282
Communication: between patient and healer, 46; importance among investigators, 290; importance in therapy, 233
Community: alcohol remedies, 4, 255, 256; control and coercion of deviant behavior, 30, 255, 256; demands in treatment, 249, 255, 256; developed tolerance in treatment, 32; drinking behavior valued by, 3–6, 29, 30, 255, 256; and drinking controls, 5, 256, 257; mental health services, 138, 204, 246; psychiatry, 21, 272, 276, 277
Conditioned: autonomic drive (CAD), 112; aversion, 100, 117ff; aversion reaction to alcohol, 124–126, 130; reflex treatment, 130
Conditioning: adaptation to punishment in, 105; by, (a) apomorphine, 125, 126, (b) disulfiram, 130ff, (c) emetine, 127ff; interoceptive, 254; and learning, 100ff; operant-aversive, 115; proximity in, 105; by strength of punished response, 105
Conflict, unconscious, 80ff
Consolidated Edison Company of New York, Consultation Clinic for Alcoholism, 220
Consultants: for general hospitals, 284; in other institutions, 284, 285; services, 53, 54
Copenhagen Institute of Forensic Psychiatry, 146, 147
Correctional facilities (*see also* Jails), 150ff
Counter-transference, 31, 242; responses defined, 86
Criminality (*see also* Homicide), in alcoholism, 18, 42, 239
Crisis: periods, 240; theory, 205; treatment, 180, 276, 286

Cultural: differences and conditioning, 107; values and treatment, 10
Cyclazocine, 196

D

Dancing, 145, 154, 168, 170
Day centers, 138, 275, 280
Death: accidental, 194; symbolic, 197, 198
Delirium tremens, 19, 193
Depression, 18, 91, 120, 174, 194, 240
Deviant behavior, 3, 5, 6, 9, 10, 29–32, 248, 256
Diagnosis: dynamic, 286; in progressive care, 279; and secondary prevention, 285ff; social, 286
Diagnostic: consensus, 229ff; reliability, 33
Didactic: groups, 143ff; methods, 302; therapy, 143
Diphenhydramine, 131
Disulfiram, 116, 117, 130ff, 205, 207; aversion treatment, 130ff; dangers in use of, 131, 132; definition of, 130; effects of, 131; ethanol combination, toxicity of, 131; psychosis, 122; sensitivity to, 131; treatment, 21, 130ff, 185, 186, 202, 252, 255, 301, 305
DMSO (dimethylsulfoxide), 255
Dreams, 15, 141; analysis of, 85; production of, 85, 86
Drinker (*see also* Alcoholics, Ex-alcoholic): escape-oriented heavy, 36, 39, 40; homicidal, 9; nonconforming, 28–30
Drive-reduction, 101
Drugs (*see also* under generic names): antidepressant, 194, 202; antidipsotropic, 133, 135; dependency, 19, 38, 39, 40, 42, 43, 45, 52, 194, 202, 253; environment and interactions, 199, 200; therapy, (a) adversive conditioning, 125ff, (b) general considerations, 193ff, (c) medical dangers of, 193, (d) pros-

Name Index

367

372 NAME INDEX

SHEA, J., 95, 96, 229, 244
SHEINBERG, J., 39
SHERIF, M., 140
SHOBEN, JR., E. J., 108
SIEGEL, S., 97, 98, 179, 184
SIGERIST, H. E., 277
SILBER, A., 13, 96–98, 223
SILLMAN, L. R., 13, 223
SILVERMAN, M., 6, 35, 38, 39, 308
SIMMEL, E., 90, 91
SIMMONS, L. W., 277
SIMMONS, O. G., 64, 205, 277, 301
SKINNER, B. F., 100, 107
SKOLNICK, J. H., 37
SKRAM, RUTH, 262
SLACK, C. W., 61
SLAVSON, S. F., 141, 170, 171
SMART, R. G., 200
SMITH, C. M., 198
SNYDER, C. R., 35, 39
SOLOMON, P., 284
SOLOMON, R. L., 102–105, 107
SPENCE, K. W., 100
SPIER, LESLIE, 196
STAEHELIN, J. E., 126
STANTON, A. H., 64, 277, 291
STAUFFER, DOROTHY, 262
STECK, H., 110, 120
STERNE, MURIEL W., 219
STEVENSON, I., 116
STONE, A. R., 226
STORM, T., 200
STRACHEY, J., 180
STRAUS, R., 35, 45, 214, 285
STRUPP, H. H., 264, 268, 269, 271
SULLIVAN, H. S., 141, 180
SYME, L., 42

T

TAYLOR, JO ANN T., 135
THIESSEN, D. D., 267
THIMANN, J., 129, 130, 244
THOMAS, D., 257
THOMPSON, G. N., 130
THOMPSON, T., 311
THORNDIKE, E. L., 107
THRASHER, F., 140

TIEBOUT, H. M., 163, 186
TITMUSS, R. M., 64, 248, 277
TOKARSKY, B. A., 119
TOLMAN, E. C., 100
TRICE, H. M., 56, 164, 165
TUKE, W., 8
TURK, R. E., 131

U

UHLENHUTH, E. H., 268, 299
ULETT, G. A., 262
ULLMAN, A., 108
UNGER, S. M., 198

V

VAGO, S., 262
VAN DER VEEN, F., 233
VANDERWATER, S. L., 108
VAN PELT, S. J., 187
VISPO, R. H., 196, 198
VOEGTLIN, W. L., 105, 126–128, 133, 267
VON FELSINGER, J. M., 17, 201
VOTH, A. C., 190, 191
VOTH, H. M., 190, 191

W

WALLERSTEIN, R. S., 124, 133, 185, 188, 268
WEBER, M., 6
WARREN, O., 311
WEDEL, H. L., 223, 224
WEIJL, A., 13, 92, 197
WEISS, V., 144
WEITZENHOFFER, A. M., 117, 124
WENNEIS, A. C., 225
WEST, L. J., 124
WHEELER, L., 201
WHITEHORN, J. C., 15, 299
WHITING, J. W. N., 106
WILLIAMS, L., 56
WILLIAMS, R. J., 22
WINEMAN, D., 62
WINSLOW, W., 158
WITKIN, H. A., 42, 189–191
WOLBERG, L. R., 117, 120, 185, 186
WOLF, A., 141, 181, 183
WOLF, I., 284